WRITE ALL THESE DOWN

# WRITE ALL THESE DOWN

ESSAYS ON MUSIC

Joseph Kerman

UNIVERSITY OF CALIFORNIA PRESS    BERKELEY   LOS ANGELES   LONDON

ML
60
.K37
1994

University of California Press
Berkeley and Los Angeles, California

University of California Press, Ltd.
London, England

© 1994 by
The Regents of the University of California

Library of Congress
Cataloging-in-Publication Data
Kerman, Joseph, 1924–
  Write all these down : essays on music /
  Joseph Kerman.
      p.   cm.
  Includes bibliographical references and
  index.
  ISBN 0-520-08355-5
  1. Music—History and criticism.
  I. Title.
  ML60.K37   1994
  780—dc20                          93-1876
                                      CIP
                                      MN

Printed in the United States of America
9  8  7  6  5  4  3  2  1

The paper used in this publication meets
the minimum requirements of American
National Standard for Information Sciences—Permanence of Paper for Printed
Library Materials, ANSI Z39.48-1984. ∞

*To Anna Sophia*

# CONTENTS

# PREFACE

While books generally focus on a single topic, collections of essays can display the author's range: can, in my case, cover work on the different music I have been occupied with over the years—William Byrd and his associates, Beethoven and Verdi, to a lesser extent Mozart and Wagner—and also illustrate some diversity of approach, method, and voice. As usual with anthologies of this kind, the contents also reflect a certain anxiety that work originally published in out-of-the-way places, such as festschrifts, may not have found its true harmonic resonance on the great monochord of musicology. On the other hand, two old essays that were widely noticed and reprinted elsewhere are absent; it seemed right that they should make room for others here.[1] The new is well represented. Six of the present items date from the last five years, and several of them are appearing in print for the first time. "Mozart's Piano Concertos and Their Audience" is part of a larger project, on the concerto, that I am still working on.

The book's opening section collects tracts from the 1960s to the 1980s about musicology, criticism, and analysis: put differently, about the right response to the traditional canon of Western music. I hope that the repetitions, overlaps, and cross-references will not be too intrusive, and that reading these essays as a unit may qualify the answers proposed at the time and deepen the inquiry. That I was not happy to rest with those answers will appear from some later essays, such as "Taking the Fifth" and "Mozart's Piano Concertos and Their Audience."

The articles on Verdi are earlier yet; indeed, "Verdi's Use of Recurring Themes," published in the festschrift for Oliver Strunk in 1968, goes back to a paper delivered a dozen years earlier. (There is a private story attached to this which explains why the paper was foreordained for that publication and why it remains a personal favorite. In 1955, when my Ph.D. dissertation on the Elizabethan madrigal—under

Strunk—was only four years behind me, he wrote to me officially on behalf of the American Musicological Society, asking me to speak at the Society's annual meeting at Princeton that Christmas. Strunk added coolly that he hoped the topic would not fall in the Renaissance period; the Renaissance was oversubscribed. All this was tantamount to a command, of course. Having done a little research at Berkeley on Verdi under the eye of Manfred Bukofzer, whose tragic final illness—he died in December 1955—left me with a fall-semester seminar to prepare in a hurry, I chose Verdi as the topic, and with much help from the students, and some more help from a flying visit to the New York Public Library, put together a paper in time for Christmas. It was my first scholarly outing past the Renaissance. I have always felt very thankful to Strunk for the push, and, for a while, it became in my fantasy an emblem of the special approval from him that was craved by all his students.)

Also included here are two of the twenty-odd articles, reviews, and review-articles that I published in the *Hudson Review* between 1949 and 1965 (mostly in the period 1949 to 1955). My late friend William Arrowsmith, who introduced me to *Hudson* almost as soon as it commenced publication, was a formative influence on my intellectual makeup, and the encouragement I received from the editors, especially Arrowsmith and Frederick Morgan, was decisive for my career as a writer. When a *Hudson Review Anthology* was published in 1961, covering fiction, poetry, and criticism, I must say I was overwhelmed to find myself included, along with many great eminences.

These early critical efforts deserve a place in this book on their merits, I trust, and I also hope that they may help the reader to understand or at least locate my later writings. For a start, they should help account for the diversity of "voice" referred to above. The *Hudson Review* pieces addressed a (vaguely imagined) literate, even specifically literary readership interested in music but not professionally involved with it. Examples in music notation were hardly ever used, and technical language was kept to a minimum. On the matter of range in the *Hudson* pieces, as music critic for the journal—for that is how I saw myself, in the early years—my self-image was that of a generalist, at home with all of classical music, including of course contemporary music.[2] Opera was a natural subject; many sections of my first book *Opera as Drama* first appeared in *Hudson*. The mode was descriptive and evaluative, often enthusiastic and often judgmental.

After the mid-1950s my work was addressed less to the *Hudson Review* readership and more to musicologists (and, one always hopes, to practical, performing musicians). There were a number of reasons for this career change—for in a limited sense, that is what it was. Disciplinary pressure must have been one reason, though not, incidentally, institutional pressure; never once did my older faculty colleagues Manfred Bukofzer or David Boyden register disapproval of criticism as against scholarship. But Berkeley *had* hired me as a musicologist, and as such I began to yearn for a fundable project that would make my next sabbatical leave transatlantic.

On another level, the need to speak technically—that is, in close detail—about music began to seem a more urgent matter than the intellectual and artistic common ground that I felt (or vaguely imagined) I shared with the *Hudson* readership. I was also experiencing more and more difficulty coping with contemporary music—music past Elliott Carter—and felt as a result more and more uncomfortable with my stance as a generalist critic. The fundable project turned out to be a study of the sacred music of William Byrd; this led after many delays and many preliminaries to a comprehensive book, *The Masses and Motets of William Byrd* (1981), part of a projected three-volume study of all Byrd's music in collaboration with Philip Brett and Oliver Neighbour.

The scholarly voice cultivated after around 1960 was not a new voice—it had already been used for a dissertation and an AMS paper, *inter alia*—but it was now heard more often. The mode was descriptive, objective, and measured. The audience shifted. Studies of documents, such as the manuscripts containing Byrd's motets and Beethoven's sketches; histories of compositional devices and practices, such as Renaissance counterpoint, Beethoven's tonality, and *primo ottocento* lyric forms; analyses of the liturgical and non-liturgical text repertory of Elizabethan music with Latin words; and close readings of motets and songs, fugues and symphonies—these are not exercises that the non-musician wants to be subjected to in any detail, let alone the detail they seem to require.

The other voice, however, was not abandoned. It wavered, and at the node of maximum wavering, I wrote a book about the Beethoven string quartets which seems to have been loved and hated in about equal measure. In any case, institutions and journals from outside music as a profession or discipline who have approached me have not usually been refused. As a result of all this, there is a kind of bivocality, polyphony, or (some will say) ventriloquism that comes through in this book. In the section devoted to Byrd, for example, the opening biographical essay originated as a general academic lecture and was published in a non-specialist journal, the *New York Review of Books,* whereas the detailed analytical study of a Byrd song, "Retire, My Soul," was commissioned for a volume of specialized *Byrd Studies.*

But the polyphony is not of the strictly non-imitative variety, as in a San Martial organum or a ballade by Machaut. Motivic connections can be traced between the voices. For from the start my study was always to ground criticism in historical knowledge (that was why I went off to Princeton to study musicology) and to leaven scholarship with criticism. This even developed into an explicit program, as I gradually pulled out of the *Hudson Review,* backed away from my ambition as a generalist critic, and confirmed my ties with the academy. The first item in this book, "A Profile for American Musicology," a paper delivered at another AMS annual meeting, in 1964, urged upon the membership a reorientation of our discipline around criticism. This talk attracted unusual notice, thanks mainly to an older scholar, Edward E. Lowinsky, whose formal response at the meeting turned out to be a long, strong attack. So the issue was joined in the sharpest possible way, with the paper and the response published along with a rebuttal. Still, it took another twenty years and another harangue from the same soapbox[3] before criticism really caught the attention of American musicology.

The 1979 paper "How We Got into Analysis, and How to Get Out," though it formed part of a series of philosophical lectures, was really addressed to music theorists, who around that time were setting themselves up as a new subdiscipline, with their own society and their own journal.[4] The pitch was much the same: musical analysis, theory's practical wing, should reorient itself around criticism. And just exactly what is it that you mean by criticism? Different things, and changing things, as I had tried to say in "Profile":

> Criticism is the way of looking at art that tries to take into account the meaning it conveys, the pleasure it initiates, and the value it assumes, for us today. Criticism deals with pieces of music and men listening, with fact and feeling, with the life of the past in the present, with the composer's private image in the public mirror of an audience. At worst criticism is one man's impressionism—like bad art—and at best it is an uneasy dialectic. Allen Tate says that criticism is a perpetual impossibility and a perpetual necessity; and he adds stonily that in this it resembles all our other ultimate pursuits.[5]

This attempt at a definition, apart from the heavy hint about the New Criticism, and the regrettable sexist tinge to the language, still strikes me as right as far as it goes, but incomplete, and I am sure it would be futile to try to complete it. One cannot define criticism; one must be content with exemplifying it—bearing witness, as it were—and, sometimes, with writing around it, as at the end of "How We Got into Analysis."

The polemic thrust or undertone to my writing has been regretted by persons whom I greatly respect, and so I feel uneasy about it; but there it is. If its reinforcement through twenty chapters proves to be irritating, I can only offer my own regrets. As to method, in "How We Got into Analysis" and elsewhere I make a point of opposing any and all ideologically held methodologies; my own ideology would have to be described as methodological eclecticism. The 1973 essay on Beethoven's song cycle *An die ferne Geliebte* may perhaps be regarded as emblematic in this regard, drawing as it does on biography and psychobiography, musical and literary history, study of the sketches and the autograph, literary and musical analysis, style history, and even, near the end, just a trace of music theory. The idea is to get the best illumination for the matter at hand by using as many spots and gels as one can assemble and manipulate.

Close readings are not favored nowadays, and there are good reasons for that, but I think highly of my detailed studies of music which is seldom read closely, music of the sixteenth century, music by William Byrd. Rather reluctantly, I include only one of my extended essays in this genre, the most recent, on "Retire, My Soul"; earlier essays deal with the motets *Emendemus in melius* and *Tribue, Domine*.[6] (*Emendemus in melius* is the most novel of the extraordinary batch of motets contributed by Byrd to the Tallis–Byrd *Cantiones sacrae* of 1575, his first publication; *Tribue, Domine* is the most archaic.) "Verdi's Use of Recurring Themes" and "Beethoven's Minority" are samples of another kind of study that has worked well for me, the longitudinal style study. One example of a performance review has been included, partly because it fits so conveniently into a composite item on early Verdi operas, and partly because when people think of music criticism they think of the assessment of live music: and they can't be all wrong.

It remains to thank various people in connection with the present project. I am especially grateful to Walter Frisch, for proposing it and even offering to carry it through, an ordeal which could not be countenanced; to Ann Pescatello, for releasing me from another commitment; to Doris Kretschmer, for her support up front and back stage; and as ever and ever more so to Vivian Kerman and Gary Tomlinson, for advice on the selection of essays. The selection has also been influenced by publishers' readers, whose wise comments I appreciate very much. In the few cases where the original texts have been added to or altered, beyond simple correction or clarification, this is signaled by brackets.

*Zur Widmung:* this book was already in production when our son Jonathan Kerman died unexpectedly, leaving a one-year-old daughter. I lovingly inscribe the essay on *The Magic Flute,* Chapter 14, to his memory; he loved Mozart, and I choose this item also because it brings us back together over the longest time.

---

### Notes

1. Joseph Kerman, "A Romantic Detail in Schubert's *Schwanengesang*" and "On William Byrd's *Emendemus in melius,*" *Musical Quarterly* 48 (1962): 36–49, and 49 (1963): 431–49, reprinted in *Schubert: Critical and Analytical Studies,* ed. Walter Frisch (Lincoln, Neb., 1986), and *Analyse und Chormusik,* ed. Heinrich Poos (Mainz, 1983), respectively.
2. Strangely, as it now seems, "early music" prior to Bach was not in the picture. Nearly half of the *Hudson* pieces dealt with twentieth-century music, by Schoenberg, Stravinsky, Berg, Britten, Sessions, Copland, and Carter.
3. Joseph Kerman, *Contemplating Music: Challenges to Musicology* (Cambridge, Mass., 1985).
4. See "Comment and Chronicle," *19th-Century Music* 2 (1978–79): 90–91; 284–85.
5. See p. 5.
6. Joseph Kerman, "Old and New in William Byrd's *Cantiones sacrae,*" in *Essays on Opera and English Music in Honour of Sir Jack Westrup,* ed. F. W. Sternfeld et al. (Oxford, 1975), 25–43; see also n. 1.

# CRITICISM

I

# A Profile for American Musicology

"What is the purpose of humanistic scholarship? What, in fact, does the humanist scholar do?" These sanguine editorial questions introduce and define the scope of the Princeton "Studies of Humanistic Scholarship in America"—fourteen books-in-progress appraising the condition of the various humanistic disciplines in this country. "The aim of these volumes is to present a critical account of American humanistic scholarship in recent decades. They have been commissioned by the Council of the Humanities, Whitney J. Oates, Chairman, of Princeton University and were made possible by a grant from the Ford Foundation."[1] Certain of the books may be thought to glut certain of the fields, but the one on musicology fills a void; the joint study by Frank L. Harrison, Mantle Hood, and Claude Palisca has been welcomed and very rightly praised as a milestone in the history of the discipline. There have been few deeply considered statements about American musicology—distressingly few, I should say, in recent years. The general unselfconsciousness of American musicology perhaps reflects its newness as a field of study; much more discussion of aims and principles and premises is needed, as well as of actual working methods. Starting discussion is the first great virtue of the *Musicology* volume, to which I am gratefully paying a small tribute in the form of the present address.

"What is the purpose of humanistic scholarship? What, in fact, does the humanist scholar do?" The *Musicology* volume answers the second of these questions far

An address delivered at a plenary session of the 1964 annual meeting of the American Musicological Society in Washington, D.C.; published in *Journal of the American Musicological Society* 18 (1965): 61–69.

better than the first. The field has been defined in very comprehensive ways, as Professor Palisca points out, but when all is said and done, "the musicologist is first and foremost a historian." What serves this particular variety of historian as a goal or as a goad, Palisca never makes very clear; perhaps that is tacitly contained in the term "history," or perhaps musicologists themselves are not so very clear about it. As for Dr. Harrison, he frankly set himself the job not of just answering questions, but of casting around and nudging us a little in one particular direction. That direction is toward a "social aim." Without such an ideal, Harrison remarks in a terrifying aside, musicology seems merely "to create and protect a reserve for specialized and uncommunicative scholarship"; instead the aim should be the understanding of man: "enlarging man's knowledge of himself by widening the bounds of historical writing and so throwing light on Western man's cultural and intellectual development." According to this concept, musicology should first "contribute to the understanding and re-creation of music by a close analysis of the composer's musical thought and style in the light of the technical and aesthetic principles of his day"; but although this may be the first task, the ultimate goal becomes "the study of men in society insofar as they express themselves through the medium of music. . . . Looked at in this way, it is the function of all musicology to be in fact ethnomusicology, that is, to take its range of research to include material that is termed 'sociological.'"[2] With this view, reasonably enough, Professor Hood's essay on ethnomusicology finds itself in cordial agreement.

After making various necessary allowances, and noting sadly the substitution of the word "function" for the word "purpose," we shall probably assent to this general formulation. The more thoughtful American musicologists are doing studies which they gingerly fit into one corner or another of the cultural and intellectual history of Western man. The less thoughtful ones are collecting all kinds of information in the vague expectation that someone—someone else—will find it useful in the same great undertaking. This view of musicology is neither surprising nor novel. Before it hardens into orthodoxy—I might say, before the milestone becomes a millstone—I should like to suggest another possible view or orientation.

It treats the same material and uses the same terms. However, works of art are not studied as a means of furthering "the study of men in society." The terms are just turned around. Men in society are studied as a means of furthering the comprehension of works of art. This may be described as a critical orientation, to differentiate it from the sociological orientation. It is of course no more novel or surprising than the other.

In this conception of musicology, history and sociology are not valued as ends, but as means. Even style analysis, which often gets the place of honor (or at least lip service) in discussions of musicology, is pursued not for general evidence about an era, but for contextual evidence about the artistic individuality of a particular piece. Each of the things we do—paleography, transcription, repertory studies, archival work, biography, bibliography, sociology, *Aufführungspraxis,* schools and influences, theory, style analysis, individual analysis—each of these things, which some scholar somewhere treats as an end in itself, is treated as a step on a ladder. Hopefully the top step affords a platform of insight into individual works of art—into Josquin's *Missa Pange lingua,* Marenzio's *Liquide perle,* Beethoven's op. 95, Stravinsky's *Oedipus rex.* These works cannot be understood in isolation, only in a context. The infinitely laborious and infinitely diverting ascent of the musicologist should provide this context.

The insight that I am referring to, critical insight, has never been easy to define, and it has always been as urgent as it is problematic. Urgent, because criticism is the way of looking at art that tries to take into account the meaning it conveys, the pleasure it initiates, and the value it assumes, for us today. Criticism deals with pieces of music and men listening, with fact and feeling, with the life of the past in the present, with the composer's private image in the public mirror of an audience. At worst criticism is one man's impressionism—like bad art—and at best it is an uneasy dialectic. Allen Tate says that criticism is a perpetual impossibility and a perpetual necessity; and he adds stonily that in this it resembles all our other ultimate pursuits.

Now the serious study of criticism is barely mentioned by Palisca or Harrison, even in their more speculative passages. Whether or not this depresses us, it will not much surprise us, for in musical parlance criticism always seems to refer only to daily newspaper writing, a field that has the reputation of an intellectual jungle, in spite of recent efforts by some musicological missionaries. However, the lacuna *will* surprise and may depress the non-musical reader of the book, such as, for example, the experienced academic person with no knowledge of the musical situation (the type is common enough). It will surprise him particularly if he has just read the companion book on *Art and Archeology,* our closest neighbor discipline. Starting out flatly with the proposition that "the [art] historian must be a critic as well . . . since fundamental values in the work of art are inaccessible to historical method," the essay on Western art history goes on to devote an entire chapter to "The Historian as Critic." To quote:

> As long as the work of art is studied as a historical document it differs
> from the archival document only in form, not in kind. The art historian
> should be interested in the difference in kind, which is immanent in the
> capacity of art to awaken in us complex responses that are at once intellec-
> tual, emotional, and physical, so that he needs, in addition to the tools of
> other historians, principles and methods specifically designed to deal with
> this unique mode of experience.

According to the writer,

> The philosophy of art history of the last generation could be called anti-philosophical; it taught nonintervention, not only in the sense of avoiding value judgments, but in the sense of minimizing the factor of creativity in historical scholarship. . . . I look on criticism not as an additional technique to be adopted by historians but as a challenge that forces us to re-examine the fundamental philosophical principles by which we operate.[3]

The writer of this is, of course, no outside activist but (like most of the Princeton Studies authors) a member of the younger academic establishment—a Harvard professor, authority on Michelangelo, sometime editor of the *Art Bulletin,* and a veteran of several formidable art-historical institutes.

The lacuna will very greatly surprise the non-musical academic reader if he is a professor of English. In English departments of American universities, criticism has been living alongside of historical scholarship for twenty-five years. Two volumes of "Studies of Humanistic Scholarship" are needed, one on *English Literature* and one on *Modern American Criticism.* In the 1920s, the field was committed to philology and literary history as firmly as music is now committed to similar pursuits; how the change came about is a long story—too long for the present occasion—and an instructive one. Although the "New Criticism" has been forcefully attacked for its excesses, these excesses seem to have diluted with time, and in any case were never shown to be more absurd than those of some so-called scientific research. Dozens of Ph.D. theses in literary criticism, as well as in literary history, are processed in a perfectly responsible scholarly fashion every year. The undergraduate curriculum of the department at the University of California at Berkeley builds on a basic junior course in "Methods and Materials of Literary Criticism." The catalog description reads: "Explication and evaluation of literary texts and study of the various principles of literary judgment."

The lacuna would also surprise a classicist. The oldest of the humanistic disciplines is on that account the most open to the charge of pettifoggery—and from time to time this charge is made with positively Dionysiac vehemence. At the present time, a revisionist quarterly magazine called *Arion* is attacking root and branch the alleged Byzantinism of conventional classical studies, and pleading by polemic and by example for a critical approach to Greek and Latin literature. Along with learned critical essays and translations, *Arion* indulges in such alarming exploits as the defense of Nietzsche against Wilamowitz, and the silent exposure of noted classicists by the device of selective quotation. It is notable, again, that the impetus comes from within the academy. The magazine, published by the University of Texas Press, includes on its last page a discreet listing of the faculty in classics at Texas, from which it draws its editors.

But there is probably no need to continue rehearsing all this fairly familiar academic lore. In the humanistic disciplines, criticism is a feature, or a fixture, or at least an issue. It should become an issue in musical studies. Until this comes about, our confident cries of maturity among the other liberal arts will fall on somewhat skeptical ears.

Criticism does not exist yet on the American music-academic scene, but something does exist which may feel rather like it: theory and analysis. Theory, says Professor Palisca with some understatement, "is a field that needs definition almost as badly as that of musicology itself."[4] The shadowy, fluid state of the field; its problematic relation to analysis; the sporadic nature of the published material; the small number of practitioners—these features, which are only to be expected in a new field, certainly make it hard to get hold of and discuss with confidence. However, I think we realize that those practitioners, if they ever paid the least attention to traditional musicology, might fairly claim achievements ranking in rigor and importance with those of the historians. One can also discern the typical stages of academic infiltration: the key appointments, the prestige courses, the doctoral degrees, and the establishment of a *Journal of Music Theory*. One can also remark that in general, theory and analysis—like the various processes of traditional musicology—are still being treated as ends rather than as steps on the ladder to criticism. Like musicology, analysis seems too occupied with its own inner techniques, too fascinated by its own "logic," and too sorely tempted by its own private pedantries, to confront the work of art in its proper aesthetic terms. Theory and analysis are not equivalent to criticism, then, but they are pursuing techniques of vital importance to criticism. They represent a force and a positive one in the academic climate of music, and tactful efforts should be made (on both sides, let us sincerely hope) to arrange a rapprochement with musicology. In point of fact, this is just what is happening at a number of leading universities.

The lack of due consideration of theory and analysis in the *Musicology* book has been noted by Lewis Lockwood in a discerning (and doubly diplomatic) review published in *Perspectives of New Music*.[5] The authors class theory and analysis apart from musicology, and so they are classed in the schools; but as Professor Lockwood suggests, these subjects could certainly fall under the ample canopy of *Musikwissenschaft* as defined by the Germans. We need to stress the breadth of musical studies. The intimation that theorists and analysts might be called musicologists, however, strikes me as both touchy and a little specious; better abandon the word "musicology" altogether—who ever heard of "artology" or "literology"? No wonder we are getting mixed up with the social sciences. The book ought to have been entitled *Musical Scholarship*, within which broad study ethnomusicology, historical scholarship, theory, analysis, and even criticism should all have found a place.

In the end, though, whether theory is subsumed under musicology, or musicology under cultural history, or ethnomusicology under anthropology, are more questions of tactics than of substance. I could cheerfully argue, with Northrop Frye, for a general field theory of criticism in which historical criticism, analytic criticism, sociological criticism, and so on, would figure as subtypes. What does seem to me of substance is that we come around to recognizing the critical orientation as legitimate and fruitful—at the *very least*—in serious musical studies. It is my strong suspicion that the main incentive that brought most musicologists to musicology, and most theorists and analysts to their fields, was something close to the critical urge—not the scientific fervor for research, nor a curiosity about Western man and his history and sociology, nor an abstract speculative bent, but a passion for Bach or Josquin or Beethoven or Stravinsky. Certainly we continue to listen to this music, and play it, and get sustenance from it, and try to pass on that sustenance in our daily undergraduate teaching. Yet our scholarly writing is of a kind that can make even a friendly outside examiner like Frank Harrison speak (not once but several times) about "musicology that has lost touch with music." For reasons of time and timidity, I pass over the trivia that occupy good minds while Beethoven's sketches remain unanalyzed (the Germans are only *transcribing* them) and spurious works lurk scandalously in the Josquin canon. Suffice it to say that the gap between music and musicology is neither fortunate for public relations nor in the least necessary. There should be more work on the great masters (among the 1800-odd members of the American Musicological Society, one is hard pressed to name more than two Handel experts, one Monteverdi expert, one Mozart man. We probably harbor more Wagnerians than any organization west of Seventh Avenue—but so far as I am aware, no professed Wagner specialist). And given the critical orientation, work on all other music, however obscure and unstudied, would automatically be brought toward a sphere of general relevance. Even minutiae could be read with pleasure and profit if they could be shown to be making a minute contribution to our essential musical experience.

A parallel situation exists on the level of the students. In the contemporary American scene there is little to motivate them initially in the direction of "pure" scholarship. What brings young men and women to musicology is an original commitment to music as aesthetic experience. Does this become desiccated, somewhere in the graduate curriculum, and can we, their teachers, maintain an altogether clear conscience in this matter? Again and again one sees the best students veer toward analysis, which promises real involvement with musical essences. Again and again one sees them taken aback by the analysts' narrow intellectual structure. Then one sees them drag their feet on historical dissertations which, be it admitted, are sometimes merely laborious rather than intellectually or musically challenging. What they want—I am still talking about the best students—is a discipline that will allow them to work, with rigor and intelligence, close to the music that moves them. Failing this, they can turn into very half-hearted scholars.

Dr. Harrison has urged us all to be sociologists—but I must not lay at his door this little sociological speculation about musicologists and their students. I may be completely wrong about it, in which case I apologize to the Society for wasting its time. But if I am right, the situation is not a healthy one. Far better if our scholarly interests were bound in with our musical interests. Far better if our original musical passions were sublimated, rather than repressed, in our research.

It may be objected that a lack of commitment to scholarship in the abstract on the part of Americans or some Americans is no reason for musicology to change, to swerve from the true objective path which the German scholars stamped out generations ago, and have been marching on so powerfully ever since. I am afraid, though, that until American musicology catches something of the resonance of the American personality, it will remain an echo of the great German tradition—and I should not be too sanguine about recent signs of international recognition, welcome and deserved as these may be. That tradition was not dictated by objective truths of nature, it arose out of a certain national current of thought at a certain point in its history. Other European nations, in spite of all temptations—proximity, propaganda, immigration—developed styles of scholarship appreciably different from the German. Presumably we too should be echoing our own current and our own time.

None of this must be taken as chauvinism. The thanks we owe to German musicologists and German-trained musicologists are too obvious, the debt too great and too deep-rooted and (at least in my case) too affectionate. All the same, our identity as scholars depends on growth away from an older alien tradition into something recognizably our own. European observers have a very simple recipe for national integrity: study your own American music, they say, as we have built our musicology around *Stamm* and *Liederbuch,* Risorgimento opera and Elizabethan madrigal, Bulgar folk song, and the like. The critically inclined scholar has a very simple answer: unfortunately, American music has not been interesting enough, artistically, to merit from us that commitment. Even so experienced a visitor as Harrison fails to see the extent to which the American mind dwells in the present, and how little in the past; and the critical attitude is exactly that which takes the past up *into the present,* rather than admiring it as an antiquity. The student of Beethoven feels concerned with the present because the music is (as we say) "alive"; the student of Marenzio or Louis Couperin is concerned with music that can be brought to life; but Francis Hopkinson or Lowell Mason or Theodore Chanler— surely they would defy all efforts at resuscitation. Man, they are dead. About jazz, Harrison has a real point, but such an extremely complex one that I ask leave to pass over it in the present discussion. It does not appear to me that a characteristically American musicology can be built on native repertory. It can be built only with a native point of view.[6]

Characteristic or not, the recent growth of musicology in this country has been headlong, in terms of the numbers of scholars and students, opportunities, facilities, recognition, support, and all the other rituals which foreshadow coming-of-age. In the years since World War II, the membership of this Society has more than tripled, and Helen Hewitt's dissertation index has nearly quadrupled itself in length. The postwar generation is now coming strongly into prominence—writing the articles, running the seminars, editing our journal, speaking to and for the Society—as the relatively small group of older scholars is thinned by time and retirement. Harrison, Hood, and Palisca all made their scholarly careers in the postwar period. We really must not ask the prewar German scholars or American scholars to guide us any more. They do not ask to guide or to restrain us.

Someone has spoken about the growth of American musicology from infancy to adolescence; the metaphor is irresistible. Yet as many readers have noticed with a twinge, only Mantle Hood's essay on ethnomusicology conveys the sense of horizon, excitement, experimentation, and just plain kicking around that one associates with even the most docile adolescents. Has historical musicology somehow skipped this phase? I hope instead we are still in infancy. The critical profile envisaged here for American musicology would supply some of this excitement. It would neither replace nor slight our traditional scholarly pursuits, but would on the contrary depend upon them and thereby strengthen their rationale. It would follow a template familiar to the humanistic disciplines in this country and would, I believe, match our temperament as well as smooth the accommodation which must come to theory and analysis. I even believe that such a profile would bring musicologists closer to the celebrated "composer's point of view," and help fill the even more celebrated gap between the scholar and the general public.[7]

In conclusion, though, let me not unduly stress psychological, political, and sociological considerations above philosophical ones. Most of all I believe James Ackerman, the author of the essay on Western art history, when he recalls that a work of art differs in kind from an archival document. That difference makes it art, and that difference ought to dictate our response to it. The term "art object" has always seemed to me offensive; works of art are not things, they are human acts, and while it may be appropriate to study things by means of some -ology or other, human acts make a further demand. They demand sympathy, in the etymological sense of the word, and they demand judgment. The very nature of our chosen material, then, calls for the critical stance if that material is to be granted its full dignity. Critical judgments are no more easily made than moral judgments; doubtless they can be more easily avoided, but it does not seem to me in the last analysis more moral to avoid them. Habitually to treat music as something less than art is to dehumanize music, and even to dehumanize ourselves. "I look on criticism," writes Professor Ackerman, "not as an additional technique to be adopted by historians but as a challenge that forces us to re-examine the fundamental philosophical principles by which we operate."

*Notes*

1. Frank L. Harrison, Mantle Hood, and Claude V. Palisca, *Musicology* (Humanistic Scholarship in America: The Princeton Studies, Richard Schlatter, ed.; Englewood Cliffs, N.J., 1963), iv.
2. Ibid., 6; 8; 74; 19; 80.
3. James S. Ackerman and Rhys Carpenter, *Art and Archeology* (Humanistic Scholarship in America: The Princeton Studies, Richard Schlatter, ed.; Englewood Cliffs, N.J., 1963), 131; 131; 142; 243.
4. Claude V. Palisca, "American Scholarship in Western Music," in Harrison, Hood, and Palisca, *Musicology,* 110.
5. Lewis Lockwood, Review of *Musicology,* in *Perspectives of New Music* 3 (1964): 119–27.
6. [This paragraph requires comment. In 1964 I was right, I think, to wish to distance American musicology from German musicology, and to acknowledge ambivalence about this wish in some way. But past those moves, the argument takes one wrong turn after another, probably under the pressure of that ambivalence. After accepting that a critically oriented musicology can take its impetus from a national repertory, I denied that such a repertory exists in America, injected jazz into the argument only to withdraw it at once, and finally implied that the critical impulse itself is peculiarly American. This made and makes no sense.]
7. See the exchange between Charles Rosen and myself in *Perspectives of New Music* 1 (1962): 80–88, and 2 (1963): 151–60.

## 2

# How We Got into Analysis, and How to Get Out

As a matter of general usage, the term "criticism" is applied to music in an anomalous and notably shallow way. This is regrettable but not easy to change so long as the usage has the consent of musicians and non-musicians alike. When people say "music criticism," they almost invariably mean daily or weekly journalistic writing, writing which is prohibited from the extended, detailed, and complex mulling over of the matter at hand that is taken for granted in the criticism of art and especially of literature. Journalistic writing about music is posited on and formed by this prohibition. The music critic may accept it grudgingly, keeping a higher end in view, or he may depend on it to hide what may gently be called his lack of intellectual rigor; in any case, the prohibition is central to his métier. The music critic's stock-in-trade consists of the aesthetic question begged, the critical aphorism undeveloped, the snap judgment.

In fact, a body of less ephemeral, more accountable professional criticism does exist in this country and elsewhere: which is the first thing I wish to argue (or just point out) in this paper. The discipline in question is called by musicians "analysis," not criticism, and by non-musicians it is seldom recognized or properly understood—this for a number of reasons, one of which is the simple matter of nomenclature. In conjunction with music theory, musical analysis enjoys a relatively long academic history going back to the nineteenth-century conservatory curricula. Today all university as well as conservatory musicians are into analysis. They all

⬩ Presented as one of the 1978–79 Thalheimer Lectures in Philosophy at The Johns Hopkins University, and published in *On Criticizing Music: Five Philosophical Perspectives,* ed. Kingsley Price (Baltimore: The Johns Hopkins University Press, 1981), 38–54, under the title "The State of Academic Music Criticism." The present version appeared in *Critical Inquiry* 7 (1980): 311–31.

have to study it and generally do so with much respect. Many practice it, either formally or, more often, informally. They do not, however, like to call it criticism—and one reason for *that* may be traceable to phobias in the profession at large caused by prolonged exposure to journalistic critics.

Thus even those who have dealt most thoughtfully with music criticism in recent years have shown a marked reluctance to affiliate criticism and analysis. I am thinking of such commentators as Arthur Berger, Edward T. Cone,[1] David Lewin, Leonard B. Meyer, Robert P. Morgan, and Leo Treitler. Indeed, some words of my own, written about fifteen years ago, can perhaps be taken as representative:

> Criticism does not exist yet on the American music-academic scene, but something does exist which may feel rather like it: theory and analysis. . . . Analysis seems too occupied with its own inner techniques, too fascinated by its own "logic," and too sorely tempted by its own private pedantries, to confront the work of art in its proper aesthetic terms. Theory and analysis are not equivalent to criticism, then, but they are pursuing techniques of vital importance to criticism. They represent a force and a positive one in the academic climate of music.[2]

Fifteen years later, I can only regard this as waffling. According to the *Harvard Dictionary of Music,* the true focus of analysis, once it gets past the taxonomic stage, is "the synthetic element and the functional significance of the musical detail." Analysis sets out to discern and demonstrate the functional coherence of individual works of art, their "organic unity," as is often said, and that is one of the things— one of the main things—that people outside of music mean by criticism. If in a typical musical analysis the work of art is studied in its own self-defined terms, that too is a characteristic strategy of some major strains of twentieth-century criticism. We might like criticism to meet broader criteria, but there it is. Perhaps musical analysis, as an eminently professional process, fails to open access between the artist and his audience, and perhaps it does indeed fail "to confront the work of art in its proper aesthetic terms"—such failures, too, are not unknown in the criticism of literature and the other arts. Many tasks are ritually urged on criticism that cannot be incorporated into the concept of criticism itself. In other words, I do not see that the criteria suggested above can be included in a definition of criticism that corresponds to the practice of modern critics. We may consider it very desirable that criticism meet these criteria, but we cannot reasonably insist on it. What we have here is a matter for adjustment between music critics of different persuasions rather than some sort of standoff between adherents of distinct disciplines.

It may be objected that musical analysts claim to be working with objective methodologies which leave no place for aesthetic criteria, for the consideration of value. If that were the case, the reluctance of so many writers to subsume analysis under criticism might be understandable. But are these claims true? Are they, indeed, even seriously entered?

Certainly the original masters of analysis left no doubt that for them analysis was an essential adjunct to a fully articulated aesthetic value system. Heinrich Schenker always insisted on the superiority of the towering products of the German musical genius. Sir Donald Tovey pontificated about "the main stream of music" and on occasion developed this metaphor in considerable detail. It is only in more recent times that analysts have avoided value judgments and adapted their work to a format of strictly corrigible propositions, mathematical equations, set-theory formulations, and the like—all this, apparently, in an effort to achieve the objective status and hence the authority of scientific inquiry. Articles on music composed after 1950, in particular, appear sometimes to mimic scientific papers in the way that South American bugs and flies will mimic the dreaded carpenter wasp. In a somewhat different adaptation, the distinguished analyst Allen Forte wrote an entire small book, *The Compositional Matrix* (1961), from which all affective or valuational terms (such as "nice" or "good") are meticulously excluded. The same tendency is evident in much recent periodical literature.

But it scarcely goes unnoticed that the subject of Forte's monograph is not a symphony by Giovanni Battista Sammartini or a quartet by Adalbert Gyrowetz but a late sonata by Beethoven, the Sonata in E Major, op. 109, a work that Forte accepts without question as a masterpiece—without question, and also without discussion. Indeed, this monograph sheds a particularly pure light on the archetypal procedure of musical analysis. This branch of criticism takes the masterpiece status of its subject matter as a *donnée* and then proceeds to lavish its whole attention on the demonstration of its inner coherence. Aesthetic judgment is concentrated tacitly on the initial choice of material to be analyzed; then the analysis itself, which may be conducted with the greatest subtlety and rigor, can treat of artistic value only casually or, as in the extreme case of Forte's monograph, not at all. Another way of putting it is that the question of artistic value is at the same time absolutely basic and begged, begged consistently and programmatically.

In fact, it seems to me that the true intellectual milieu of analysis is not science but ideology. I do not think we will understand analysis and the important role it plays in today's music-academic scene on logical, intellectual, or purely technical grounds. We will need to understand something of its underlying ideology, and this in turn will require some consideration of its historical context. Robert P. Morgan is an analyst who has reminded us on a number of occasions that his discipline must be viewed as a product of its time—a corollary to his conviction that it must also change with the times. The following historical analysis owes something to Morgan's but is, I think, framed more radically or at any rate more polemically.

# II

By ideology, I mean a fairly coherent set of ideas brought together not for strictly intellectual purposes but in the service of some strongly held communal belief. Fundamental here is the orthodox belief, still held over from the late nineteenth century, in the overriding aesthetic value of the instrumental music of the great German tradition. Of this, the central monuments are the fugues and some other instrumental compositions of Bach and the sonatas, string quartets, and symphonies of Mozart, Beethoven, and Brahms.

Viennese or Pan-German in origin, and certainly profoundly guided by nationalistic passions, this ideology took hold in other countries depending on the strength or weakness of their native musical traditions. It took no hold in Italy, some hold in France, strong hold in Britain and especially in America. The ideology drew to itself many familiar currents of nineteenth-century thought about art and music. Among these were an essentially mystical notion of spontaneity and authenticity in musical performance, a Romantic myth (owing much to the example of Beethoven) which cast the artist as sage and suffering hero, and—most important for the present purpose—a strain of Hegelian aesthetic philosophy, which now runs from Schopenhauer to Susanne K. Langer with an important backtrack by way of Eduard Hanslick.

For Hanslick, instrumental music was the only "pure" form of the art, and words, librettos, titles, and programs which seem to link music to the feelings of ordinary, impure life were to be disregarded or deplored. Music, in Hanslick's famous phrase, is "sounding form in motion." Later aestheticians such as Langer have labored to preserve this central insight without denying, as Hanslick did, that music was anything more than that. The concept is an important one for the essential criterion of value that is built into the ideology. For if music is only "sounding form," the only meaningful study of music is formalistic; and while Hanslick was not an analyst, later critics took it on themselves to analyze music's sounding form in the conviction that this was equivalent to its content. To these analyst-critics, needless to say, content (however they defined it) was not a matter of indifference. The music they analyzed was that of the great German tradition.

The vision of these analyst-critics was and is of a perfect, organic relation among all the analyzable parts of a musical masterpiece. Increasingly sophisticated techniques of analysis attempt to show how each aspect or "parameter" or "domain" of the masterpiece performs its function for the total structure. Critics who differ vastly from one another in their methods, styles, and emphases still view the work of art ultimately as an organism in this sense. From the standpoint of the ruling ideology, analysis exists for the purpose of demonstrating organicism, and organicism exists for the purpose of validating a certain body of works of art.

I do not, of course, ignore that broader philosophical movement of the late eighteenth and early nineteenth centuries which focused on organicism and which some musicologists have recently been trying to relate to the development of musical style. But together with this historical process went an ideological one, in the service of which the concept of organicism began to lead a charmed existence. Organicism can be seen not only as a historical force which played into the great German tradition but also as the principle which seemed essential to validate that tradition. The ideological resonance of organicism continued long past the time of its historical impetus.

The origins of the ideology can be traced back to the famous biography of Bach published in 1802 by J. N. Forkel, director of music at the University of Göttingen and the first real German musicologist. "Bach united with his great and lofty style the most refined elegance and the greatest precision in the single parts that compose the great whole," wrote Forkel in his exordium to this work. "He thought the whole could not be perfect if anything were wanting to the perfect precision of the single parts. . . . And this man, the greatest musical poet and the greatest musical orator that ever existed, and probably ever will exist, was a German. Let his country be proud of him; let it be proud, but, at the same time, worthy of him!"[3] We can see the concept of the musical organism taking form with the new attention given to fugue in the early nineteenth century. There was a swift Viennese co-option only a few years later, when E. T. A. Hoffmann began to view Haydn, Mozart, and Beethoven with much the same reverence we do today and began to marvel at the way works such as Beethoven's Fifth Symphony seem to grow from a single theme as though from a Goethean *Urpflanz*. The first great ideological crisis was precipitated by Richard Wagner—Wagner, who could not launch a paper boat without making waves, let alone a revolutionary theory of opera. As Wagner asserted his claim to the Beethovenian succession, the youthful Brahms and his imperious friend Joseph Joachim proclaimed their opposition to symphonic poems, music-dramas, and other such novelties. Hanslick had already closed ranks around the concept of purely instrumental music. He soon came to support Brahms, the most instrumental-minded as well as the most traditional-minded of all the great nineteenth-century composers.

But the ideology did not receive its full articulation until the music in which it was rooted came under serious attack. This occurred around 1900 when tonality, the seeming linchpin of the entire system, began to slip in Germany as well as elsewhere. Lines of defense were formed at what Virgil Thomson used to call "the Brahms line," first in opposition to Richard Strauss and then to Arnold Schoenberg. The situation was exacerbated after 1920 when Schoenberg, in an astonishing new co-option, presented himself and his music as the true continuation of the Viennese tradition. It is against the background of this new crisis that we must see the work of the founding fathers of analysis.

Schenker was born in 1868, Tovey in 1875. The first significant writings of both men, which appeared shortly after 1900, are peppered with polemics and were obviously conceived as a defense against the new modernism. Tovey was no Viennese, of course—Balliol was his beat, and before that Eton—but over and above the general reliance of Victorian England on German music and musical thought, he himself was deeply influenced by the aging Joachim. Concentration on the sphere of harmony and the larger harmony, namely, tonality, led Tovey ultimately to the organicist position, though he was never as dogmatic in this regard as the Germans. In his major essays on the Schubert Quintet and the Beethoven Quartet in C-Sharp Minor, op. 131, he went beyond his usual terminus, the individual movement, and saw tonality inspiring the whole work, with each "key area" conceived of as a functional element in the total structure. And in what he called the "superb rhetoric" of Bach's F-sharp-minor setting of *Aus tiefer Noth* in the *Clavierübung,* part 3—a chorale in which the melodic and rhythmic substance of the given cantus firmus is drawn into all of the polyphonic voice parts according to a rigorous system, so that every note is practically predetermined by an external scheme—Tovey found unshakable evidence that form in art is equivalent to content. "The process miscalled by Horace the concealment of art," wrote Tovey, "is the sublimation of technique into aesthetic results."[4]

In many ways Tovey was a typical product of the *litterae humaniores* at the Oxford of Benjamin Jowett and F. H. Bradley. He came by his neo-Hegelianism honestly. Schenker, on the other hand, was a typical product of the Vienna Conservatory, where the great systematic theorist Simon Sechter had been the teacher of Bruckner, himself the teacher of Schenker. Slowly, stage by stage throughout his career, Schenker labored to construct a grandiose general theory to account for all the music of the great tradition. Tovey's analytical method may be said to involve a reduction of the melodic surface of music to the level of the articulated system of tonality. Schenker's method involved a much more systematic reduction to the level of a single triad, the tonic triad. In his famous series of formalized reductions, he analyzed music on "foreground," "middleground," and "background" levels—the latter comprising the *Urlinie* and the *Ursatz,* a drastically simple horizontalization of the vertical sonority of the tonic triad. (We shall see an example of such an *Ursatz* later.) The concept of hierarchies or levels and the technique of their manipulation constituted Schenker's most powerful legacy to the structuralist future.

Beethoven occupied the dead center of both Schenker's and Tovey's value systems. Schenker's most exhaustive studies concern Beethoven's Third, Fifth, and Ninth Symphonies and the late piano sonatas. Indeed, the list of some fifty compositions which Schenker discussed formally and at full length presents a striking picture of musical orthodoxy. With a few exceptions (including most honorably those late Beethoven sonatas), they are drawn from the stable of symphony orchestra war horses and from the piano teachers' rabbit hutch. In his tacit acceptance of received opinion as to the canon of music's masterpieces, Schenker exemplifies more clearly than any of its other practitioners one aspect of the discipline of analysis.

His work looms so large in academic music criticism of the recent past that analysis is sometimes equated with "Schenkerism," as it is called. The movement is much broader, however, and therefore more significant than any intellectual current which was the province of just one man and his followers could be. Schenker is not the only impressive and influential figure among the older analysts. I have already mentioned Tovey. Rudolph Réti, a disciple at one time of Schoenberg and later an emigré to America, developed a nineteenth-century strain of analysis based not on tonality, line, or triad but on motif. Réti's demonstrations of the hidden identity of all themes in a musical composition—a sort of poor man's organicism—has had a particular impact in Britain. Alfred Lorenz, also originally from Vienna, extended organic analysis over a larger span than had been thought possible and into forbidden territory, the four great music-dramas of Wagner. While modern Wagner scholars seem not to tire of disproving and rejecting Lorenz's work, it receives sympathetic attention from the Verdians, among others. It is possible that both Réti and Lorenz have been written off a little too hastily by modern American academics.

More important—indeed, crucial—is the role of Schoenberg himself in our story. In his relatively limited body of writings on music, Schoenberg showed himself to be a brilliant theorist and critic, and, justly enough, the fact that he was the composer he was gave those writings immense authority.

Schoenberg's really decisive insight, I think, was to conceive of a way of continuing the great tradition while negating what everyone else felt to be at its very core, namely, tonality. He grasped the fact that what was central to the ideology was not the triad and tonality, as Schenker and Tovey believed, but organicism. In his atonal, preserial works written just before World War I, Schoenberg worked out a music in which functional relations were established more and more subtly on the motivic, rhythmic, textural, and indeed the pitch level, with less and less reliance on the traditional configurations of tonality. So for Schoenberg, Brahms was the true "progressive" of the late nineteenth century—Brahms, who had refined the art of motivic variation, rather than Wagner, who had refined and attenuated tonality to the breaking point. Twelve-tone serialism was not far off, and indeed in retrospect one can see implicit from the start the ideal of "total organization" which was to be formulated by the new serialists after World War II.

Schoenberg himself was never interested in developing the sort of analysis that has subsequently been practiced on his own and on other serial music. But once he had entered his formidable claim for inclusion within the great tradition, it was inevitable that a branch of analysis would spring up to validate that claim. For analysis, I believe, and as I have already said, exists to articulate the concept of organicism, which in turn exists as the value system of the ideology; and while the validation provided by analysis was not really necessary for the Viennese Classics, it became more and more necessary for the music of each succeeding generation. What Schenker did for Beethoven and Lorenz did for Wagner, Milton Babbitt and others did later for Schoenberg, Berg, and Webern.

The universal impetus behind analysis was expressed with particular innocence by Réti when he recalled asking himself as a young student why every note in a Beethoven sonata should be exactly *that* note rather than some other. Réti dedicated his career as an analyst to finding an objective answer to this question. And questions of the sort can indeed be answered in respect to the totally organized serial music of the 1950s. Every pitch, rhythm, timbre, dynamic, envelope, and so on can be derived from the work's "precompositional assumptions" by means of simple or slightly less simple mathematics. Whether this derivation provides the *right* answer—that, to be sure, is another question. But the answer provided by serial analysis is, undeniably, objective.

III ·   I come at last, after this lengthy historical digression, to the current state of music criticism in the American academy. Analysis, as I have already indicated, is the main, almost the exclusive, type of criticism practiced in music departments today. I believe also that analysis supplies the chief mental spark that can be detected in those departments.[5] Musicology, a field considerably larger and better organized than analysis, involving mainly historiography and quasi-scientific scholarly research in music, is also cultivated; but American musicology in its academic phase—which has now lasted about thirty or forty years—seems to me to have produced signally little of intellectual interest. What it has assembled is an impressive mass of facts and figures about music of the past, codified into basically non-evaluative histories, editions, bibliographies, and the like. One is reminded of the state of literary studies in the 1930s. Musical analysis has also reminded many observers of the New Criticism which arose at that time. This analogy, though it is not one that will survive much scrutiny, does point to one of the constants of intellectual life as this applies to the arts: as intellectual stimulus, positivistic history is always at a disadvantage beside criticism. It is precisely because and only because analysis is a kind of criticism that it has gained its considerable force and authority on the American academic scene.

Still, as the years and the decades go by, the predominant position of analysis grows more and more paradoxical; paradoxical, because the great German tradition of instrumental music, which analysis supports, no longer enjoys the unique status it did for the generation of Schenker and Tovey and Schoenberg. There is no need to enlarge on the various factors that have so drastically changed the climate for the consumption and appreciation of music today. They include the wide variety of music made available by musicological unearthings on the one hand and recording technology and marketry on the other; the public's seemingly insatiable hunger for opera of all sorts; the growing involvement with non-Western music, popular music, and quasi-popular music; and also a pervasive general disbelief in hierarchies of value. It is not that we see less, now, in the German masters. But they no longer shut out our perspective on great bodies of other music, new and old.

Another factor contributing to this change in our musical climate stems from the crisis in which musical composition has for some time found itself. Heretofore the great tradition had been felt to exist in a permanent condition of organic evolution, moving always onward (if not always upward) into the future, into what Wagner's contemporaries called "Die Musik der Zukunft" and what we were still calling "New Music" with the same upbeat accent in the 1950s. Forkel saw the German tradition originating with Bach; Hoffmann saw Beethoven following from Haydn and Mozart; and Schumann, when he turned resolutely from songs and piano pieces to fugues and symphonies, tactfully added his own name. Less tactfully, Wagner did the same. Hanslick countered with Brahms, Adorno nominated Mahler and Schoenberg, and it was still possible in the 1960s to think of Karlheinz Stockhausen, followed at a discreet distance even—who could tell?—by some non-German figures. Now that there are no candidates from the 1970s, a void has been discovered very close to the center of the ideology.

The paradox has been working itself out in recent American analysis. True, a newly published anthology of *Readings in Schenker Analysis* holds primly to the traditional core of J. S. Bach, C. P. E. Bach, Mozart, Beethoven, Schubert, Schumann, and Brahms. But for more and more analysts it has become a matter of importance—perhaps of supreme importance—to extend the technique to all the music they care deeply about. That is the impetus behind serial analysis, the most impressive American contribution to the discipline at large, which was developed under the general inspiration of Babbitt at Princeton in the late 1940s and 1950s. It is the impetus behind efforts such as those of Morgan and others to extend analysis to the so-called non-teleological music of the 1960s and 1970s. At the other end of the historical spectrum, analyses of pre-Bach, pretonal music were published as early as the 1950s by Felix Salzer, Schenker's most influential follower in this country. Salzer has also sponsored other such analyses in the periodical *Music Forum*. More or less Lorenzian methods have been applied to the Verdi operas. Not only opera but also other music with words and programs has been subjected to analytical treatment: the Schumann song cycle *Dichterliebe,* for example, and the Berlioz *Requiem* and *Symphonie fantastique.* The blanket extension of analysis to genres with words and programs has important theoretical implications, of course. For in spite of Hanslick, the verbal messages included with a musical composition have a strong prima facie claim to be counted in with its content, along with its analyzable sounding form.

These new analyses are, as always, conducted at different levels of sophistication and insight. Even the best of them leave the reader uneasy. They come up with fascinating data and with undoubtedly relevant data; yet one always has a sinking feeling that something vital has been overlooked. For however heavily we may weight the criterion of organicism in dealing with the masterpieces of German instrumental music, we know that it is less important for other music that we value. This music may really not be "organic" in any useful sense of the word, or its organicism may be a more or less automatic and trivial characteristic. Its aesthetic value must depend on other criteria. Cannot a criticism be developed that will explain, validate, or just plain illuminate these other musical traditions?

The obvious answer would seem to be yes, and indeed one can point to a number of recent efforts along these lines. These efforts have not been followed up to any significant extent, however—at least not yet. Musicians in the academic orbit have always dragged their feet when it comes to developing alternative modes of criticism. This is as true of the musicologists as of the analysts and of the large, less clearly defined group of musicians whose inclinations may be described as broadly humanistic and who care about musicology and analysis without having made a full commitment to either (one could point, for example, to the constituency of the College Music Society). Among these many people, it is not uncommon to hear criticism invoked, discussed in general terms, sometimes praised, sometimes even practiced, and occasionally even practiced well. But there seems to be a general disinclination or inability to formalize—much less to institutionalize—the discipline on any scale broader than that of analysis.

There is a real problem here which I do not believe can be attributed entirely to some massive failure of imagination or intellectual nerve. I should prefer to believe that at least part of the problem stems from the prestige of analysis—or, to put it more accurately, from the genuine power of analysis which is the source of that prestige. For analysis, taken in its own terms, is one of the most deeply satisfying of all known critical systems. "Music has, among the arts, the most, perhaps the only, systematic and precise vocabulary for the description and analysis of its objects": that is an envious quotation from Stanley Cavell, a philosopher and critic well versed in music, who knows how much more fully one can fix a melodic line as compared to a line in a drawing, or a musical rhythm as compared to a poetic one, or even an ambiguity in harmony as compared to an ambiguity of metaphor. The discipline of analysis has made a very good thing out of the precise, systematic vocabulary which music possesses. But as Cavell goes on to remark, thinking of the non–existence of what he calls a "humane criticism" of music, "Somehow that possession must itself be a liability; as though one now undertook to criticize a poem or novel armed with complete control of medieval rhetoric but ignorant of the modes of criticism developed in the past two centuries."[6] The liability must stem from the power of analysis and its consequent seductiveness. Its methods are so straightforward, its results so automatic, and its conclusions so easily tested and communicated that every important American critic at the present time has involved himself or implicated himself centrally with analysis.

Not all these critics would consider themselves primarily analysts, and some would probably be begrudged that epithet by the analysts themselves.[7] Charles Rosen, for example, prefaces *The Classical Style: Haydn, Mozart, Beethoven* (1971) with a critique of analytical systems en masse: the limitations of Schenker, Tovey, Réti, and others are cataloged incisively. Nevertheless, Rosen's procedure in the book is basically analytical, if by analysis we mean the technical demonstration of the coherence of individual pieces of music. He also presents a trenchant, controversial, historical interpretation and a steady stream of brilliant aperçus on all aspects of music. But at heart his book is a wonderfully readable and original essay in musical analysis. Rosen speaks not of organicism but of "balance" and "coherence," and it is his sensitivity to the harmonic and melodic determinants of these criteria that provides *The Classical Style* with its greatest power.

Leonard B. Meyer, in his impressive first book *Emotion and Meaning in Music* of 1956, proposed a comprehensive theory of musical aesthetics. A wide-ranging scholar, he moves on in his fourth book to spell out his recipe for criticism (*Explaining Music: Essays and Explorations*, 1973). Again there are telling arguments against Réti and Schenker, and again the proof of the pudding turns out to be analysis—a detailed exemplary study of the first twenty-one bars of a Beethoven sonata according to the author's own analytical principles. (An even more detailed analysis of another German masterpiece has since appeared in *Critical Inquiry*.)[8] Meyer sees musical events as embodying multiple implications for other events that will ensue, implications which are realized or not in various ways. This follows perfectly the model of an overriding system of relationships between all musical elements which has always animated analytical thinking.

To turn now from the sublime to the confessional, my own criticism has returned repeatedly and, as I now think, immoderately to the manner and method of Tovey. There have been digressions to the left and to the right, but in its biggest manifestations, my work, too, has been centered in a kind of analysis.

Finally, I cannot resist mentioning the recent *Beyond Schenkerism: The Need for Alternatives in Music Analysis* (1977) by a younger writer, Eugene Narmour. This is probably the sharpest, most comprehensive attack on Schenker that has ever appeared; and it culminates in the modest proposal of a new analytical system developed by the attacker. The musician's instinctive tendency is always to choose among rival analytical systems or principles rather than to look for a broader alternative to analysis itself. Where we should be looking is not only Beyond Schenkerism but also Beyond Narmourism.[9]

IV ·     I dislike seeming to preach in the abstract, especially when I seem to be preaching against, so I shall now sketch out some conceivable alternatives to analysis in reference to the criticism of one particular short piece of music. I have chosen a familiar, standard German-masterpiece-type example, hoping to show how much can and should be done even where analytical methods traditionally work best.

The piece is from Schumann's song cycle *Dichterliebe,* the second number, "Aus meinen Thränen spriessen" (example 1). The poem is from Heine's *Lyrisches Intermezzo* in the *Buch der Lieder.* I have chosen it partly because, in the somewhat overheated words of the analyst Arthur Komar, "In recent years, the song has aroused an extraordinary amount of interest, much of which can be attributed to its selection as the principal illustration of Schenker's analytic technique in Allen Forte's important introductory article on Schenker's theories."[10] In my view, Schenker's analysis of this song, which bids fair to attain exemplary status, shows up the limitations of the discipline as a whole with exemplary clarity. It constitutes a strong argument for alternatives.

Those unacquainted with the Schenker system will be interested to see his analysis of the song (figure 1). From the "foreground sketch," on the bottom line, more than 75 percent of the notes in the actual song have already been reduced away. Only those considered structurally most important remain, with their relative structural weight indicated by the presence or absence of stems, by the note values—half-note forms are more important than quarter, and so on—and by the beams connecting certain groups of quarter and half notes (in this sketch). Above it, the "middleground sketch" carries the reduction one step further, and above that the "background sketch" completes the process. The basic structure of the song is indicated by the unit at the top right of this *Ursatz:* a simple three-step arpeggiation of the A-major triad, going from the third degree C♯ to the tonic A by way of B as a passing note in the middle. The unit at the left shows the original thrust toward this same *Urlinie* interrupted at the midpoint; the motion is then resumed and completed as shown at the right. Every middleground and foreground detail can be seen to play its organic role as subsumed by the *Ursatz.* And indeed the *Ursatz* is indicative of organicism on a higher level yet: for the *Ursätze* of all musical compositions in the great tradition are essentially the same. Although naturally the interruptions differ, and sometimes the tonic triad is arpeggiated $\hat{5}-\hat{3}-\hat{1}$ or $\hat{8}-\hat{5}-\hat{3}-\hat{1}$, rather than $\hat{3}-\hat{1}$, as here, in principle the *Urlinie* always consists of a simple downward arpeggiation of the tonic triad, which Schenker took to be the "chord of nature."

EXAMPLE I

It seems interesting, incidentally, and possibly significant that this apparently simple song still leaves room for debate as to the precise location of the principal structural tones. Schenker put $\hat{3}$ on the upbeat to bar 1, $\hat{2}$ on the upbeat to bar 9, $\hat{3}$ on the upbeat to bar 13, $\hat{2}$ and $\hat{1}$ in bar 15. Forte proposed a modification: the second $\hat{3}$ on the C♯ in bar 14 (beat 2). Komar accepts this and proposes another modification: the first $\hat{3}$ on the C♯ in bar 2. More serious interest might attach to this debate if someone would undertake to show how its outcome affects the way people actually hear, experience, or respond to the music. In the absence of such a demonstration, the whole exercise can seem pretty ridiculous.

As is not infrequently the case with Schenkerian analyses, the fragile artistic content of this song depends quite obviously on features that are skimped in the

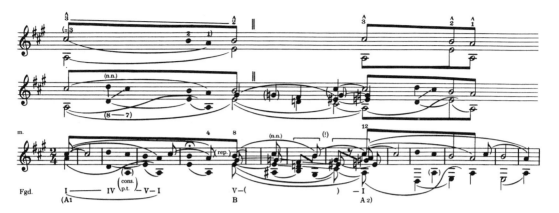

FIGURE I  From Heinrich Schenker, *Free Composition,* ed. and tr. Ernst Oster
(New York, 1970), Supplement: fig. 21b. Reprinted with permission of
Schirmer Books, an imprint of Macmillan Publishing Company, © 1979.

analytical treatment. The song's most striking feature—practically its raison d'être,
one would think—is the series of paired cadences in the voice and then the piano
at the conclusion of lines 2, 4, and 8 of the poem. How are these rather haunting,
contradictory stops to be understood (or "heard," as musicians like to say) at the
two points within the body of the song? And how are they to be heard at the end?
From Schenker's foreground sketch one gathers that in bars 4 and 8 he counted the
voice's half cadences as primary, whereas in bar 17 he counted the piano's full
cadence. But there is no explanation for this disappointingly conventional interpretation, nor any appreciation of the whole extremely original and suggestive
situation, nor indeed any relic of it on the middle- and background levels. The
*Ursatz* confuses the issue, for in bars 4 and 8 the cadences lack status because they
are regarded simply as details of prolongation, along with many others, and in bars
16–17 they are trivialized because true closure is conceived as happening a bar
earlier.

Forte and Komar, with their *Ursatz* revisions, do nothing to help the situation.
Ambiguities such as those set up by Schumann's cadences are likely to strike a critic
as a good place to focus his investigation, to begin seeing what is special and fine
about the song. The analyst's instinct is to reduce these ambiguities out of existence.

Another prime feature of the music skimped by Schenker is the climax at the
words "Und vor deinem Fenster soll klingen," in line 7. This Schumann achieved
by a classical confluence of thickened piano texture, intensified rhythms, a crescendo, and harmonic enrichment by means of chromaticism; for a moment the
emotional temperature spurts up into or nearly into the danger zone. Schenker's
foreground sketch, so far from "explaining" the chromaticism here, barely ac-

knowledges its existence. Once again his very first reduction employs too coarse a sieve to catch something of prime importance. Schenker seems often to have derived a sort of grim pleasure from pretending not even to notice certain blatant foreground details in the music he was analyzing.

In this case, the pretense was too much for Forte, and he draws attention to what he rightly calls a "striking" chromatic line, an inner line, and to its parallelism to others in the song. The emotional temperature, however, does not interest him any more than does the symbolism (of which more later); he is interested only in the fact that the line serves as "an additional means of unification." Forte finds a particularly vexing problem in the G♮ of bars 12–13. Komar too dwells on this as the "major analytic issue" of the whole song.

Neither of these analysts troubles to say (though they surely must see) that both this chromatic G♮ and also the chromatic F♮ in bar 14 give the word "klingen" a richer emotional coloration than "spriessen" and "werden" at the parallel places earlier in the song. Sooner or later we shall have to retrace the course taken by the composer himself and peek at the words of the poem:

Aus meinen Thränen spriessen
Viel blühende Blumen hervor,
Und meine Seufzer werden
Ein Nachtigallenchor.

Und wenn du mich lieb hast, Kindchen,
Schenk' ich dir die Blumen all',
Und vor deinem Fenster soll klingen
Das Lied der Nachtigall.

"Klingen" is a verb applied by the man in the street to coins, wine glasses, and cymbals; poets apply it to the song of nightingales. Was Schumann trying to insist on the poetic credentials of this verb? He certainly declaimed it strangely: the vowel should be short, as of course he knew perfectly well. Also harmonized very richly is the parallel word in the previous couplet—the assonant and no doubt hugely significant word "Kindchen." So presumably the curious accents in lines 2 and 4 on the words "spriessen" and "werden" (rather than on "Thränen" and "Seufzer") were planned with "Kindchen" and "klingen" in mind. Schumann's personal reading of the poem begins to take shape. That reading may fairly be suspected of having influenced his musical decisions.

A good deal more can be done along these lines. Musico-poetic analysis is not necessarily less insightful than strictly musical analysis, whether of the Schenkerian or some other variety, as is evident from the subtle and exhaustive analyses of Schubert songs by Arnold Feil and Thrasybulos Georgiades in Germany.[11] In

America, unfortunately, the one serious recent study of the German lied is valuable mainly as shock therapy. In *Poem and Music in the German Lied from Gluck to Hugo Wolf* (1971), the late Jack M. Stein prods all the great nineteenth-century lieder composers for their misreadings of poetry; our song, for example, he dismisses on account of its "mood of naiveté and sentimental innocence." There is often something in what Stein says. But while Schumann certainly comes dangerously close to sentimentality in his setting of the word "klingen," we should also reckon on the clipped and dryly repetitious musical phrase that returns unvaried for "Das Lied der Nachtigall." Does this not effectively undercut the sentimental tendency? On this occasion, at least, Schumann has not smoothed away the celebrated irony of his poet.

Komar's criticism of Schenker and Forte as regards the *Ursatz* stems from his reading of the song in conjunction with the preceding song in the cycle, "Im wunderschönen Monat Mai," the beautiful and well-known opening number. He is right as far as he goes, though he does not go so far as to make the obvious point that since "Aus meinen Thränen" directly follows the famous arpeggiated C#$^7$ chord on which that opening song is left hanging, its first few notes do not announce an unambiguous A major, as Schenker so brutally assumed, but rather, for a fleeting moment, the expected resolution in F-sharp minor. So even the first half-prominent gesture in the song, the articulation of the word "spriessen," sounds more poetic and less naive, less sentimental, than Stein would have us believe.

Komar says that Schumann forged the two songs "virtually into a single entity" from a strictly musical standpoint. If so, that shows that, unlike his analysts, Schumann cared that the two poems also form a unit:

Im wunderschönen Monat Mai,
Als alle Knospen sprangen,
Da ist in meinem Herzen
Die Liebe aufgegangen.

In the beautiful month of May
when all the buds were bursting,
it was then that in my heart
love broke through.

Im wunderschönen Monat Mai,
Als alle Vögel sangen,
Da hab' ich ihr gestanden
Mein Sehnen und Verlangen.

In the beautiful month of May
when all the birds were singing,
it was then I confessed to her
my longing and desire.

Aus meinen Thränen spriessen
Viel blühende Blumen hervor,
Und meine Seufzer werden
Ein Nachtigallenchor.

From my tears there sprout
many flowers in bloom,
and my sighs become
a nightingale chorus.

Und wenn du mich lieb hast, Kindchen,
Schenk' ich dir die Blumen all',
Und vor deinem Fenster soll klingen
Das Lied der Nachtigall.

And if you can love me, dear child,
I will give you all the flowers,
and your window shall resound
with the song of the nightingale.

The "Knospen" of the first song open into "blühende Blumen" in the second, the "Vögel" identify themselves as "Nachtigallen," and so on. In terms of critical methodology, Komar's emphasis on the cycle's continuity merely transfers his organicist investigation from the level of the song to the higher level of the cycle. Still, there is some use to his procedure in that it indicates a broadening out, and one may ask what the real subject of the critic's attention should be—that G♮ which Komar calls the "major analytic issue" of the song, or the total music of the song, or its music taken together with its words, or the full sixteen-song *Dichterliebe* cycle, or perhaps the entire output of Schumann's so-called song year, 1840. As is well known, *Dichterliebe* was composed along with about 120 other songs in a single burst of creative energy lasting for eleven months, a period which encompassed the composer's marriage, after agonizing delays, to Clara Wieck.

All the songs of 1840 were written for Clara, and many of them were written directly to her. *Dichterliebe* begins in the way that Schumann's earlier Heine song cycle, op. 24, ends: with a song of dedication. The poet-composer offers his work to his beloved, work that is formed out of his love and his longing. Heretofore, however, Schumann had been transforming his longing not into nightingale songs but into piano pieces—which suggests a new irony to the word "klingen," a double (or by now a triple) irony if one thinks of the shallow virtuoso pieces by Herz and Pixis on which Clara was making her reputation as a pianist while Robert was attacking them angrily in his journalism, crippling his hand in a mechanism designed to strengthen it, and bit by bit relinquishing his own ambitions as a performer. The sixteen songs now dedicated to Clara speak of love's distress, not of love's happiness. Clara, incidentally, was twelve years old when Robert first turned up as her father's student, already a sick man and a rather alarmingly dissolute one. "Aus meinen Thränen" is the only one of Schumann's love songs which includes the word "Kind" or "Kindchen."

The comprehensive study of the Schumann songs by the English critic and cryptographer Eric Sams has not been much noticed in this country.[12] Sams takes a strong antianalytical line and also puts people off by his somewhat brazen pursuit of a special theory about Schumann's compositional practice. This theory centers on the composer's use of a complicated network of private musical symbolism; thus Sams identifies several secret "Clara themes" in "Aus meinen Thränen," among them the expressive descending-scale figure on the word "Kindchen" which was mentioned above. The analysts cannot do anything with data of this kind. As far as they are concerned, the same notes in the same musical context ought always to produce the same sounding form, whether written by Schumann or Schubert or Mendelssohn. But it is not unusual for composers to nurture private musical symbols. Berg is a famous case in point. Schumann is unusual, perhaps, only in the large number of studied clues he left around for future decoders. No doubt Sams goes too far. But if what we value in an artist is his individual vision, rather than the evidence he brings in support of some general analytical system, we shall certainly want to enter as far as possible into his idiosyncratic world of personal association and imagery.

Looking again, more broadly yet, at Schumann's songs and the tradition from which they sprang, one must come to a consideration of characteristics inherent in the genre itself. An artistic genre has a life of its own in history; criticism cannot proceed as though history did not exist. The nineteenth-century German lied began with a firm alliance to a romantically conceived *Volksweise*, and while from Schubert on the history of the genre is usually seen in terms of a transcendence of this ideal, composers have never wished to transcend it entirely. Evocations of the *Volkstümlich* were handled excellently, in their different ways, by Beethoven, Schubert, Brahms, and even Wolf, to say nothing of Mahler. But Stein was right: Schumann's evocations are always tinged with "sentimental innocence." Some further examples may be cited: "Volksliedchen," op. 51 no. 2; "Der arme Peter," op. 53 no. 3; "Marienwürmchen," op. 79 no. 14; "Lied eines Schmiedes," op. 90 no. 1; "Mond, meine Seele Liebling," op. 104 no. 1; and "Hoch, hoch sind die Berge," op. 138 no. 8.

Sams makes the same point and also stresses that in addition to word cyphers and musical quotations, Schumann was also addicted to disguises, of which the impulsive Florestan and the introspective Eusebius are only the most public—so much so, that in works like *Carnaval* and *Dichterliebe* one sometimes feels impelled to ask the real Robert Schumann to please stand up. In *Dichterliebe,* by contrast with the song cycles of Beethoven and Schubert, not all but very many of the songs seem to assume different personae: think of "Aus meinen Thränen" in contrast with "Ich grolle nicht," "Wenn ich in deine Augen seh'," "Ich hab' im Traum geweinet," and others. Schumann's self-consciousness as regards the implications of genre and subgenre must be taken into account for any comprehensive understanding of his artistic intentions.

The term "persona" has been borrowed from literary criticism by a musician whose commitment to analysis has never blinded him to what Cavell calls a "humane criticism of music," Edward T. Cone. In *The Composer's Voice,* Cone's argument, which ultimately goes much further than the lied repertory, begins with Schubert's "Erlkönig." He first inquires who it is that sings the various "voices" in this well-known song and next invites us to distinguish the vocal persona or personae from that of the piano part which underlies and binds the whole together. This seems a fruitful line to take with "Aus meinen Thränen." At first the vocal and instrumental parts run closely parallel, but they pull apart at those ambiguous cadences to which attention was drawn earlier. The voice and the piano stop in their own ways and in their own sweet times; how are we to conceive of their coordination? A highly suggestive question that Cone asks about songs is whether the pianist hears the singer and vice versa (more precisely, whether the instrumental persona hears the vocal persona). There is no doubt that the pianist hears the singer in bar 12 of "Aus meinen Thränen." But I am less sure that he does so in bar 4 and pretty sure he does not in bar 17. At this point, the attention of the instrumental persona is directed elsewhere, toward some arcane and fascinating musical thought process of its own.

Can analysis help us here? Cone always likes to address his musical criticism to musical performance, and I believe that a resolution of this question of the vocal and instrumental personae will also resolve one performance problem with this song, this small, fragile, and haunting song: namely, the treatment of the fermatas in bars 4, 8, and 16.

v ·    The alternatives that I have suggested to traditional musical analysis—in this case, to Schenkerian and post-Schenkerian analysis—are not intended, of course, to exhaust all the possibilities. They are merely examples of some lines along which a more comprehensive, "humane," and (I would say) practical criticism of music can and should be developed. Nor is the term "alternative" to be taken in an exclusive sense. One cannot envisage any one or any combination of these alternative modes of criticism as supplanting analysis; they should be joined with analysis to provide a less one-dimensional account of the artistic matters at hand. What is important is to find ways of dealing with other kinds of aesthetic value in music besides organicism, ways of dealing responsibly.

I do not actually think we need to get out of analysis, then, only out from under.

As I mentioned above, there are a number of pressures today leading to a new breadth and flexibility in academic music criticism. Of these, one of the most powerful emerges from efforts to come to terms with the newest music. The position of Robert Morgan, for example, seems not far from that outlined in the present paper, though the way he formulates that position is certainly very different. The traditional concept of analysis as "the elucidation of a sort of teleological organism," Morgan feels—the language is derived from Cone—must be made broader; the analysis of new music

> must examine the composer's intentions in relation to their compositional
> realization, must discuss the implications of the compositional system in
> regard to the music it generates, consider how the resulting music relates
> to older music and to other present-day music, examine its perceptual
> properties and problems, etc. There is really no end to the possibilities that
> could enable this list to be extended.

Indeed, "a pressing responsibility of present-day analysis is to indicate how new music reflects present-day actuality."[13]

Within the narrow confines of the music-academic community, this call for analysis to examine, discuss, and indicate what it never thought of examining, discussing, or indicating before may well prove to be perplexing. Outside the community, the only thing that will perplex is Morgan's clinging to the term "analysis." What he seems clearly to be talking about is criticism, and he is talking about it in a way that must surely enlist sympathy.

---

*Notes*

1. [But soon after this essay was written, Cone brought criticism and analysis together in an impressive comprehensive essay, "The Authority of Music Criticism" (1981), reprinted in his *Music: A View from Delft,* ed. Robert P. Morgan (Chicago, 1989), 95–112.]

2. See p. 7.

3. *The Bach Reader,* ed. Hans T. David and Arthur Mendel, rev. ed. (New York, 1966), 352–53.

4. Donald Francis Tovey, *The Main Stream of Music and Other Essays* (New York, 1949), 165.

5. [This was written, of course, around 1980.]

6. Stanley Cavell, *Must We Mean What We Say?* (New York, 1969), 186 (from ch. 7, "Music Discomposed").

7. "Work . . . by 'one-off' analysts like Rosen or Kerman [is] frequently held to be suspect in its theoretical focus," writes Jonathan M. Dunsby. "They seem to embed the most penetrating and original insight about specific musical objects in an all-embracing cultural critique that can be ultimately confusing, without the deep-rooted convictions—often hard to live with but always comprehensible—of the Schoenbergian analytical tradition" (Review of *Beyond Orpheus* by David Epstein, *Journal of the Arnold Schoenberg Institute* 3 [1979]: 195).

8. See Leonard B. Meyer, "Grammatical Simplicity and Relational Richness: The Trio of Mozart's G-Minor Symphony," *Critical Inquiry* 2 (1976): 693–761.

9. Another younger writer, David Epstein, prefaces his *Beyond Orpheus: Studies in Musical Structure* (Cambridge, Mass., 1979) with this statement about "the limitations imposed on the [analytical] studies that follow": "First, they are concerned with music written within the era commonly known as classic-romantic, in effect from Haydn and Mozart through the middle nineteenth century, as delimited by Brahms. Secondly, these studies are restricted to music in what might be called the German-Viennese tradition—the most seminal body of music that emerged during this broad period. Third, they are confined to absolute music. . . . A fourth and final limitation: the matter of 'expression' in music is beyond the confines of these studies" (p. 11). One hears the sound of windows closing.

[The quip about Beyond Narmourism can be read today in reference to Narmour's *The Analysis and Cognition of Basic Melodic Structures: The Implication–Realization Model* (Chicago, 1990).]

10. Arthur Komar, "The Music of *Dichterliebe:* The Whole and Its Parts," in *Robert Schumann, "Dichterliebe,"* ed. Arthur Komar (Norton Critical Scores, New York, 1971), 70–71.

The article in question, "Schenker's Conception of Musical Structure," one of Forte's earlier writings, first appeared in *Journal of Music Theory* 3 (1959): 1–30, and has since been reprinted in Komar's casebook (pp. 96–106) and as the first item in *Readings in Schenkerian Analysis and Other Approaches,* ed. Maury Weston (New Haven, 1977), 3–37. In a graded list of "Initial Readings in Schenker" prepared by another leading analyst, Richmond Browne, for the journal *In Theory Only* 1 (1975): 4, Forte's article appears as the second entry from the top.

11. [Samples appear in *Schubert: Critical and Analytical Essays,* ed. Walter Frisch (Lincoln, Neb., 1986).]

12. Eric Sams, *The Songs of Robert Schumann,* rev. ed. (London, 1975).

13. Robert P. Morgan, "On the Analysis of Recent Music," *Critical Inquiry* 4 (1977): 40; 51.

3

# A Few Canonic Variations

1 · *Thema*  "Canon," to musicians, means something else. "Wir haben ein Gesetz." That may
be the one reason we feel awkward, even a little uneasy, about using the term as it
is used in the other arts, to mean (roughly) an enduring exemplary collection of
books, buildings, and paintings authorized in some way for contemplation, admiration, interpretation, and the determination of value. We speak of the repertory,
or repertories, not of the canon. A canon is an idea; a repertory is a program of
action.

A deeper reason, I think, has to do with some simple and well-known truths
about music's evanescence, that evanescence which makes for special difficulties
when we try to talk about music's history. Certainly it is difficult to talk about a
canon without also talking about history. Perhaps I can begin a discussion of these
difficulties through some simple words once spoken by Mantle Hood, following
one of his gracefully polemical seminars. Hood had just urged, in effect, that
Western art music be viewed not in terms of a canon but rather as a field of social
and cultural activity.

> Music persists as it is only to the extent that interlocking requirements
> allow it to. . . . When a culture has finished with any [musical] tradition,
> when it no longer communicates or ceases to fill whatever function it
> has filled esthetically or otherwise, then it will most certainly disappear,
> particularly in cultures where there is no form of written record of such
> things. In our culture I think many traditions have not completely

➤ From *Critical Inquiry* 10 (1983): 107–25, and *Canons,* ed. Robert von Hallberg (Chicago: University of Chicago Press, 1984), 177–95.

disappeared because we do have some kind of written record. I suspect that in many ways, however, their real identities are gone. I think we are looking at skeletons, without being sure what kind of flesh they ought to be clothed in.[1]

Music is process, action, activity; but once it is written down it yields up an object (a score) and is itself on the way to becoming objectified. The concept of a musical work or composition, to say nothing of a canon, depends on such objectification, at least to some extent—on writing, which is not a musical but a graphic mode. What Hood wants to stress is that "some kind of written record" is neither necessary nor sufficient to assure the "real" maintenance of a musical tradition. As long as a tradition persists, musicians continue to internalize the music by a long and, to them, rewarding process of attending to it, absorbing it, imitating it, learning it, and repeating it. There may or may not be written aids to this, but essentially the tradition is passed on orally from musician to musician and from musician to listener.

It is not surprising to find this model for music insisted on by ethnomusicologists. Coming to an alien music cold, or more or less cold, and perhaps finding that some sort of notation has been developed for it, an ethnomusicologist such as Hood becomes only too sharply aware of how little the documents tell him about time and tempo, nuance and sonority, the limits of improvisatory practice—everything that gives the music of the Javanese puppet theater, say, its particular arcane identity. Often enough the ethnomusicologist finds nothing at all in writing to help him with his work, whether this consists of describing music or learning to perform it—often through lengthy apprenticeships—in order to achieve some measure of the internalization on which that identity depends.

None of this may seem like much of a problem to those of us who stick to our own tradition. We have been internalizing this music ever since our fathers sang us Beatles songs and our mothers shoved our playpens in front of the TV. It is only on the basis of this unconscious internalization that musicians can easily learn to read musical scores straight off—with the feel of other such music in their fingers and throats and with its sound in their ears. But music in this sense, as must be clear, does not extend back very far in history. Music in this sense (which is Hood's sense) does not *have* much history. In the absence of an internalized performance tradition, the interpretation of written records of Western music going back two hundred years is already equivocal, five hundred years highly speculative, and a thousand years in certain serious ways hopeless. The notation symbols of the ninth and tenth centuries—staffless neumes—do not even specify pitch or (so far as scholars agree) rhythm, let alone tempo, tone quality, ornamentation, or dynamics—only certain aspects of melodic contour.

So it is not surprising, once again, that among students of Western music the greatest sympathy for the ethnomusicologists' dilemma, and the greatest interest in their model, has been shown to date by medievalists. Leo Treitler now conceives of the history of medieval music in terms of a by no means simple or unilateral transition from what he calls the "medieval paradigm" to the "modern paradigm" or "paradigm of literacy."[2] Gregorian chant was first sung in monastic communities according to an oral, formulaic system, internalized by cantors of ritual texts whom Treitler has compared to Albert Lord's singers of tales. The complex polyphonic music of later centuries was written down by composers—Pérotin, Petrus de Cruce, Machaut, Dufay—to be sung, more or less "by the book," by musicians who could read music as well as words. Treitler's medieval paradigm helps explain many things, including some puzzles about the interpretation of the earliest Gregorian chant notation—a notation invented, it is clear, in order to meet Charlemagne's determination to import and standardize the music that went with the canonical words of the Roman Mass and office services. He ran into trouble, which is reflected in the chant manuscripts. While the words could be sent to him, it took some time before he could be satisfied about the music, for it was not clear in Rome how an oral tradition could be, in fact, canonized.

Charlemagne's program was the first instance of canon formation in Western music, and one thing to keep in mind about it is that it called for texts, for written records. This was a new idea as far as music was concerned. When a fresh redaction of the Gregorian canon was demanded by the Counter-Reformation papacy, things went much more smoothly since people were by then accustomed to using musical texts like verbal texts, musical notation was much more highly developed, and, of course, the distribution of texts was now much more efficient. The next official redaction of the Gregorian canon was carried out by the scholarly Benedictines of Solesmes in the nineteenth century. This was interesting both because of the sophisticated philological principles on which it rested and also because its authority was extended to cover not only the notes on the page but also the way they were to be sung. The Solesmes phenomenon is an early instance of re-creating a historical performance tradition—putting flesh or clothes on those skeletons. I shall return to it later.

II · *Canon perpetuus*    With some qualifications Richard L. Crocker, another medievalist, accepts Treitler's medieval paradigm for the early Gregorian period but not his paradigm of literacy for the later Middle Ages and beyond.[3] Impressed by work such as Hood's, he does not consider that a musical tradition changes in any essential way under the impact of writing or literacy. Crocker is even ready to take on the art music of the nineteenth century—though if there ever was a time when a canon was consolidated in music outside of the Church, this should be it. Even in the nineteenth century, musicians operated more or less as they always had, relying primarily on the internal dynamic of tradition rather than on the external authority of composers' ideal texts. The points Crocker makes about this are worth summarizing. As he says, performers were (and still are) taught by word and gesture and example those all-important, unwritten nuances that would completely elude someone from Java schooled simply in note reading, although such nuances are required for even the most elementary level of performing competence. Nineteenth-century instrumental and vocal virtuosos improvised freely and often played fast and loose with the text before them. "Throughout the nineteenth century we know of the important role of the performer as 'interpreter,' under which rubric he or she could do and did an endless variety of individual things to whatever written record there was." Scores were neither sacrosanct nor stable; well-liked music was arranged—that is, recast, rescored, and recomposed—into multiple versions for different performing groups. Famous composers kept revising their famous texts, too; so much so, in Verdi's case, that of his twenty-six operas, seventeen (including *Oberto,* the first, and *Falstaff,* the last) exist or existed in more than one version. "The fact that a work can be established to have one original, authentic, final form may not reflect the composer's final authoritative determination, but only that he was never occasioned by performance opportunities to rethink it."

This is spirited and salutary; though for the purposes of his own polemic, Crocker lights up only one face of a notoriously two-faced century. Verdi also wrote contracts stipulating that his operas were to be performed note for note according to the materials supplied by his publisher. Very few are the compositions by Brahms that he allowed to survive in more than one version. No one called Clara Schumann a *virtuosa* or observed her monkeying with a text. The same nineteenth century that spawned all those innumerable arrangements also nurtured the first musical variorums (Bischoff's edition from the 1880s of Bach's keyboard music, now published by Kalmus, is an example that many will know).

What seems to me more significant about the nineteenth century is the fundamental change that took place during this period in the nature of the Western art-music tradition or, more precisely, in the way this tradition changed. In previous centuries the repertory consisted of music of the present generation and one or two preceding generations; it was continuously turning over. Thus in the fifteenth century the insufferable Johannes Tinctoris could announce that there was no music worth listening to that hadn't been written in the last forty years (about his own age at the time); in seventeenth-century Venice, though the opera houses may remind us of a modern city's movie theaters, there were no rerun houses for Monteverdi as there are for Fellini; and Bach's music dropped out of the Leipzig repertory at his death no less promptly than that of his far less eminent predecessors. Under such conditions of evanescence the idea of a canon is scarcely thinkable.

After around 1800 or 1820, however, when new music entered the repertory, old music did not always drop out. Beethoven and Rossini were added to, not replaced. Increasingly the repertory assumed a historical dimension; music assumed a history. There were even conscious efforts to extend the repertory back into the evanesced past.

For "repertory" I should have written "secular repertories"; as has already been noted, the Catholic church had its enduring canon, periodically revised, and by 1800 the Lutheran and Anglican rites also supported musical traditions extending back (even if only tenuously, as the Leipzig case reminds us) two hundred years or more. In the secular sphere an interesting exception is Jean-Baptiste Lully, whose operas held the stage in France for nearly a hundred years after their composition. This exception is revealing because special social-political and also special literary-academic reasons can be adduced for it with such clarity. On the one hand, there was Lully's extraordinary and, it seems, even posthumous power in controlling the resources of artistic monopoly and patronage under the Sun King. On the other, there was the French academic establishment, which took the composer and his librettist Philippe Quinault if not exactly into its heart at least into its canon, even devising a special literary genre, *tragédie lyrique,* to validate the canonization. Quite exceptionally for operas in the seventeenth century, sumptuous scores were printed of the Lully works.

That the new longevity enjoyed (or suffered) by repertories depended on the new social configuration that was formed for music in the nineteenth century is obvious. It may be less obvious that it also depended on the literary phenomenon of canonization. Why would the new social scene for music—the concert series and the virtuoso, the bourgeois as audience and amateur, the freelance composer and critic—in itself have frozen and extended repertories? The social scene exacted, perhaps, its ideology. In any case, the ideology supporting the notion of a canon in music was one of the first precipitates of the post-Kantian revolution in music criticism and aesthetics. Like the expanding, historical repertory, the canon was one of music's legacies from early Romanticism.

Repertories are determined by performers, canons by critics—who are by preference musicians, but by definition literary men or at least effective writers about music. Literary models lie close at hand for the categories that music critics have to manipulate. When E. T. A. Hoffmann in 1810 proclaimed Haydn, Mozart, and Beethoven as the three great Romantic composers—though Beethoven was clearly *primus inter pares*—an idea that caught so much of the resonance of contemporary aesthetics itself resonated hugely into the future. "Romantic" was a term taken from literature (and Hoffmann the arch-Romantic novelist did his unfortunately rather premature best to compose Romantic operas also). What Hoffmann called "Romantic" we call "Classic," to be sure: a term conflating a stylistic discrimination between these composers and a later generation, which Hoffmann did not live to see, with the honorific that Hoffmann actually intended, whatever his terminology. For him, Haydn, Mozart, and Beethoven constituted the canon.

Literary, too, was the model for the status Hoffmann meant to bestow on his musical trinity. He wanted to erect pedestals for them like those supporting the three great Greek tragedians, thrones like those still being warmed by at least one of the Weimar classics. Beethoven was compared, inevitably, to Shakespeare. The canonization of the Greek tragedians and Shakespeare depended on written texts; there was no concern about the internalization of theatrical performance traditions, nor as yet about recovering such traditions. Hence scores in the nineteenth century assumed a new importance, over and above that of providing guidance for conductors (less anachronistically: leaders of group performances) or fodder for student composers. Scores were now seen as texts for criticism, like literary texts.

Hoffmann's program as a music critic combined metaphysical speculation, Romantic rhetoric, and legislation about the canon with specific, sometimes bar-by-bar musical descriptions—an early form of musical analysis modeled once again on the modes of literary criticism. Hoffmann must be the first of many authors who have badgered journal editors with demands for more and more music illustrations; it is extremely important, he kept saying, for his readers to be able to see the scores—scores which he himself had to prepare, incidentally, since the music he was discussing was issued not in scores (to be studied) but in separate band parts (to be played from). His famous Beethoven reviews were not of live performances but of published sheet music, texts dead on the page save for Hoffmann's internalized musical imagination and that of his readers.[4]

As in the case of plainchant in the ninth century, canonization in the nineteenth was bound up with the whole matter of musical records. Inexpensive *Taschenpartituren* found their way into the pockets of serious concertgoers, while expensive fifty-volume critical editions of great composers' scores in folio were prepared by musicologists, a new brand of scholar marching along dutifully in the footsteps of literary historians and philologists. The Romantics did not think like today's ethnomusicologists, for whom the ultimate reality of music resides in the social activity of musical performance. They were idealists enough to see musical scores as primary texts of which performances, or "readings," were successively imperfect representations.

And if this idea was not always spelled out frankly, one reason was, I think, that it clashed with another idea or ideal that was dear to the Romantics. This was the spontaneity of the artist—the performing artist as well as the composer. The performer was thought to have something inspired of his own to bring to any music; yet the underlying assumption was that he should be representing the composer's inspiration and doing his best to convey this faithfully, "authentically." In a similar way, as M. H. Abrams pointed out many years ago, the idea of the work of art growing organically and inevitably as though from a seed clashed with the ideal of the poet's spontaneity, and indeed put in question his very role in making the poem.[5] These conflicts were unresolvable and grew more explicit as the discipline of musical analysis was refined from its adumbrations in the work of Hoffmann. Analysis shows why this sequence of notes in the score is important and that sequence is not, why the main downbeat is here and not there, and why this phrasing is right and that one wrong. Unless the critic conceives of his work as purely theoretical, these are veiled instructions he is issuing to the performer. The analysts' insights, said Edward T. Cone in a famous article, "reveal how a piece of music should be heard, which in turn implies how it should be played. An analysis is a direction for a performance."[6] The idea of a canonical work of music has to imply the idea of a canonical musical performance.

All this was possible, no doubt, only because an entire high culture intoxicated by music had internalized it to so high a degree. Crocker observes that where Treitler's paradigm of literacy works best is in reference to the seemingly perpetual twentieth-century cultivation of nineteenth-century masterpieces:

> If we turn to classical instrumental music—symphonies, chamber works, and solos—especially in twentieth-century institutionalized performances, then indeed we seem to be dealing with the "paradigm of literacy." . . . The most important point about this instrumental repertory seems to me to be that it involves a very specific, restricted list of symphonies, string quartets, sonatas preserved long after origin in a kind of Meistersinger environment—one in which we could imagine the authority of the stan-dard version to derive . . . from factors of reverence for impressive, beloved compositions.[7]

This sounds like a pretty fair definition of a canon, except that Crocker is really speaking about a repertory; but in this case, at least, the canon is at the core of the repertory. It need not be restricted to instrumental music. Equally canonical are vocal works by the instrumental masters—*Don Giovanni, Dichterliebe, Ein deutsches Requiem*—as well as works by other masters who specialized in opera or lieder.

The idea of a canon had taken hold powerfully during the nineteenth century, as the canon itself grew by the accretion of more and more music—though of course the growth was never entirely linear. While Beethoven always stayed at dead center, Haydn and much of Mozart dropped or at least faded out, to be reinstated later, and a major issue developed over the inclusion of Wagner or Brahms or both. Liszt's claim was never properly adjudicated; indeed, members of non-Teutonic nations grew increasingly restive over the difficulty of gaining places for their heroes. For from Hoffmann's time on, the ideology which nurtured that growth included a strong component of nationalism along with historicism, organicism—

a concept applied not only to individual artistic structures but also to the canon itself—and what Carl Dahlhaus has aptly called "the metaphysics of instrumental music." This ideology is something I have touched on in an earlier article, which also includes something about the canon and a good deal more about the academic critics—that is, musical analysts—who validated it.[8]

Formed at the outset of Romanticism, this ideology seems to have reached its fullest articulation as a reaction to the advent of modernism, at the very time when the ideology itself came under question. The first of the influential writings of Heinrich Schenker and Donald Francis Tovey appeared in the early 1900s. Of all early twentieth-century critics, Schenker was the most rigidly committed to the concept of a canon, which for him consisted of J. S. and C. P. E. Bach, Handel, Haydn, Mozart, Beethoven, Schubert, Schumann, Mendelssohn, Chopin, Brahms, and no further. Tovey was a little more flexible, partly because, unlike Schenker, he was a practicing musician all his life and, as such, had to deal with the day-to-day reality of repertories—but not much. Both men, incidentally, spent much time editing authoritative editions of Beethoven and the two Bachs.

It is worth repeating that repertories are determined by performers, canons by critics. How much effect critics have on actual repertories is a matter of much ill-natured debate. In any case, conservative critics at the turn of the century did not all agree on the exact prospectus of the canon, any more than they agreed on correct methods of musical analysis. That would hardly have been natural, would have left hardly anything to argue about. What they did all agree upon was that Western music should be viewed in terms of a canon and that some form of analysis of the scores was the means of determining what music belonged in.

III · *Per motum contrarium*    A contrary way of viewing music, perhaps even directly opposite, has made great headway in this century. It fixes arts policy in Marxist societies. In the West this view has been building up somewhere in between, I believe, two other contrarieties, which have become fully articulate only when formulated as attacks. One is an attack in the marketplace, an attack on the nineteenth-century repertory. The other is an attack in the academy, an attack on musical analysis.

A nonpareil marketplace warrior was Virgil Thomson, ever since the fine fury of his campaign against "the appreciation-racket" and "the fifty pieces" in *The State of Music,* which burst on the scene in 1939. Many critics have followed him—most recently, and most gently, Edward Rothstein of the *New York Times*—in deploring the anacondalike hold that nineteenth-century music persists in maintaining on today's repertory.[9] It is a quixotic attack, for the beast is more likely to laugh all the way to the bank than to holler out "Virgil!" and roll over belly up. Some of the animus here—certainly for Thomson's generation—stems from the anti-Romantic reaction following World War I. People turned against the high emotional and sententious tone that is the hallmark of Romantic music—in Wagner quintessentially, but also even in Beethoven. Those who remember Aldous Huxley's novel *Point Counter Point* may remember how accurately that always trendy author expressed the anti-Beethoven fashion of the 1920s, this by means of the episode in which Maurice Spandrell, dejected after Mark Rampion has listened with him to the *Heiliger Dankgesang* movement of opus 132 and pontificated about its metaphysical emptiness, walks into his self-prepared suicide trap. As his friends rush to the door to confront his assassins, the needle is heard scratching away at the end of the record. The end for Spandrell, it seems, is also the end for Beethoven.

Many needles have scratched on Beethoven records since that fictional day. However, the standard repertory has regrouped appreciably, and with it, the canon, as indeed had been happening all along. Berlioz, Musorgsky, and Verdi have assumed some of the former luster of Mendelssohn and Brahms, as we know, to say nothing of Rachmaninoff and Sibelius. It is surely no accident that the most conspicuous new addition to the repertory, Mahler, should be almost Nietzschean in the combination of nausea and nostalgia which he expresses for nineteenth-century music.

Another outcome of the anti-Romantic reaction that worked against the nineteenth-century repertory was an interest in older, "pre-Bach" music (which did not, however, develop as a major force until after World War II, at a time when the anti-Romantic reaction was waning). More serious than any of this, I suspect, was the dawning realization after World War I that the repertory was no longer growing by the addition of new or at least modernist music. The reasons are well known. Modernist composers, like other modernist artists, dissociate themselves from any audience other than one made up of other artists; listeners have not been able to internalize much modernist music; and performers, since so much of it is extremely difficult to execute, often do not persevere with material they find unrewarding in several senses of the word. In this situation modernist music is played on relatively few occasions by a relatively small cadre of contemporary-music specialists. It belongs in *their* repertory but not in *the* repertory. The Berg *Altenberg Lieder* does not figure in the corpus of music that sopranos are taught they must master to achieve professional status; the same is true of the Stravinsky and Schoenberg concertos for violinists, the Boulez sonatas for pianists, and even the Elliott Carter quartets for string quartets. These are works we may ache to see included in the canon, but we cannot say they are included in the repertory.

The musical tradition has changed diametrically, both in the music played and listened to and in the social conditions under which playing and listening take place. At first the repertory was nearly all contemporary. Then it extended from some point in the past up to and including the present. Now it seems to hang suspended like a historical clothesline between two fixed points in the past. This new state of affairs must first have caused apprehension and then something like terror; fears for the very life of music seem to underlie attacks on the nineteenth-century repertory as much as any explicit commitment to modernism. I do not suppose people really begrudged the repertory the right to send down taproots, but some seem to have felt like ripping them up when they saw the trunk was no longer growing new leaves and flowers. The repertory was no longer functioning like an organism.

For that matter, was the individual work of art, the autonomous musical structure itself, still functioning like an organism? Had it ever? There has always been a current of opposition to the dominant strain of academic music criticism, analysis, which stands or falls on this very issue of organicism. But these questions were not forced until fairly recently—until the 1960s, when new music in the so-called non-teleological mode began to be taken seriously, and until the 1970s, when various currents of dissatisfaction with or revaluation of Schenkerian analysis finally began finding their way into print.[10] However, it is not only the Schenkerians and the neo-Schenkerians (Eugene Narmour's term for the more system-minded of Schenker's followers) who think in terms of a canon of great works. So does a polemical anti-Schenkerian like Narmour and so do analytically inclined critics of all shades, schools, and descriptions. That categorization covers, I trust, the great majority of musicians who are trying to practice criticism in the academy today. It has been phrased broadly enough, in any case, to cover critics with a wide range of commitment to analysis and of course an equally wide range of methodological preference.

The most coherent attack on this well-entrenched academic position comes from ethnomusicologists of the anthropological school and some systematic musicologists, Americanists, and students of popular music. Scholars who see the reality of a musical tradition in its social function within a supporting culture can only regard the activity of poring over revered scores "in a kind of Meistersinger environment" as not only elitist and compulsive but myopic (and possibly chauvinistic), a deflection of scrutiny from where it belongs. "I am convinced," writes the ethnomusicologist John Blacking, "that an anthropological approach to the study of *all* musical systems makes more sense of them than analyses of the patterns of sound as things in themselves."[11]

Again there is something quixotic about this attack. It may be that Gregorian chant as we now know it is best studied in terms of Frankish culture and politics and that country music yields most as an expression of everything that Robert Altman put into *Nashville*. But if nineteenth-century music is to be approached on the same basis, that is, in terms of its own culture and ideology, the force exerted by the idea of the canon must be recognized and so must the practice of analysis which was developed to validate it. We shall certainly *not* feel bound to study and appreciate this music exclusively in the terms it evolved for itself, and I have argued elsewhere against the exclusive use of formalistic analytical methodologies in current academic music criticism. On the other hand, it would be flying in the face of history to try to view the nineteenth-century musical tradition as though its performers and listeners, let alone its composers, were innocent of the idea of a canon.

It is another question, of course, whether earlier music or very recent music should be viewed in the same way. That might indeed be thought to go against history. As far as older music is concerned my answer to this is rather simple. There was assuredly no canon in the early days; the musical tradition was essentially contemporary and extended back, so Tinctoris assures us, no more than a few generations. Yet from the beginnings we have the names of celebrated composers, wistfully memorialized even though their music was mute. Why? Notker, Léonin, Pérotin, Machaut, Dunstable, Dufay, and Ockeghem (Tinctoris himself mentions these last three)—even their names were probably read infrequently, for their music was no longer sung and its archaic notation could no longer be deciphered, even if anyone had the mind to do so and could have found the written records. In the lifespan of these composers and for a time thereafter they had great reputations, it seems, like those of contemporary artists and writers. For a time their music was considered outstanding, great, canonical.

We can now read archaic notations better. Old written records have been searched out and found, codified and transcribed. For some time we have been experimenting with the performance of old music, which is to say experimenting with the internalization of past musical traditions; I shall return to this matter later at greater length. It is not an ahistorical task to seek to explain and exemplify those evanesced reputations. On the contrary, I would say it is one of the primary goals of historical criticism.

IV · *Per augmentationem*    What Spandrell did he would not have been able to do if *Point Counter Point* had been written just a few years earlier. Feeling it a matter of life and death to hear a certain Beethoven movement, he played it on a record. The record, he carefully explained to Rampion, had just been issued. Even if Huxley had decided to have the Flonzaley or the Léner Quartet doing a concert that afternoon at Wigmore Hall, it would not have helped Spandrell, who needed to hear just the *Heiliger Dankgesang* and needed to hear it again and again. In an earlier age he would have reached in his extremity for the Bible or the *Imitation of Christ*.

Sound recording has increased such options. The new form of musical records that this century has developed has changed musical life in the most comprehensive way. One paradox is that although our new records are not in writing at all but in sound, they have brought music in one important sense close to the condition of literature. Once sound recordings can be used as freely (or almost as freely) as books, music can be absorbed as freely (or almost as freely) as literature. No wonder the audience for music has expanded.

We have all gasped at tales of how recording technology and marketing made the careers of such artists as Elvis Presley and set in motion whole waves of popular music. The effect of records on the nineteenth-century repertory must have been and must continue to be enormous, too, though I don't recall ever seeing this discussed systematically. Clearly, the standard repertory would not have regrouped in the way it has without records. Would it even have frozen to the extent it has without records? What is discussed most frequently is the effect of sound recording—usually judged to be dire—on the canonization of musical performance. A symptomatic figure in this regard was B. H. Haggin, a critic who was still writing in the 1980s but whose main period of influence was from around 1935 to 1955. For Haggin, the canon took on the aura of a Great Composers' Club every bit as exclusive as that of Tovey (whom he admired) and Schenker, though the membership list had been revised with the aid of some anti-Romantic blackballs. Haggin's most important book, *Music on Records,* attempted to set forth not only the full canon of music as he saw it but also the full canon of musical performance as frozen on 78 rpm records. Indeed Haggin also took in jazz, a kind of music he probably never would have known if not for records.

In 1938, when Haggin's book first came out, about ten years after the development of electrical recording, there were still few enough commercial records issued so that his project seemed like a feasible one. It did not survive the next technological breakthrough, the development of the long-playing record. Thirty years and several more breakthroughs later, it seems generally agreed that recordings have contributed to canonization in a way that the older generation may not have foreseen. It is not just a question of influential critics upholding Toscanini records; the prestige of certain recordings has led them to be studied in detail and systematically imitated by other performers. As more and more works are recorded again and again, there is a noticeable tendency toward standardization in every aspect of the performer's craft. The loss of spontaneity (for the performer) and variety (for the listener) is often deplored. But for the ideal listener in the ideal sound archive—with its disc collection extending back to Nikisch, Joachim, and Caruso augmented yearly by new recordings of any work holding a secure place in the repertory, with its piano rolls and off-the-air tapes, and now with its CDs and videodiscs—there is probably variety and spontaneity enough.

Sound recording has worked otherwise with music that does not hold a secure place in the repertory. Of this the most vulnerable category is twentieth-century modernist music, as has already been remarked. It is seldom played in public. The music is evanescent. If a recording of a new piece is issued, the *actualité* far exceeds that provided by a single performance or a single season of performances or by publication of the score (a less likely windfall, in any case, for a composer today). A second recording may never be issued; unless the first was a disaster, this is an eventuality that can be borne. It may be worrying that on the single recording the music always sounds exactly and unspontaneously the same; but it sounds, it sounds, it continues to sound. As one composer, Roger Reynolds, has put it: "The singular representation—the existence as sound (though inflexible)—has a tendency to *become* the work, even for the composer. The authority of sound prevails over the abstract prescription in score. The goal (let alone the fact) of multiple realizations fades, and the creative person's aims are inevitably re-directed."[12]

It becomes possible after all, then, to conceive of works that figure in the canon of music but not in the repertory. There exist key works of contemporary music that are never performed at all because they were composed on tape by means of electronic generators and computers, works which have consciously renounced (or given up on) the flexibility and spontaneity of "multiple realizations." Could not such works enter the canon? And then how would they differ in status from earlier, performed works fixed on tape after the event?

Perhaps we need a new paradigm for music, one centered on the activity—or, if you prefer, the passivity—of listening to music on tapes and records. This modern paradigm would start with the listener but also implicate the performer and the composer, whose "aims are inevitably re-directed." It would not supplant the older paradigm which starts with the performer. Music as action or praxis, also implicating the composer (if any) and the listener, a form of behavior whose continuity is assured not by records in writing or sound but by means of an internalized oral tradition—this describes much non-Western music as well as Western popular music (however much this may be affected by sheet music and records). It would not supplant Treitler's paradigm of literacy, which starts with the composer. As even Crocker grants, this describes the standard nineteenth-century repertory as preserved and presented today. What the new paradigm covers is something that now coexists with the above: modernist music and, with some qualifications, older music resuscitated from the past. Music happens in different ways and means different things under these paradigms. Contrast the Javanese puppet theater, a social event loud with cultural resonance for the improvising musicians, puppeteers, and audience alike; the symphony orchestra rehearsal, a highly professional "reading" of the score and parts—the text—of a canonical masterpiece by the conductor and the players; and the solitary willed experience of music in the hi-fi den.

"That which withers in the age of mechanical reproduction is the aura of the work of art. . . . The technique of reproduction detaches the reproduced object from the domain of tradition."[13] Walter Benjamin, who died in 1940, did not talk about music reproduced on records, but T. W. Adorno, who lived to see the LP explosion, hated it. And mandarins of fine printing cannot look at a photoset, ragless page like this one without regretting its detachment from tradition. The rest of us look where we can for the compensations of art without aura. Asocial, amateur, existential, blanketed in anomie, the passive listener to records nonetheless chooses in a way that the Javanese theatergoer and the Western orchestra musician do not. He does not always choose new and old music in favor of standard fare, obviously—rather the reverse. But those are the categories of music that need him the most.

v · *Quaerendo invenietis*     Since the idea of a canon seems so closely bound up with the idea of history, there should be something to be learned from the persistent efforts that have been going on for nearly two hundred years to extend the musical repertory back in time. What is involved here is nothing less than a continuous effort to endow music with a history. From the workings of this process in the nineteenth century, we learn that where the ideology is right the past can indeed yield up a canon of works and even a canon of performance.

Bach, to take the most weighty example, would appear to have entered the canon—Hoffmann's canon—before entering the repertory. The history of the nineteenth-century Bach revival begins as a triumph of ideology over practice. Only after J. N. Forkel, in his famous biography, canonized Bach as the archetypal German master was *The Well-Tempered Clavier* published for the first time—and if any one work of music deserves to be called canonic, it would have to be *The Well-Tempered Clavier*.[14] (But when did it really enter the repertory? Not really until the formation of a new repertory, the repertory of the modern harpsichord, in our own time.) Gradually other Bach works, works which fitted better into nineteenth-century concert life, did enter various nineteenth-century repertories; Mendelssohn's revival of the St. Matthew Passion is a well-known landmark, and various piano transcriptions and orchestral arrangements, not to speak of Gounod's "Ave Maria," followed in due course. Bach was made to sound like a premature Romantic. There was as yet no call for historical "authenticity." But I do not think it was Bach that Hood was thinking of when he complained of musical traditions of the past whose "real identities are gone." The skeleton may not have been bodied out with authentic flesh and blood, but it was made into a handsome waxwork which was quite real enough for the nineteenth century.

The Solesmes monks made Gregorian chant, too, sound Romantic. There is a considerable irony here, since in editing the chant texts they went back to the earliest neumes and subjected them to the full rigor of nineteenth-century historical philology. The Church authorities were duly impressed; but for the Solesmes performance style, which was promulgated as zealously as were the texts themselves, the historical underpinnings were much more speculative—and once again, in this matter there was as yet no call for rigor. After successfully making their case for canonization at the turn of the century, the monks made their first commercial records of plainchant as early as 1930. To this day, thanks at least in part to these canonical recordings, Gregorian chant is always sung in their admirably lifelike wax-museum version, even though this certainly reflects the ideals of the Cecilian or Pre-Raphaelite movements more closely than anything that can conceivably be imagined from the ninth century.[15] And if the Church itself saw in sound recordings an important means for stabilizing its canon, sound recordings were to prove even more important for the revival of past secular music.

This is shown graphically, if negatively, by the story of Arnold Dolmetsch, an intimate of William Morris, George Bernard Shaw, and William Poel, who was involved in old music long before the reaction against Romanticism. Equal in crankiness to any of the old-music specialists who followed him, in universality he outdid them all—Dolmetsch not only played the first modern harpsichords, recorders, and viols, he also made each of these instruments and more in his own workshop. And he wrote a landmark study of *The Interpretation of the Music of the Seventeenth and Eighteenth Centuries* as early as 1915. The point is that while the instruments he made in the 1900s were unmatched for historical authenticity, sensitivity, and beauty of sound until the 1950s, the old-music revival that might have taken off from his work, both as maker and player, did little more than mark time until the age of LP records. Then it exploded.

The effect of LP records on the dissemination of older music, especially Baroque music, is clearer and possibly more dramatic than on music of any other kind (popular music excepted). Think of the Pachelbel Canon; but think more seriously of the enormously expert and artistic re-creation of past performance styles that has been recorded by the direct and indirect followers of Dolmetsch. What has happened is not so much an expansion of existing repertories as a sudden addition of new ones (though perhaps each is as marginal as the contemporary-music repertory, using this term broadly for music played by contemporary-music specialists): repertories for the harpsichord, the countertenor, the Baroque orchestra, and so on. These repertories, incidentally, have proved to be *less* susceptible to canonization of performance than has the nineteenth-century repertory in one way and modernist music in another. A single recording of a modern piece can attain canonical status because usually the composer has been involved with it, at least indirectly; while the result may not do full justice to the composer's conception, it will probably come close enough not to offend him. This is exactly what we do not know about with performances of old music. In this area, performance styles change almost as frequently, it sometimes seems, as fashions change in clothes—precisely because what to do with those skeletons is the subject of so much busy debate and experiment. Although some years ago it was generally felt that the cause of "authenticity" was best served by an anodyne and mechanical style of playing, today there is probably more variety and vitality of performance to be heard on old-music records than on those of the standard repertory.

And what about the canon of old music? This is not, in fact, a question that seems to interest most old-music performers. They approach whatever old music attracts them with internalization in mind, not discrimination.[16] It will be historians or, rather, historical critics who will be interested in establishing or clarifying the canon of old music, as I have already suggested. The problem is that historians of music have typically veered away from criticism. To go with Hood's irresistible metaphor once again, their best work has been a sort of musical paleontology devoted to restoring the skeletons; they have not even gone forward very often to assume the role of those ingenious taxidermists who make the animals we see in museums of natural history, nor of those artists who create the delectable swamp and tundra scenes in which they are exhibited. That work has been left, by and large, to musicians and craftsmen like Dolmetsch and his successors, who have mostly tended to pick up just a little from the research of scholars, a little from the lore of cabinetmakers, and a little more from their own continuous exercise of the aural historical imagination.

Still, there have always been some maverick musicologists—I count Treitler and Crocker in that category—and I believe that in the last half-dozen years there has been a real tropism toward criticism in the musicological community.[17] Symptomatic of this is Treitler's discussion of the interrelations of history and criticism in his article "History, Criticism, and Beethoven's Ninth Symphony," the powerful argument of which falters only very occasionally.

> This discussion provokes reflection on the possibility of practicing criticism with respect to the music of the Middle Ages and even the Renaissance, that is, of having historical knowledge of it in Croce's and Collingwood's sense. It sometimes seems that we can hope to do no more than identify the range of choices that performers and composers *could* make, without being able to count on any persuasive hypotheses for the choices they *did* make. That would be a way of saying that their traditions are no longer alive.[18]

This thought is expressed tentatively, by Treitler's standards, and is relegated to a footnote, but in any case the pessimism he appears to be flirting with here seems to me unfounded. Like Hood, he speaks of traditions that "are no longer alive" without acknowledging the accomplishments of today's old-music revivers and their allies in the recording industry. Modern performers of medieval and Renaissance music are making choices with increasing confidence and persuasiveness.

Those accomplishments seem to me as remarkable and as historically significant as those of the Bach and Solesmes revivals in the nineteenth century. Dufay was no longer alive in 1950 just as, I suppose, Theocritus was no longer alive in 1450. But after musicologists like Guillaume de Van and Heinrich Besseler have reconstructed the skeletons, and after Charles Hamm, Craig Wright, and David Fallows have polished them up, and after performers like Thomas Binkley, Fallows, Michael Morrow, and Alejandro Planchart have provided flesh or clothes—it does not matter which—Treitler himself as well as Patricia Carpenter and Don M. Randel have started a criticism for Dufay which can indeed lay the basis for the kind of knowledge Treitler seeks. Oliver Neighbour and I have done the same for William Byrd. Winton Dean has done the same for Handel's oratorios and operas. Crocker has done the same for the earliest sequences, chants whose witness and first critic was the ninth-century monk Notker of St. Gall.

There has been more about the history and the ontology of the canon in these remarks than about the philosophy and politics of canon formation. They are coming to an end at a point where many readers, I rather think, would have liked to see them begin: *How* are canons determined, *why,* and on *what* authority? The situation in music, in my view, is such that we have first to build up serious criticism so that when we ask these questions of critics, we can ask them seriously. My closing point, and I am sorry if it seems a self-serving one, is that the old music which now occupies so large a part of our sound-world needs a sensible criticism. But a sensible criticism for Boulez and Carter is needed only slightly less than for Gregorian chant, Dufay, Byrd, and Monteverdi—and there is certainly no reason to exclude the authors of the St. Matthew Passion and the Ninth Symphony from this list. Everyone now sees that analysis cannot serve as the sole critical methodology, not even for the nineteenth-century canon, in aid of which it was developed, let alone for earlier and later music. Those critics who still believe in the canon must work to keep it viable, and work freshly.

### Notes

1. Mantle Hood, *Perspectives in Musicology,* ed. Barry S. Brook, Edward O. D. Downes, and Sherman Van Solkema (New York, 1972), 203–4.
2. Leo Treitler, "Transmission and the Study of History," *International Musicological Society, Twelfth Congress, Berkeley 1977: Report* (Cassel, 1981), 202; cf. his "Oral, Written, and Literate Process in the Transmission of Medieval Music," *Speculum* 56 (1981): 471–91.
3. See Richard L. Crocker, "Is There Really a 'Written Tradition' in Music?" (paper delivered at the Music Colloquium, University of California, Berkeley, May 1982).
4. Hoffmann's role in the history of criticism has been analyzed with great perspicacity by Carl Dahlhaus; for a summary, see "The Metaphysics of Instrumental Music," in *Nineteenth-Century Music,* tr. J. Bradford Robinson (Berkeley and Los Angeles, 1989), 88–96.

5. Some of Abrams's ideas are placed in a music-historical context by Ruth A. Solie, "The Living Work: Organicism and Musical Analysis," *19th-Century Music* 4 (1980): 147–56.

6. Edward T. Cone, "Analysis Today," in *Music: A View from Delft*, ed. Robert P. Morgan (Chicago, 1989), 41.

7. Crocker, "Is There Really a 'Written Tradition'?"

8. See pp. 12–32.

9. See Edward Rothstein, "Does Music Have an Avant-Garde?," *New York Times*, 15 July 1982, C17.

10. See, e.g., my "How We Got into Analysis"; Eugene Narmour, *Beyond Schenkerism: The Need for Alternatives in Music Analysis* (Chicago, 1977); Charles Rosen, "Art Has Its Reasons," *New York Review of Books*, 17 June 1971, 32–38, and *The Classical Style: Haydn, Mozart, Beethoven*, rev. ed. (New York, 1972), 33–36; Solie, "The Living Work"; Leo Treitler, "History, Criticism, and Beethoven's Ninth Symphony," *19th-Century Music* 3 (1980): 193–210; the posthumously published lecture by T. W. Adorno, "On the Problem of Musical Analysis," tr. Max Paddison, *Music Analysis* 1 (1982): 169–87; and Carl Dahlhaus, *Analysis and Value Judgement* (1970), tr. Siegmund Levarie (New York, 1983), 8–9. The magisterially critical essays on Schenker written by Roger Sessions in the 1930s (". . . Talmudic subtleties and febrile dogmatism") were reprinted in 1979 in *Roger Sessions on Music: Collected Essays*, ed. Edward T. Cone (Princeton, 1979). Perhaps David Epstein's *Beyond Orpheus: Studies in Musical Structure* (Cambridge, Mass., 1979) should be added to this list; see the review by Arnold Whittall and correspondence in *Journal of Music Theory* 25 (1981): 319–26, and 26 (1982): 208–12.

11. John Blacking, *How Musical Is Man?* (Seattle, 1973), xi.

12. Roger Reynolds, "Thoughts on What a Record Records," in *The Phonograph and Our Musical Life*, ed. H. Wiley Hitchcock (New York, 1980), 33.

13. Walter Benjamin, "The Work of Art in the Age of Mechanical Reproduction," tr. Harry Zohn, in *Marxism in Art*, ed. Maynard Solomon (Detroit, 1979), 554.

14. This point is made by Crocker, "Is There Really a 'Written Tradition'?"

15. For an excellent summary of the nineteenth- and twentieth-century chant movement, see the *New Grove Dictionary of Music and Musicians*, s.v. "Plainchant," by John A. Emerson. To him I owe the astonishing information that a recording survives of demonstrations of chant performance by the Solesmes pioneers and others at the Gregorian Congress of 1904 (available on Discant DIS 1-2). The effect of recordings on canonization may have been more decisive in this case than anyone realized.

   Efforts to perform Gregorian chant in a more "authentic" fashion have been few, but there are some on records: the remarkable performances from the 1930s for the Anthologie Sonore under Guillaume de Van and Curt Sachs (reissued in the 1950s by the Haydn Society, AS-1) and recently those by the Schola Antiqua, *Tenth-Century Liturgical Chant* (Nonesuch H-71348). See Lance W. Brunner, "The Performance of Plainsong," *Early Music* 10 (1982): 317–28. [I would now add recordings made at the Benedictine Abbey of Muensterschwartzach, under Father Godehard Joppich (DGG Archiv 410 658, etc.), as well as private recordings by Richard Crocker.]

16. Just recently, however, some complaints about this situation have begun to surface in "early music" circles; see Philip Brett, "Facing the Music," *Early Music* 10 (1982): 347–50, and David Z. Crookes, "A Turinese Letter . . . ," *Music Review* 42 (1981): 169–73.

17. See the group of "state-of-the-art" papers read at the American Musicological Society annual meeting in 1981 and published as *Musicology in the 1980s: Methods, Goals, Opportunities*, ed. D. Kern Holoman and Claude V. Palisca (New York, 1982).

18. Treitler, "History, Criticism," 208 n.35.

4

# Critics and the Classics

Late eighteenth-century music is called Classical *not* because it has anything to do with the issues of classicism and neoclassicism that so occupied literary and artistic theory at the time. We call this music Classical (as the eighteenth century did not) not because of what it looked back to, but because of the way we look back at it. For a variety of reasons it has assumed for musicians an authority as great as, however different from, that of the literary and artistic monuments of ancient Greece and Rome for later poets, architects, painters, men of letters, and historians of the fine arts. This authority was achieved very rapidly in the early decades of the nineteenth century. In the later decades it was personified by the powerful figure of Brahms and embodied in his oeuvre. It is still felt today in any musician's education and in the conduct of his or her professional life.

As a consequence, any music critic or scholar who makes any claim to generality, even if he is not a specialist in the eighteenth century, as I am not, thinks he has something to say about Haydn and Mozart. It is a little like the situation in literary studies, where so many people seem to be ready and eager to talk about Shakespeare. Further, the criticism of this music can be taken as a fair spectrum of modern attitudes toward music in general. There has been intensive and distinguished work in other fields too, of course, but in none other, I believe, have different and sometimes divergent theories jostled so powerfully. My intent here is to examine critically the work of several important authors, in order to trace the main outlines of a developing modern view of Classical music.

➤ Presented at the 1980–81 lecture series of the William Andrews Clark Memorial Library in Los Angeles and published (under the title "Theories of Late Eighteenth-Century Music") in *Studies in Eighteenth-Century British Art and Aesthetics,* ed. Ralph Cohen (Berkeley and Los Angeles: University of California Press, 1985), 217–44.

Let us begin with Charles Rosen's *The Classical Style: Haydn, Mozart, Beethoven* (1971), a book which offered, without much doubt, the freshest prospect on this music that had been seen since the dissertations of Kurt Westphal and Rudolf von Tobel in the 1930s, or—if we may take a viewing-point across the Channel—since the collecting and publication of Sir Donald Tovey's program notes and essays, starting around the same time.[1] Charles Rosen is principally a pianist, of course. As a critic he has adopted much from many quarters, and a broad kinship between his work and that of Tovey has often been observed. Later we shall discern another influence—perhaps less conscious, perhaps more profound.

In any event, whether or not Rosen's eclecticism demonstrates sound common sense, and even if it betrays a regrettable lack of rigor, as some of his critics evidently feel, it probably accounts for the consensus of approval that has been accorded to *The Classical Style*. There is something in the book for everyone. Especially in view of the book's broad sweep, then, we will do well to identify clearly at the start the intellectual tradition to which the author owes his central allegiance.

This is the tradition that musicians call "analysis." American academic music criticism today, as distinguished from journalistic criticism, is dominated by analysis; and as I have argued elsewhere, all the various methodological currents and eddies of musical analysis flow from a single theory, indeed from a single guiding ideology.[2] The theory is the analogue in music of a closely related pair of aesthetic theories that have been examined richly in the work of M. H. Abrams.[3] The "contemplative" theory of art, developed primarily in reference to painting, and the "heterocosmic" theory, developed in reference to poetry, especially narrative poetry, can be traced back to the eighteenth century, though, as we know, it was in the nineteenth century that they surged and in the twentieth that they threaten to engulf us. (They do, at least, in music.) According to the contemplative and heterocosmic models, a work of art may be analyzed "as having distinctive elements, made coherent by a variety of internal relations, and unified by subordination to an internal end"; this pithy characterization by Professor Abrams applies just as well to the vision of the musical analysts. The problem of artistic form and content is solved (when it is posed at all) by equation, by decreeing that expression, meaning, beauty, and so forth, must reside in the music's internal relations and nowhere else.

Some analysts explain the autonomous perfection of the musical masterpiece according to the familiar metaphor of an organism, others do not. But analysis as a critical theory can absorb organicist theories of art much more easily than other theories we have learned to identify through Abrams's work—more easily than expressive theories, for example, or than the mimetic, imitative, didactic theories that still dominated the thought of the late eighteenth century. Music analytic writings say nothing about the work of art as an expression of the composer's imaginative vision, his ideology, or indeed any other such personal category. They say nothing about how music might uplift, educate, or please the nonprofessional listener. I shall return to these lacunae later. Analysis is a strictly professional type of criticism and it is essentially a formalist type of criticism. Analysts deal with internal musical relations in technical language, and their values are expressed in such terms as coherence, integration, and unity—not infrequently, organic unity.

And so with Rosen, although "organic" is a word he tends to stay strictly away from. Like most serious analysts and other music critics, he takes up a position at some distance from the full-fledged organicist theories that are still current. *The Classical Style* begins with a number of polemic chapters disposing of some ideas that the author thought needed to be countered. Chapter 2 (entitled, significantly, "Theories of Form") offers a convenient point of entry to his own position.

*Formenlehre* is the German term for the doctrine of form taught in the old conservatories and modern music-appreciation mills, with its patterns of A and B sections and phrases, its abstract norms and categories. Among the components prescribed for Classical sonata form are the first and second "subjects," the modulatory bridge section, the development section consisting of motivic working-out, and so on. Rosen begins with a spirited destruction of this naive account and holds it up to ridicule on more than one occasion later in his work. Though as he himself admits, this is "a game too easy and too often played": indeed, it was Tovey, seventy-five years ago, who polemicized decisively against what he called the "jelly-mold" view of sonata form, form conceived as something prior and rigid into which musical material is mindlessly poured. Nonetheless, the appreciation of Classical music that Tovey instilled depends on form fundamentally. Music exists in time—time is its primary level, what Susanne Langer calls its primary illusion; musical sounds experienced in time create the contrasts, balances, and symmetries we call form; we cannot do without it, we must only try to understand it as flexibly as did the masters. Near the end of his preliminaries Rosen remarks, somewhat wistfully, that "an understanding of the sense of continuity and the proportions of classical style would enable us largely to dispense with a further discussion of 'sonata form.'"[4] It was not to be. Two chapters later he presented a concise, essentially conventional summary of the various sonata forms. Nine years later he published another book, actually called *Sonata Forms* (1980), in which such taxonomic urges are carried to unusual and surprising lengths.

Also somewhat equivocal are Rosen's attacks on what he describes as the most sophisticated theories of form developed in the twentieth century, those of the *Urlinie* and *Ursatz* on the one hand, and of *Substanzgemeinschaft* on the other. Of these two eminently Germanic, unabashedly organicist theories,[5] Schenker's *Ursatz* was, I think, less to Rosen's purpose, except insofar as he felt inclined to take account of high fashion in the academy, and is indeed less to the purpose of anyone concerned with Classical music. I therefore forgo the nearly impossible task of trying to characterize it briefly. For all the "considerable validity" of Schenkerian analysis, Rosen remarks, "the rate of progression from one point of the basic line [*Urlinie*] to another and the proportions of the form . . . are completely irrelevant to the theory."[6] And for him any account of Classical music that slights movement, proportions, and temporal symmetries—in short, form—goes clearly and outrageously against the basic postulates of the style.

More significant are theories of *Substanzgemeinschaft,* or, as we would do better to call them, thematicist theories. Thematicist critics see the unity of musical compositions in the community of thematic or motivic material among their various parts or levels. While in criticism this idea can be traced at least as far back as E. T. A. Hoffmann's famous reviews of Beethoven in the early 1800s, thematicism did not really come into its own until this century, especially under the impetus of Gestalt psychology. Tracing deep-level thematic relationships, which may not be easily or immediately perceived, has become the characteristic pursuit of modern thematicists. The figure best known in this country, Rudolph Réti (at one time a follower of Schoenberg, Réti emigrated to America and wrote several books in English), is also the most extreme, the most vulnerable, and in consequence possibly the most frequently attacked of any modern writer on music. But Schoenberg himself, in some rather shadowy comments he made about the derivation of musical compositions from a single *Grundgestalt,* or "basic shape," provided a less systematic but highly suggestive theory along the same lines. The analogue between thematicist theories of criticism and the development of twelve-tone composition is obvious enough and has often been remarked.

Rosen approaches theories of *Substanzgemeinschaft* or thematicism obliquely, by first undermining the antithematicist position in the person of its most outspoken adherent, who was Tovey. As I have suggested elsewhere,[7] ideology appears to have got in the way of Tovey's ear in this matter; he was so determined to rest art upon a bed of Victorian verities that he refused to admit the evidence of his senses in respect to any thematic relationships that were not made absolutely clear by the composer. Once one accepts the obvious possibility that composers may not have wanted to make their intentions all that clear, one is free to accept more imaginative thematicist insights. But Rosen is no gentler on Réti than he is on Tovey. When the extreme thematicists treat music as a purely relational field that is static and nondirectional (or, as is sometimes said, "ontic"), they do not recognize that relational structure in music is created by sound in time. Even more than Schenker, Réti minimizes (even denies) the importance of form in Classical music. Compared to these men, Rosen can even begin to look like a *Formengelehrter.*

At a closer look he will be discovered on middle ground. Like many critics of this century, he has worked out for himself a critical practice that tries to reconcile the claims of both "inner form" and "outer form," in the dialectic formulation of the German theorist Ernst Kurth. These claims have been recognized ever since sonata form was categorized, a little uneasily, by A. B. Marx in the 1840s;[8] for however deeply some critics have wished to view Classical compositions as autonomous individual works of art, none except the most ideologically committed have been able to ignore those compositions' recourse to patterns, formulas, and even molds on a variety of different compositional levels. When Tovey equated "freedom" with "normality" in music, and when Schoenberg contrasted "musical prose" with "poetry" (as *patterned* discourse), each was dealing in his own way with this same basic dialectic.[9]

Rosen is less inclined to address it in theoretical terms; his strength is as a practical critic, not as a theorist. But in his criticism, a key concept is the relation between material and structure, between the detailed musical gesture and large-scale formal proportions. All the elements of style—line in Schenker's sense, motif in Réti's, tonality, harmony, rhythm, phrasing, texture, figuration, dynamics—work together to produce that most perfect and autonomous of musical objects, the masterpiece of Classical music. Or as Edward T. Cone put it in a well-known article from 1961, in reference to what he called "the Golden Age of functional tonality,"

> The tension between detail and whole was here brought into equilibrium; musical suspense was under complete control; the shapes demanded by the respective needs of melody, harmony, and rhythm were integrated into a rich, multidimensional whole. . . . Everywhere we look, whether at general proportions, at phrase structure, at harmonic rhythm, or at rhythmic motifs, we find patterns interesting not only for their own sake but also, and especially, for the way in which they control, and are controlled by, the other elements.[10]

The elucidation of this central insight occupies focal chapters in each of Rosen's books, "The Coherence of the Musical Language" in *The Classical Style* and "Motif and Function" in *Sonata Forms*. This drawing together of so many elements in an eclectic and comprehensive sweep is no doubt the most impressive aspect of Rosen's work.

How much, for Rosen, coherence depends on deep-level thematic connections appears from his treatment in the latter chapter of Beethoven's "Lebewohl" motif in the Sonata in E Flat, op. 81a, as compared to Tovey's. However, thematic connections do not enter at all into his discussion of the first movement of Mozart's C-major Concerto, K. 503, the coherence of which is demonstrated in terms of mass, rhythm, and modality. Here his discussion is much closer to Tovey's well-known essay than to the elaborate thematicist attack on it by Hans Keller, a follower of Réti.[11]

We have the sense, says Rosen in a striking sentence, that in Classical music "the movement, the development, and the dramatic course of a work all can be found latent in the material, that the material can be made to release its charged force so that the music . . . is literally impelled from within."[12] This seems a classic statement of the organicist's creed of an entelechy generating a work of art from within. Yet once again, where Rosen wants to apply this idea is in the sphere of form, sonata form. The sonata exposition's inevitable modulation in the bridge passage is not to be thought of as a prescriptive "rule" or formula but as the outcome of charged forces latent in the particular opening theme. The nature of the so-called second group, after the modulation—its thematic substance, its graded series of cadences—emerges from all that has preceded it. The development section dilates upon thematic, tonal, and textural conflicts established in the exposition. As for the recapitulation section, its true function is that of "symmetrical resolution"—a catch phrase of Rosen's that seems to me a little clearer when turned around as "resolving symmetry." Symmetry is a requirement of all eighteenth-century art; what the sonata required was a symmetry that would also reinterpret material so as to resolve prior tensions—a resolving symmetry rather than the purely decorative symmetry of earlier musical genres such as the da capo aria.

In summary, the following seem to me to be the main points about Rosen's view of late eighteenth-century music. While his stance as a critic is eclectic, his central concern—like that of other analysts—is with the internal coherence of works of art conceived of as autonomous entities. While he grumbles a good deal about sterile formalism as applied to Classical music, his own criticism holds stubbornly to the concept of form. But his is a concept of form growing out of and articulated by musical material, by musical material in all its aspects, all seen (and shown) as working together, without dogmatic emphasis on any single one.

III ·
When *The Classical Style* appeared in 1971 it was received with mixed feelings, if not outright distrust, by many musicologists in the academic establishment. It was a foregone conclusion that historians of eighteenth-century music would find at least one of the book's basic postulates unacceptable.[13] For musicologists style is a normative concept; for Rosen it is an ideal one, embodied perfectly only in the works of Haydn, Mozart, and Beethoven—whose names form, indeed, the subtitle of his book. Other composers are almost completely ignored in *The Classical Style*. More attention is paid to history in *Sonata Forms*. But even assuming that the differences with the historians have been papered over—which would be assuming too much[14]—there still remain other problems with Rosen's theory of Classical music. His Classical synthesis is a powerful but not an easy concept, which shades easily from the demonstrable to the mystical. How does one distinguish purely formal or merely tautological resemblances among artistic phenomena from manifestations of vital coherence? Exactly what is meant by "impulsion," "latency," "emergence," even symmetry? What does Cone mean by "control"? What tests are offered for the validation of these qualities?

I shall attempt to deal with some of these questions later, in reference to an actual piece of music. Before doing so, however, I should like to show how they are avoided in more orthodox accounts of Classical music. Let me take as an example the article "Sonata Form" written for the *New Grove Dictionary of Music and Musicians* by James Webster, a leading younger specialist in the music of Haydn and his contemporaries. That a major statement specifically about sonata form may fairly be taken as indicative of a total conception of Classical music will be clear from what has already been said. It is also clear that while Webster has read Rosen with care and appreciation, he is prepared to follow him only so far.

Webster begins, as one does in dictionary articles, by casting the net wide:

> Like any form in tonal music, a sonata-form movement creates its designs in time. The form is a synthesis of the tonal structure, the rhythmic organization and the development of the musical material. . . . The meaning of each event depends both on its function in the structure and its dramatic context. Sonata form is thus not a mould into which the composer has poured the contents; each movement grows bar by bar and phrase by phrase.

This is unexceptionable, and it is only after reading the article to the end that we notice not much more is said about the synthesis. Whether or not this was due to the compression inevitable in such articles, it seems that for Webster the matter of synthesis cannot be crucial. He delivers a routine slap at the jelly-mold theory of sonata form, but just how each movement grows bar by bar and phrase by phrase is something he does not enlarge upon.

Also noticeable is a disparity in treatment between the three elements of the Classical synthesis—"the tonal structure, the rhythmic organization, and the development of the musical material." Tonal structure receives adequate coverage, considering the limited amount of space Webster allows himself for a discussion of "Principles of Sonata Form" (most of his article deals with its history). The main business of the sonata-form exposition is to establish "a large-scale dissonance (Rosen) that must be resolved"; the development should be viewed as "a (gigantic) transition from the end of the exposition to the beginning of the recapitulation," and this beginning counts as "the central aesthetic event in the entire movement [produced by] a return to the main theme . . . timed to arrive simultaneously with the return to the tonic [key]." Rhythmic organization is also given its due, if not in the actual prose—rhythm is an extremely difficult thing to write about—at least in the annotations provided along with Webster's main musical example, which is the whole first movement of Mozart's *Eine kleine Nachtmusik,* K. 525, in a skeletal reduction. In Classical music, "sections vary in phrase rhythm, level of activity, harmonic structure and cadential strength; this sense of varied pace is essential to the style," writes Webster, and that is exactly what is revealed graphically by his rhythmic analysis of the Mozart. See figure 1. We shall return to this figure later.

RECAPITULATION
76–98 = 1–23;   24–5 omitted;   99–100 = 26–7, now on V, not V/V;   101–127 = 28–54 transposed to I

FIGURE 1 Mozart, *Eine kleine Nachtmusik*, first movement (reduction). From James Webster's article "Sonata Form" in *The New Grove Dictionary of Music and Musicians* (London: Macmillan, 1980). Reproduced by permission.

It is "the development of the musical material"—that is, the melodic, thematic, and motivic material—which comes off less well. The Mozart example is furnished with thematic as well as rhythmic and harmonic annotations—the usual themes 1 and 2, a, b, c, c', etc.—but some of them are unpersuasive and none of them illuminates the relation of the material to the structure. Nor in the rest of the article is there much to be learned about why tunes or motifs come when they do, or how they function, or what role they play in the synthesis. The bias noted here is characteristic. Historical musicologists of past generations nearly always regarded anything that smacks of thematicism with suspicion. And American musicologists of today, confronted by the two great Germanic "rigid linear dogmatisms," as Rosen calls them, those of the *Urlinie* and of *Substanzgemeinschaft,* have proved more hospitable to the former, more resistant to the latter. As I have tried to show, Rosen stands considerably to the right of dogmatic organicist critics such as Schenker or Réti. He is still too far to the left for most musicologists.

And if (as it appears)[15] Webster regards Rosen as a somewhat radical thematicist, he is not alone. In a recent study issuing from another sector of the music-academic establishment, the theorist David Epstein specifically associates Rosen with Réti and Réti's followers Keller and Alan Walker. To be sure, he absolves Rosen from the one-sided emphasis on melodic shapes that characterizes the Réti school, and by drawing attention to the discussion of Haydn's intertwining of shapes and key structures in *The Classical Style,* he acknowledges the book's broader thrust.[16] As well he might, for Epstein's own study, *Beyond Orpheus: Studies in Musical Structure* (1979), is probably the most forthright assertion that has yet appeared of a modern all-embracing organicist position in musical criticism.

This study is not one we should pause over, for though it includes illuminating material about Haydn, Mozart, and Beethoven, it does not deal centrally with Classical music, still less with Classical style or form. Epstein walks the long gallery of modern music from Haydn to Brahms, with the door left invitingly open, in more ways than one, to Schoenberg. The focus is not critical or historical but theoretical—that is, in the last analysis, philosophical, so that insights about music are secondary to ideas about order. In view of what has been said above about Rosen's eclecticism, however, it is interesting to see Epstein set out programmatically to synthesize Rosen's two "linear dogmatisms," to infuse life into both of them, jointly, under the aegis of an arching theory of rhythm. It is also interesting to see him place as antithesis to Schenker's linear reductionism not Réti's simplistic "thematic process" but rather Schoenberg's much subtler concept of the *Grundgestalt*. A *Grundgestalt* or "basic shape" is not exactly equivalent to a melodic configuration; it is that and also something more abstract. Thus when Rosen, in discussing Haydn's Quartet in B Flat, op. 55 no. 3, shows how a "dead" semitone interval between the first two four-bar phrases infects other themes and controls formal junctures, he is dealing not with a motif but a "shape," a Gestalt. Likewise his point about the opening orchestral sonority of Mozart's Sinfonia Concertante, K. 364 (320d), and how this prefigures the music to come, recalls the point made by Epstein and others about the two opening chords of the *Eroica* Symphony. These are observations worthy of Schoenberg; they are beyond the range of the systems of Réti or Schenker.

Of various influences on Rosen's criticism, the one that has struck people most often is that of Tovey, whom Rosen seems clearly to admire in everything but his antithematicism.[17] Once past an initial skirmish on that score, which I have already mentioned, *The Classical Style* includes references to Tovey in far greater number than to any other author. Tovey too never tired of proclaiming the equation of artistic form and content; but Tovey tied himself into paradoxical knots by refusing to admit any but the simplest kinds of thematicism. Consequently he was never quite able to translate his organicist ideology into his actual criticism, as Schoenberg did in his fugitive but brilliant analytical aperçus—to say nothing of what he revealed (though not to Tovey) through his own music. It is probably no accident that next after *The Classical Style* Rosen wrote a book for the "Modern Masters" series on Schoenberg.

IV ·

To move from Epstein's *Beyond Orpheus* to the book by Leonard G. Ratner, *Classic Music* ( 1980), is to move from theory to history; it is also almost like moving into history. Ratner is a musicologist who has spent a lifetime studying eighteenth-century writers on music theory and composition. He has studied them so devotedly—so uncritically, I am afraid—that he has ended up by absorbing not only their limited insights but also their limitations. This is true even in a narrow chronological sense. Not much gets quoted in Ratner's *Classic Music* that was written later than around 1820.

The book's subtitle is *Expression, Form, and Style;* whole sections are devoted to "Expression," "Rhetoric," "Form," and "Stylistic Perspectives." This bold seizing of the category "expression" is unnerving. Nothing of the sort happens in any of the other recent literature; bring up the subject and Epstein throws up his hands, Webster pretends not to hear, and Rosen waxes Johnsonian (" 'Expression' is a word that tends to corrupt thought"). But since the subject was the first brought up by systematic writers on music in the eighteenth century, Ratner makes it his first order of business too. What interests most twentieth-century listeners who come to Classical music is also, I think, expression—at least, expression in some sense. Granted that this word is used by different people to mean different things, some of them perhaps regrettably imprecise. But given the general retreat from anything but technique as the subject for current American music criticism, one turns with eager anticipation, even yearning, to any account that offers to deal seriously with expression in almost any of its meanings.

The trouble is that on the subject of musical expression, Ratner's late eighteenth-century authorities stumble and skim, pontificate and prevaricate. Although the century was a time of unparalleled speculation about psychology and feeling, as we know, not much of this rubbed off onto the writers of treatises on music and manuals of practical composition. There were no minds of the stature of a Rameau, a Kirnberger, or an Emanuel Bach among the music theorists at the end of the century. They were mostly modest individuals, who had enough trouble keeping up with the latest trends of music in Vienna and Paris without attempting serious contributions to musical aesthetics (a subject, let us remember, that still eludes thinkers of the present century, who have a good deal more to go on). The most conscientious and thoughtful among them was a violinist of Rudolstadt, a little town in Thuringia, named Heinrich Christian Koch. In 1793 Koch mentions Mozart ("der sel. Mozard") in a single sentence; he had heard of Mozart's six quartets dedicated to Haydn, but it is not clear that he had heard them. He discusses in detail only one Haydn symphony, from twenty years earlier—that is, from a quite early stage in the composer's career.[18]

What these men remembered was the baroque *Affektenlehre,* the doctrine of affects derived ultimately from Descartes, and still current in watered-down forms, which associated certain musical tropes with certain standardized sentiments. You could always convey the required sentiment by employing the correct trope; you could, indeed, do it just as well as Johann Sebastian Bach or George Frideric Handel, for it was no part of the doctrine to distinguish between one user of these universal nostrums and the next. Likewise analysis of later eighteenth-century music in terms of what Ratner calls "topics" gives us no way to distinguish between Haydn and Pleyel, Mozart and Süssmayr—or between Haydn and Mozart. This is a more serious shortcoming because of a significant change over the course of the century. As is well known, musical expression becomes less emblematic and more personal. Even traditionalists who still thought in terms of the affects could no longer limit a musical composition or a movement to a single affect, as in the earlier period. Music was now made up of contrasting sections, sections with contrasting affects. This meant that musical expression became a function of musical form: another significant change, or another aspect of the first one.[19]

Ratner's procedure is to identify as many as possible of the topics or *topoi* which were used again and again at the time and therefore universally recognized. They are mostly melodic or rhythmic configurations—a thoroughly miscellaneous collection of tags, signals, and formulas to which he gives names such as minuet, contredanse, brilliant style, learned style, military music, Turkish music, Storm and Stress, and fantasia. And it is unnerving indeed to see the first-movement exposition of a late Mozart quintet, the E-flat major, K. 614, partitioned into successive segments labeled hunt, brilliant style, sensibility, learned style, brilliant style again, singing style, gigue, learned, brilliant, fanfare, and finally sensibility.[20] But what is most seriously wrong is that no topic label acknowledges the later reinterpretation of the first so-called brilliant passage: in the recapitulation section, Mozart turns this into something rich, unbrilliant, and deliciously chromatic. Expression in Mozart's music, if not in Bach's, is controlled by such reinterpretations. We can see this more clearly, perhaps, than could theorists of the time, to whom this music was new and exciting but also different and difficult.

Under the broad heading of "Rhetoric" Ratner discusses the construction, juxtaposition, and enjambment of musical phrases, techniques closely dependent on the placement and weighting of cadences. These are the areas that the instruction books dealt with most successfully and in the greatest detail. Hence Ratner's historically based account of sonata form, amply bolstered by contemporary citations, resembles Webster's in its bias toward the rhythmic and harmonic elements of the "classic synthesis" at the expense of the thematic. (Though perhaps this is putting the matter the wrong way around; Webster too has read Koch, and he has also read Ratner.) There is no use searching in this author for the ritual attack on the jelly-mold theory of sonata form; he is too close to the composition manuals, which were designed not for the Haydns and Mozarts of this world but for readers who needed, expected, and welcomed rules and patterns to follow. As he says, music of the time undoubtedly "had to be composed quickly, for immediate use, [and] composers relied on familiar and universally accepted formulas for its organization and handling of detail." Ratner likes to tell of the *ars combinatoria* that is promulgated by some of his writers, whereby standard phrases and even individual bars can be juggled around in many different permutations and combinations

EXAMPLE I

to produce plausible little Classical compositions.[21] It is all very matter-of-fact. Perceptive critical comments and coarse ones rattle disconcertingly together.

A curious book, and never more curious than in its final chapter, "Beethoven and the Classic Style," which is given over to a continuously perceptive discussion of one piece, the first movement of the String Quartet in F, op. 59 no. 1, the first "Razumovsky" quartet. This dates from 1805, early in Beethoven's so-called second period, shortly after the *Eroica* Symphony. Here, clearly, it was the author's laudable intention to break out of the heavily systematic manner adopted to explicate late eighteenth-century music in order to suggest horizons beyond. He breaks out with a vengeance: for now eighteenth-century terms such as "topic" and "rhetoric" are abandoned for the vocabulary of present-day analysis. After the "opening chord of the movement sets the mood" (I am now quoting almost entirely Ratner's own words), the first four measures, which "appear as an expansion or elaboration of this [chord]," are perceived as "a pattern for the whole movement." This is because the opening scale figure "can be trimmed to various lengths" and quickened or slowed in such a way as to "penetrate and saturate the melodic action, contributing to the broad flow and unity of the movement." When Ratner sees "the 'vertical' and 'horizontal' exchang[ing] roles . . . to fuse even more strongly the continuous flow," he seems to look past the immediate technical point he is making to an almost ecstatic organicist vision; and when he derives the development section's fugue subject from the second theme of the exposition, as in example 1, he comes before us in a new guise, as a thematicist to be reckoned with. There is no labeling of topics in this chapter. Nor, for once, is there a single citation from a contemporary authority. The unsuspecting reader might suppose that the insights presented here into Beethovenian unity are the product of a twentieth-century ear, not an eighteenth- or early nineteenth-century one.[22]

However, Ratner's historical credentials are entirely in order. He might easily have cited E. T. A. Hoffmann's appreciation of Beethoven's music, which was referred to in passing above. The following familiar sentences appeared in a musical magazine as early as 1810, and then circulated widely in the *Kreisleriana* section of

*Fantasiestücke in Callots Manier* of 1814. In Beethoven's Fifth Symphony, Hoffmann wrote, "The internal disposition of the sections [*Sätzen*], their working-out, orchestration, the way in which they succeed each other, all is directed toward a single point. But it is particularly the close relationship of the themes to each other which provides the unity that alone is able to sustain *one* feeling in the listener." But lest we think that under the impact of Beethoven's V-for-victory motif Hoffmann is expressing no more than a superficial thematicism, he adds that although "this relationship frequently becomes clear to the listener when he hears it in the similarity between two passages, or discovers a bass pattern which is common," nevertheless "a deeper relationship that is not demonstrable in this way speaks only from the heart to the heart."[23] Hoffmann is a good contemporary witness, all the better because he is not a theorist but a practicing artist—an important composer and a very important novelist and critic. Unlike the theorists, moreover, who notoriously write for the most prosaic of human beings, namely students, Hoffmann writes for the most audacious, the most imaginative, the most poetic: "But what if it is only *your* inadequate understanding which fails to grasp the inner coherence of every Beethoven composition? What if it is entirely *your* fault that the composer's language is clear to the initiated but not to you, and that the entrance to his innermost mysteries remains closed to you?"[24]

In spite of Hoffmann's taunts, sensitive critics from his time to the time of Ratner have seldom missed that "inner coherence" in compositions by Beethoven. Beethoven's music was made to order for the burgeoning organicist theory of music, and so was the music of the boldest composers who followed him in the nineteenth century. Even Brahms, widely considered to be one of the less bold, was shown by Schoenberg to have developed his own type of thematic procedure, what Schoenberg called "developing variation"; and Professor Webster, in an important two-part essay on sonata form in Schubert and Brahms, points to imaginative thematic relationships in Brahms of a kind unmentioned in his *Grove* article.[25] Here Webster goes beyond Schoenberg to touch on the dialectic between "inner form" and "outer form" in the work of this composer—that is, on the way Brahms's developing variation technique was made to meet the demands (as he saw them) of traditional sonata form. This topic is further developed with much sensitivity by a younger scholar, Walter Frisch, in a recent study.[26]

Rosen's major effort in regard to Classical music can be viewed in similar dialectic terms, as I have already suggested. And what has always been provocative about Rosen's *The Classical Style* is that he has carried a familiar Romantic dialectic back to the eighteenth century—back to Mozart's first great piano concerto, the E-flat Concerto, K. 271, of 1775, which Alfred Einstein characterized as Mozart's *Eroica;* back especially to Haydn's op. 33 quartets of 1781 and his symphonies of the late 1770s. Speaking of the "deeper structural import between shape, as local idea, and its correspondence through tonal plan," David Epstein remarks that these relationships "are most striking, perhaps, in the music of Haydn, though the idea was adopted and extended by his successors throughout the next hundred years."[27] This would not have been said, I think, before the appearance of *The Classical Style.*

v · I should now like to focus this discussion by means of a specific musical composition, and also to extend the base of the argument somewhat. To introduce the extension, here is another familiar quotation, this one from a letter from Mozart to his father, in 1782. Mozart is writing about his earliest Viennese piano concertos.

> These concertos are a happy medium between what is too easy and too difficult; they are very brilliant, pleasing to the ear, and natural, without being vapid. There are passages here and there from which connoisseurs alone can derive satisfaction; but these passages are written in such a way that the less learned cannot fail to be pleased, though without knowing why.[28]

Ratner, who reminds us of this letter, thinks that when Mozart refers to difficult passages for connoisseurs he means passages in the topic he calls "learned style." This may be right, but it seems to me admissible also to read the passage in a broader context. If modern connoisseurs claim to derive satisfaction from the interpenetration of material and structure in Haydn's music, this is not likely to have escaped Mozart's attention. He may have been referring to compositional subtlety rather than contrapuntal ostentation. Can we perhaps locate the two poles between which Mozart found his "happy medium" not only in his most ambitious and personal works, such as his piano concertos, but also in more modest, less learned, seemingly routine Classical compositions? Can we locate them in a work like *Eine kleine Nachtmusik?*

Webster's selection of this particular work as his paradigm of sonata form gives pause. The piece belongs to the category of the serenade, a popular genre, *Gebrauchsmusik* for the open air, the minimalist art of the late eighteenth century. It was a genre abandoned by Mozart long before he came to write *Eine kleine Nachtmusik* in 1787, the year of *Don Giovanni;* and why he wrote it remains a mystery, for no record survives of its commissioning or its performance. "Vapid" it is not, but it breathes a refined simplicity of form, content, and procedure as the essence of its genre.

*Eine kleine Nachtmusik* would not, then, have been the obvious choice for an author who wanted to show the subtle synthesis of melody, harmony, and rhythm in Classical music. In fact, I do not believe it would have been chosen by any true hater of jelly molds. Tovey, at all events, did not choose such an example for his "Sonata Forms" article in the old *Encyclopaedia Britannica,* an article that must haunt

EXAMPLE 2

any later writer on the subject. What Tovey chose was the first movement of the *Eroica* Symphony (all 689 measures of it, requiring three full folio pages in a condensed score). This is a movement that gloriously illustrates the horizons of Classical form. The *Nachtmusik* would seem, at least at first glance, to exemplify its lowest common denominator.

What is more, the *Eroica* includes Tovey's favorite case of a pregnant thematic detail that is expanded into the total structure. Both Rosen and Epstein also write about it.[29] The famous dissonance in the *Eroica* main theme (bar 7) acts initially as a disturbance, a source of those charged latent energies that drive the music on and on through its extraordinary journeys. At the beginning of the recapitulation (bar 402) the dissonance is reinterpreted enharmonically so as to move the music in lyric, static, poignant directions. In a coda or final section of unprecedented extent it is finally accorded heroic resolution. There is nothing of this kind going on, surely, in *Eine kleine Nachtmusik*.

Or perhaps there is something. Not that much can be made of the neutral, formulaic opening theme shown in Webster's line 1 (see figure 1; in this figure each new staff corresponds to what Webster calls a new "sentence" in the music). Label it "fanfare." Line 2 is the merest busywork, and the modulatory phrase of line 4 is such as to cause a delicate critic discomfort, discomfort heightened by the suspicion that Mozart may be grinning at him. As for the charming melody in line 5, it would take a deeply committed thematicist to propose its derivation from the latent charge of anything ahead of it. Ever so gracefully, it might have been poured into a mold.

Halfway through this sentence, however, Mozart's interest became engaged. The first-violin part at bar 32, starting as an extended ticktock accompaniment—thirteen eighth-note As—takes over the main melodic role as the A moves up the scale to echo the modulatory phrase and to prepare the cadence. There is a magical integration of the functions of theme and accompaniment here.[30] Then in line 6 this line is played backwards (more or less) to disclose another melody (see example 2). The scale-figure backward—that is, going down, not up—also occurs in the cadence figure (line 7, end) and stands out there because of the cadence figure's extreme brevity.

In this sonata exposition, then, there is a sense in which the end of the second group (lines 6 and 7) can be said to "emerge" out of its beginning (line 5, end).

To demarcate and initiate the second large section, the fanfare theme appears again, but with a harmonic change (spelled out in figure 1 by Webster's bracketed chords at the end of line 8). Instead of the original neutral motion from tonic to dominant harmony, from I to $V^7$, the fanfare now goes from I (in D major) to $V^7$ of ii, from the tonic toward the supertonic. The important difference is the note D♯. This is slightly less neutral. For to an exposition of astounding harmonic simplicity, this same V-of-ii chord built on D♯ had brought the one even slightly disturbing element. The chord had come twice, in two not unrelated passages, both of them repeated.

The harmonic content (slim as it is) of the exposition can therefore be said now to have infected the fanfare theme and thus to have "impelled" the first harmonic gesture of the development section.

The nature of this impulsion well illustrates the wit and also the sense of balance that are so important to the Classical style. Whereas in the exposition the V-of-ii chord always resolved normally to ii, in the development section it resolves deceptively to the lowered VII degree, C major. Once this slightly surprising harmony has been proposed, it is maintained as the central plateau of the whole little section. And the route off of this plateau is by way of a long bass E♭, the punning equivalent (or enharmonic reinterpretation) of D♯.

So if we may venture a little further into metaphorical language, the "latent force" injected by D♯ in the exposition can be felt not only in the first gesture of the development section but over its entire course.

As for the melodic material in this section, it did not take a composer of Mozart's genius to decide on using the little up-and-down scale figures of lines 5 and 6. They are, after all, the most—perhaps the only—interesting material at hand. As the scales are treated rather intensively, at least by the standards of this piece, it was a good idea to liquidate them rather definitely at the end of the section. Mozart does this by carrying the upward scale up farther, by slowing it down, and by introducing chromatic steps (B♭–B–C–C♯–D) which seem to trivialize the upward thrust at the same time as the slowdown tends to make it more imposing. It is another very witty place. And the thematic procedure here—the liquidation—can certainly be said to be coordinated with the form. It can also be said to articulate the form. Perhaps it can be said, without undue solemnity, to "engender" the form.

Rosen's term "reinterpretation," however, does seem too solemn for what happens to the exposition material in the recapitulation. This passage, fifty-five bars long, is altered by a mere flick of the wrist in the modulatory section (line 4) at bars 99–100 and by an extension to the tiny cadence figure (line 11). The only sense of resolution conveyed by this facile symmetry is the outcome of one of Mozart's characteristic setups, as transparent as it is delightful. In the exposition he holds the cadence figure down to two bars, which is really too brief to discharge the

EXAMPLE 3

relative intensity of the music just preceding it (line 7). (This intensity itself depends on parallelism with a less intense earlier passage, as Webster indicates.) We are so used to the *Nachtmusik* that we may not notice—but Koch would probably have recommended four bars for the cadence figure, not two (example 3).

So in the recapitulation the composer of *Don Giovanni* resolves this rhythmic imbalance by the sort of expandable vaudeville exit repetitions that come so naturally to Leporello, and Figaro and Bartolo before him (line 11). Instead of the insinuating "voi sapete . . ." phrases of the Catalog Aria, Mozart makes final reference to his much-used up-and-down scale figures—a "resolving" reference in that the upward chromatic line from the end of the development section now runs harmlessly down, and a comic one in that a diatonic scale now seems to grow out of a chromatic one. Since six bars have been used up by this, overshooting the required four, the further rhythmic imbalance requires further discharge in an overlapping six-bar coda. Though why the discharge takes the particular noisy and vacuous form it does here is not altogether easy to say, unless Mozart is grinning at us again. Label it "raucous."

VI ·

How much of this was apprehended and appreciated by the man in the street who happened upon the (undocumented) first performance of Mozart's serenade, one night in 1787, we cannot say, nor what effect it all has on his progeny who are still listening to Mozart in our own time. Perhaps what Mozart's "less learned" listener enjoyed in *Eine kleine Nachtmusik* was indeed "expression" in the sense of an agreeably varied series of "topics" that he could identify with comfortably: fanfare, busywork, charm, ticktock, vaudeville exit, and the rest. Symmetry in art always pleased him, especially in recapitulations, where things are not obscured by improvised ornamentation as in the da capo arias he had grown weary of because of their fussy elaboration and faintly indecorous display. That he cared about the recapitulation resolving or reinterpreting anything is vastly to be doubted. He would have appreciated the raucous passage at the end of the first movement, and also the parallel place at the end of the last movement; at any rate, these we can at least feel fairly sure he would have apprehended. Mozart must have written them purposely to drown out the likely street noise.

As for the features of this music for the connoisseur, I suppose I am making two contrary points about them. They can be missed by the connoisseur, the specialist, or the musicologist who concentrates on Kurth's "outer form," on formula and pattern, at the expense of "inner form." However, in a Classical work of this kind they amount to no more than occasional touches. They can hardly be said to permeate the entire fabric of the music.

Rosen likes to give the impression that the Classical style depends critically on the perfect integration of melody, harmony, rhythm, and texture, something the minor composers of the time could scarcely achieve. Tovey wrote a major essay purporting to show the essential "freedom" of the one Beethoven sonata which looks suspiciously as though it were poured into a mold.[31] Yet I do not think we can seriously doubt that in writing his serenade Mozart relied, in Ratner's words, "on familiar and universally accepted formulas for its organization and handling of details." He would have lost his audience otherwise. I might mention parenthetically that even in the organization of the *Nachtmusik*'s development section around D♯ and E♭ Mozart was relying on a formula that he used in several other compositions, among them the E-flat String Quintet. When thirty years later Beethoven began to depart radically from accepted norms he did indeed lose his audience; Beethoven being Beethoven, the late sonatas and quartets were accorded a measure of mystical respect, but they were not understood for nearly fifty years after his death.[32] His earlier works that retained their enormous popularity did not depart too far from norms, despite Hoffmann's enthusiastic proclamations. And it is probably true that what made the Fifth Symphony a favorite with contemporary *Nichtkenner* was its series of powerful topics: fate knocking at the door, Storm and Stress, the hunt, consolation, mystery music, military music, fanfare—particularly, in those Napoleonic times, military music and fanfare.

By insisting in their matter-of-fact way on the importance of topic and formula, musicologists provide a corrective to esoteric modern theories of Classical music. Whatever late eighteenth-century art was, it was not (and is not) esoteric. Immersion in the treatises and manuals of the time has at least allowed Ratner to keep the common touch, for while those books were written by and for professionals, in the eighteenth century no professional musician or writer on music ignored the essential audience for music as is the case in our time. Analysts like Schenker, Réti, and Epstein write as though the non-professional world did not exist, and it is this, when all is said and done, not the particular details of their theories, that makes them so profoundly unhistorical. Here too Rosen occupies middle ground, for his criticism is addressed to an educated lay public—to an elite public, if you will, but at least not to music professors. He is, in the best sense of the word, a popularizer of advanced modern critical insights. He writes for the same public he plays to.

There is still something to learn from Tovey in this matter, I believe. Tovey's final appeal was always to what he called the "naive listener," the interested, earnest non-musician whom he could cajole again and again into appreciating the subtleties of tonality, invertible counterpoint at the twelfth, and so on. Tovey's very limitations as a critic were probably due, in part, to his refusal to venture into certain areas where he feared the non-professional would not be able to follow the professional. This naive listener, this amiable abstraction, this eminently Victorian invention—clearly he is a grandchild in concept of the cultivated man of common sense to whom eighteenth-century writers addressed their work. Can we postulate a great-great-grandchild for our own time?

We need him to keep our criticism honest, and we will continue to appeal to him most urgently in respect to the music of the late eighteenth century, to the music we call Classical. This is no longer for us, as it still actually was for Tovey, a touchstone for musical composition. It remains a touchstone for ideas about how music is to be apprehended and appreciated.

*Notes*

1. On the German tradition, see Jens Peter Larsen, "Sonatenform-Probleme," in *Festschrift Friedrich Blume zum 70. Geburtstag,* ed. Anna Amalie Abert and Wilhelm Pfannkuch (Cassel, 1963), 221–30; on Tovey, see "Tovey's Beethoven," pp. 155–72.

2. See "How We Got into Analysis," pp. 12–32.

3. See, for example, M. H. Abrams, "From Addison to Kant: Modern Aesthetics and the Exemplary Art," in *Studies in Eighteenth-Century British Art and Aesthetics,* ed. Ralph Cohen (Berkeley and Los Angeles, 1985), 16–48.

4. Rosen, *The Classical Style: Haydn, Mozart, Beethoven,* rev. ed. (New York, 1972), 53.

5. See Ruth A. Solie, "The Living Work: Organicism and Musical Analysis," *19th-Century Music* 4 (1980): 147–56.

6. Rosen, *Classical Style,* 36.

7. In "Tovey's Beethoven" (see n. 1).

8. See Ian Bent, "Analytical Thinking in the First Half of the Nineteenth Century," in *Modern Musical Scholarship,* ed. Edward Olleson (Stocksfield, 1980), 151–66. Many writers, including Rosen, have misjudged Marx's role in the ossification of sonata-form theory.

9. Donald Francis Tovey, "Normality and Freedom in Music," in *The Main Stream of Music and Other Essays* (New York, 1949), 183–201; Arnold Schoenberg, *Style and Idea* (London, 1976), 415.

10. Edward T. Cone, "Music: A View from Delft," in *Music: A View from Delft,* ed. Robert P. Morgan (Chicago, 1989), 21–22.

11. Hans Keller, "K. 503: The Unity of Contrasting Themes and Movements" (1956), repr. in *Mozart: Piano Concerto in C Major, K. 503,* ed. Joseph Kerman (Norton Critical Scores; New York, 1970), 176–200.

12. Rosen, *Classical Style,* 120.

13. See especially the review by Edward Olleson in *Musical Times* 112 (1971): 1166–67. For criticism on somewhat different historical grounds, and from a less strictly academic position, see Alan Tyson in *New York Review of Books,* 15 June 1972, 10–12.

In America *The Classical Style* was given the silent treatment by the "official" scholarly journals; no reviews appeared in *Journal of the American Musicological Society, Musical Quarterly, Music Library Association Notes,* or *Journal of Music Theory.*

14. See the review of *Sonata Forms* by Jan LaRue in *Journal of the American Musicological Society* 34 (1981): 557–66.

15. "As it appears": as it appears to me on the basis of careful analysis and my best understanding of Webster's article. It should be said, however, that Webster does not broach this issue in his review of *Sonata Forms* in *Musical Times* 122 (1981): 301–4.

16. David Epstein, *Beyond Orpheus: Studies in Musical Structure* (Cambridge, Mass., 1979), 53 n. 7. Rosen is linked with Réti, etc., on pp. 10 and 37.

17. A lengthy review of *The Classical Style* was entitled "Better Than Tovey?" (*Hudson Review* 25 [1972–73]: 633–46); to William H. Youngren, "Tovey's catalyzing influence" was "apparent on virtually every page of Rosen's book." See also the review of *Sonata Forms* by Joseph Kerman, *New York Review of Books,* 23 October 1980, 50.

18. Heinrich Christian Koch, *Versuch einer Anweisung zur Composition* (Leipzig, 1782–93), 3:326–27, 179–90. There is a growing literature on Koch, who was first studied intensively by Ratner; recent items include *New Grove* articles on Koch (Ratner) and analysis (Bent), and Nancy Kovaleff Baker, "Heinrich Koch's Description of the Symphony," *Studi musicali* 9 (1980): 303–16. Baker discusses Koch's Haydn analysis in detail and remarks that when Koch analyzes a more modern symphony, by Rosetti, he misattributes it to Pleyel (!).

19. "It is largely in the music of Haydn and Mozart after 1775 that structure replaced ornamentation as the principal vehicle of expression" (Rosen, *Classical Style,* 395).

For the difficulties experienced by late eighteenth-century theorists and aestheticians with the element of contrast in contemporaneous music, see Bellamy Hosler, *Changing Aesthetic Views of Instrumental Music in Eighteenth-Century Germany* (Ann Arbor, 1981), esp. ch. 5, "Contrast, Change, and the Worth of Instrumental Music: Sulzer—Junker—Forkel."

20. Leonard G. Ratner, *Classic Form: Expression, Form, and Style* (New York, 1980), 237–46.

21. For a fresher view of this matter, see Bent, "Analytical Thinking."

22. Ratner, *Classic Form,* 423–31.

23. *E. T. A. Hoffmann's Musical Writings,* ed. David Charlton, tr. Martyn Clarke (Cambridge, 1989), 100, 250–51.

24. Ibid., 98.

25. James Webster, "Schubert's Sonata Form and Brahms's First Maturity," *19th-Century Music* 1 (1978): 18–35, and 2 (1979): 52–71.

26. Walter Frisch, *Brahms and the Principle of Developing Variation* (California Studies in Nineteenth-Century Music, no. 2; Berkeley and Los Angeles, 1983).

27. Epstein, *Beyond Orpheus,* 41.

28. *The Letters of Mozart and His Family,* tr. Emily Anderson (London, 1938), 3:1242.

29. Rosen, *Classical Style,* 80; Rosen, *Sonata Forms,* 277–80; Epstein, *Beyond Orpheus,* 124–25. Tovey's music example is reprinted in his *Musical Articles from the Encyclopaedia Britannica* (London, 1944), 221–28; see also his *Essays in Musical Analysis,* vol. 1, *Symphonies* (London, 1935), 30–31.

Incidentally, Schenker's non-treatment of this central matter in his book-length study of the *Eroica* has become a *locus classicus* for showing the limitations of his system; see p. 168 and Milton Babbitt's remarks in the foreword to Epstein, *Beyond Orpheus,* x.

30. This is a style feature in Classical music that has been repeatedly illuminated by Rosen (*Classical Style,* 115–18; *Sonata Forms,* 174–80). Rosen sees this feature as a key criterion of the style, and he sees it used consistently by Haydn and Mozart only after 1775–80. Hence

he dates the beginning of the Classical style from that period (cf. n. 18) rather than from around ten years earlier—a point of issue between him and other scholars (see the reviews by Tyson and LaRue, nn. 13 and 14).

A little-noticed passage in one of Tovey's earliest essays draws attention to this same style feature. The finale theme in Haydn's great Sonata in E Flat "begins with a purely rhythmic figure on one note. If this rhythm is treated as an accompaniment (and Haydn so treats it from the outset), that accompaniment is *ipso facto* alive and thematic. . . . It is interesting to note that Beethoven, in his 'second period', developed a strong predilection for such rhythmic figures in his themes, and used them constantly as a most powerful means of giving life to inner parts without the necessity for the [introduction of independent] counterpoint" (*Essays in Musical Analysis,* vol. 7, *Chamber Music* [London, 1944], 104). The words in brackets are my attempt to fill in an evident lacuna in the text.

31. Opus 22: see Tovey, "Some Aspects of Beethoven's Art Forms," in *Main Stream,* 271–97.

32. See Amanda Glauert, "The Double Perspective in Beethoven's Op. 131," *19th-Century Music* 4 (1980): 113–20.

BYRD, TALLIS, ALFONSO FERRABOSCO

# 5

# William Byrd and Elizabethan Catholicism

Until fairly recently the history of Catholicism in Elizabethan and Jacobean England was conceived largely in terms of hagiology. From the first history of the English Jesuits, by Father Henry More, grandson of Sir Thomas, in 1635, to the biography of the Blessed Edmund Campion by Evelyn Waugh, written exactly 300 years later, Catholic historians concerned themselves mainly with saints and martyrs, men of action and men of vision, with the pious great and the pious poor. They said little about poets and even less about artists or musicians; traditional historians have never been much interested in the arts. No doubt if they had found a Shakespeare among the faithful they would have made much of him. But they did not. They found only the Jesuit poet Robert Southwell; and it seemed rather beside the point to award Father Southwell the laurel since God had reserved for him the vastly greater glory of a martyr's crown of thorns.

In fact the English Catholic community had among its members a much more brilliant ornament in the field of the arts. William Byrd, the premier figure of Elizabethan and Jacobean music, was also one of the greatest of all European composers of the time and arguably the greatest English composer of *all* time. But the art of music has been slow to acquire the prestige of poetry; when music did gain it (or something like it) Byrd's music was no longer well known or easy to

---

➤ The 1978 Faculty Research Lecture at the University of California at Berkeley ("William Byrd at Fifty"); published in *New York Review of Books,* 17 May 1979, pp. 32–36.

Placed in a broader context, this material also appears in chapter 1 of *The Masses and Motets of William Byrd,* The Music of William Byrd, vol. 1 (Berkeley and Los Angeles, 1981), where the complete texts and sources of the motets and references for the biographical data may be found. See also Edmund H. Fellowes, *William Byrd,* 2d ed. (London, 1948), and *New Grove Dictionary of Music and Musicians,* s.v. "Byrd, William."

come by; and when this music at last became more generally available, the key to its interpretation as a Catholic statement was still lacking. And so Catholic historians have paid Byrd almost no attention.

Music historians, though they have paid more attention, have failed or refused to see the composer clearly enough against the background of his religion. It is not that his religious convictions have ever been in the slightest doubt. He wrote great quantities of Latin liturgical music for Catholic services, and a high proportion of the records of his life that have come down to us concern his Catholic activities and activism. So many, indeed, that in the standard life-and-works by E. H. Fellowes, which has three chapters on the life, one of these chapters is devoted entirely to "Byrd's Association with the Catholics." But as the word "association" in this context perhaps already suggests—would one speak of "Milton's Association with the Puritans"?—Byrd's Catholicism was something that Fellowes could never take quite seriously. A decidedly stiff-necked Victorian clergyman, the author of a major work on Anglican cathedral music, he never missed an opportunity of pointing out that Byrd also wrote admirable music for the Church of England liturgy—though to be sure, there was very much less of this than of the Catholic sacred music. In the early part of this century Fellowes performed wonders in the publishing and publicizing of Byrd's music, but he did this in an ecumenical spirit which seriously obscured its fundamental sectarian nature.

Thanks partly to Fellowes's work, it is now customary, at least in English and American musical writings, to rank Byrd with the main masters of late sixteenth-century music—with Palestrina, Lassus, and Victoria. He is so ranked, for example, in Howard Mayer Brown's *Music in the Renaissance* (1976). This is not, I think, a case of mere chauvinism on the part of English scholars and critics, and mere superstition on the part of Americans. A study of *The Consort and Keyboard Music of William Byrd,*[1] by Oliver Neighbour, illuminates sharply the greatness of Byrd's instrumental music; he was the first major composer to devote a substantial effort to music without words. Getting Byrd's Latin sacred music into correct focus—a Catholic focus—will allow a clearer view of another body of his music which is equally great. And when this music is in its correct focus it also will be seen to illustrate the responses of the Elizabethan Catholic community in a unique way. Resources are available to art and to artists that are not available to even the greatest saints and heroes of traditional Catholic history.

II ·    The course of Byrd's life and the history of Elizabethan Catholicism intersect most dramatically in 1580–81, at the time of the fateful Jesuit missionary expedition of Fathers Robert Persons and Edmund Campion. These were two very remarkable men, and Campion, especially, who had been the most brilliant figure at Oxford in the 1560s, seemed to have a disquieting success among the country gentry, the clergy, and academics. After about a year he was betrayed, apprehended, interrogated with the help of the rack, and finally condemned to die with two other priests at a great public execution in London. Campion started his final address from the scaffold with words of St. Paul to the Corinthians, "Spectaculum facti sumus Deo, angelis, et hominibus" (We apostles are made a spectacle unto God, unto His angels, and unto men)—but this was brutally cut short. The three men were hanged, drawn, and quartered, and their dismembered bodies nailed to a gate on Tyburn Hill.

This triple execution rocked England and set off a storm of protests from abroad. There had been nothing like it since the days of Mary Tudor. Tracts were written back and forth about the event, and stories began to grow up around it. One of these concerned a young Catholic gentleman named Henry Walpole—"Cambridge wit, minor poet, satirist, flaneur, a young man of birth, popular, intelligent, slightly romantic," as Waugh describes him. Standing near the scaffold when Campion's body was being butchered, he saw a drop of blood spurt onto his coat. Profoundly shaken, he went home and sat up that night writing an extremely long, anguished poem about Campion, "Why Do I Use My Paper, Ink, and Pen," which caused a scandal. The printer of it had his ears cut off, and Walpole had to flee the country. Eventually he became a Jesuit himself and returned to England to meet the same fate as Campion.

Byrd set this notorious poem to music, and the setting certainly did not escape notice. Another future Jesuit, Thomas Fitzherbert, remarked that "one of the sonnets [on Campion's death] was presently set forth in music by the best musician in England, which I have often seen and heard," and no doubt Fitzherbert heard it before 1582, when he too left England. Also, at around this same time, Byrd wrote an extended Latin motet, *Deus venerunt gentes,* which must also rage and lament for Campion under the cover of some blameless verses from Psalm 79:

Deus, venerunt gentes in hereditatem tuam, polluerunt templum sanctum tuum, posuerunt Ierusalem in pomorum custodiam; posuerunt morticinia servorum tuorum escas volatilibus coeli, carnes sanctorum tuorum bestiis terrae; effuderunt sanguinem ipsorum tanquam aquam in circuitu Ierusalem, et non erat qui sepeliret. Facti sumus opprobrium vicinis nostris, subsannatio et illusio his qui in circuitu nostro sunt.

O God, the heathen have set foot in thy domain, defiled thy holy temple and laid Jerusalem in ruins. They have thrown out the dead bodies of thy servants to feed the birds of the air; they have made thy saints carrion for the wild beasts. Their blood is spilled all around Jerusalem like water, and there was no one to bury them. We suffer the contempt of our neighbors, the gibes and mockery of all around us.

We have here the unburied bodies nailed to the gate, the blood that spurted on Walpole, the protests from "our neighbors" abroad, and even an allusion to Campion's speech from the scaffold: for the last verse begins in Latin, "Facti sumus opprobrium vicinis nostris," and I do not think it can be a coincidence that this comes so close to Campion's "Spectaculum facti sumus Deo, angelis, et hominibus."

It is likely enough, I suppose, that Byrd too stood in the rain and the mud at Tyburn to witness Campion's martyrdom. It seems very likely that this affected him much as it affected Walpole. Not that he ever went abroad to become a missionary; Byrd was one of those who stayed at home, and prospered, and made his uneasy peace with the system. But after 1581 his religious commitment hardened decisively. Whether it is technically correct to speak of a "conversion" in his case, as in Walpole's, is not clear. But with Byrd as with Walpole we cannot fail to detect a profound new sense of devotion to the Catholic faith and the Catholic cause.

Born in 1543, Byrd was just old enough to have been brought up as a choirboy under the old religion—the old religion which Mary Tudor restored, between 1553 and 1558, with special zeal. His first position was in the new Anglican disposition; he was appointed organist-choirmaster of Lincoln Cathedral in 1562. The personality that we are able to glimpse from Lincoln records is not distinguished by any unusual spirituality, but rather by a certain contentiousness and a precocious talent for the great Elizabethan art of applying influence—a talent that obviously stood him in very good stead during his later, intransigently Catholic years. Lincoln appointed him at a higher salary than his predecessor, with a lease of land thrown in to sweeten the contract, and when he left for the Chapel Royal in 1572 he pulled strings from London so that he actually continued to draw a salary from Lincoln for nearly ten years more.

In London Byrd's star rose rapidly. He made connections with powerful lords such as the earls of Essex and Northumberland, and acquired more leases. He was appointed joint organist of the Chapel Royal, sharing the post with his master Thomas Tallis, who was then around seventy years old. With Tallis, too, he secured a patent from the Crown for music printing—a trade with little history in Britain up to this time. The monopolists' debut was a joint publication of Latin motets, the *Cantiones quae ab argumento sacrae vocantur* of 1575, dedicated to Queen Elizabeth and designed to show the world what excellent music Britain could produce. So at least we are told by the elaborate prefatory matter, which goes on for six pages. And influential persons were enlisted to fill these pages: a youthful courtier and dilettante composer named Sir Ferdinando Heybourne, and the important educator Richard Mulcaster. One has the feeling it was Byrd, not the aging Tallis, who did the enlisting.

So far it had been a worldly career, with scarcely any signs of Catholic leanings. In 1577, however, Byrd's wife was first cited for recusancy, that is, for refusing to attend Church of England services as required by law. It was a common pattern for Catholic wives to stand on principle while their husbands, who had much more to lose, attended the required services as "church-papists." After 1580 the signs multiply. Clearly the authorities were now more vigilant, but clearly also Byrd was more engaged.

His house was watched and on one occasion searched. His servant was caught in a raid. One of his surviving letters sues on behalf of a beleaguered Catholic family. In 1586 he was one of a small group assembled to welcome two notable Jesuits to England, Fathers Southwell and Henry Garnet. Byrd must have been highly regarded among the Catholics to have been summoned on this occasion.[2] He himself was cited for recusancy in 1585, and bound in recognizance of the staggering sum of £200 for the same crime two years later. (He may never have paid it.) Still to come, in his declining years, was the accusation that he had "seduced" certain servants and neighbors away from the Church of England; but Byrd seems always to have stayed clear of actual arrest or serious harassment.

III ·    Byrd's new religious conviction was expressed in music—in a remarkable series of Latin motets composed in a new style, and with texts of an entirely new kind. These texts seem to voice prayers and protests, which are sometimes general and sometimes more specific, on behalf of the Elizabethan Catholic community.[3]

Some of these motets speak of a "congregation" or "God's people" who await liberation. Thus *Domine praestolamur:*

Domine, praestolamur adventum tuum ut cito venias et dissolvas iugum captivitatis nostrae. Veni, Domine, noli tardare, relaxa facinora plebis tuae. Et libera populum tuum.

O Lord, we await thy coming, that you may at once dissolve the yoke of our captivity. Come, o Lord, do not delay. Break the bonds of your servants, and liberate your people.

Byrd harps on the theme of the coming of God in various moods—supplicatory, as in the text above, or confident, in *Laetentur coeli:*

Laetentur coeli, et exultet terra, iubilate montes laudem quia Dominus noster veniet, et pauperum suorum miserebitur.

Let the heavens rejoice and the earth exult, let the mountains sing forth praise, for the Lord is coming and will have mercy on his destitute ones.

or didactic in *Vigilate:*

Vigilate, nescitis enim quando dominus domus veniat, sero, an media nocte, an galli cantu, an mane; vigilate ergo, cum venerit repente, inveniat vos dormientes. Quod autem dico vobis omnibus dico: Vigilate.

Keep awake, for you do not know when the master of the house is coming, evening or midnight, cock-crow or early dawn. Keep awake, then; if he comes suddenly, he must not find you asleep. And what I say to you, I say to everyone: Keep awake.

Several impressive motets refer to the Holy City, Jerusalem, and the Babylonian captivity: a transparent metaphor for the Catholic situation in Britain, though of course it could also be turned in other directions. *Ne irascaris Domine,* which is dated 1581 in two independent manuscripts, was and still is the most popular of these "Jerusalem" motets.

Other texts, of which the most sensational is *Deus venerunt gentes,* the Campion lament mentioned above, are more explicit in reference. Two of Byrd's greatest motets, *Haec dicit Dominus* and *Plorans plorabit,* tell in the one case of the progeny of lamenting Rachel who are promised their patrimony, and in the other of the king and queen who hold the Lord's flock captive—this motet appeared as late as 1605—and whose proud crowns have fallen. Both texts are drawn from Jeremiah; both seem frankly political in intent.

Boldest of all, perhaps, is *Circumspice Ierusalem,* a text from the Apocrypha which can only refer to the Jesuit missionaries:

Circumspice, Ierusalem, ad orientem et vide iucunditatem a Deo tibi venientem. Ecce enim veniunt filii tui, quos dimisisti dispersos, veniunt collecti ab oriente usque ad occidentem et verbo sancti gaudentes in honorem Dei.

Look around toward the East, o Jerusalem, and see the joy that is coming to you from God! Behold, your sons are coming, whom you sent away and dispersed; they come gathered together from the East to the West, at the word of the Holy One, rejoicing in the glory of God.

"Whereas I have come out of Germany and Boëmeland," wrote Campion in the document known as Campion's Brag, a powerful open letter to the Privy Council, "being sent by my Superiors, and adventured myself into this noble realm, my dear country, for the glory of God and benefit of souls. . . ."[4]

Interestingly enough, there is a contemporary acknowledgment of Byrd's covert use of Latin motets for personal or political statements. It is a covert acknowledgment, of course. In 1583 a grandiose motet was sent to him by the great Netherlandish composer Philippe de Monte, chapelmaster to the Holy Roman Emperor. The motet's words are pointedly rearranged from the most famous of the psalms of captivity, "Super flumina Babilonis" (By the waters of Babylon, Psalm 137):

> Super flumina Babilonis illic sedimus et flevimus dum recordaremur tui Sion. Illic interrogaverunt nos, qui captivos abduxerunt nos, verba cantionum: Quomodo cantabimus canticum Domini in terra aliena?

> By the rivers of Babylon, there we sat down, yea, we wept, when we remembered Zion. There they that carried us away demanded of us a song. How shall we sing the Lord's song in a strange land?

A year later Byrd sent back a magnificent answering motet as though to a challenge:

> Quomodo cantabimus canticum Domini in terra aliena? Si oblitus fuero tui, Ierusalem, oblivioni detur dextra mea; adhaeret lingua mea faucibus meis, si non meminero tui; si non proposuero Ierusalem in principio laetitiae meae.

> How shall we sing the Lord's song in a strange land? If I forget thee, o Jerusalem, let my right hand forget her cunning. If I do not remember thee, let my tongue cleave to the roof of my mouth, if I prefer not Jerusalem above my chief joy.

Byrd's *Quomodo cantabimus* includes a three-part canon by inversion: as though to assure Catholic Christendom that he had not hung up his harp, that his faith was firm, and that his hand had lost none of its cunning. Seldom does the murk of under-documentation allow so sharp an insight into the Elizabethan musical condition as is afforded by this exchange between two great Catholic composers.

IV ·   Byrd's motets of the 1580s employ a new musical style, on which his whole political endeavor depended. (We should speak more strictly of a maturing of tendencies already evident in the *Cantiones sacrae* of 1575—a brilliant, experimental, uneven group of compositions.) There is much that is historically important about this style, as far as the development of English music is concerned: its refinement of the basic medium of imitative polyphony, its command of the subtle distinctions between various homophonic and half-homophonic textures, and in general its superb native reinterpretation of the classical mid-century idiom of Continental Europe.

But perhaps its most important new feature is its new sensitivity to verbal texts. It is only with the Tallis–Byrd *Cantiones sacrae* of 1575 and especially with Byrd's motets of the next decade that English music is "framed to the life of the words," as Byrd himself was to express it some time later. This "framing" we usually associate with the madrigal, a secular genre which had served Italian composers since the 1530s as an endlessly fertile field for the investigation of word–music relationships. But madrigals are not known to have been written in England before the 1590s. Ahead of the English madrigalists, Byrd was already practicing the expressive and illustrative rhetoric of Continental music in his sacred motets of the 1580s.

This rhetoric made for their impact. Byrd did more than provide significant texts with beautiful music. It was music of a rhetorical vividness that was all but unprecedented on the English scene, and so it was music of unprecedented power. Again and again, when the motets break into their great supplications—"Have mercy on us, o Lord," "Lord, do not forget thy people," and the like—the music breaks out of the prevailing polyphonic discourse into powerful chordal passages of direct outcry. When the text of *Ne irascaris Domine* says "Zion is a wilderness" Byrd frames these words with harmonies and textures that are unforgettably bleak and hollow. When the Lord is urged to arise ("Exsurge Domine") the melody mounts up the scale in excitement, and when it is promised that he will not delay ("et non tardabit") the rhythm races in frantic double-time note values. And when St. Mark warns us to be wakeful, lest when the Lord arrive he find us sleeping, Byrd with grim humor writes music that drones or snores and is then cut short by vivid shouts of "Vigilate! vigilate! vigilate!"

The stylistic point is important to make because, of course, the expressive style is at the heart of Byrd's unique contribution to these motets. The texts themselves may not have been his personal choice. They could have been given to him by his patrons or his priests (though some I believe he must have chosen himself, because only a musician would have been likely to know their sources). Whoever chose the words, however, Byrd brought them to life in a way that had previously been unknown in English music. These motets must have seemed extraordinarily moving and powerful to their first listeners. Indeed they still seem extraordinarily moving and powerful today.


v ·   At the end of the 1580s Byrd for the first time began issuing his music in a systematic way. He published two books of English songs and two of Latin motets, and also supervised a beautiful manuscript collection of his virginal music, *My Lady*

*Nevells Booke.* It is hard to escape the impression that the composer was setting his house in order—writing *finis,* as it were, to a chapter of his creative career. And indeed in his fiftieth year, 1593, Byrd obtained a farm in the village of Stondon Massey in Essex and went there to live. After this move, the music that he wrote was of a different kind than he had cultivated before.

Situated between Brentwood and Chelmsford, the county town, Stondon is about twenty-five miles from Westminster—that is, about twice as far as Byrd's previous home (which was at Harlington, Middlesex, near the present Heathrow Airport). The farm was a good-sized one, and it looks as if the composer were going into a semi-prosperous semi-retirement. Though he certainly did not resign his position in the Chapel Royal, it seems he was not often there, for his name is usually missing from the memorials and petitions signed by all the other members. His printing monopoly was not renewed; henceforth he is not much heard of around London. But I believe that this semi-retirement was not the prime consideration, but rather a symptom, and that the real significance of the farm at Stondon was not its remoteness from London but its proximity to the great manor house at Ingatestone, just a few miles distant.

Ingatestone Hall had been built by Sir William Petre, secretary of state under Henry VIII, Edward VI, Mary, and Elizabeth. His son Sir John was a circumspect Catholic and a patron of Byrd's. (The first document linking their names dates from the fateful year 1581.) Lady Mary was less circumspect. The Petres presided over a Catholic community centered on their Essex estates of Ingatestone and Thorndon; and what I suspect is that Byrd moved from Harlington expressly to join this community and participate in the Catholic life there. If so, this clearly marks a new deeper commitment by William Byrd to his religion.

The social historian John Bossy has given us a remarkably full picture of Catholic life in England at this time.[5] A large proportion of the Elizabethan gentry retained Catholic sympathies, and those that were really serious about religion found it possible to work out a *modus vivendi* within the system. They had to stay out of public life and retire to their country estates, and they might have to put up with fines and harassment—and they were well advised to stay clear of their inflammatory sons and cousins who went abroad to become Jesuits and returned, like Henry Walpole, to make life difficult for the authorities and for the Catholic minority alike. That is a lot. But if they were prepared to make these sacrifices, the Catholic gentry were pretty much left to supervise the lives of their families, servants, and tenants according to Catholic principles as they saw them.

The main principles, and the main preoccupations, according to Bossy, were three. First, the Catholic gentry were naturally determined to raise their children in the faith. Second, they labored to institutionalize a daily routine in accordance with the elaborate Catholic calendar of those days, with its feast and fast days, its rogation times, and its seasons of abstinence from meat. The daily texture of their lives grew more and more distinct from that of the Anglican majority. Third, they struggled to maintain undercover Catholic services. They set up "Mass-centers" in attics and barns, furnished with the necessary consecrated church furniture, vestments, and the like, and they harbored traveling or circuit priests, even sometimes resident ones. Mass was celebrated strictly according to the Roman liturgy, of course. On great occasions such as Christmas and Easter, it was desirable for Mass to be sung with a choir in as festive and ornate a fashion as one remembered from the days of Henry VIII and Queen Mary. Then the Petres were inclined to seek out the quiet of Ingatestone, away from the main road and less public than their principal seat at Thorndon.

The impression that Byrd entered into a life of this kind rests not only on the fact that he moved to Stondon—it appears, incidentally, that he brought his entire extended family along with him—but also on the kind of music he wrote after the move. Instead of covert political motets and the other types that he had cultivated in the 1580s—mainly settings of penitential texts, which were widely popular in the sixteenth century, with a few didactic homilies and general songs of praise—he now turned almost exclusively to liturgical items for particular Catholic services. And once again, as at the beginning of the 1580s, the change in text repertory was accompanied by a change in musical style.

His three settings of the Ordinary of the Mass date from 1592–95. They contain the music by which he is perhaps best known today: direct, concise, eminently "functional," even austere, yet infused with a remarkable quiet fervor. In the next decade he produced his magnum opus the *Gradualia,* a great collection of more than a hundred motets for the Proper of the Mass (those sections of the service which change according to the season). The entire Church year is covered; one remembers Bossy's point about the Catholics' preoccupation with the Church calendar. There are motets for Christmas, Epiphany, the Purification, Easter, Ascension, Whitsun, Corpus Christi, All Saints, and various feasts of the Blessed Virgin Mary—as well as two feasts of special importance to the Catholics, Sts. Peter and Paul and St. Peter's Chains. Byrd sets the communion of these two feasts, *Tu es Petrus,* with the greatest of verve: "You are Peter, the rock, and on this rock I will build my Church."

Liturgical music is written to be used in a liturgy. Byrd's Masses and *Gradualia* motets were written for services held at the clandestine Mass-centers of Catholic England. He says plainly, when dedicating book two of the *Gradualia* to his patron, that its contents "have mostly proceeded from your house, which is most friendly to me and mine"—Ingatestone Hall, where Byrd and his family must have worshipped regularly. "These little flowers are plucked as it were from your gardens and are most rightfully due to you as tithes." But the fact that this music was printed shows that it was destined to be sung elsewhere, too. "We kept Corpus Christi Day with great solemnity and music," writes Father Garnet in 1605, "and the day of the Octave made a solemn procession about a great garden, the house being watched, which we knew not until the next day." Was the music taken from the Corpus Christi section of the *Gradualia,* published only a few months earlier? A few months later Garnet, who had an "exquisite knowledge of the art of music," was together with Byrd at a musical gathering in London.

And a few months later than that, the Gunpowder Plot had brought down Garnet and all possible Catholic hopes for a new restoration. It should already have been clear enough after the defeat of the Armada in 1588 that the best that could be hoped for was the maintenance of a Catholic way of life in a minority status. In the 1580s, when many Catholics still regarded the eclipse of their faith as a temporary aberration, Byrd spoke for them in motets of extraordinary power. Then in the 1590s he turned from these motets of anguish and anger to motets and Mass sections celebrating the Catholic rite in perpetuity. In this turn we may see a new acceptance of the inevitable on the part of his essential patrons among the Catholic gentry.

His own acceptance can be seen in the move to Stondon, the withdrawal from artistic life in London, and the establishment of closer ties with the Catholic community under the Petres. There is one non-liturgical motet in the *Gradualia* that deserves special notice—one non-liturgical motet among a hundred that are strictly bound to the liturgy:

Unam petii a Domino, hanc requiram, ut inhabitem in domo Domini omnibus diebus vitae meae, ut videam voluntatem Domini et visitem templum
eius.

One thing I ask of the Lord, one thing I seek, that I may inhabit the house of
the Lord all the days of my life, to reflect on the will of the Lord and to seek
him in his temple.

These words from Psalm 27 would seem to speak with uncommon directness of Byrd's own condition.

VI ·  One might say that Byrd had come full circle, in that he was now treating the same Catholic liturgical texts that he had come to know as a choirboy in the time of Queen Mary. But of course the music he wrote for these texts in the 1590s was not like the music he sang in the 1550s. Much as the Catholics may have wished to return to the medieval order, they could not do this in their music any more than they could in their political accommodation. The clandestine Masses at Ingatestone, always in danger of exposure by spies, had no leisure for the grandiose, drawn-out, florid music of Tallis and his generation. Byrd's Masses are a great deal simpler and more concise. Some of his *Gradualia* motets are positively aphoristic.

There could also be no return to the older Tudor composers' attitude toward the words. For them, the actual *meaning* of the words in a liturgical text mattered less than the *function* of that text as a unit in the ritual. But for Byrd the word was primary. "There is such a profound and hidden power to sacred words," he observes in the dedication to the *Gradualia*—it is a famous and beautiful statement—"that to one thinking upon things divine and diligently and earnestly pondering them, the most suitable of all musical measures occur (I know not how) as of themselves, and suggest themselves spontaneously to the mind that is not indolent and inert." The expressive rhetoric that he had developed in the 1580s still illuminates the liturgical texts of the *Gradualia*—texts such as *Ave verum corpus, O magnum misterium, Iustorum animae,* and *Tu es Petrus,* to mention only some of the most familiar. It even illuminates the words of the Ordinary of the Mass, which served Catholic composers on the Continent as the commonest of clay for the building of one purely musical construction after another. But Byrd was a Catholic composer who could not and did not take the Mass for granted.

His late Latin sacred music was, in short, Catholic liturgical music in a new manifestation: just as Ingatestone was not really a continuation of the old late-medieval order, but the beginning of a new regime of Catholic life which would, in fact, continue with relatively minor modifications until the nineteenth century.

Anyone who knows anything of the *Gradualia* will remember the luminous "alleluia" sections in *Sacerdotes Domini, Non vos relinquam orphanos, Constitues eos,* and many other pieces. Byrd's treatment of these alleluias—there are nearly eighty examples—can perhaps be taken as emblematic of his whole endeavor in the late sacred music. He never thought to cut corners by writing a da capo indication for one of these alleluias, though in many cases the liturgical rubrics would have made this perfectly appropriate; he seems to have been fascinated by the problem of setting the same word in dozens of different ways, as though absorbed in the mystery of the inexhaustible renewal of praise. The language of the Seven Penitential Psalms and the Book of Jeremiah echoes through the texts of Byrd's earlier motets. What stays in the mind from the *Gradualia* is the endlessly repeated, endlessly varied acclamation "alleluia" and the act of ritual celebration which it embodies.

Notes

1. Oliver Neighbour, *The Consort and Keyboard Music of William Byrd,* The Music of William Byrd, vol. 3 (Berkeley and Los Angeles, 1979).
2. [When this was written I was still thinking of Byrd as an outsider drawn into Catholic machinations—still thinking too much like Fellowes. Documents recently brought to light indicate that Byrd was at the very storm center of the movement. Many letters place him

in close contact with Lord Thomas Paget of Beaudesert, Staffs., who was implicated in the Throckmorton Plot of 1583 and later attainted. One letter, sent from Clopton, Northants., at the end of 1581, tells Paget that "Of Mr. Byrd you are not worthy, and we take comfort in him as a lean-to by whom we are relieved upon every casual wreck"; the writer, Ralph Sheldon, was arrested in 1581, at the same time as Paget; otherwise unknown, he must be related to Hugh Sheldon of Staffordshire, a Jesuit lay brother who became Garnet's servant or factotum. See Christopher Harrison, "William Byrd and the Pagets of Beaudesert: A Musical Connection," *Staffordshire Studies* 3 (1991): 61, and Craig Monson, "William Byrd and the Catholics: A Reexamination," publication pending.]

3. The argument justifying such an interpretation of Latin motet texts—texts which are in many cases drawn directly from the Bible—is an intricate or at least a laborious one, which I first made in "The Elizabethan Motet: A Study of Texts for Music," *Studies in the Renaissance* 9 (1962): 273–306; see also Joseph Kerman, *The Masses and Motets of William Byrd,* The Music of William Byrd, vol. 1 (Berkeley and Los Angeles, 1981), ch. 1.

4. [Would not this have been ideal music for the welcome party for Southwell and Garnet? I owe this suggestion to Craig Monson.]

5. John Bossy, *The English Catholic Community, 1570–1850* (Oxford, 1976).

6

# Byrd, Tallis, and the Art of Imitation

*For Gustave Reese*

The history of imitation is a key topic in Renaissance musicology. Our understanding of "the central musical language" owes a great deal to analyses of minutiae of imitative technique, to hypotheses about its evolution, and to interpretations of its changing structural role. In England, away from the center, imitation like everything else developed in its own fitful way, with one eye on older Continental practice, and the other eye turned insular-inward. "The English were in no haste," as Gustave Reese puts it, "to adopt the main musical characteristic of the Late Renaissance."[1] Laggard or not, however, the development must presumably be well charted before any serious stylistic exploration can be made of Tudor music. The groundwork has been laid in *Music in the Renaissance*. More recently details have been filled in by Frank L. Harrison, in the later chapters of *Music in Medieval Britain*—English historians are in no haste to terminate their Middle Ages—and in his admirable chapters for *The New Oxford History of Music*.[2]

Around 1500, Robert Fayrfax and the composers of the Eton Manuscript were not employing much imitation in their most important compositions. These were elaborate Masses, Magnificats, and votive antiphons for five, six, or even more voices, composed with or without cantus firmus in alternating sections for full choir and for semichoir *a 2, a 3, a 4*, and so on. Taverner, who is said to have quit music by 1530, employed the technique more freely, but in "full" sections imitative writing is still only incidental. The large antiphons of Thomas Tallis and William Mundy, however, come to drop the cantus firmus altogether and rely on imitation almost constantly both in "full" and in semichoir sections. Heir to the great votive

From *Aspects of Medieval and Renaissance Music: A Birthday Offering to Gustave Reese,* ed. Jan LaRue et al. (New York: Norton, 1966), 519–37.

antiphon in the 1550s and 1560s was the extended psalm setting. Composed first of all in the very same prolix sectional form, this was gradually shortened and homogenized into a moderately scaled motet *a 5* or *a 6* characterized by "continuous full treatment in imitative style." Such works are—at last—directly comparable to Continental motets of the same time, in text, form, scope, and, at least in a general way, in style.

Imitation in "full" sections of the votive antiphons tends to be flexible and unsystematic. Individual lines often run into long melismas, and no scheme controls the spacing or pitch placement of the entries. Imitation does not seem to have been viewed yet as an architectural device, but rather as another form of rich decoration to the leisurely flow of alternating sections—as though an invisible cantus firmus were still assuming structural responsibility. With the psalm settings, however, a very marked change takes place toward terseness of material and toward regularity, even squareness, of imitative technique. A probable impetus for this came from much smaller, simpler four-part motets, which circulated increasingly during Henry VIII's reign, and which absorbed something from the Franco-Netherlandish tradition. Tallis and Mundy, in any case, tightened their imitative style as they turned from the votive antiphon to the psalm and to the smaller motet. When they thought that imitation had to bear the weight of the structure, they could only think to make it as rigid as possible. Or so one is tempted to suppose: these composers extend phrases by means of strict, symmetrical repetitions of one kind or another. Very rarely indeed do they significantly *develop* a contrapuntal idea within the course of an imitative section.

As an example, the beginning phrase of Tallis's motet *Salvator mundi*[3] may be quoted. (See example 1a.) This is the first of two settings of these words in the *Cantiones quae ab argumento sacrae vocantur*, 1575, an important joint publication by Tallis and Byrd which marked the first appearance in print for both composers. (Some of the music it transmits must have been written a good deal earlier.) The construction of Tallis's phrase is simplicity itself. The subject imitates tonally, forming a contrapuntal unit five semibreves long; this unit repeats itself systematically down through the five voices, without transposition. No effort is made to provide a sixth entry to fill out the third unit. Perhaps on this account, and in any case to good effect, a beat is skipped, and then the entire contrapuntal complex returns voice by voice, with only an occasional light alteration of the opening note of the subject or the answer.

Tallis even stresses the symmetry by leaving the bass silent in bar 9, so that this measure corresponds exactly to bar 4; though in adding new lower voices in bars 6–7, he shows himself excellently sensitive to potentialities of variation. Notice the beautiful new B-flat and E-flat sonorities. The phrase does not cadence firmly, but tapers punctually to a close in the last bar of the repetition. Here new imitations on the next text fragment enter overlapping.

EXAMPLE 1

a. Tallis, *Salvator Mundi* I

A crude line diagram may be devised to show the spacing and placement of these entries at a glance:

$$G_2\,D_4 \qquad G_2\,D_4 \qquad G_5 \qquad G_2\,D_4 \qquad G_2\,D_4 \qquad G$$

Letters refer to the initial note of the entry, subscript numbers denote the number of beats between the entry and the next one, and the spaces between letters are kept roughly proportional to the length of time between entries. Much is ignored in a diagram of this type—tonal answers, octave registers, the individual voices involved in the imitations, and the delicate variations introduced during the counter-

EXAMPLE I

b. Byrd, *Memento, homo* (see page 96)

exposition or second set of entries (indicated on the diagram by italics). Nevertheless, with the aid of such diagrams one can readily grasp the determined regularity of the opening phrases of those Tallis motets in the *Cantiones sacrae* which involve "continuous full treatment in imitative style":[4]

a 7:     *Suscipe, quaeso, Domine*
$GC_9$              $F_{11}$                $C_{11}$              $GC_9$           F

$2^a$ pars: *Si enim*
$GC_4$     $GC_4$     $GC_4$     GC
(The subscript number "1" is omitted from the diagrams)

a 5:    *In manus tuas*
        GD$_7$            GD    (the tenor does not really imitate)

        *Salvator mundi* (I)
        G$_2$ D$_4$    G$_2$ D$_4$    G$_5$    G$_2$ D$_4$    G$_2$ D$_4$    G

        *O sacrum convivium*
        G$_2$ DDGG$_2$ D$_2$ DG$_2$ DDGG

        *Absterge, Domine*
        G$_2$ CGDGG$_2$ CGD

        *Mihi autem*
        D$_3$    D$_3$    D$_3$    D$_3$    G$_7$        *d$_2$  d$_2$  d$_2$  d$_3$   g*

        *Derelinquat impius*
        G$_4$    E$_4$    C$_4$    A$_6$    ₲D$_2$₵

In *Mihi autem,* a slightly sophisticated case, the small letters on the diagram denote a free diminution of the original subject, but the counter-exposition in diminution follows almost the same strict pattern as that of the first exposition, even down to the order of the voices. Only *Derelinquat impius* is anomalous, very obviously; not only do as many as five different pitches figure as initials for the entries, but symmetry is knocked out by two *very* free syncopated stretto entries (shown by "₲" and "₵" on the diagram). Quaintly enough, these unique features are associated with the words "Let the wicked forsake his way," from one of the Lenten responsories. This point of imitation is quite literally—even didactically—the exception that proves the rule.

The rule, or rather, the general principle of regularity in imitation, was followed by Tallis in his other continuously imitative motets, not printed in the *Cantiones sacrae. O salutaris hostia* affords a very striking example. The principle was also followed in one way or another by Tallis's younger contemporaries, such as Robert White, active from the late 1550s until his death in 1574, and William Mundy, active from the 1550s until his death in 1591.

The fearful symmetry of much of White's writing has been recognized ever since his music was published in volume 5 of *Tudor Church Music.* "At times," the editors remarked, "we feel that he is composing by specific, mechanically, even pompously," and they went so far as to single out certain compositions in which White's "formal instinct is shown at its coldest and most calculating."[5] Mundy, who was presumably closer to Tallis and Byrd, since all three men were in the Chapel Royal, writes with only a little more variety. One of his motets opens with an imitative phrase rather along Tallis's lines:[6]

a 6:    *In aeternum*
        A$_4$    E$_5$    A$_2$ A$_3$    A$_4$    E$_5$    A$_4$    E$_5$    A$_2$ A$_3$    A$_4$    E

one shows a different but even more aggressive sort of regularity—the lower-case letters here referring to a free inversion of the brief opening subject:

a 6:   *Adolescentulus sum ego*  $e_2$  $e E e E e_2$  $e E e E e_2$  $e b_3$  $b$

one is very short, skipping a counter-exposition and therefore precluding large-scale symmetry:

a 6:   *Domine, non est exaltatum*  $CF_4$   $FB\flat_5$   $F_3$   C

and one is very long, with strong hints of regularity (but the tenor voice of this piece is lost; the starred entries have been fitted in by Harrison):

a 6:   *Domine, quis habitabit*
       $C_4$  $F_8$      $\star CF_9$        $CF_9$        $\star CF_6$   $G_2\, CF_9$         $CF$

All this looks very different from the practice of William Byrd, even in his earliest motets.

II ·   Born in 1543, some thirty-five years after Tallis, Byrd joined him on an equal basis in the *Cantiones sacrae* of 1575, and enjoyed along with him the compliments of such important persons as Richard Mulcaster and Sir Ferdinando Heybourne in the prefatory matter of the publication. Byrd had obviously made a great impression in London in a period of only three years after arriving there from Lincoln Cathedral. That Byrd's music for the print is vastly different from Tallis's goes without saying; one might not have expected it to differ so strongly from that of White or Mundy, who were no more than ten or fifteen years his senior. Of the seventeen numbers that he contributed, eight of which are continuously imitative motets, only one shows any concern for the symmetry that preoccupied his contemporaries:[7]

a 6:   *Laudate, pueri*   $F_2$ $C_2$ $F_2$ $C_2$ $F_2$ $CF_3$ $F_2$ $C_2$ $F_2$ $C_2$ $F_2$ $CF$

This runs the "principle of regularity" into the ground. However, *Laudate, pueri* stands in a class by itself. It is not originally a motet but an adaptation of a fantasia; hard pressed, perhaps, to supply as many as seventeen numbers, Byrd fell back on an instrumental piece to which he added (none too skillfully) a pastiche of various cheerful psalm verses. The lockstep structure, so reminiscent of the canzona, characterizes the remaining phrases of the composition also.

The fantasia shows, of course, that Byrd was perfectly aware of the symmetrical tendencies in contemporary English polyphony. But he seems to have considered them applicable to a major vocal work only as a makeshift; in the other seven motets, the imitations are kept studiously *irregular* in their spacing and in the pitches employed, at least within the conspicuous opening phrases. The simplest motet, *Memento, homo*[8] (see example 1b), bears a similarity to Tallis's *Salvator mundi*. At the back of Byrd's mind, I believe, was a two-voiced unit consisting of subject and tonal answer, to be repeated down through the other voices—as is the case with the older composition. But the following differences are to be noted: (1) Byrd inverts voices in his unit and (unlike Tallis) foreshortens it, from its initial seven beats to six to five; (2) he complicates his second unit with a full-fledged extra stretto entry, starting at the end of bar 4 of the example; (3) so far from writing a counter-exposition mirroring the exposition proper, Byrd instead introduces one more unit constructed not of subject plus tonal answer, but of answer plus answer, so arranged that a new note B♭ appears in the bass as the initial of the last true entry. This being the subdominant, and being reinforced by another B♭ in the top voice, it provides a cumulative strength to the section as a whole which is altogether different in spirit from Tallis's level ideal.

A diagram would run as follows:

a 6:     *Memento, homo*  $C_3$     $F_4$      $C_3$    $F_2$ $FF_5$      $F_3$    B♭

However, a diagram of this type is helpless to indicate (4) the remarkable number of very free syncopated entries which Byrd jammed in, it would seem, at every possible occasion. (On the examples, these are marked with small brackets.) They have a distinct tendency to group themselves in pairs (bars 3 and 4: A or F–C; bars 5 and 6: C–F; bars 8 and 9: A or G–C). The three free strettos in bars 8 and 9 seem calculated to add to the sense of climax imparted by the harmonic weight of the B♭ in the bass, and by the strongly cadential urge of the concluding bars.

If an artistic judgment were in question, one would not hesitate long between the two phrases that have been quoted. Tallis is sober, assured, deeply individual; Byrd is coarse, busy, brash, and rather anonymous in feeling. But his piece is more advanced in many ways—in the brilliance (or intended brilliance) of contrapuntal action; in the harmonic lucidity; and in the clear concern for climax, which is to say in the dramatic shaping of the phrase. More fundamentally, whereas with Tallis the contrapuntal structure is the be-all and end-all of the phrase, with Byrd other considerations determine the form. The imitative units serve rather as underpinning to a guiding polarity of the outer voices. Yet as a whole *Memento, homo* is one

EXAMPLE 2    Tallis, *Suscipe, quaeso, Domine* (*Tudor Church Music*, 6:222)

of the more awkward of Byrd's early compositions; and it is most curious to see the second and last phrase of this little motet ruled by symmetrical contrapuntal thinking.

In the first phrase, it should be observed that although the complete text handled is "Memento, homo, quod cinis es," only the first two words are articulated thematically. The second text fragment, "quod cinis es," though sung more than a dozen times, never attaches itself to a consistent musical idea; clarity in this matter was sacrificed, evidently, to the rather excessive joy in strettos. Tallis, when dealing with a text phrase of some length, ordinarily defines it clearly enough (see example 2). This imitates almost canonically all the way through in all seven voices. But when any one of the voices subsequently repeats the second text fragment "vocem confitentis," free counterpoint is used; what Tallis does not do is divide his long subject in two and develop the two parts in flexible conjunction. One would speak of a single long subject, not of a first and second subject treated as a "double imitation" of any sort.

In certain of Byrd's imitative motets of 1575, he works deliberately—if not always successfully—with independent second subjects within his imitative phrases. At the beginning of the large six-part motets *Da mihi auxilium* and *Domine, secundum actum meum,* for example, clearly separate subjects are used together for the text fragments "Da mihi auxilium / de tribulatione" and "Domine / secundum actum meum." Something similar appears to be evolving at the opening of the *secunda pars* of *Libera me, Domine, et pone me juxta te* for the words "Dies mei / transierunt." And although the effort seems rather to have defeated the composer, *Aspice, Domine* actually involves three subjects at once, for the text fragments "Aspice, Domine, / quia facta est / desolata civitas." Examples can be multiplied from later phrases within many of the 1575 motets. By the time of Byrd's own individual *Cantiones sacrae* of 1589 and 1591, the technique of "double imitation" has been normalized and is employed with a power and variety that precludes any thought of technical difficulties.

In the *Plaine and Easie Introduction to Practicall Music* of 1597, Byrd's pupil Thomas Morley actually states that the best way to begin a song is with "two severall points in two severall parts at once, or one point foreright and reverted," preferably the former alternative: "this way of two or three several points going together is the most artificiall kinde of composing which hetherto hath beene invented either for Motets or *Madrigals,* speciallie when it is mingled with revertes, because so it maketh the musick seeme more strange."[9] However, the example that so awes Philomathes and Polymathes is less "strange" in Morley's sense than plain clumsy, and in any case stylistically much more like an instrumental fancy than a madrigal, let alone a motet. In going about his example—like all his other examples—without any consideration of the words, Morley effectively disqualifies himself on this topic. For of course the technique arose not from any purely musical impetus, but from the desire to differentiate, articulate, and contrast successive fragments of a text phrase within the unity of a single musical section. This explains the staple role of double imitation in the Continental and especially in the Italian madrigal and motet; a fine example would be the opening of Palestrina's famous seven-part motet *Tu es Petrus* (published in 1567). It is natural to inquire whether foreign influence had anything to do with Byrd's introduction of double imitation into English music.[10]

Some time ago the present writer worked through the madrigals of Alfonso Ferrabosco, a minor Italian composer active at Queen Elizabeth's court on and off between 1562 and 1578, in the hope that they would throw some light on the English madrigal development.[11] They throw some, but not much—in spite of the abnormally wide circulation of Ferrabosco's madrigals in Elizabethan England, and in spite of Morley's recommending him in the same breath as Marenzio as a "guide" for madrigal composition. By the time native musicians began writing madrigals and reading Morley, in the 1590s, they had more up-to-date models than the rather humdrum works of a man who had long since disappeared from the local scene.

The case was quite other in the 1570s, when Ferrabosco was very much in evidence, and when the style of his music must have struck London musicians such as White, Mundy, Tallis, and Byrd as extremely radical, or perplexing, or suggestive—depending on their individual temperaments. It is possible that Morley's pious attitude toward Ferrabosco traces back to Byrd, for there can be little doubt that on Byrd Ferrabosco's influence was a good deal more telling than on madrigalists of a later generation. Certain of Byrd's more singular experiments in the 1575 *Cantiones sacrae* derive from Ferrabosco;[12] and his usual, normal contrapuntal style, notably in this technique of double imitation, also owes much to the example of "Master Alfonso."

A pair of motet openings by Byrd and Ferrabosco illustrates the technique well (see example 3).[13] The melodic figures for the words "non secundum" (Ferrabosco) and "secundum actum meum" (Byrd) were conceived from the start as separate or separable elements, so much so that they are chiseled out of the texture by means of preliminary rests. These figures enjoy rich imitative life of their own both independent of and simultaneous with the "Domine" figure; this can be seen in the passages shown and even more extensively in the concluding parts of the phrases, which are not quoted here because of their considerable length. In both pieces, a voice may make its very first entrance not with the opening words and the opening subject, but with the second subject. In bar 11 of Ferrabosco's motet, he is even beginning to treat a third subject independently, for the words "peccata mea."

The imitative ground plans are, of course, irregular. Even if the composers had desired symmetry—which they did not—symmetry would hardly allow the kind of contrapuntal complexity which they did desire. The following diagrams cover the entire opening phrases, but are able to indicate only *full entries* of the first plus the second subject:

| FERRABOSCO | $A^\dagger D_9$ | $A^\dagger_3$ $D_{11}$ | $(A^\dagger)A^\dagger D_8$ | $DD^\dagger_{12}$ | $D^\dagger_2$ $G_2$ $G$ |
|---|---|---|---|---|---|
| BYRD | $B^\dagger E^\dagger_7$ | $E^\dagger_2$ $E^\dagger_8$ | $E^\dagger A^\dagger_{11}$ | $A^\dagger_{12}$ | $A_3$ $E_3$ $E^\dagger_5$ $A_{11}$ |

The first (unitalicized) expositions are still built out of units combining two entries each, but neither composer cares to standardize the stretto interval within his units, nor the length of time between units, and Byrd moves restlessly through various different pitches to begin his subject. The counter-expositions (italicized) are unsystematic to the point of omitting one of the six voices. Both composers introduce heavy, deliberate strettos before cadencing in the subdominant thirty-one bars (in each case) from the beginning.

In the above diagrams certain letters have been provided with daggers: these indicate those entries in which the second subject involves a semitone step above the note of the "Domine" monotone. This is more typically the case with Byrd, who is working with a real answer, than with Ferrabosco, who builds his "unit" with a free answer substituting the interval of a third for a second (D–F answering A–B♭). At his eighth entry, however, Ferrabosco moves from his customary D not to F but to E♭. This carefully calculated introduction of a new affective interval finds a parallel in Byrd's sixth entry, where A–B♭ is added to the previous semitone arsenal B–C and E–F. Although both composers have concocted themes dwelling on a semitone by repetition, Byrd certainly seems more in love with the interval. Still, he too finds a use for the alternating second and third suggested by Ferrabosco's "unit"—though at the end of his total phrase, not at the beginning. Expansion of the subject "secundum actum meum" from A–B♭– to A–C– and from E–F– to E–G– gives the ending stretto (which is not quoted, but whose letters *lack* daggers in the diagram) an appropriate rugged touch.

EXAMPLE 3

a. Ferrabosco, *Domine, non secundum peccata mea*

Subjects hinging on an expressive semitone step are important in Byrd's work, and decidedly rare in earlier English music. Sooner or later Byrd always brings in a third semitone, a B♭ or an E♭ which artfully lacerates the modal purity. Ferrabosco's *Domine, non secundum peccata mea* may seem to provide a model for the procedure—for of the two motets I should not hesitate to accord his the priority. Still, deliberate manipulation of an impressive subject featuring a semitone occurs already in Byrd's *De Lamentatione,* a work which on other stylistic evidence one would date earlier than the 1575 motets. *De Lamentatione* was presumably written before Byrd's association with Ferrabosco in London after 1572.

III · Whether Ferrabosco "guided" Byrd or whether he simply confirmed his prejudices is unimportant compared to what emerges as the central historical fact here: the wonderful widening of horizons in British music of the 1570s at the hands of the young composer from Lincoln. There is a new freedom of imitative counterpoint, along with a new variety and expressivity of melodic material; also a remarkable series of experiments in affective homophony, in which Tallis seems to participate;

EXAMPLE 3

b. Byrd, *Domine, secundum actum meum*

and at just the same period a new personal attitude begins to be assumed toward the choice of words for a motet. In the 1575 *Cantiones sacrae* Byrd occasionally departs from "standard," liturgical texts such as hymns and responds in favor of individual, direct selections from the Bible and elsewhere—a tendency that becomes the rule in his two later volumes of *Cantiones sacrae* (1589 and 1591).[14] In a very short time Byrd attained the mastery attributed to him by Mulcaster and Heybourne and amply forecast by the motets of 1575. Though imitative technique is only one element of that mastery, it remains a central one for Byrd through the period of the Masses in the 1590s. Only with the *Gradualia* in 1605 and 1607 does imitation start to recede as the principal driving force of his work.

The opening phrase of Byrd's motet *Domine, praestolamur adventum tuum* (1589),[15] shown in example 4, employs means similar to those of *Domine, secundum actum meum* more freely, more concisely, and more dramatically. The irregular ground plan would appear in a diagram as follows:

a 5:  *Domine, praestolamur* $E_4$    $A_3$   $A_5$    $A_{10}$          $AEA_4$   $A_{12}$

EXAMPLE 4    Byrd, *Domine, praestolamur adventum tuum*

But it is time to throw out these diagrams (and throw out bland Alfonso Ferrabosco, too); they and he no longer take account of the essentials. The second subject, "adventum tuum," is not merely a separable element with contrapuntal potential of its own, but an element that takes powerful control of the phrase both at its center and at its conclusion. Which is only just: in a dramatic reading of the text, emphasis ought to fall not on "Lord we await" but on "Thy advent." The two themes cleave admirably to the words, too, though the treatment is less obvious than that of *Domine, secundum actum meum,* with its monotone apostrophe and its guilt-ridden semitones. "Lord we await" mounts rockily up the Phrygian scale, conspicuously *minore* in sonority; "Thy advent" makes a delicate lyric contrast by the relatively sudden descent of a fourth curling back on itself, suggesting a major sonority. Anticipation is a somber matter for Byrd; we greet the Advent with something like an intimate gesture of gratitude and release, not with jubilation, rapture, complacency, triumph, humility, or whatever.

The first exposition counts as quite free, for the soprano does not even sing the first subject, entering directly with the second instead (as we have also seen happen with some voices in the related pair of motets by Ferrabosco and Byrd). The ecstatic stretto rush of the second or counter-exposition is superbly lifted up by a free version of the second subject (bars 13–14). Fourths and fifths leap up to a held A which seems to be stretched higher yet by the held F above it (bars 14–15, across the barline), the climax of an almost perfect syncopated entry.

As for the second subject, "adventum tuum," that is handled throughout with the greatest flexibility and imagination. Inverted and syncopated entries occur, but the chief device seems to be repetition in and around the same note (bars 4, 6, and 8: E–F; bars 9, 10 *bis*, and 11: B or A–C; bars 16, 17, and 18: G or B–C; bars 18, 19, and 20: E or D–G). This tendency toward ostinato, already noted in connection with the untidy strettos of *Memento, homo,* is very characteristic of Byrd, and evidently an inheritance from earlier English polyphony. Interestingly, the final form of the second subject (bars 18, 19, and 20) replaces the original semitone step E–F– by the interval of a third, E–G–: a modification that recalls the rugged expansion of a subject involving the step E–F in *Domine, secundum actum meum.* The new note G is elegantly supported. Byrd introduces it in bar 18 over a G triad which stands out because it is the first G triad in the piece, and because it is rhythmicized so freshly. Then at the end he dissolves his insistent motivic G by clashing it away against the G♯ of the cadence—the sharp being expressly marked in the print. The famous old cadential cross-relation is turned to aesthetic capital; how carefully, too, the dissonance level is released in bar 21.

Paradoxically, Byrd finds the leisure to duplicate bars 7–10 quite closely in bars 15–18. Yet the distance traveled from the parallelisms of Tallis's day is immeasurable: this repetition sounds not like retracing ground, but like touching ground prior to a climactic vault. Craft and expression, in the motets of 1589 and 1591, stand in very sophisticated equilibrium.

There is much more to say about these motets, and about Byrd's contrapuntal style in general. Perhaps, though, enough has been said to clarify some not unimportant points about the development of imitation into Elizabethan times. In the later Middle Ages, imitative writing was essentially a decorative or a special device. Then when imitation came to be the guiding structural principle in large-scale composition, English musicians tended to work with schematic patterns which still recall, in a dim, curious way, something of the medieval mentality. Within seventeen years after the accession of Queen Elizabeth, contrapuntal structure had grown a great deal more subtle and was beginning to serve more dramatic, imaginative goals in the shaping of the individual phrase. The technique of double imitation, determined by the words, goes hand in hand with a new interest in subjects that "express" the words. The great figure here is William Byrd, and a shadowy figure in the background is Alfonso Ferrabosco, with whom Byrd entered into a "friendly æmulation" not only in devising canons, as Morley tells us, but also in composing complex expressive motets, as we have been able to see.

That Byrd was now exercising much more personal choice in taking texts for his motets is certainly no accident. One way or another, the text is the new guiding principle in late Tudor music. "In sacred words," Byrd observes in a much-quoted preface, "as I have learned by trial, there is such a profound and hidden power that to one thinking upon things divine and diligently and earnestly pondering them, all the fittest numbers occur as if of themselves."[16] Like so much else in late Renaissance music, the maturing of the art of imitation in England stemmed from a passion to make music match the quality of the word, phrase, sentence, sonnet, or psalm: to make music rhetoric.

## Notes

1. Gustave Reese, *Music in the Renaissance,* rev. ed. (New York, 1959), 778.
2. Frank L. Harrison, *Music in Medieval Britain,* 2d ed. (London, 1963); *New Oxford History of Music,* vol. 3, *Ars Nova and the Renaissance (1300–1540),* ed. Anselm Hughes and Gerald Abraham (London, 1960), ch. 9, and vol. 4, *The Age of Humanism (1540–1630),* ed. Gerald Abraham (London, 1968), ch. 9.
3. Tallis's motets are published in *Thomas Tallis,* vol. 6 of *Tudor Church Music,* ed. Percy C. Buck et al. (London, 1928); *Salvator mundi* is on pp. 216–18.
4. The fine motet *In ieiunio et fletu* is not included here, since the opening in declamatory stretto cells, almost homophonic in feeling, seems to me rather different in principle. The diagram would go

$B^\flat E^\flat G_7$     $AFD_5$     $A^\flat A^\flat C$

5. *Robert White,* vol. 5 of *Tudor Church Music* (London, 1926), xv.

6. Mundy's motets are published in *Early English Church Music,* vol. 2, ed. Frank L. Harrison (London, 1963). See my review in *Musical Quarterly* 50 (1964): 251–56.

7. Byrd's motets of 1575 are published in *The Byrd Edition,* ed. Philip Brett, vol. 1, *Cantiones sacrae* (1575), ed. Craig Monson (London, 1977); *Laudate, pueri* is on pp. 82–96.

8. *Byrd Edition,* 1:97–103.

9. Thomas Morley, *A Plaine and Easie Introduction to Practicall Music,* ed. Alec Harman (London, 1952), 276.

10. The best discussion of double imitation I have found occurs in H. K. Andrews, *An Introduction to the Technique of Palestrina* (London, 1958), ch. 8.

11. Joseph Kerman, *The Elizabethan Madrigal: A Comparative Study* (American Musicological Society Studies and Documents, no. 4; Philadelphia, 1962), ch. 3.

12. [See Joseph Kerman, *The Masses and Motets of William Byrd* (Berkeley and Los Angeles, 1981), 35–36, 101–6, 115–18, 122.]

13. *Byrd Edition,* 1:132–50, and *Alfonso Ferrabosco the Elder (1543–1588), Opera Omnia,* ed. Richard Charteris (Stuttgart, 1984), 1:167–74.

14. See Joseph Kerman, "The Elizabethan Motet: A Study of Words for Music," *Studies in the Renaissance* 9 (1962): 273–305.

15. *The Byrd Edition,* vol. 2, *Cantiones sacrae I* (1589), ed. Alan Brown (London, 1988), 15–31.

16. William Byrd, *Gradualia* (1605); see Oliver Strunk, *Source Readings in Music History* (New York, 1950), 328.

# 7

# "Write All These Down": Notes on a Song by Byrd

*A song that is well and artificially made cannot be well per-
ceiued nor understood at the first hearing, but the oftner you
shall heare it, the better cause of liking you will discover.*

WILLIAM BYRD, *PSALMES, SONGS, AND SONNETS,* 1611

The first major body of music by William Byrd that I came to know was the
vernacular music of the English songbooks. I was studying the English madrigal,
and students in those days took issues of stylistic taxonomy rather seriously. It
seemed very important to distinguish Byrd's songs from madrigals, to separate
them off more clearly than had been done by E. H. Fellowes in his book *The English
Madrigal Composers,* and with firmer musicological apparatus than had been deployed by Edward J. Dent in the article "William Byrd and the Madrigal."[1]

But Byrd's songs refused to be moved tidily aside. The chapter in which this was
supposed to happen took on a life of its own. It even acquired a certain dense,
knotty quality, possibly a result of enigmatic stylistic emanations from its subject
matter.[2]

What impressed me first of all, as I recall, was the massive stylistic control of the
texted consort songs published in the 1588 songbook. One of the songs, "La virginella," soon to be republished with a translation in *Musica Transalpina,* was set to
an ottava rima stanza from Ariosto—and this verse, Einstein assured us, was a
favorite among the Italian madrigalists.[3] But "La virginella" was certainly not to
be classified as a madrigal. On the other hand "This Sweet and Merry Month of
May," published not much later, certainly was. The stylistic crux adumbrated here
grows more intense in the later Byrd songbooks. The musician in me was fascinated, and the musicologist a bit worried, by those songs which I thought I could
see winding a precarious course between the stylistic norms of the consort song
and the madrigal.

➤ From *Byrd Studies,* ed. Alan Brown and Richard Turbet (Cambridge: Cambridge University
Press, 1992), 112–28.

One song it appears I didn't see clearly at all: "Retire, My Soul," no. 17 in the *Psalmes, Songs, and Sonnets* of 1611. It needed hearing oftener. I can now see it as an entirely unprecarious Byrd masterpiece.

II · *What Genre?*    "Unprecarious," because intuitively the musical style of the piece feels entirely normal and right, straightforward, almost unremarkable (see example 1). One does not have to be deeply knowledgeable about the music of Byrd or indeed any other music of his time to feel this, I think. But what can be said about the genre? In a note to his edition, John Morehen writes that "The poor word-setting in some of the lower voices, combined with several avoidable melodic inelegancies, suggests strongly that this composition originated as a solo song."[4] Inelegancies? sir! beyond a tenor octave and a limping alto line in bar 4, some odd underlay in bars 33–34, and perhaps the repeated f[1] in bar 30, I hear nothing to offend. On the other hand, the putative melody of this song—Morehen speaks of it as a "conflate" of the song's two soprano parts—is not of a quality that would in itself inspire superlatives, as song melodies by Dowland or Gibbons ("Ah, Dear Heart") might, for example.

In fact, no arguments are adduced in the editorial matter to place the piece within the tradition of the consort song, or, rather, the consort song with words adapted to the instrumental parts. (The sorts of changes that Byrd routinely made in the adaptation process can be studied by comparing the originals with their texted versions in the 1588 *Psalmes, Sonets, & Songs*.)[5] And "Retire, My Soul" does not quite look like any other Byrd song. Not one of its eight musical phrases entails systematic "pre-imitations" in Byrd's usual manner. When Morehen describes the piece elsewhere as "close to the consort song in spirit" (p. ix)—not the same as proposing its genesis as an actual consort song—the ghost of the taxonomist in me rests more easy. At some places in the song the basic conception seems less melodic than genuinely polyphonic. At other places (and at some of the same ones) the text in the lower voices is too carefully declaimed to be understood as a later addition, however *ben trovato*. Surely Byrd composed this song—as he appears to have composed others—for five actual voices, albeit with the stylistic norm of the consort song sometimes dimly, sometimes less dimly in mind.

As Byrd's song style developed, a second soprano is introduced more and more often in the five-part choir. This tended to break down solo texture in favor of more even-handed polyphony. However, "Retire," though scored for two sopranos, is *less* polyphonic than the two-soprano songs of 1588 and 1589. More to the point, perhaps, it is more concise; in the earlier songs the composer seems to have used the two-soprano texture as a way to expand his pieces, as much as to vary their texture. I shall touch on the question of genre again later in this essay, when comparison with an actual consort song will suggest itself.

It remains to say at this point that if "Retire" is less expansive than many of Byrd's middle-period songs, it is also less madrigalian than some of the late ones. Neither its rhythmic nor its harmonic style, nor its treatment of the words, owes much to the madrigal. Yet Byrd's response to the words in this song is unusually deep and affecting.

III · *Sizing Up the Poem*    "Retire, My Soul" is an aphoristic six-line stanza in which, as usual, the quatrain sets forth the conditions of the argument and the couplet points the moral. As poetry, this verse is considerably more accomplished than most song texts set by Byrd, characteristic as it may be in content:

> Retire[,] my soule, consider thine estate,
> And iustly summe thy lavish sinnes account,
> Times deare expence, and costly pleasures rate,
> How follyes grow, how vanities amount.
> Write all these down in pale Deathes reckoning tables,
> Thy dayes will seeme but dreames, thy hopes but fables.

The poet draws upon the lexicon of accounting and finance to enjoin his sinful soul to prepare its spread-sheet: "estate," "sum," "account," "dear expense," "costly," "rate," and "amount." The couplet begins solemnly, as heavy monosyllables pronounce a new, summarizing injunction: "Write all these down." Then at the end of line 5, though we are still hearing about "reckoning tables" (a "reckoning book" is a ledger), these tables are now "pale Death's"—no great surprise, after mention of retirement and estate. Under death's shadow, line 6 urges the soul to consider the illusion (seeming, dreams, fables) of that which it has amassed, of its hopes.

When this song was published, by the way, Byrd was a fairly rich man of sixty-eight. From drawing up his will probably on more than one occasion, he would have become familiar with the long process of inventorying his material assets, no less than with that of weighing his spiritual ones.

Six-line stanzas are typically set in two sections, with the second section (covering the final couplet) repeated so as to hammer home the "point." What I have called the summarizing gesture in line 5, "Write all these down," appears to have encouraged the composer to plan for especially heavy parallelism between the beginnings of the two sections. Acting on this hint, he also made them parallel in other ways. Both sections go to F in their second phrase and to V/D minor in their third. And both contain four musical phrases, each ending with clear cadences, even though the first section sets four lines of verse and the second sets two.

EXAMPLE I

# Retire, My Soul

William Byrd

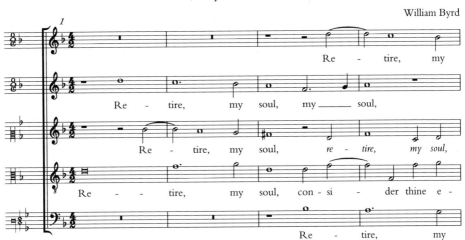

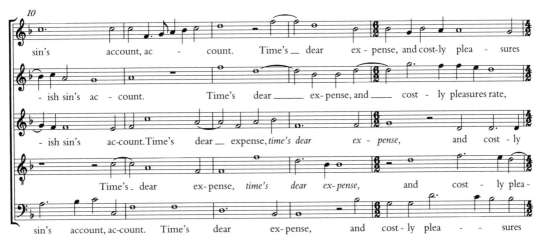

*(continued)*

EXAMPLE I   (*continued*)

EXAMPLE I    (*continued*)

The overall plan for the song is nothing if not economical (lower-case letters here denote minor keys):

| TEXT LINE | 1 | 2 | 3 | 4 | 5a | 5b | 6a | 6b |
|---|---|---|---|---|---|---|---|---|
| MUSICAL PHRASE | 1 | 2 | 3 | 4 | 5 | 6 | 7 | 8 |
| CADENCES | (d?)(1/2g?) | F | 1/2d | g ‖: | d,F,1/2d | F | 1/2d | d :‖ |
| LENGTH (SEMIBREVES) | 13 | 9 | 9 | 15 | 6 | 6 | 8 | 14 |

If I am right to think Byrd wanted four phrases in each section of the song, his strategy was simple enough. He fashioned his phrases in the quatrain out of full lines, and those in the couplet out of half lines. The two sections of the song are symmetrical, then, though not proportional; no doubt he wanted more speed and intensity in line 5 than in lines 1 and 2. Between the two parts the ratio is approximately 4:3 or, rather, 2:3 when the repeat is included. While tallying of this kind can seem both mechanical and elementary, to the tallier as well as to the reader, the fact remains that such precompositional calculations underpin the form of the song and hence its rhetoric. It also seems to be a fact that systematic setting of half lines in this fashion distinguishes "Retire" from any other of Byrd's songs.[6]

In the present case, of course, reducing the text-setting unit in the couplet to the half line makes every kind of rhetorical sense. The caesura in line 6 practically demands such setting. And although line 5 does not have a caesura, when the composer in effect creates one of his own—he even supplies the text in all the voice parts with a comma—the rhetorical effect is to delay and hence dramatize the evocation of death.

In the quatrain, setting each whole line to its own rather long melody might have led to diffuseness; this is often a danger in Byrd's consort songs. Possibly with this in mind, it seems that the composer looked out for lines that break into two parts with caesuras, once again; he still set these lines as single musical phrases, unbroken by cadences, but he set both parts of the line to the same motif. The phrases in question, then—lines 1 and 4, "Retire, my soul, consider thine estate" and "How follies grow, how vanities amount"—are rather densely knit motivically, and far from diffuse. With line 4, where the caesura marks off two parallel "how" phrases, the effect is immediately plausible as rhetoric. The text repetitions in this line also extend the phrase so as to end the section strongly: after four appearances of the motif adapted to each of the two half lines "how follies grow" and "how vanities amount," there are two freer entries at the end. The added soprano entry—a sort of free augmented stretto—is particularly expressive, and the motif also undergoes expansion of its interval structure. This is a detail that we can return to at more leisure later.

With line 1, however, was it somewhat arbitrary of Byrd to have used one and the same motif for both parts of the line, "Retire, my soul" and "consider thine estate"? There is no parallelism here. This too is a point that I should like to defer and return to later.

IV · *Mapping the Form*    First, since form has to do with tonality, a word about the modal situation. The music is in a D mode with one flat in the signature, transposed Aeolian;[7] a standard high-clef combination is used, $C^1$, $C^1$, $C^2$, $C^3$, $F^3$. The D-Aeolian mode with this cleffing—a combination of features that Harold S. Powers calls a "tonal type"—occurs more often than any other in the *Gradualia*, notably in the large group of Marian Masses of book one.[8] It should be noted that one modal pattern expected in this tonal type is the cadential figure F–E–D–C♯–D. Byrd must have been quite conscious of never having his trebles sing this figure anywhere in the first part of the song (it is sung twice in the tenor).

What Byrd writes instead is B♭–A–G–F♯ and he writes it three times: not just as a pattern, but as a motif. His setting of line 1 consists of three similar musical cells employing this motif: "Retire, my soul" twice, plus "consider thine estate" once. (See example 1, bars 1–7. It is a nice point whether the listener actually hears this, and if so how, though I take it there is less of a problem of perception for the singers themselves. We hear first the prominent upper counterpoint, D–C–B♭–A. Then, as the texture increases from three voices to four to five, and the rhythm grows progressively more complex, we notice B♭–A–G–F♯ in the bass range, where there is nothing to hide the diminished-fourth outline. The motif is heard most clearly when it is adapted to the new words "consider thine estate" with a dotted rhythm—and when the upper counterpoint disappears.) The whole opening leans toward the subdominant, and presages the rather elegiac close of the song's first section on G.

The same motif is employed in diminution for the beginning of the song's second section, at line 5. As I have said, Byrd planned a heavy parallelism here (bars 21–24). Besides the common motif, the two phrases have in common their triple reiterative character, also their use of the F♯/F cross-relation in adjacent D-major and B♭ chords (a sound not heard elsewhere in this piece). The cells that start part 2 are of course shorter—two breves long, rather than four and five—and clearer—all in three voices. This underlines a new urgent tone to the poet's new injunction. And while the first cell replicates the B♭–A–G–F♯ line of the earlier cells, a new C♯ (over the G) already dilutes the subdominant feeling. Then the second and third cells modulate.

V · *Setting "Dreams"*    The third cell modulates decisively to a half cadence in D, on an A-major chord, and finally brings the expected modal formula F–E–D–C♯ in the treble range. This formula now seems to permeate the rest of the song. It comes several times in the last phrase as the kernel of the melodic cadences. It also comes in the penultimate phrase, in bars 29–30, when the alto sings the word "seem" on $c\sharp^1$, forming the third of another A-major chord. This place, the song's expressive climax, deserves our close attention.

There is one and only one line in the poem where the caesura or the natural line break comes after the third metrical foot, rather than after the second. This climactic effect is saved for the poem's last line; an inner rhyme which Byrd certainly heard—"Thy days will *seem* but *dreams,* thy hopes but fables"—stresses the new metric situation. In setting the half line "Thy days will seem but dreams," Byrd does not devise a motif covering all six of the words. He sets up a little ostinato just for the words "Thy days will seem," C (or F, or B♭)–F–D–(?)—which has the effect of stressing the word "seem"—changing the ending harmony each time to "modulate." The music modulates back from F (the cadence point of the previous phrase "in pale Death's reckoning tables") via C to an A-major chord, as already mentioned.

Perfectly placed, in close position, this A-major chord in bar 30 turns out to be Byrd's trump card for the word "dreams." Four suddenly converging voices sing "dreams" for the first time on this chord. The word glistens (and we surely want it sung by four voices, not by one voice accompanied by viols). This is the word that articulates the fresh caesura. Of all the words in the poem, too, it is probably the most remote in feeling from the original fiscal vocabulary, with its accounts and reckoning tables.

Let us listen oftener, more closely. The first voice to sing the ostinato motif is soprano 2; being the voice that initiates the text fragment, it is also the one voice to utter the word "dreams" before the others converge upon it. Although soprano 2 sings the word very beautifully on a descending fourth $d^2$–$a^1$, it is somewhat obscured by soprano 1 beginning the ostinato motif in the same high range. And soprano 1 treats the key word in its own new beautiful way, with a pregnant rest before it: "Thy days will seem—but dreams." The slowdown continues. On the cadential A-major chord, soprano 1 and the tenor sing a breve (as does, a moment later, soprano 2). After this weighty cadence is sounded, free imitations on the motif (and words) of the first half line continue for five minims more before there is any sign of the second half line commencing.

Given Byrd's time scale, this certainly counts as a profound caesura. Previously he has never interposed more than a single minim's space between one phrase and the next. Occasionally he has arranged for an overlap.

Most gorgeous, of course, is the cross-relation formed when soprano 2 returns to the words "but dreams," making a kind of subdued echo, an afterbeat to the extraordinary focus of declamation on the "dream" chord (bar 31; to *play* the $c\natural^2$ here and not sound the word would be a great pity, once again). It was certainly unusual to end the point "Thy days will seem but dreams" with murmuring imitations on the main motif *after* the ostensible final cadence. It was even more unusual to allow the aphoristic notes $a^1$ and $c^2$ of the second soprano's "but dreams" to anticipate the motif for the next point, "thy hopes but fables": for as first presented, the motif for that point begins with the identical pitches $a^1$–$c^2$. Unusual, because a non-motif for a loose word does not ordinarily presage a true motif for the next phrase.

VI · *Ending the Song*    Of all the phrases in the song, the last one is the least clearly "melodic," and not only because the second soprano voice now jostles more seriously with the first. There are really two soprano motifs which fit together contrapuntally as a cadential unit (the less sharply defined motif involves the characteristic modal pattern F–E–D–C♯–D). What is more, imitations in the lower voices are more numerous and more closely organized here than in any of the earlier phrases, as I shall now try to show. I hope I shall not also try the reader's patience; the analysis necessarily becomes more dense at this point. There is value sometimes in looking quite closely at refinements of contrapuntal structure.

While the five-part texture of this last phrase is imitative, and therefore essentially homogeneous, a rather clear distinction exists between the high and the low voices. The tenor and bass are always simpler, because they never sing motif 2, with the repetition of the words "but fables"; they are also stronger, because of their long high notes: "Thy *hopes* but FA---bles." The tenor's long high note is his melodic peak, the only high $a^1$ in the entire part. As for the alto, that evinces less distinctive character, but makes up for it by providing a scrumptious dissonant flurry for the final cadence.

The first entry, in soprano 1, establishes an attractive hemiola cross-rhythm repeated by soprano 2: "Thy *hopes* but FAbles, but *FAbles*" (bars 31–33). If we were to listen downward, as it were, from the soprano lines, we would catch a large 3/1 meter defined by appoggiatura-like accents that are occasioned by strong feminine cadences in bars 33 and 34. This is where the motifs come together—an effect adumbrated in bars 31–32. However, it is the strong low voices that define the large metrical organization. We can perhaps hear them organizing the total point of imitation into three similar cells, built around a stretto of motif 1 at the upper fifth. Each of these cells is a little more fully scored than the last, and each ends with a strong cadence. The cadences fall into a i–iv–i pattern. Motif 2 also figures in these cells, kept in its appropriate range—including high $f^2$—by means of double counterpoint at the twelfth where necessary.

Cell 2 overlaps with cell 1, forming a large 3/1 pulse. Cell 3 restores a leisurely duple pulse, as traces of soprano cross-rhythm evaporate and the piece eases into its final slowdown. We can track this slowdown in various subtle details: soprano 1, by means of an absent-minded rest, delays the second, climactic part of her line and dilutes the hemiola feeling; soprano 2 declines to sing "fables" in the established

EXAMPLE 2

cadential rhythm, instead dragging the last syllable forward; and the tenor, after arriving on cue in bars 34–35, gets involved with the alto and bass in a sort of stammering stretto, with the result that his line is completed only in bar 37 (and an octave lower, in the bass). What the stammer prepares or emphasizes is the pitch (pitch class) F, which is about to put in its last appearance in the soprano. Compare the opening of the point, where two "amorphous" lines stressing C—without, however, giving away the word "hopes"—prepare the $c^2$ in the first entry of the new text, sung by the soprano.

Example 2 shows the structural cells in this point. The "extra" motifs are bracketed.

Byrd scrupulously refuses to extend the final amphibrach "but fables"; in fact, he emphasizes the feminine rhyme-word in bars 33 and 34 by means of offbeat cadences. He might have allowed the anomaly to evaporate in cell 3, where the slight augmentation has the effect of changing the feminine cadence to a masculine one. But at the very end of the song the second soprano insists on the feminine afterbeat—a sort of metrical reversal of her action in bar 33. The effect is a little bleak.

Is it fortuitous that the accented high $f^2$s in the second section of the song all come to *a* sounds: "pale," "day," and "fables"?

VII · *"Why Do I Use My Paper, Ink, and Pen"*    Of the various phrases of "Retire, My Soul," the second, third, and sixth are most easily construable in terms of Byrd's earlier work. Half-homophonic phrases of this kind would not be out of place in the more concise of the *Psalmes, Sonets, & Songs* of 1588. Phrases 1 and 5, with their repetition of brief cells, will strike us as most remote from the consort song repertory. But while such cells cannot be found in earlier songs by Byrd, they can be understood without too much difficulty as refinements of resources that had already been drawn upon in those works. A case in point occurs in one of his best-known songs, "Why Do I Use My Paper, Ink, and Pen," set to a poem on the martyrdom of Edmund Campion in 1581. The consort version was adapted to words in the 1588 songbook.

Byrd was probably anxious to do something special with the lame couplet that ends this highly charged poem's first stanza (example 3a):

Why do I use my paper, inck, & pen
and call my wits to counsel what to say,
Such memories were made for mortal men,
I speak of Saints, whose name cannot decay,
An Angel's trump, were fitter far to sound
their glorious death, if such on earth be found.

With the words "an Angel's trump," Byrd's route to rhetorical emphasis was no doubt conventional enough—a sequential repetition of the motif in the "first singing part" (the alto), and a flurry of stretto entries fitted into the other voices. This mildly climactic effect is capped by the emphatic setting of the phrase "Their glorious death." Here the words are repeated as an ostinato. The motif comes three times at the same pitch: twice in the first singing part, pre-imitated by the contratenor, and once at the upper octave, with the other voices deployed not imitatively but half-homophonically, so as to form slightly fuzzy semichoir cells. As the texture fills out from three to four voices to five, the rhythm marches, accelerates, then stops for a moment, to underline the word "death" at its terminal appearance.

A composer who had written a reiterative structure of this sophistication could probably go on and write the beginning of "Retire, My Soul." The last line of "Why Do I Use" can also be usefully compared with the later song's ending (see example 3b). As a rhetorical effect, singing "death" again and again on A-major chords in the ostinato passage, as in "Why Do I Use," may or may not be preferred to saving both the word and the chord for one main moment, as in "Retire." But in any case, the last time "death" is sung in the ostinato its effect is vitiated by the declamation in the other voices—not a weakness Byrd seems to have minded when he texted the earlier song, but also not one that he condoned when he composed the later one. Notice, also, how in "Why Do I Use" the cross-relation performs a purely technical function, canceling the C♯ so that some B♭s can be worked in easily

EXAMPLE 3

a. "Why Do I Use"

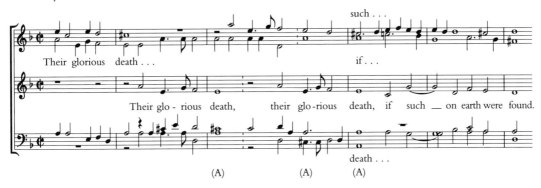

b. "Retire, My Soul"

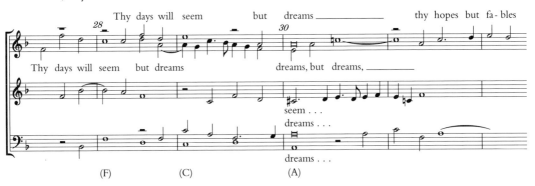

before the final cadence. In "Retire," where the cross-relation is introduced in much the same way, the texting makes it uniquely expressive.

The generic point to be made about "Retire" is that it is a single-stanza song. No extra stanzas are provided, and just because consort songs are strophic we must not postulate extra stanzas of "Retire" which have somehow got lost and which could not possibly fit the music. It is true, and it is well known, that later stanzas of Byrd's strophic songs often do not fit the music very well. His setting of "Why Do I Use," determined by the poem's first stanza, makes amiable nonsense out of most of what turns up at the end of later stanzas (compare "An Angel's trump . . . Their glorious death" with "As his Apos(tles) . . . With many more . . ." and "That we therefore . . . Pray we to Christ"). But this is as nothing compared to the carnage that new words would occasion added to the music of lines 1, 4, 5, and 6 of "Retire."[9]

EXAMPLE 4

a. "Why Do I Use"

And call ___ my wits

(9   8   ♯   6 - 5)
             5   4   ♯

b. "Retire, My Soul"

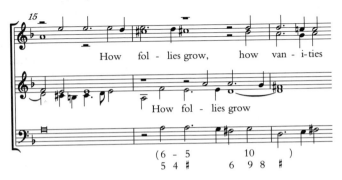

How   fol - lies grow,   how   van - i-ties

How   fol - lies grow

(6 - 5          10        )
 5   4   ♯      6   9   8   ♯

VIII · *Some Harmonic Details*    It has already been mentioned that the cross-relation in line 1—F♯/F between D-major and B♭ triads—is used structurally, as a way of linking the two sections of the song through their opening phrases (phrases 1 and 5).

Line 2 could be described as a loose, hastily syncopated canon between tenor and soprano 1. Here the word "lavish" caught Byrd's ear, as well it might. When the tenor's high f¹ for "*lav*ish" is imitated by the soprano f², a momentary dissonance (an augmented triad) supplies a touch of irony, perhaps. Then an even more biting dissonance is sounded against the second soprano's B♭ for this syllable; the graceful *échappée* that resolves the dissonant ninth sounds like a little gasp of relief. In line 3 it is the word "pleasure"—continuing the irony?—that is first sung hastily, as before, before supporting rich dissonances in three of the other voices.

Another fleeting dissonance appears in line 3, in bar 17. Once again, comparison with "Why Do I Use" shows a growing refinement of technique (example 4). What was used routinely in the early song is used here to initiate a formal process, for in

"Retire" the dissonance arises in the first stage of a motivic expansion: beginning as a unison, the first interval of the motif grows to a minor second, a third, and a fourth.[10] Growing out of this motivic expansion, a little rush of upward leaps in the sopranos in bar 20—a sort of snowballing diminution—imitates the trope by which several of the voices paint the word "amount." This lone madrigalian conceit contributes to the power of the expansion process and also has its own formal value, in that it helps destabilize the central cadence (on g rather than G).

The third and last augmented sound in this song delicately colors the word "pale" on its first appearance (bar 24). "Pale Death" probably counts as the poem's most stereotyped image, but that very fact makes it curiously momentous.[11] There is something faintly ominous, perhaps, about the bland near-homophony used by Byrd for this whole phrase, and the slightly slowing harmonic rhythm.

The common melodic progression 6–5 over a stationary bass occurs in only a few places (for example, F–E in bars 8, 19, 31). The most striking case is the most delicate: the progression A–G (and back to A) in bar 29. The anomalous sixth was Byrd's exquisite way of lingering on the word "dreams" in its first presentation— the obscured soprano 2 entry that I referred to above. The contrast between the open scorings of the 6-chord (c c$^1$ a$^1$ e$^2$ and c a c$^1$ c$^2$ e$^2$) and the close-position A-major chord (A a c$\sharp^1$ e$^1$ a$^1$) adds yet another nuance to the setting of "dreams" in bar 30.


IX · *Write All These Down*    "Retire, My Soul" inscribes all that we have come to admire most in Byrd's art. Especially admirable is the balance between rhetoric and structure. This is a quality that I and others have pointed out frequently in Byrd compositions, frequently enough to prompt questions whether this critical category may not be anachronistic and even illicit. It may have been smuggled in to the sixteenth century by the twentieth-century observer; who can say if our mental metal detectors are sensitive enough to ideological baggage bearing the name-tags of other composers in other centuries? Yet observe the music. Does not the heavy parallelism between the two parts of the song—a unique feature, it seems, in the repertory of Byrd songs—establish an unusually strong shape to the music, and does it not also establish the basis for the rhetoric on the largest level?

For while phrases 1 and 5 are closely linked by their triple repetitive quality, the repetitions have quite a different effect in each case. In phrase 1, the unchanged fundamental pitch structure of the cells gives a feeling of mulling over, meditation, consideration. In phrase 5, that the faster-moving cells modulate gives a feeling of action, urgency, drama. It was perhaps exactly in order to magnify this contrast that Byrd used the same motif in setting the two different text fragments (the half lines) of phrase 1. The progress between the two cell-organized phrases of the song from meditation to action—from "retire" to "write"—is mirrored also by the different feeling of its two fully polyphonic phrases: elegiac in phrase 4, energetic in phrase 8.

"Write all these down": one can say that with the three cells he composed here Byrd was inscribing, repeating, accounting for everything that had been said in the piece so far. Positioned by the G minor of the central cadence, the first cell reinstates the *motif* of phrase 1. The second cell resumes the *harmonic goal* of phrase 2. The third cell recalls the *melodic outline* of phrase 3, which starts on high $f^2$ and works down through canonic chains of thirds to a half cadence in D (an A-major chord, bar 15. This cadence should be heard as the strongest in the piece up to that point: note the 6–8 progression between soprano and bass).

I have spoken of the formula F–E–D–C♯ which is introduced at this point. The important new note is C♯, and Byrd makes $c♯^2$ doubly fresh by prefacing it with a $c♮^2$ at the start of a superbly inflected counterpoint in the second soprano. "*Write all—these down.*" The rhythmic intensification works powerfully for the rhetoric, once again. (Byrd has not finished with the C♯–C♮ crux; it returns again in the next line at the word "dreams," and echoes repeatedly in the song's conclusion.) First articulated by the soprano to mark the rhetorical climax of phrase 5, F–E–D–C♯ now echoes through the rest of the song as an element of its form. With this figure the song clarifies or achieves its true modality, which is perhaps to say its true identity.

The figure also marks the rhetorical climax of the entire song, as we have seen, when the alto sings "Thy days will seem" on the notes $c^1$–$f^1$–$d^1$–$c♯^1$, and $c♯^1$ becomes the third of the "dream" chord. The preparation of this chord, its declamation and sonority, the way it is canceled when the words "but dreams" are sung again, on the notes $a^1$–$c♮^2$—all this has been discussed above. C♯ paints the seductiveness of dreams, then the cross-relation registers their vanity, then comes a three-minim wait. . . . Not many madrigalists could match this for subtlety and impact.

John Ward could not, in his setting of a poem rather similar to Byrd's:

Retire my troubled soule, rest, and behold
Thy dayes of dolour, dangers manifold,
See, life is but a dreame . . .
Begun with hope . . .[12]

Like Byrd, Ward moves to a striking chord on the word "dream"—a C-major triad, in a madrigal that stays largely in a Dorian A-minor region. He returns to C major for "hope," again following Byrd, whose figure $a^1$–$c^2$ for "but dreams" anticipates the motif for the words "thy hopes. . . ." But Ward reserves his most dramatic gesture for the vocative "See"—a mannerist move, privileging the form of an assertion over its substance. Byrd, more classical, focuses upon the dream, and his associating of dreams with hopes also fulfills a formal function. In line 4 he had underlined the parallelism between the half lines that are separated by the caesura in a rather direct fashion. By equating dreams and hopes in line 6, he found a richer way of doing the same thing.

The rhetoric in these two phrases—the two polyphonic phrases which end the song's two parts—is a rhetoric of reiteration: but reiteration comes in many varieties with many shades of affect. In phrase 4 the repetitions of "how follies grow" and "how vanities amount" are rather placid in themselves, elegiac, even bleak, but the motif that repeats them is varied so that the feeling deepens. As a result of the manipulations of the motif, which I have traced above, we can hear the words of this phrase declaimed in four ways: "How follies grow," "*How* follies grow," "How *vanities* amount," and "HOW—*vanities* amount" (soprano 1, bars 18–20). Not often is rhetoric that is as quiet as this so urgent. Nor can it be accidental that Byrd arranged for a similar variety of declamation in the next phrase, too: "Write all these down," "Write *all* these down," "*Write* all—these down."

As for phrase 8, that is the first to be truly blanketed by reiterations. The word "fables," which Byrd had to interpret (fairly enough) as the poem's clincher, is pressed on our consciousness ten times; within each of the three cells, the word occurs in a complex concatenation on several overlapping levels:

Thy hopes but *fa*bles, but FA— — — — — —bles
thy hopes but *fa*bles
Thy hopes but *FA*— — — —bles

In the final cell, there is also the stammering effect of "thy hopes" sung in close stretto. Density of imitation, extension of register, augmentation—these are classic devices used by sixteenth-century composers to add weight to the cadential sections of their pieces. These formal devices can also be used expressively. With a little help from Byrd, the technique of imitation itself is used here to point up the obsessive yet confused persistence of hopes, their wispiness and ultimate futility.

It is the trajectory, finally, that is so impressive. A formal archetype for Byrd and his time was to begin a piece in a relatively homophonic style and close with relatively rich polyphony; one hears this in works ranging in time from the early motet *Emendemus in melius* to *Ave verum corpus* and from the Sidney elegy "Come to Me, Grief, Forever" to the song that we have just now been admiring. Byrd has the capacity and the imagination to reuse such archetypes in widely different expressive contexts, in much the same way that later composers could manipulate archetypes such as sonata form. Or, to venture a closer analogy—for it is the text that inspires—the way Mozart could manipulate sonata-like procedures in opera ensembles. Byrd seldom absorbed an English text and transmuted it into music so profoundly as he did in "Retire, My Soul."

## Notes

TEXTUAL NOTE: The editions by E. H. Fellowes (*The English Madrigal School*, vol. 16 [1920]) and Thurston Dart (revised edition of the Fellowes editions [1964]) have now been superseded by that of John Morehen in *The Byrd Edition*.

In bar 10, Fellowes liked the beautiful alto *échappée* $c^2$, it seems, for he let it stand, even though he believed that "C in the original edition is probably a misprint for A," in the words of his note. Dart's addition to this note was "though the printing is generally accurate"; still, he endorsed Fellowes's conclusion that the C was probably a misprint—and kept it anyhow. Morehen thinks the *échappée* is an error and emends it away, though unlike Dart he does not suspect a misprint, concluding instead that the error was in the compositors' copy.

1. Edward J. Dent, "William Byrd and the Madrigal," in *Musikwissenschaftliche Beiträge: Festschrift für Johannes Wolf zu sienem 60. Geburtstag*, ed. W. Lott et al. (Berlin, 1929), 24–30. It is a powerful article.

2. Joseph Kerman, *The Elizabethan Madrigal: A Comparative Study* (Philadelphia, 1962), ch. 4.

3. Alfred Einstein, "The Elizabethan Madrigal and 'Musica Transalpina,'" *Music & Letters* 25 (1944): 66–67.

4. *The Byrd Edition*, vol. 14, *Psalmes, Songs, and Sonnets* (1611), ed. John Morehen (London, 1987), 183.

5. The original consort versions have been available since 1976 in *The Byrd Edition*, vol. 16, *Madrigals, Songs, and Canons*, ed. Philip Brett (London, 1976).

6. The closest is "Penelope That Longed," no. 27 of the *Songs of Sundrie Natures*, though there is no real cadence or change of style between the half lines of its final couplet. Also as in "Retire," the second section of this song lasts longer than the first, thanks to the addition of a codetta:

| "Retire" | *lines 1–4*: 23 breves | *lines 5–6*: 34 (2:3) |
| "Penelope" | *lines 1–5*: 62 | *lines 6–7*: 75 (5:6) |

7. The music does not draw on the characteristic Dorian resource of using both natural and flat forms of the sixth degree. The alteration B♮ occurs on only three occasions, once as a tierce de Picardie (bar 21) and twice in nonharmonic situations (auxiliary, passing notes) involved with A-major harmony (bars 15 and 19).

8. See Harold S. Powers, "Tonal Types and Modal Categories in Renaissance Polyphony," *Journal of the American Musicological Society* 34 (1981): 428–70, and Joseph Kerman, *The Masses and Motets of William Byrd* (Berkeley and Los Angeles, 1981), 68–72, 218.

9. Over and above this, the song's sectional proportions (2:3, as tallied above) suggest a one-stanza song. Such proportions are found only in such other sectional songs by Byrd as survive with only one stanza, such as "Compel the Hawk" and "Penelope That Longed" from the 1589 *Songs of Sundrie Natures*, and manuscript elegies such as "In Angel's Weed."

10. Unisons—S2 and S1, bars 15–16; minor seconds—T, bar 16; S1, bar 17; and A, bars 17–18 (here the new words are given to the motif, and the music itself is progressively

inverted); thirds—S1 and S2, bar 18; and a fourth—S2, bar 19 (compare B, bars 17 and 18–19, and T, bars 17–18).

11. Some of the imagery of "Retire, My Soul" occurs in a lute song by Robert Jones:

> Life is a Poets fable,
> And all her daies are lies
> Stolne from deaths reckoning table. . . .

Byrd's poem would appear to be the model for Jones's, though the latter was published earlier, in Jones's *First Booke of Songes & Ayres* of 1600.

12. John Ward, *The First Set of English Madrigals* (1613), no. 19.

8

# The *Missa Puer natus est* by Thomas Tallis

*For Oliver Neighbour*

Thomas Tallis appears to have written comparatively few compositions on a monumental scale, though these include his famous tour de force *Spem in alium*—"Mr. Tallis's 40 parts Anthem," as Thomas Tudway called it in 1718: "tis unic made. . . . I had often been told of this Composition, but could never believe ther was any such thing."[1] Besides this, we have only four extended votive antiphons by Tallis and two large Masses: a five-part Mass based on the antiphon *Salve intemerata virgo* and another, incomplete Mass for seven voices.

All of these works were made available for the first time in the Tallis volume of *Tudor Church Music,* in 1928. The seven-part Mass seems to have been completely unknown before that time. It had not figured in the worklist compiled for the 1904 edition of *Grove's Dictionary of Music and Musicians,* which benefited from the contributions of some of the best Victorian musical antiquaries; probably Dr. E. H. Fellowes discovered the work in a set of incomplete partbooks at St. Michael's College, Tenbury, some time after 1918, when he was made Honorary Librarian there. He and the other *Tudor Church Music* editors published those sections of the Mass that appear in Tenbury MSS 341–44 (three sections out of a probable total of nine), leaving blank staves for the missing voice parts.[2] They would have noticed what was evidently a rhythmicized cantus firmus in one of the sections, but since this extended to only half a dozen pitches, it is not surprising that the basis for the Mass was not identified.

⏤ From *Sundry Sorts of Music Books: Essays on the British Library Collections, Presented to O. W. Neighbour on His 70th Birthday,* ed. Chris Banks, Arthur Searle, and Malcolm Turner (London: British Library, 1993), 40–53. The beginning has been slightly expanded.

In 1960, most of the rest of the Mass (though still not all of it) was found among the manuscripts in the library of the Madrigal Society, which had just recently (in 1954) been placed on extended loan in the British Museum. Mass sections appear in no fewer than three sets of Madrigal Society partbooks, all of them related, and all of them lacking attributions to composers. If Fellowes had not drawn such emphatic attention to Tallis's Mass by printing extended fragments, doubtless the new sections would still be slumbering anonymously in the Society's collection, for this still awaits cataloging.

The work's cantus firmus is the Christmas introit *Puer natus est nobis*. The advanced style of composition points to a relatively late date; to mention only the most obvious (but also the most remarkable) feature, this Mass is in principle "full" throughout, not segmented into semichoir and full-choir sections like Tallis's *Missa Salve intemerata virgo*, Taverner's *Gloria tibi Trinitas*, Sheppard's *Cantate*, Tye's *Euge bone* (in a slicked-down version), and every other large-scale, festal Tudor Mass. One assumes it was composed during Queen Mary's reign, and a hypothesis due to Jeremy Noble, that the Mass was planned for the Queen's well-publicized but false pregnancy in late 1554, shortly after her marriage to King Philip II of Spain, has been generally accepted. David Wulstan has remarked on the unusual, un-English scoring—in the clefs $C^1$, $C^2$, $C^3$, $C^4$, $F^3$, $F^4$, and $F^4$—and suggested that the work was planned for joint performance by the Chapel Royal and the king's famous Capella fiamenca.[3] This would help explain not only the work's scoring but also its modern style and its special artifice; Tallis would have done all he could to impress for such an occasion.

Sally Dunkley and Wulstan issued a modest-looking but scholarly performing edition in 1977. They reduce time values by half and transpose the music up a minor third; I follow their voice nomenclature, bar numbering, and reduction in my music examples, but in the text refer to original note values and pitches. In the same year a fine recording was issued by the Clerkes of Oxenford.[4]

II · *Sources*  We know Tallis's Mass only from copies made half a century after its composition. All four of its sources stem from the scriptorium of Edward Paston, who was well known in his own time for his music, and renowned in ours for his voluminous, even maniacal music copying. Philip Brett's article of 1964 is still our main source of information about Paston.[5] Tenbury 341–44 (*T*; five voices survive in the four partbooks) bears his name and may be the earliest of his surviving manuscripts, dating from the 1590s. It is written in what Brett calls the "lute" group of hands, because the copyists worked mostly with lute music (*T* and the Petre Manuscript, Essex Record Office D/DP Z6/1, are their only known partbooks).[6]

*T* contains over a hundred English motets for five, six, and seven voices, mostly by Byrd and Alfonso Ferrabosco Senior. It also transmits an unusual section of

Tallis hymns and a group of three-part fragments of larger English compositions—Masses and votive antiphons—notated *en regard*. Of the few foreign items in this source, *Ego flos campi* by Clemens and *Decantabat populus* by Lassus were probably included to bolster the slender seven-voice section, which also contains Tallis's great seven-part motet *Suscipe, quaeso, Domine*, copied from the 1575 Tallis–Byrd *Cantiones sacrae*.

The Madrigal Society sources are more specialized collections, of the kind Paston turned to more and more after the turn of the century. Two very similar manuscripts, G 16–20 (*MA;* five surviving voices) and G 21–26 (*MB;* six surviving voices), each transmit about fifty motets, most of them for six and seven voices, and almost all of them foreign. None of the music is attributed. In handwriting, both manuscripts belong to Brett's "Group A"; they share about a dozen concordances; their original bindings are alike; and although they pick slightly different selections from the Tallis Mass—apparently it never occurred to Paston to transmit the whole piece—both include *Suscipe, quaeso, Ego flos campi,* and *Decantabat populus*. The text of the Mass is the same as that of *T*.

G 9–14 is a motet collection for seven and eight voices; again most of the motets are foreign. While the Madrigal Society has only seven of the partbooks, the eighth survives as British Library Additional MS 34,000. G 9–14 plus Add. 34,000 will be designated as source P. The handwriting is that of "Group B"; *Suscipe, quaeso* and *Ego flos campi* are absent, and this source records a slightly different textual tradition for the Tallis Mass. In the four movements transmitted by P, there are about a dozen small rhythmic variants in the tenor, and further variants—rather fewer—in the other six voices.[7] A more significant variant that shows up in the sources will be discussed below, under "Mensuration."

Figure 1 is provided as much to show which movements and voice parts have survived, and where, as to set forth the simple stemma. Square brackets enclose hypothetical complete sources, italics indicate that one or more voice parts are missing in the source, and capitals indicate unica. I shall keep italic type in reference to incompleteness throughout this article.

In summary: the Et in terra, Qui tollis, Pleni, and Benedictus are complete and voice parts are missing from the *Et expecto, Sanctus, Agnus I,* and *Agnus II,* though one can be fairly confident about reconstructing them. The Patrem omnipotentem movement, or possibly two movements constituting the Patrem, is or are still lost; this section may well have been very long, long enough to discourage collectors or copyists. On the other hand, the *Et expecto* seems to owe its survival to its brevity, for it fills a half-used page in most voice parts of *T*.[8]

III · *Cantus Firmus Treatment*    Tallis segmented the chant as follows: "[1] Puer natus est nobis, [2] et filius datus est nobis: [3] cuius imperium super humerum eius: [4] et vocabitur

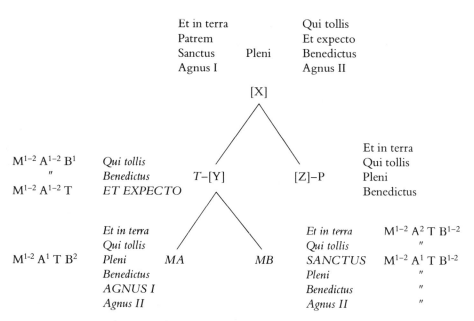

FIGURE I Sources and stemma for the *Missa Puer natus est*.

nomen eius, [5] magni consilii [6] angelus." The cantus firmus is presented in two cursus, one extending through the Gloria and Credo and the other through the Sanctus and Agnus Dei, always in the tenor voice.

The length of the tenor notes (not of the rests) is derived according to a plan that is quaint or learned, according to taste, and simple enough once one has caught on to it and discounted the rhythmicization applied to the longer notes in order to accommodate the Mass text. John Caldwell has recently shown how it works in one movement, the Et in terra.[9] Tallis assigned a factor to each cantus firmus note according to the vowel chanted in the introit (a = 1, e = 2, i = 3, o = 4, u = 5) and also assigned a time unit to each Mass movement; the length of each tenor note is the time unit multiplied by the vowel factor. Thus in the Et in terra, where the assigned time unit is the semibreve, the chant's opening translates into Tallis's tenor as shown in example 1.

In the first cursus (Gloria and Credo), the unit in the Et in terra, covering cantus firmus segments 1 and 2, is the semibreve, in the Qui tollis (segment 3) it is the breve, and in the *Et expecto* (segment 6) the dotted semibreve in tripla proportion (₵ 3). The missing Patrem omnipotentem (segments 4 and 5) probably used the dotted semibreve in regular mensuration as its time unit. Even allowing for text omissions, Tallis would have needed a leisurely cantus firmus here to allow for all the words.

EXAMPLE I

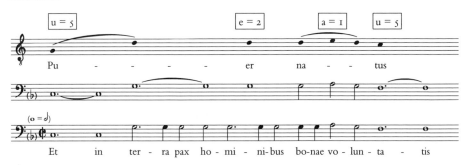

The second cantus firmus cursus (Sanctus and Agnus) employs various refinements, in addition to the numerical vowel code. Three of the five movements use the time unit of the minim, and since this covers ground rather rapidly, these movements all treat their cantus firmus segments to some kind of repetition. In the first two movements of the Sanctus, the repetition is in retrograde, either straightforward or somewhat involved—straightforward in the Sanctus, which presents cantus firmus segment 1 at the minim unit followed by the same in retrograde, and somewhat involved in the Pleni. Here the cantus firmus segment (segment 2) consists of six ligatures and three puncta, and after each ligature is sung (still in the minim unit), it is repeated in retrograde before going on to the rest of the chant. The puncta are not repeated.

The Benedictus, using cantus firmus segment 3 with the semibreve unit, reverses the code so that e = 4, i = 3, and u = 1. Segment 3 includes no *a*s or *o*s.

*Agnus Dei I* covers cantus firmus segment 4 in the original code, with the longest time unit yet, the dotted breve, changed later to the dotted semibreve. Although there is no break or big formal cadence within this movement, the cantus begins the second statement of "Agnus Dei . . . miserere nobis" at the exact halfway mark, where the unit changes. The climax of complication comes with *Agnus Dei II*. Again the minim unit is employed, along with a bizarre repetition scheme, which can be indicated by the series $n^1\ n^2\ n^1\ n^2\ n^3\ n^2\ n^3\ n^4\ n^3\ n^4\ n^5\ \ldots\ n^{20}\ n^{21}\ n^{22}\ n^{21}\ n^{22}$, where $n^1$, $n^2$, and so on up to $n^{22}$ represent the successive notes of cantus firmus segments 5 and 6. The numerical code still applies, of course. Example 2 shows the chant,[10] the "ideal" cantus firmus written in small notes an octave higher, and—at pitch—the actual, rhythmicized tenor with words as adapted.

IV · *Mensuration*    Elizabethan and later scribes, including the "lute" music scribe of *T*, regularly replaced the signature for perfect time (Φ) in older music with ₵, adjusting dots, coloration, and ligatures as necessary.[11] Copying the Benedictus from an

EXAMPLE 2

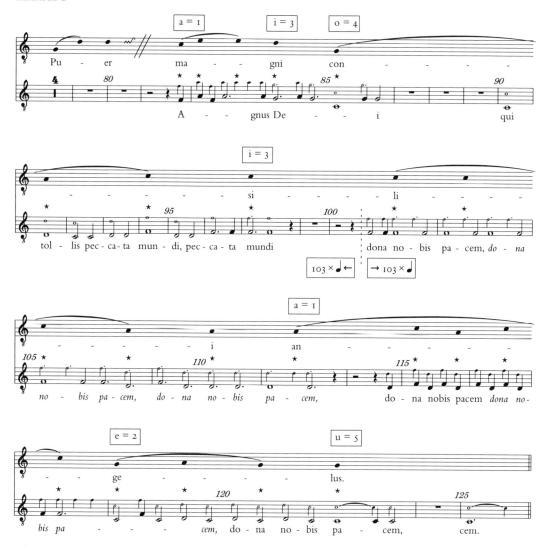

earlier source [Y], our scribe is caught in the act. In MSS 341 and 342 he reproduced the Φ signature, but in 343 and 344 omitted any signature, so the singer can only assume that the ¢ signature from the preceding Qui tollis continues.[12] All later sources sign the Benedictus and all other movements with ¢.

So the Benedictus, the final movement of the Sanctus, was originally notated in perfect time, like the *Et expecto,* the final movement of the Credo. I suspect, in fact, that the whole of *Missa Puer natus est* was originally in perfect time, for two

EXAMPLE 3

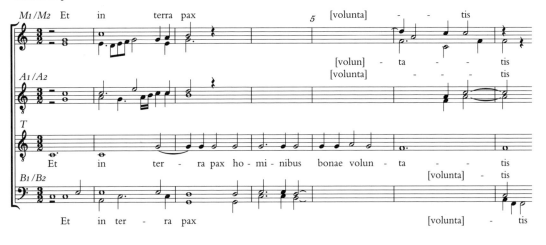

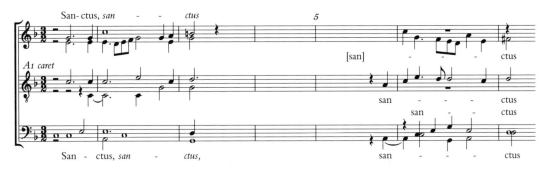

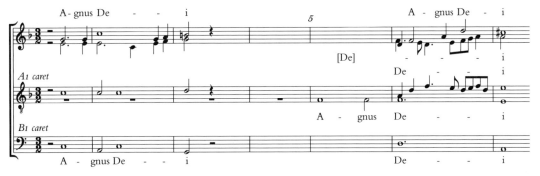

principal reasons. First, the imposing "head theme" in the surviving initial movements falls so naturally into triple meter—especially the first six semibreves, but
to some extent also the first eighteen. (See example 3.) Second, if (and only if) the

breves are read as perfect, containing three semibreves rather than two, certain of the movements display striking numerical proportions.

This is a controversial area of argumentation, and I hasten to make clear that the only breves in question are final breves—"ideal" breves, which are hardly ever to be seen in the sources at all (the scribes usually write longs). What is more, in some cases the proportions are calculated to include the finalis in the tenor voice, and sometimes the finalis in other voices, voices which stop later than the tenor. The modern researcher must bear patiently the charge that he is having it both ways by counting different voices in different situations. Though one can suggest that maybe it was the original composer who had it both ways, one cannot expect to convince.

Nevertheless, in several movements, if the finalis is counted as a perfect breve, lasting for three semibreves rather than two, a major segment of the tenor begins at the exact halfway point, after a rest that would evidently have been calculated to achieve these exact proportions. Thus the *Sanctus* extends 132 minims up to the finalis in the tenor (and in the second alto—bars 1–33 in VM); the retrograde statement of the cantus begins after 69 minims. *Agnus Dei I* extends for 147 semibreves up to the finalis in all four surviving voices *except* the tenor, which stops sooner (bars 1–74); the second statement of "Agnus Dei," with its new time unit, begins after 75 semibreves. *Agnus Dei II* extends for 200 minims up to the finalis in the tenor (coinciding with four other voices—bars 75–124); "dona nobis pacem" is first sung in the tenor after 103 minims. (See example 2.)

More number magic is at work in *Agnus Dei I*. Each 75-semibreve half of this movement divides in the ratio 48:27, though in each half the division is accomplished in a different way. (No doubt Tallis considered this more elegant than making the two divisions in the same way.) The first half totals 48 semibreves of notes and 27 of rests. The second half runs for 48 semibreves up to, and 27 after, a change of time signature in the tenor to C. The new signature was evidently introduced in bar 62 (rather than 61, as one might possibly have expected on rhythmic grounds) in order to achieve this division, and overall a division according to squares—25:16:9 in perfect breves. The tenor in this movement moves very naturally in triple meter throughout.

I have made no attempt to track the traditional symbolism of the numbers that Tallis contrived here.[13] If numerical proportions exist in the other movements, they are more complex, and an amateur had better not mess with them.


v · *Musical Style: Agnus Dei II*    While the sources, cantus firmus treatment, and mensuration of the *Missa Puer natus est* can be discussed usefully in a short space, or so I hope, this is not true of the musical style. A complex, richly varied work, the Mass resists direct stylistic comparison to other music by Tallis because of its unique texture:

imitative counterpoint over a cantus firmus consisting of long, irregular notes occurs in no other Tallis work.[14] Rather than attempting a general description, then, I shall focus on a single movement, *Agnus Dei II,* perhaps the most unusual of all and also perhaps the one which Tallis was proudest of. In addition to the intricate cantus firmus plan and the numerical proportions, mentioned above, this movement also features a strict canon between the two mean (upper) voices— strict, though the canon changes time intervals after about a third of the movement and "breaks" after two-thirds. Furthermore the cantus firmus is involved more closely with the imitative matrix here than in any other movement. A skeletonized score is provided as example 4.

Bar 80    "Agnus Dei": the motif appears in the canonic voices (the means) after having been sung by the two basses and the surviving alto (also surely by the second, lost alto in the otherwise completely void bar 1). Imitation extends to the tenor, which doubles the first four notes of the *comes* at the lower tenth.

83    "Qui tollis peccata": a new motif introduced by the *dux* is repeated in expanded form to include the word "mundi." Hence the means sing this motif four times in all.

92    "Peccata mundi": these words generate another new motif. Yet neither one of these motifs is imitated in any of the surviving lower voices. For twelve breves or more, then, the texture is polyphonic but not consistently imitative; the music feels amorphous, and it would probably be a mistake to try to alter this quality by imaginative reconstruction of the missing alto.

97    "Qui tollis . . .": the *dux* introduces a triadic motif, other voices imitate it, and the canonic interval changes from three semibreves to four. Tallis seems to be trying to get the composition back on track; the canonic voices repeat the triadic motif, so that it is heard four times in the means, like the earlier "qui tollis" figure, but on this occasion there is an ostinato effect. The words "dona nobis pacem," adjusted to the second pair of entries, are now heard constantly until the end, as the motif is developed.

105    The motif expands (downward) from a fifth to a sixth, and is then moved up and reformulated in pitch contour and rhythm. A process of simplification is setting in, first in rhythm: this now consists of absolutely even minims ($d^1$–$f^1$–$bb^1$–$a^1$–$d^1$–$f^1$–$bb^1$–$a^1$), and a hypnotic ostinato gets under way, aided by the two bass voices in stretto imitation at the lower octave. The monorhythm continues for fifteen bars, to the end of the Mass, for even though the alto varies the rhythm after bar 119 (and doubtless the

EXAMPLE 4

lost second alto did also), the means and basses stay almost entirely with minim motion.

114  The canon breaks: instead of waiting for two bars, the *comes* intrudes after one bar, and a third higher than the *dux*. At this climactic point, the tenor again joins the imitative fabric, in much the same way as it did at "Agnus Dei," by doubling the treble at the lower tenth. But instead of lining out the kernel of the motive and then stopping, it bizarrely continues oscillating between d and f at a semibreve interval: d–f–d–f–d–f–d–f–d–f–. Melodic simplification matches and intensifies the rhythmic simplification.

There is no further melodic development; the canon collapses into strettos at a two-semibreve interval, prolonging the hypnosis with a five-bar ostinato (bars 118–23). The decaying "dona" motif in tenths shifts upward by thirds, from a starting point $d/f^1$ to F/a to $A/c^1$, though the overall

EXAMPLE 4    (*continued*)

pitch drops. This makes a harmonic climax of a sort, to add to the rhythmic and melodic ones, and of course allows Tallis to follow the chant from a "Dorian" beginning to an "Ionian" conclusion.

What is interesting about all this is how close the music comes to being mono-thematic. The opening "Agnus Dei" motif in the canonic mean voices is essentially a rocking figure of a third, $a^1$–$c^2$–$a^1$–$c^2$; when the tenor enters, doubling the *comes* at the tenth, the centrality of the rocking figure is really hammered home. So the intertwining triadic pattern that enters in bar 97, $f^1$–$a^1$–$f^1$–$a^1$–$c^2$–$a^1$, and so on, clearly recalls the original "Agnus Dei" motif; indeed, one could read it as a linear composite of the original $a^1$–$c^2$–$a^1$–$c^2$ doubled by f–a–f–a.

Then this motif is developed successively in several stages, as we have seen. The climactic entrance of the cantus firmus with its oscillating figure reminds us (forcibly!) of the derivation of the various "dona" motifs from the rocking third. Two further details seem calculated to strengthen the monothematic concept. First, a rather striking melodic figure within the "free" section of the piece (bars 94–95 and 95–97) foreshadows the insistent outline of the final "dona" motifs, a sixth. Second, the concluding bass statement in minims, A–c–F–c–A–c–A–c–A–, echoes the unforgettable tenor oscillation, heard eight bars earlier.

Along with monothematicism goes seamlessness; this movement is virtually without cadences until the end. In the absence of the second alto, the only strong-beat dissonances come in bars 82 (weak cadence), 91 (noncadential), and 124 (the final cadence).[15] The whole Mass is very consonant, but the climactic *Agnus Dei II* is more so than the rest.

Finally, to return for a moment to the matter of cantus firmus treatment, it should be observed that the intricate, even convoluted repetition scheme used by Tallis in this movement must have been chosen precisely in order to generate those oscillating minim ostinatos.

VI · *Personalia* — The identification of sections of the *Missa Puer natus est* in the Madrigal Society manuscripts was made by the present writer, engaged at the time (1960) in a survey of English library holdings bearing on motets by William Byrd. The presence of the Madrigal Society collection at the British Museum was by no means well publicized, but I was tipped off by Jeremy Noble, who had already guided and helped me on that research project in more ways than one could imagine. As the collection was housed in the Music Room, not in the Manuscript Room, which was my regular beat, this was actually my first visit to that sanctum in the back of the Museum. I had not met Oliver Neighbour before, and he must have made a great impression, for I remember him and details of the scene clearly, even though our friendship and collaboration was not to develop until some time later.

That was my first encounter with the *Missa Puer natus est*. In later years I spent a good deal of time with this work and others by Tallis, both in the study and in the seminar room, because of an agreement to edit Tallis's Latin church music for the series Early English Church Music. The edition never happened—to be frank, it defeated me; and while this was unfortunate from one standpoint, in that the edition was inordinately delayed, it was fortunate from another, in that the project is now in much better hands.

My last encounter with the *Missa Puer natus est* was of a less scholarly sort, but the story is worth telling on the twin slim pretexts that it informs about the work's reception (actually, more like *receipts*) and that it involves Neighbour, once again. In 1982 I received an unexpected telephone call from a motion-picture functionary who was trying to locate a score of the Tallis. It seems that David Wulstan's recording had made such a deep impression on a well-known Hollywood director that he had decided to use the work as background music for a feature film. I told my caller to get the Voces Musicales edition, but that was not accessible to him, he would not quite say why. (The reason may have been that the performing forces decided on were not the Clerkes of Oxenford but Tangerine Dream, the German new-age group.) He had "contacted" the British Library, and a Mr. Neighbour had referred him to me. Did I not have a score, at least of the Gloria? It was very important, also important that it reach them by the next Monday.

I did not, not yet, but by Sunday night an untransposed score in 3/2 time was expressing its way to the Southland. After a number of months the film opened, failed massively, and was immediately withdrawn. I phoned Hollywood. The Tallis had never been used at all. And what of my time, my trouble, my expertise, my dreams of a second career? What would I suggest? What I suggested may not, I fear, have been appropriate, for it was agreed to without so much as a murmur and remitted at once.

## Notes

1. Thomas Tudway, quoted in *Thomas Tallis,* vol. 6 of *Tudor Church Music,* ed. Percy C. Buck et al. (London, 1928), xx.
2. Ibid., 49–61.
3. David Wulstan, *Tudor Music* (London, 1985), 295–96.
4. *Thomas Tallis, Missa Puer natus est nobis,* reconstructed and ed. by Sally Dunkley and David Wulstan, Voces Musicales, ser. I, vol. 1 (Oxenford Imprint, 1977: obtainable through Blackwell's Music Shop), referred to below as VM. *Thomas Tallis, Messe "Puer natus est," Motets "Suscipe quaeso Domine" et "Salvator mundi,"* Clerkes of Oxenford, dir. David Wulstan (Calliope LP, CAL 1623, 1977; reissued as Nonesuch H 71378, 1980).
5. Philip Brett, "Edward Paston (1550–1630): A Norfolk Gentleman and His Musical Collection," *Transactions of the Cambridge Bibliographical Society* 4 (1964): 51–69.
6. For a facsimile from *T,* see E. H. Fellowes, *William Byrd,* 2d ed. (London, 1948), plate facing p. 142. Samples of the Group A and Group B hands (see below) appear in Philip Brett and Thurston Dart, "Songs by William Byrd in Manuscripts at Harvard," *Harvard Library Bulletin* 14 (1960): Plates I and II, between pp. 350 and 351. Sigla in italics refer to sources that are incomplete, missing some partbooks.
7. For details, see the Critical Commentary of VM.
8. In Tenbury 341 *Et expecto* begins on staff 5 of fol. 62$^r$, in 343 on staff 6 of fol. 61$^r$, and in 344 on staff 6 of fol. 62$^r$. In 342, which transmits two voice parts, the scribe found himself starting at the tops of pages (75$^r$ and 76$^r$); he did not fill all the staves.
9. John Caldwell, *Oxford History of English Music,* vol. 1, *From the Beginnings to c. 1715* (Oxford, 1991), 298–99.
10. Compare *The Use of Salisbury,* ed. Nick Sandon, vol. 2 (Newton Abbott, 1986), 54. The cantus firmus of the Mass will make sense on the assumption that Tallis read liquescents as reiterations, for in both the *Et expecto* and *Agnus Dei II,* the neume consisting of torculus ACA and cephalus (liquescent clivis) CB on "an[gelus]" becomes DFDFF, and in *Agnus Dei II* the liquescent torculus CED on "ma[gni]" becomes FAA. This is similar but not identical

to the way Byrd treated liquescents in his early cantus firmus motet *Christus resurgens:* the cephalicus FE on "ul[tra]" and "[alle]lu[ia]" becomes FEE, and the cephalicus ED on the next alleluia becomes EDD. See Philip Brett's note in the Textual Commentary to *The Byrd Edition,* vol. 6b, *Gradualia I (1605): Other Feasts and Devotions,* ed. Philip Brett (forthcoming). The chant line in example 2 gives note reiterations, not liquescents as in *The Use of Salisbury.*

It should be noted that Sandon provides an edited composite version of chant, which differs slightly from the version in the printed Graduals from 1507 to 1532 and from that in Frere's *Graduale sariburiensis* (London, 1894). VM reproduces the latter without indicating liquescents. Professor Brian Trowell has kindly collated graduals for me.

11. Thus, for example, in Tenbury 342 all but one of the thirty-odd three-part fragments are signed for imperfect time, including those that were originally in perfect time. In most cases, the change of signature probably occurred long before *T* was copied; but one fragment lacks any time signature, the opening trio from Tallis's *Ave Dei patris,* and one may suspect that this was copied directly from a perfect-time original, like the Benedictus.

12. This is reported incorrectly in the VM Critical Commentary. In *Tudor Church Music* the signature is normalized to $\Phi$ throughout, in VM to $\mathbb{C}$.

13. See the remarkable essay by Brian Trowell, "Proportion in the Music of Dunstable," *Proceedings of the Royal Musical Association* 105 (1978–79): 100–141.

14. Struck by the nearly continuous imitative style, Paul Doe has suggested the influence of Gombert, which is probably right, though it would be hard to say whether the influence came directly from the master of the Capella fiamenca himself, or from one of the host of composers whose styles are said to have been formed by his. And in accommodating Tallis to the "international" style, a qualification must be made as regards his proclivity for ostinato; while in the present work this was encouraged (indeed required) by the marathon pedals produced by the cantus firmus, Tallis's fondness for ostinato is well known from other music too. Doe ingeniously adduces and cites the seven-part Agnus Dei II—with the added cantus firmus *Ecce sacerdos magnus*—of Gombert's six-part *Missa Quam pulchra es.* But Gombert's cantus firmus treatment here is very different from that of Tallis, and the music is, exceptionally, largely non-imitative (Paul Doe, *Tallis,* 2d ed. [Oxford Studies of Composers, no. 4; London, 1976], 20–25).

Tallis may, however, have learned something from Gombert's Mass or others like it— namely that Continental composers anticipated that the last movement of a Mass would contain fireworks.

15. The final cadence can make an odd effect, especially if one hears that a breve rest has been inserted in the cantus firmus to allow for it. It is my suspicion that the hushed tone adopted by Wulstan in his recording of this movement was an effort to mitigate this effect; but it also militates against the brilliance I feel sure Tallis intended.

9

# An Italian Musician in Elizabethan England

For a student of English Renaissance music, the invitation to present a "case history" of a Mediterranean musician in the North points inevitably to one individual. He is Alfonso Ferrabosco, who served Queen Elizabeth I on and off for sixteen years at the beginning of her reign, from 1562 to 1578, and enjoyed extraordinary renown as a composer long after he returned to Italy, indeed long after his death. In the annals of European music, "Master Alfonso," as the English called him, gets scarcely a mention. But in England his music was repeatedly praised by musicians and amateurs, posthumously published, and anthologized widely in retrospective manuscripts of the early seventeenth century.

Alfonso's story has been told many times, most recently by the Australian musicologist Richard Charteris,[1] and if it is told a little differently here, that is mainly as a result of two analyses that I have attempted. One deals with the sources of Alfonso's music, and the other with his affiliations—that is, with the many well-known persons who are associated with him in the archival records relating to his life. If the first of these analyses proceeds cautiously and the second the opposite of cautiously, I think that in each case the strategy helps thicken the description.

II · The Ferrabosco family of musicians from Bologna was a mobile one. Domenico Maria, ousted from the Cappella Sistina in 1555, along with Palestrina, has been

‌  Paper for a round table on "The Events of the 1570s and 1580s and the Changes in Musical Balance between the Mediterranean Countries and Northern Europe" at the 15th Congress of the International Musicological Society, Madrid, 1992. To be published in *Actas del XV Congreso de la SIM Madrid '92*.

The invitation referred to in the first sentence was issued by Professor Ludwig Finscher, chairman of the round table, in a communication to the participants.

located during the early 1560s in Paris, where he was engaged in collecting information on behalf of the Bolognese Cardinal Paleotti.[2] He also gained a more powerful patron, Charles de Guise, Cardinal of Lorraine; under his sponsorship, three Ferrabosco children sang at a Paris wedding in 1559. One of them may have been Anfione, who turns up later in the service of Henri III. Alfonso, the oldest son, appears in England[3] as "one of the Q. Musicons" before he is twenty. His cousins Matthia and Costantino settled in Graz and Nuremberg respectively; both were minor composers.

Alfonso was not only mobile, he was also upwardly mobile, a courtier as well as a musician. He was sponsored in England by Giambattista Castiglione, a trusted servant of Elizabeth since her youth, her teacher of Italian, and now a groom of her privy chamber who was sometimes entrusted with minor diplomatic errands. By 1576 Alfonso too was a groom of the chamber, acting as an intermediary between the Queen and Venetian visitors; later in life he called himself a *gentiluomo* at the court of Carlo Emanuele I of Savoy. (In one Spanish document he is described overoptimistically as "noble saboyano.") Alfonso was paid more than the other royal musicians, presumably because Elizabeth thought so highly of him, and perhaps because of his proficiency in theatrical entertainments and in extracurricular political operations. Like many of the other musicians, he seems to have used court influence to "feather his nest," as G. E. P. Arkwright put it, judging from obscure financial claims he tried to assert after leaving the country. Unlike many (or perhaps any) other court musicians, Alfonso also attached himself to the most powerful lords of Elizabethan England.

It was not impossible for an Italian to do this, despite a good deal of anti-Italian feeling in England at this time.[4] The first serious plot against Elizabeth, in 1569, is named for the Florentine banker Ridolfi, and in 1570 the Queen was excommunicated by Pope Pius V. Yet Italian arts, scholarship, statecraft, popular philosophy, and manners held an irresistible fascination for the Elizabethans. And there was a distinguished group of Italians in London, mostly Protestants and refugees from the Inquisition, some of them resident since the time of King Edward VI. Among them were John Florio, the translator of Montaigne; the historian Pietro Bizzarri; the reformer Iacopo Aconcio, a close friend of Castiglione; the scholar and illuminator Petruccio Ubaldini; Claudio Conti, author of a famous treatise on horsemanship; and—at a later period—the eminent jurist Alberico Gentili, and of course Giordano Bruno. Alfonso was introduced to court by Castiglione. Shortly afterwards he traveled back from Italy in the company of Conti (for Alfonso returned several times to his homeland). Later still, he was on close terms with Ubaldini, as we shall see.

Conti was master of the horse to the Earl of Leicester, Elizabeth's first favorite, and indeed most of the Italians mentioned above relied on the earl's patronage. While Alfonso seems to have relied on Leicester's good offices all through his stay in England, he also sued for the favor of Leicester's rival, the Earl of Sussex, whom he addresses as "mio Patricio e Prottetore" in one letter. Other famous names crop up in the correspondence: Alfonso complains that he has been robbed by a former page of "S$^r$ Carlo Havvard," the future Lord Howard of Effingham, and bewails the accusation that he has murdered a young servant of Sir Philip Sidney. Can we infer from this that Alfonso associated with these important persons? The Sidney connection, at least, was not entirely casual, for Alfonso was able to get both Sidney and Leicester to take his side and intercede on his behalf with the Queen.[5]

Leicester was the greatest patron of his time—over a hundred books were dedicated to him—and whether or not he counts as a musical Maecenas on the scale of Henry Fitzalan, Earl of Arundel, as David Price claims, his largess was certainly tapped by music for the theater. He engaged William Hunnis and Edward Johnson to compose music for his famous Kenilworth entertainment of 1575 (and received a dedication from Hunnis in return), and supported a band of traveling musicians in conjunction with "Leicester's Men," his even more famous acting company.[6] However, the real music lover in the family was Leicester's son-in-law Philip Sidney, and in the mid-seventies Sidney in effect took over as the dominant figure in English cultural life. Sidney's emphatic interest in Italian poetry and music is well known; he wrote poems to be sung to the music of Italian villanellas, which he may well have heard at court.[7] William Byrd was probably in touch with the Sidney circle, and the poet Thomas Watson, Byrd's collaborator, almost certainly was. It makes every kind of sense that Alfonso would have had some connections here, however slight.

Besides Leicester and Sussex, the main recipient of Alfonso's surviving letters was William Cecil, Lord Burghley, Queen Elizabeth's secretary of state ("mio Procuratore e Protetore"). Burghley employed Alfonso as a secret agent on his trips abroad (and, for all we know, at home too). And when Alfonso left England for good in 1578, his adventures read like a bad historical novel—the jewels and huge purses he was delivering to Burghley's Italian spies; his consorting with the infamous Egremont Radcliffe, brother of Sussex, and Leicester's double-dealing servant Sylvanus Scory;[8] his methodical entrapment by the Papal Nuncio in Paris, Dandino; Catherine de Medici's letter on his behalf to the Pope; and his imprisonment by and somewhat banal confession to the Inquisition.[9] But Alfonso's later career is not to our purpose here.

III ·

We need instead to inquire about his music. Some lute music and a few French chansons by Alfonso have survived, as well as essays in native genres such as the consort song, the anthem, and the In nomine. More impressively, seventy-odd Latin motets and a like number of Italian madrigals are transmitted in English sources, in retrospective manuscript anthologies dating from the early seventeenth century. This was twenty years after Alfonso had died, thirty years after his final return to Italy. Grateful as we are for the survival of this unusually large repertory, we need to subject the unusual conditions of that survival to careful analysis. Can we tell which of this music was known during his years in England?

At court one would assume Alfonso was admired as a lutenist, though he is never mentioned as such; probably he was a singer to the lute.[10] In a minor way, he was a composer for the instrument—the first of note in England, it would seem: in 1610 a fantasy and a pavan by "the Most Artificiall and Famous Alfonso Ferrabosco of Bologna" was printed in London, by which time the fantasy (in a corrupt version) and another one had already appeared in Besard's *Thesaurus harmonicus,* and a dozen or so works for lute and bandora had been copied into various English manuscripts. Alfonso took a prominent part in theatrical entertainments at court, so he probably wrote songs, dances, and madrigalesque compositions for the stage. If so, this music has proved to be as evanescent as the texts themselves and the stage architecture, though a secular motet survives, *Virgo per incertos casus,* which sounds as though it belonged to an allegorical entertainment.[11]

A number of sacred motets are preserved in what might be called the "mainstream" music manuscripts of the time, the miscellaneous collections of songs, motets, and instrumental music that seem to have been compiled by many amateurs and musicians. None of these "mainstream" manuscripts can be dated securely from the period of Alfonso's residence in England, but in some that date from the 1580s and 1590s, we find a couple of In nomines and chansons by him, an English song, and a handful of motets (though no madrigals).[12] One of the amateurs who compiled such a manuscript, Robert Dow, an Oxford don, peppered the partbooks with interesting annotations. Dow includes an exemplary pair of motets: *Mirabile misterium,* which he inscribes "Alfonso Ferabosco Italus," next to *Miserere mei Deus* by "Gulielmus Birde Anglus."

Other early favorites are a *Da pacem,* a setting from Lamentations, and another secular motet, *Musica laeta,* in which the speaker, returning to his homeland, bids a surprisingly affectionate farewell to a patron. "I return home, leaving you, dear friend; in these circumstances, home is scarcely pleasing": these are certainly not words Alfonso would have addressed to Leicester, but one can imagine him addressing them to Ferdinando Heybourne alias Richardson, the teenage courtier and composer-to-be who in 1575 became the first Englishman to sing Alfonso's praises (albeit an "Englishman Italianate"). The occasion was a lengthy Latin commendatory poem in that pompous publication *Cantiones sacrae* of Tallis and Byrd, dedicated to Queen Elizabeth. Probably Heybourne was Alfonso's pupil.[13]

A handful of motets, as has been said, is found in relatively early manuscripts; most of Alfonso's Latin compositions owe their preservation to later manuscripts.

Taking the Latin corpus as a whole, we note that the text repertory has a distinctly English cast. This will require a moment's explanation. The Reformation and the introduction of vernacular services did not bring with it a cessation of Latin composition, at least partly because in the hierarchy of genres motets were "the chiefest both for art and utilitie," as Thomas Morley was to say. Long settings of entire psalms were cultivated, probably by the Chapel Royal at the behest of ecclesiastical authorities, though composers from outside the Chapel also participated. There was also a somewhat mysterious tradition of composing Lamentations. William Byrd and some other composers also wrote shorter Latin works—motets—using sacred texts that lacked any obvious Catholic association.

Alfonso's seventy-odd Latin compositions include ten full or abbreviated psalms, four Lamentations, and not a single motet referring to the Virgin Mary or any other saint. And since so many of Alfonso's motets were used as models by Byrd, and one was so used by Robert Parsons who died in 1570,[14] there is no reason to doubt that Alfonso's motets were written in England for England.

Yet there is reason to doubt that they were sung at court. The Queen's Musick, consisting of instrumentalists, was strictly separate from her Chapel Royal, consisting of singers; conservative and insular, the Chapel never admitted foreigners (in conspicuous contrast to the Queen's Musick). There is a large retrospective manuscript of Latin music at Christ Church, Oxford (979–83), which is thought to transmit the Chapel Royal repertory, and among 150 works by native composers from Taverner to John Mundy, it admits just one motet each by Lassus, Sebastian Holland, and the Scotsman Patrick Douglas, and two by Alfonso. Although we can read these statistics as a modest tribute to Alfonso, if we wish, they do not suggest that his music was much sung in the Chapel Royal.

One place where it very probably *was* sung was Nonsuch, the great mansion of the powerful Earl of Arundel, head of the old Catholic party. Nonsuch has been described, perhaps a little enthusiastically, as a "flourishing outpost of continental musical fashion";[15] but there is no doubt that Arundel was far and away England's most active patron of foreign music and musicians. He supported the shadowy (but prolific) Netherlander Derick Gerarde, accepted the dedication of printed music by Lassus, and ordered manuscripts of Italian madrigals and villanellas. An inventory lists 127 musical instruments in Arundel's possession. His "solem Queer / By vois and Instruments so sweet to heer" is praised in a poem. Nonsuch also boasted a great library with an extraordinary music section; when this was cataloged in 1609, it contained mostly Continental printed music by composers from Josquin to Palestrina, as well as manuscripts by Gerarde, and the later Latin publications of William Byrd.[16]

Alfonso, whom we have seen gravitate toward Cecil, Sussex, and Leicester, would have been even more likely to ingratiate himself with Arundel; and this likelihood is increased by two more of his associations. One of them, Petruccio Ubaldini, has already been mentioned. An emigré from Edward VI's time, Ubaldini was patronized by Arundel, to whom he presented a beautiful Latin psalter in 1565.[17] Ubaldini was associated with Alfonso in theatrical activities at court,[18] and when Alfonso's wife had to escape from London, it was Ubaldini who gave her money. The other association, of course, was with Byrd. The English composer modeled composition after composition on works by his Italian friend, and joined with him to produce a much-admired lost set of canons on the *Miserere* (the lutenist Thomas Robinson proposed to publish them; Morley marveled at the composers' "vertuous contention in love"). Byrd dedicates one of his motet books to Lord Lumley, Arundel's heir, who had lived at Nonsuch since the 1550s, and there is also evidence that Byrd used the Nonsuch library.[19]

IV ·

Alfonso's Italian madrigals divide conveniently into two groups. The later group consists of those in two Venetian publications of 1587; according to their dedications, Alfonso's new patron Duke Carlo Emanuele I of Savoy had ordered him to issue (and presumably to compose) them. An earlier group is preserved only in English manuscripts; on stylistic grounds this music can be placed in the 1560s or 1570s, even though the manuscripts date from after the turn of the century. The madrigals are long, solemn pieces with a strong, even suffocating literary flavor. They look like academy exercises, and I think of Padua, that most academic of towns, and of the Paduan composer Francesco Portinaro, who published a six-part setting of Petrarch's eleven-stanza "Vergine bella" in 1568 and 1569. For Alfonso also made a six-part setting of this immense canzone—in Italy, surely; we know he was in Italy at some time between 1569 and 1571. It seems beyond coincidence that the Earl of Arundel visited the baths at Padua in these years and ordered a collection of madrigals from an associate of Portinaro, Innocenzio Alberti. (Dated 1568, this is one of very few Italian madrigal manuscripts of this period that survive in British libraries.)[20] Alfonso's whereabouts in 1568 are unknown; he figures in no English records from that year.

I very much doubt that Alfonso's "Vergine" madrigals were sung at the court of Queen Elizabeth, or, for that matter, anywhere else in her realm. There is no trace of them in sixteenth-century sources. They are transmitted only later, in the retrospective anthologies already mentioned.

This is not to say that nobody in England had copies of Alfonso's older madrigals. Somebody did, since a few of them turn up in *Musica transalpina,* the important publication of translated Italian madrigals which launched the Elizabethan madrigal development of the 1590s. But none of these copies has survived, and no Ferrabosco madrigals appear in the "mainstream" music manuscripts of the time, as has already been noted.

Dated October 1588, *Musica transalpina* includes some of Alfonso's older madrigals and also several newer ones, dedicated to the Duke of Savoy and published only seventeen months earlier in *Il primo libro de madrigali a cinque voci* of May 1587. (Clearly Alfonso kept in close touch with England. The obvious contact would have been Gomer van Awsterwyke, one of the Queen's flutists, who was bringing up the small children Alfonso had to leave behind when he returned to Italy—the future composer Alfonso Ferrabosco Junior and a sister. Alfonso tried to get the children back in 1584 and again in 1586 and 1587—he even sent an intermediary to Gomer, with money—but in vain.)

And Alfonso's *Secondo libro* of September 1587, which seems to have reached England too late for *Musica transalpina,* confirms his new popularity as a madrigalist. A group of five numbers from this set—nos. 7–8, the *proposta–risposta* "Donna l'ardente fiamma"–"Signor la vostra fiamma," nos. 11 and 12, "Non mi fuggir" and "Zefiro torna," and no. 17, "Nel più fiorito Aprile," the set's final number, also its most modern in style—are copied at the end of a manuscript that could be as early as 1598.[21] This is the first appearance of Ferrabosco madrigals in an English manuscript. The same pieces often occur (and often occur in groups) in later ones; four out of five of these madrigals also appear with translations in the second, smaller *Musica transalpina* of 1597. The four poems were all reset by English madrigalists, major (John Wilbye) and minor (Michael Cavendish, John Bennet, John Farmer). One madrigal of the group, "Zefiro torna," was actually used as the basis for a viol fantasia by John Jenkins.

Joan Wess, who made this observation, dates the Jenkins fantasia in the 1620s.[22] She also points to a fantasia by John Coprario that is modeled on Alfonso's "Come dal ciel" ("Like as from Heaven" in *Musica transalpina* I). Nor, of course, is the modeling of fantasias on madrigals restricted to madrigals by Alfonso; Marenzio and Monteverdi have also been spotted, and, as Wess remarks, "much work has yet to be done [after her impressive start] to reveal the extent of the fantasia writers' debt to the Italian madrigalists." The main historical point made by Wess is that the "emerging Jacobean fantasia" of Coprario, Thomas Lupo, Richard Mico, and Alfonso Ferrabosco Junior bears a similar relation to the madrigal as the canzona of Gabrieli and others does to the French chanson. A fringe benefit of her study is the new light it sheds on the influence of Master Alfonso.

The light it sheds on a famous statement by Thomas Morley is positively stroboscopic. Writing in 1597 for would-be madrigal composers, Morley recommends "if you would imitate any I would appoint you these for guides: *Alfonso Ferrabosco* for deepe skill, *Luca Marenzo* for good ayre and fine invention, *Horattio Vecchi, Stephano Venturi, Ruggiero Giovanelli,* and *John Croce,* with divers others." Not only did some madrigal composers submit to Alfonso's guidance, so did composers of viol fantasies—and so did composers of lute airs: for Wess also observes that John Dowland quotes from Alfonso's madrigal "Vidi pianger Madonna" at the beginning and at the end of one of his most famous songs, whose words are the *Musica transalpina* version of that madrigal: "I Saw My Lady Weep." The song appeared in 1600. As for Morley, the most promiscuous of musical modelers, his recommendation can almost be read as autobiography. Morley's ever-popular fa las "Fire Fire My Heart" and "Now Is the Month of Maying" are derived from Marenzio and Vecchi, his six-part "Oriana" madrigal "Hard by a Crystal Fountain" from Croce, and his four-part madrigal "Now Is the Gentle Season" from a madrigal which many English scribes—and so probably Morley too—thought was by Alfonso: the famous "Io mi son giovinetta" by Alfonso's father Domenico.[23] "Now Is the Gentle Season" is patently more archaic than any other of Morley's *Madrigalls to fowre voyces* printed in 1594. It could even possibly date back to a time when Alfonso was still in England; we know that Morley was writing music as early as 1576, the date attached to a motet which already shows his borrowing proclivities.[24]

No doubt Alfonso's new prominence on the English madrigal scene fed in to the extensive program of anthologizing his motets and madrigals that we encounter in manuscripts of the early 1600s. Here the key figure must be Alfonso Ferrabosco Junior, whose career was just now getting under way. There is some evidence for this in two of the manuscripts in question, Christ Church 463–67 and Tenbury 1018. The former, which contains almost exclusively music by Alfonso Senior, has the name of Junior's brother-in-law written on it, Nicholas Lanier; and the latter, after being begun as a score collection of Alfonso Senior's music, was soon utilized instead for a great variety of songs and dances for masques, by Alfonso Junior and others. Junior is also represented by a unique set of songs in Italian.

We know that the younger Ferrabosco cultivated the elder's memory by composing motets much like his—and this at a time when even Byrd had retreated from such motets to the liturgical niceties of Mass components for undercover services in remote country manors. Young Alfonso's *Incipit Lamentatio* quotes music from one of his father's works of the same title.[25] No one would be more likely than the son to have access to the father's music, and no one more interested in seeing it circulate, in promoting it both as personal publicity and as a monument to London's foreign music community. At the beginning of his career, around 1600, the younger composer had everything to gain by cultivating the myth of his father. Thomas Campion understood this, perhaps; when he praised the son in a commendatory verse as

> *Musicks* maister, and the offspring
>   Of rich *Musicks* Father
> Old *Alfonso's* Image living,

I think he was saying exactly what he knew his subject wanted to hear.

# VI

And what, finally, will history's verdict be on Old Alfonso and his achievement in England? What did he contribute to that "musical balance between Southern and Northern countries" that is the object of our present inquiry? The answer will depend, of course, on the historian.

We must not forget that after sixteen years among the heretic, Alfonso returned to Italy. In the late 1570s things were getting hot for foreigners in England, and he had certainly been shaken by the murder charge. He may have grown weary of living a religious double life, currying favor with programmatic Protestants like Leicester and Sidney on the one hand, hearing Mass at the French ambassador's on the other. He may well have hoped to get back his inheritance, confiscated by the Inquisition. About all this we do not know. But we do know that while his second cousin Matthia could be appointed "Undter Capelmaister" at Graz, no such position was open to Alfonso in London. He had reached the modest pinnacle available to him as a member of the Queen's Musick and as a groom of her chamber. For positions in the Chapel Royal, the sign read "only English need apply." And as a courtier, there was obviously more of a future for him in Italy. All that hypothetical patronage from Leicester, Sussex, Arundel, and Heybourne probably did not add up to much. It must have been occasional at best.

A glance ahead in history reveals a radically changed patronage situation. After the death of Queen Elizabeth in 1603, there were multiple courts in England that required, among other things, music: in addition to the court of James I with its lavish masques, there were those of pleasure-loving Queen Anne of Denmark and brilliant Prince Henry.[26] Patronage of music by the nobility also increased significantly. Alfonso Ferrabosco Junior, Ben Jonson's collaborator in court masques, held successively the posts of music teacher to Prince Henry, teacher to Prince Charles, and Composer in Ordinary and then Composer of Music to Charles after he became king. Nicholas Lanier grew up in the service of the Earl of Salisbury, was appointed Master of Music to Prince Charles, and later Master of the King's Musick (a new title, first recorded in 1625). Lanier, also English-born though Huguenot in origin, became a courtier of note, traveling abroad to purchase Correggios, Raphaels, Titians, and Caravaggios for the royal collection.

Alfonso the father's music made an impression on many English composers, but on none was his effect as deep as on William Byrd. Alfonso taught Byrd a great deal about motet composition; for this reason the historian whose eye is on the great composers will always estimate Alfonso highly, regard him warmly. Yet we all know that in Byrd's lifetime the sixteenth-century motet was not only careening toward obsolescence all over Europe, in England it was literally superannuated. With services sung in the vernacular, there was less and less use for sacred music in Latin. Craig Monson has argued ingeniously that in the Chapel Royal Latin survived partly for political reasons, because Elizabeth liked to invite foreign dignitaries to her very high-church services and show them how much milder her brand of Protestantism was than they would have thought.[27] All the more rapid was Latin's decline after 1603. The Elizabethan madrigal, too, was a short-lived and retrospective phenomenon. Alfonso's madrigals were liked and imitated, but his influence on the native development was much less than that of more modern masters like Marenzio and Vecchi—and Ferretti and Gastoldi.

It was a later generation of Italian and Italianate musicians—Alfonso Junior, Lupo, and Coprario—who with Nicholas Lanier moved English music decisively ahead at the beginning of an historical era, rather than at the end of one. That these men were English-born is surely significant, as is the much expanded patronage in the new era. Alfonso Junior, Lanier, and Robert Johnson pioneered the declamatory song style that would develop through John Wilson, the Lawes brothers, and John Blow to Henry Purcell. Coprario, Lupo, Richard Deering, Orlando Gibbons, and John Ward pioneered the new fantasia for viols that would develop through John Jenkins, William Lawes, Simon Ives, and Matthew Locke to Purcell, once again.

From this broader historical standpoint, we would have to view Alfonso Ferrabosco more coolly. Perhaps it is not entirely facetious to say that from this standpoint his main historical achievement in England was that of fathering a son. Nevertheless, we have seen his music imitated as late as 1600 by the greatest composer of English song after Byrd, and by important pioneers of the emerging Jacobean fantasia. Back in the 1560s, Alfonso provided Byrd with models for In nomines, as Oliver Neighbour has shown, not only for motets.[28] Alfonso's quiet or not-so-quiet influence seems to turn up everywhere. This versatile and industrious, restless and devious musician from the South was a very considerable presence for at least three generations of Northern composers.

### Notes

1. Richard Charteris, *Alfonso Ferrabosco the Elder (1543–1588): A Thematic Catalogue of His Music with a Biographical Calendar* (New York, 1984), including a comprehensive bibliography. The reader is referred to this work for references to the great majority of data in this article. Footnotes give information only about items that are not in or traceable through Charteris.

2. For new information about the Ferraboscos in Europe, I am drawing on the research of Craig Monson, who has been good enough to send me copies of letters from and to Domenico and the Inquisition documents regarding Alfonso (see below).

3. "Possibly with his uncle Girolamo," according to *Grove;* I do not know any warrant for this statement.

4. See Lydia R. Hamessley, "The Reception of the Italian Madrigal in England . . . ca. 1580–1620" (Ph.D. diss., University of Minnesota, 1989), ch. 4, "Images of Italy in Elizabethan Society . . . ," following J. V. Lievsay, *The Elizabethan Image of Italy* (Ithaca, 1964).

5. On 29 December 1577 Alfonso wrote to Sussex that Leicester had tried to clear his name with the Queen; Leicester was evidently responding to a letter from Sidney of 16 December

asking him to intervene in the (unspecified) "cace of the poore stranger musicien" who "hathe allreddy so furr tasted of yowre Lordeshippes goodnes" (*Complete Works of Sir Philip Sidney,* ed. Albert Feuillerat [Cambridge, 1923], 3:133). And the murder charge does not seem to have stuck, for it is never heard of again, not even in the dozen or so letters about Alfonso written by Dandino, who reports everything evil he can about his subject.

6. Eleanor Rosenberg, *Leicester, Patron of Letters* (New York, 1955), *passim;* David C. Price, *Patrons and Musicians of the English Renaissance* (Cambridge, 1981), 167–69; and Thomas W. Baldwin, *The Organization and Personnel of the Shakespearean Company* (Princeton, 1927), 75–77.

7. The models have been found in a manuscript belonging to Queen Elizabeth: see Frank J. Fabbry, "Sidney's Verse Adaptations of Two Sixteenth-Century Italian Songs," *Renaissance Quarterly* 23 (1970): 237–55, and "Sidney's Poetry and Italian Song-Form," *English Literary Renaissance* 3 (1973): 232–48. See also the valuable article by Katherine Duncan-Jones, "'Melancholie Times': Musical Recollections of Sidney by William Byrd and Thomas Watson," in *The Well Enchanting Skill: Essays in Honour of F. W. Sternfeld,* ed. John Caldwell, Edward Olleson, and Susan Wollenberg (Oxford, 1990), 171–80.

8. On Scory see John Bossy, *Giordano Bruno and the Embassy Affair* (New Haven, 1991), 34.

9. See n. 2.

10. Like the well-known singer Robert Hales, perhaps, who is identified in the records of the Queen's Musick only as a lutenist. Woodfill, in a composite inventory of royal musicians in 1570, includes Alfonso without comment among the lutes: Walter L. Woodfill, *Musicians in English Society from Elizabeth to Charles I* (Princeton, 1953), 184.

The distinguished lutenist Nigel North assumes that Alfonso was *not* a lutenist, for two reasons: because so little lute music by him has survived, and because although this music "'falls' on the instrument reasonably well," it is not idiomatic. This seems unconvincing, especially since according to North most of the music does not give the impression of having been written for other media and then transcribed for lute. If there is a problem here, it would seem to be explaining why there is so much surviving lute music written by a non-lutenist, not why there is so little (*Alfonso Ferrabosco: Collected Works for Lute and Bandora,* ed. Nigel North [Oxford, 1974], viii).

11. "Virgo per incertos casus terraque marique / vecta diu tandem Britanna fui, / Anglia promisit fessae solatia vitae, / sed tamen his uti fata sinistra vetant." A mythological virgin who was driven over land and sea was Io; the straits that she swam were called *bosphorus,* ox-ford.

12. Among late sixteenth-century "mainstream" manuscripts, I count British Library Add. 32377 [contains four works by Alfonso], 30840 [none], 41566 [none], 22597 [none], Christ Church 984–88 [two], Oxford, Music School 423 [two], Royal College of Music 2041 [nine], Tenbury 389 (with associated partbook in private hands) [nineteen], and 341–44 [twenty-eight]. Only the last three, dating from around 1600, include substantial cells of Ferrabosco motets, a forecast of the single-minded anthologizing to come.

Of the retrospective Ferrabosco collections, the following contain almost exclusively his madrigals and motets: Christ Church 78–82, 463–67, British Library Madrigal Society G44–47 and 49, and Add. 31417. (463–67 was copied from 78–82, which is in the same hand as G44–47/9.) On Tenbury 1018, see text. The Filmer Manuscript (Yale, Filmer 1) and Tregian's Collection (British Library Egerton 3665 plus New York, Drexel 4302) are very large manuscripts which incorporate very large Ferrabosco holdings. (Filmer has been dated "1588–1603," in Robert Ford, "The Filmer Manuscripts: A Handlist," *Music Library Association Notes* 34 [1978]: 816, but it opens with a copy of the Lassus bicinia transmitting errors that were introduced in the London edition of 1598: "prudentiam" in motet no. 2, "vias" in no. 5, "rosae" in no. 11, and "Mariam" in no. 12.)

Oxford, Music School 45–50 combines the aspects of a late "mainstream" manuscript and a Ferrabosco anthology—its main contents are thirteen motets by Ferrabosco Senior, nine by Ferrabosco Junior, seventeen fancies by Lupo and Coprario, and seventeen Italian madrigals.

This analysis has been greatly facilitated by the Charteris catalog and the availability of British library holdings through the Harvester Microfilm Series.

13. "Music laeta suum tu gaudet habere patronum / O mihi precipuos inter habende viros; / Ad patriam redeo, te dulcis amice relinquo; / Patria vix ista conditione placet." This was an elegant semi-public response (in elegiacs) to Heybourne's public encomium (also in elegiacs); no doubt Heybourne saw to it that the piece circulated. Its date of composition would be 1578.

From the lines "Temporis Alphonsum nostri Phaenica creare / Carmina, quae Phoebus vendicet esse sua" in Heybourne's poem we also gather that he saw the masque of Apollo which Alfonso was involved with in 1572; see n. 18.

14. Joseph Kerman, *The Masses and Motets of William Byrd* (London, 1981), 31, 35–36, 101–6, 115–18, 122, 175.

15. Charles W. Warren, "Music at Nonesuch," *Musical Quarterly* 54 (1968): 48.

16. See John Milsom, "The Nonsuch Music Library," *Sundry Sorts of Music Books: Essays on The British Library Collections, Presented to O. W. Neighbour on His 70th Birthday,* ed. Chris Banks, Arthur Searle, and Malcolm Turner (London: British Library, 1993), 146–82.

17. British Library Royal MS 2. B. IX, where Arundel is referred to by Ubaldini as his Maecenas. Another, earlier sample of his illumination, Royal MS 17. A. XXIV, was a presentation to Lady Lumley. Ubaldini also included an epigram dedicated to Arundel in his illuminated codex *Cebetis Thebani tabula* (Venice, 1552), and dedicated to him *Totius Regni Scotia Nova et deligentia descripto* in 1576. See J. W. Bradley, *A Dictionary of Miniaturists, Illuminators . . .* (London, 1889), 3:330–31, and G. Pellegrini, *Un fiorentino alla corte d'Inghilterra nel Cinquecento: Petruccio Ubaldini* (Turin, 1967), 16–18, and plate opposite p. 46.

18. In 1572, both men performed supervisory functions of some sort in the elaborate masque of Apollo and the Nine Muses and much else put on by Leicester and Sussex to celebrate the Treaty of Blois; Alfonso is also mentioned as a participant. I think he played (sang) Apollo: in the extensive records, he is the only actor alluded to, in connection with his special costume, buskins made of cloth of gold, and also with the chariot made for Apollo. See Albert Feuillerat, *Documents Relating to the Office of the Revels in the Time of Queen Elizabeth* (Louvain, 1908), 159–60, 453.

Then in 1576, when Ubaldini put on an Italian comedy at court, he asked for Alfonso as an actor (as well as "Claudio Cavallerizo").

19. See Joseph Kerman, "The Elizabethan Motet: A Study of Texts for Music," *Renaissance Quarterly* 9 (1962): 302.

20. British Library, Royal Appendix 59–62; see Alfredo Obertello, "Villanelle e Madrigali inediti in Inghilterra," *Italian Studies* 3 (1947–48): 97–145.

21. British Library, Additional 34050. The traditional dating of this manuscript to "ca. 1604" is based on an erroneous publication date for two madrigals in the early part of it (nos. 16 and 23).

22. Joan Wess, "Musica Transalpina, Parody, and the Emerging Jacobean Viol Fantasia," *Chelys* 15 (1986): 3–25.

23. See Joseph Kerman, *The Elizabethan Madrigal: A Comparative Study* (Philadelphia, 1962), ch. 5, and *New Grove Dictionary of Music and Musicians*, s.v. "Madrigal," sec. 4.

24. Pointed out by Philip Brett in *New Grove Dictionary of Music and Musicians*, s.v. "Morley, Thomas."

25. Compare the settings of "Ierusalem convertere" in John Duffy, *The Songs and Motets of Alfonso Ferrabosco, the Younger (1575–1628)* (Ann Arbor, 1980), 411, and in *Alfonso Ferrabosco I: Complete Works*, ed. Richard Charteris (Stuttgart, 1984), 2:146–47 (and compare p. 134).

26. For much new information about Jacobean court patronage, see *Records of English Court Music*, vol. 4, *1603–1625*, ed. Andrew Ashbee (Snodland, Kent, 1991).

27. Craig Monson, "Elizabethan London," in *Man and Music: The Renaissance*, ed. Iain Fenlon (London, 1989), 304–10.

28. Oliver Neighbour, *The Consort and Keyboard Music of William Byrd*, The Music of William Byrd, vol. 3 (London, 1978), 43–46.

BEETHOVEN

# 10

# Tovey's Beethoven

The title of this essay does not refer to Tovey's *Beethoven,* the 136-page fragment published posthumously in 1945, but more generally to Tovey's view of the composer who stood at the center of his musical experience. Tovey must still be the most widely read music critic in English-speaking countries. His work has been attacked; it has also been bypassed and tacitly contradicted; but it has never lost its broad appeal. In respect to Beethoven and the other Classical composers, in fact, it is not too much to say that Tovey's writings remained unmatched until the appearance of *The Classical Style* by Charles Rosen in 1971. And this book—the most striking book on music we have seen in a long while—owes much to Tovey, who is the one writer on music mentioned in it at all frequently. Subjected to a modern critique, certain of Tovey's insights and attitudes assume new life in *The Classical Style:* which is a signal tribute to their continuing vitality.

Tovey was born a hundred years ago, in 1875. To understand the continuing vitality of his work, and to come to terms with Tovey's Beethoven, this work should be seen as a whole both as critical theory and as critical practice, and it should be seen in its historical perspective.

II ·    When Donald Francis Tovey's career as a pianist, composer, and writer on music was launched in London in 1900, he was at once identified as a conservative figure. "His total misapprehension of what is called the modern spirit in music is simply

Written on the hundredth anniversary of Tovey's birth for *The American Scholar* 45 (1975–76): 795–805. Also published in *Beethoven Studies 2,* ed. Alan Tyson (London: Oxford University Press, 1977), 172–91.

astonishing," snapped the critic of *The Manchester Guardian* in 1903.[1] From his childhood on, Tovey came under the spell of two remarkable musicians, both adherents of the musical conservative party, Brahmsians rather than Wagnerians. He never wavered in his allegiance to their ideals.

One of them was Sophie Weisse, who took the five-year-old Eton Latin master's son into her "Dame School" and insisted on making him into a musician. Twenty years later she launched her protegé in London, and she continued to control his affairs until he escaped to the Reid Professorship at Edinburgh in 1914. It is a sobering thought that if it had not been for this immeasurably strong-willed German woman, Tovey would have gone to Eton and, most probably, followed some non-musical calling. The other great influence was Joseph Joachim, a commanding figure in both German and English musical life of the time. Tovey likened his relationship to the older man to that of Tamino to Sarastro. Through him he acquired a vicarious link with the great German tradition by way of Mendelssohn, under whom Joachim had made his memorable English debut in 1844 playing the Beethoven concerto, and especially by way of Joachim's great friend, Brahms. Whatever complimentary words Tovey ever found to say about Wagner, in his bones he felt that the great tradition ended with Brahms. He can have been under no illusions that his own classicizing musical compositions—most of them written between 1900 and 1915—carried forward the great tradition in any relevant way. And he heard no fresh music after 1900 that flowed in his famous "main stream."

Tovey's celebrated *Encyclopaedia Britannica* articles of 1906–10 read like a defense of the old order, and for his inaugural lecture at Edinburgh he lectured on—the Classics. His biographer Mary Grierson says that a grand opus on musical aesthetics which he projected as an undergraduate at Oxford and worked on from 1898 to 1900 contained the seed of all his later writing. It is not clear whether she had actual evidence for this contention, or whether she was putting two and two together, but the idea certainly feels right. Some of his *Essays in Musical Analysis* go back to 1902 and the much-admired—though not by *The Manchester Guardian*—study of "The Classical Concerto" appeared in 1903. These early efforts do not differ appreciably from his latest work in their content or quality of mind. Past the very earliest ones (the essays from 1900 and 1901 are republished in *Chamber Music,* a supplement to the six volumes of *Essays*) they do not differ appreciably in style or tone.

In dealing with Tovey, then, we are dealing with a mind that was entirely formed—that was made up—in the nineteenth century. Simply in terms of modernity of thought, it is very striking to compare Tovey to some of his German contemporaries, men of no less genius who were committed no less firmly to the Classical tradition culminating in Brahms: men such as Schenker, Schnabel, and of course Schoenberg. That Tovey's work has been attacked, bypassed, and contradicted is therefore scarcely surprising. What is more surprising—what is, on the face of it, nothing short of astonishing—is the contemporary vigor of a body of criticism so thoroughly grounded in Victorian ideas, tastes, attitudes, and inhibitions.

The systematic book on musical aesthetics was never written. However, at the end of his career Tovey endeavored repeatedly, if not systematically, to put his basic ideas on music in order, starting with the Deneke Lecture at Lady Margaret Hall in 1934 ("I regurgitate here certain platitudes which, with no pretence of originality, I was already maintaining in the year of the Diamond Jubilee")[2] and continuing with the Romanes Lecture at Oxford, the Annual Lecture on Aspects of Art at the British Academy, the Cramb Lectures at Glasgow, and the Alsop Lectures at Liverpool. In one form or another these lectures were all published, and republished, but it cannot be said that they constitute the most fortunate segment of Tovey's corpus of writings. His genius did not extend to the logical conduct of an argument, any more than it contained in it the capacity for genuine development or change. Reading Tovey's lectures, indeed, with their bright dogmatic assertions, their non sequiturs, paradoxes, and elusive digressions, one cannot escape the impression that all is not quite as it seems, that on some level he was engaged in an involved process of papering over the cracks. We should not attempt to read these lectures to grasp the coherent aesthetic philosophy that Tovey never did succeed in formulating. Nevertheless, certain elements of this philosophy penetrate deeply into his criticism. The lectures do expose the issues that concerned him most centrally, issues that we shall find were not always fully resolved in his work.

A primary belief of Tovey's was that everything of aesthetic importance in music lies within the province of his famous "naive listener." This personage has no specifically musical training, only a willing ear and a ready sensibility. Tovey maintained he could teach anyone to appreciate the aesthetic qualities of double counterpoint at the twelfth; and although he reports that he once agonized over whether he could do the same for the refinements of Classical tonality, the doubts were eventually dispelled to his satisfaction. Did Tovey really think he meant all this literally, or was the naive listener an abstraction against which to test a typically Victorian conviction that art (like knowledge) must be democratically available to all? In any case, and despite its array of technicalities, Tovey's criticism is essentially non-professional in orientation—even populist, one might say, if not for the suspicion that the naive listener has at least a pass degree from Oxford University. Now Tovey himself had an extraordinary ear and could certainly apprehend things in music beyond the range of many professional listeners, let alone non-professionals. There can be little doubt that this populist critical dogma caused him to minimize parts of his musical experience, and that this led to some of the cracks in his aesthetic system.

Many of Tovey's other ideas can be seen to cluster around another central dogma. That artistic form and content are equivalent is not an unusual concept; what is unusual is the tenacity with which Tovey held it and the way it saturated his thought. "Material and form are true functions of one another": this and other such formulations no doubt owe something to the Oxford Neo-Hegelians, among them Edward Caird, who was Master of Balliol College when Tovey was studying the traditional curriculum of classics and philosophy there. (Grierson found out that he wrote a brilliant philosophy paper in his final examination; his third-class degree was a result of failing classics.) Formalism was the practical outcome of this idealism. For a fundamental corollary of the form-content equation is the idea that absolute music represents the art in its ideal state. When Tovey discovered "perfection of form" in fugues and sonatas, which he did frequently, he conceived that he had also discovered perfection of content—in sum, artistic perfection. From here it was only one step to his well-known Pantheon of masterpieces of instrumental music.

However, some accommodation had to be made in this formalist position for music associated with non-musical ideas—the central preoccupation of nineteenth-century musical aesthetics. Tovey believed that absolute music could nonetheless digest all kinds of other "contents" (an insight that he always attributed to A. C. Bradley's Inaugural Lecture as Professor of Poetry in 1901, "Poetry for Poetry's Sake"). Music with words and program music are not lower forms of art than absolute music, for the words and the programs are absorbed into the absolute music, and this maintains its own perfection according to its own formal principles. Tovey was also persuaded that every work of art takes its own unique form from its own material or musical content, however "strict" (and therefore seemingly predetermined) that form might appear on a superficial view. Much energy was spent on a recurring polemic against the "jelly-mold" theory of musical form. In a difficult passage, which grew no less difficult as he repeated it again and again in variation, Tovey discussed the F-sharp-minor setting of *Aus tiefer Noth* in the *Clavierübung,* part 3, of all Bach's compositions perhaps the strictest in form. Did the "consummate rhetoric" of this piece stem from the strict form, or did the strict form follow from the rhetoric? Tovey could see it just as well either way, and this assured him of the equivalence of artistic form and content.

In his Deneke Lecture he wrote:

> The line between the technical and the aesthetic is by no means easy to draw, and is often, even by musicians themselves, drawn far too high, so as to exclude as merely technicalities many things which are of purely aesthetic importance. . . . The process miscalled by Horace the concealment of art is the sublimation of technique into aesthetic results.[3]

Indeed this line is by no means easy to draw, and Tovey's greatest achievement came in drawing it so cleanly so many times, and in drawing it so low. "The sublimation of technique into aesthetic results" amounts to another formulation of the identity of form and content, of course, and this formulation makes a convenient framework within which to view Tovey's actual criticism.

III · What sorts of statements and judgments does Tovey actually make about music? As an example let us consider a short passage where he is making a limited point, such as his discussion of the transition passage preparing for the finale of Beethoven's Fifth Symphony. The preparation, Tovey says, is manifestly for something new, not for some sort of return of older material. This, perhaps, is an indication of the primary aesthetic effect of the passage, and he goes on to say how this is compounded of secondary aesthetic effects. The scherzo seems "finished, exhausted, played out"—because a main section which is "dark, mysterious, and, in part, fierce" has "suddenly collapsed," after which a trio "dies away" and the return of the scherzo is "one of the ghostliest things ever written." Next, in the one sentence of the whole excerpt which a well-disposed reader might hold up as an example of real musical analysis, Tovey describes the actual transition:

> The drum, as you will see, is upon the tonic note, but the bass hovers uneasily to and fro beneath it; and, finally, we have the paradox of the tonic in the drums, quasi-dominant harmonies above it, and the dominant below it, until only at the imminent approach of the crash the top-heavy harmony straightens itself out into a dominant seventh.[4]

Yet how, the less well-disposed reader might ask, does this technical account actually relate to the aesthetic "miracle"?

Implicit in Tovey's method, I believe, if not in his theory, is the admission that we cannot plumb the mystery of his "sublimation" process. There is a genius in the machine and Tovey makes no attempt to exorcise it. That is the mission of our modern "background" analysts and musical semiologists. What he does, in his most impressive passages, is describe the technical means and the aesthetic effect and invite the reader to contemplate, if not their logical or necessary connection, at all events their simultaneity and likely association. ("I have often been grateful to a dull description that faithfully guides me to the places where great artistic experiences await me," Tovey writes.)[5] Elsewhere there is a generous measure of elision in his method. He does not spell out in detail the technical correlatives of the collapse and the dying out (matters of rhythm and dynamics) or of the ghostliness (a matter of orchestration, articulation, dynamics, and compression of form).

As for that difficult matter, aesthetic quality—it seems to have caused Tovey little difficulty. He was always ready with affective adjectives, analogies, allusions, and similes from a broad range of life and literature. Musical aesthetics, as Tovey and his naive listener experienced them, share a common world with our sense of darkness, uneasiness, and crash. The ghostliness of the Fifth Symphony scherzo da capo has "something of the thin, bickering quality of the poor ghosts that Homer describes where Odysseus visits the Land of Shadows." It is customary to say that language of this kind applied to aesthetic discourse is being used metaphorically; but Tovey's use has a very literal ring. Such language, logical positivists have reminded us, is incorrigible, and Tovey himself warns against impressionistic criticism:

> We shall do well to beware of the exclusively subjective methods of criticism so much in vogue since the latter part of the nineteenth century; methods which may be but mildly caricatured as consisting in sitting in front of a work of art, feeling our pulses, and noting our symptoms before we have taken the slightest trouble to find out whether, as a matter of fact, the language of that art means what we think it means.[6]

For Tovey, of course, the operative qualification was expressed in the concluding before-clause. Having taken no slight trouble, and having learned the language perfectly, and having written about it at length, he seems to have felt entirely at liberty to record his incorrigible symptoms.

It may all be based on a ghastly philosophical fallacy. But it is worth seeing how this view of musical aesthetics goes hand in hand with Tovey's conviction that all of music—or at least, all that counts in music—is the property of the naive listener. As there is a continuity between musical experience and the experience of ordinary life, the naive listener can move easily into the world of music without abandoning his extramusical sensibilities. They provide him, in fact, with his only sure guide to the new terrain. Tovey's populist aesthetics may also go some way to explain his repeated claim in the late lectures that music can absorb all kinds of contents. He was saying that absolute music could absorb a text or a program and still maintain its perfection, but what he was saying under his breath, I think, was that musical aesthetics could absorb the feelings of ordinary life. To the extent that this is the way that the art of literature has traditionally been regarded, Tovey's musical aesthetics can of course be seen to take their model from literature. Which is hardly surprising, for if one part of his mind was formed by Brahms and Joachim, another part of it was formed by Balliol.

Under his breath: for he was always prepared to say out loud that music makes its own effects and that these cannot be paralleled in life and literature. Yet what are we to make of this characteristic passage, in which he discusses the return of the scherzo theme within the Fifth Symphony finale:

The nearest approach to its effect in history is, I venture to think, Kipling's action in publishing his *Recessional* the day after the Diamond Jubilee, though I am far from implying that Beethoven's intention in any pieces of music can be more than dimly illustrated by anything either in history or literature; but the motto 'Lest we forget' is an admirable summary of the effect which Beethoven produces when, at the end of his development, he is preparing quite formally on the dominant for a return to his main theme.[7]

If this is "far from implying," it is hard to know what frank implication would look like.

There is certainly a problem today with Tovey's easy equation of aesthetic and non-aesthetic values and qualities. There is also a problem with his technical analyses, as exemplified in a small way by the sentence cited above describing the Fifth Symphony transition passage. Since Tovey's basic plank as a critic was that aesthetic results are sublimated from technique, discussions of technique (that is, analysis) figured prominently in his program notes from the very start. This astonished the London concert audience of the 1900s—the 47-page essay on the "Goldberg" Variations must have come as a special shock—and alienated one segment of it. Perhaps today's concert audiences would react similarly. More professional readers, however, are likely to be alienated in another way, for by comparison with the full-dress analyses published by writers as diverse as Schenker, Lorenz, Edwin Evans, Sr., Hans Keller, and Allen Forte, Tovey's analyses can seem skimpy and superficial.

On the matter of skimpiness, first of all, it is no doubt unfortunate that Tovey entitled his most famous series of books *Essays in Musical Analysis*. Many of the program notes anthologized in these seven volumes can fairly be called "analytical" program notes in that they make some analytical points, often with great insight; but they do not carry forward analysis with any kind of rigor. (An exception is the "Précis of Beethoven's Ninth Symphony" in volume 1.) Tovey did in fact prepare more rigorous analyses, but these he directed to a different readership, to music students. His *Companion to Beethoven's Pianoforte Sonatas*, subtitled *Bar-to-Bar Analysis*, was issued by the Associated Board of the Royal Schools of Music along with Tovey's handsome annotated edition of the sonatas.

In the introduction to the *Companion* Tovey put first things first:

> The first condition for a correct analysis of any piece of music is that the composition must be regarded as a process in time. There is no such thing as a simultaneous musical *coup d'oeil;* not even though Mozart is believed to have said that he imagined his music in that way. Some students begin their analysis of a sonata by glancing through it to see 'where the Second Subject

comes' and where other less unfortunately named sections begin. This is evidently not the way to read a story.[8]

That music exists as a continuous flux of time may seem like a venerable truism, but Tovey's devotion to it, or restriction to it, makes his work as an analyst distinctive. He listened to music the way one reads a story or follows a drama, not the way one reads a map or reflects upon a lyric; one can never forget the particularity of time when reading Tovey, as one notoriously can with the work of some other analysts. Although he discussed tonality more persuasively than other elements of music, tonality for him was not something primary, but only one of several important means by which composers control the larger rhythm. Tovey can be described as a "foreground" analyst par excellence, an analyst of the rhythmic surface of music. On a detailed level, his best analytical insights in the *Companion* and elsewhere will be found to concern temporal processes such as phraseology, expectation and arrival, pacing, modulation, and—within limits—Schenker's "prolongation."

It is indeed the old-fashioned, no-nonsense view of music. Tovey himself remarked that his *Companion* analyses can serve "as an example of Sir Hubert Parry's method of musical précis-writing"—an exasperatingly Tory statement—but it is not so much Parry whose presence is felt in the *Companion* as Tovey's own naive listener. Victorian scruples prevented him from admitting a gap between amateurs and professionals; even when writing for the latter, or at least for students, as in the *Companion,* he always assumed that they experience music on its rhythmic surface. For that is where he considered that its aesthetic effects are made: effects which are democratically available to all irrespective of professional training, and which he assumed to be the central interest of all listeners, whether amateur or professional.

Modern musical analysis typically appeals to some sort of background or background level, as in Schenker, and is almost always directed to a strictly professional readership. Little sympathy is expressed for the surface view of music (or for the naive listener) in Hans Keller's sustained attack on Tovey, which takes as its text the article on "The Classical Concerto" with its partial analysis of Mozart's Piano Concerto in C, K. 503:

> Faultless descriptions are Tovey's speciality: his 'analyses' are misnomers, even though there are occasional flashes of profound analytical insight. Otherwise, there is much eminently professional tautology. I have no doubt that Tovey was a great musician. His writings are a symptom of a social tragedy, for they are both a function of the stupidity of his audiences, the musical *nouveaux riches,* and too much of a mere reaction against the unmusicality of his academic forebears. . . . 'The pianoforte enters', reports Tovey, 'at

first with scattered phrases. These quickly settle into a stream of florid melody. . . .' But why are they scattered? How are they scattered? Why are they scattered in the way they are scattered? What, in short, is the compositorial cause of these absolutely unprecedented, utterly 'new' triplets?[9]

Tovey did not look for "compositorial causes" in this sense. What concerned him was causality on another level, as we have seen: how does the music cause aesthetic effects? Rather than looking backward from the music he described to compositorial causes—a matter of primary interest to composers and other professionals, presumably—Tovey looked forward from the music to its aesthetic effect.

Neither causality, it may be remarked, can be demonstrated very well to unbelievers. With Tovey, for all the illuminating things he has to say about the technical makeup of music and about its effect, one has to take "the sublimation of technique into aesthetic results" pretty much on faith. Nevertheless, this is at the heart of his effort and the key to the individuality of his writing. Certainly his analysis is superficial in the literal sense that he deals with the foreground of music—and deals with it very well. But even if he had delved into backgrounds, too, that would not be the essential point. To object that he was insufficiently sensitive to thematic relationships, to phraseology on larger levels, to the force of register and tone color is also beside the main point. It is the constant link with musical effect that distinguishes Tovey's analytical method, not the details of the analysis itself.

IV ·     "It is as certain as anything in the history of art that there will never be a time when Beethoven's work does not occupy the central place in a sound musical mind."[10] Only a Victorian clergyman's son, perhaps, could have written with such confidence about eternity and soundness. But Tovey was writing accurately enough about the central place occupied by Beethoven in his own mind. Besides articles, lectures, and program notes, he undertook two larger works of criticism and analysis, and they are indeed both on Beethoven: the *Companion to Beethoven's Pianoforte Sonatas* and the posthumously published book on the composer. One of his most important articles, which we shall examine in a moment, concerns Beethoven, who also received the lion's share—nearly 250 pages—of the *Essays in Musical Analysis.*

This will not come as any surprise, for Tovey made up his mind about music at the very height of Beethoven's prestige, at a time when this composer occupied a central place in many or most people's musical universe. Joachim was the first honorary president of the Beethoven-Verein at Bonn. Mahler conducted a massed choir of Viennese workers and a brass band in the "Ode to Joy" to inaugurate the grandiose Beethoven shrine of Klimt and Klinger. Romain Rolland wrote *Jean-*

*Christophe*. And Schenker too published his most exhaustive studies on works by Beethoven: the Third, Fifth, and Ninth Symphonies, and the late piano sonatas.

Yet Schenker's work—or at least his essential contribution—is imaginable without Beethoven, in a way that Tovey's is not. One has the impression that Tovey's whole aesthetic grew out of his experience of Beethoven (which may even have been true in a very simple sense: the most vivid childhood impression that he relates was his first hearing of the Violin Concerto). Looking at the matter from the other side, it stands to reason that a critical method that concentrates on the articulation of time will work best with music whose large-scale rhythmic effects are emphatic and varied. Tovey explained cogently, on more than one occasion, the distinction between the "dramatic" style of sonata and symphony and the "architectural" style of concerto grosso and fugue. His own activity as a performer was centered on music in the sonata style, and his best critical energy was devoted to the composer whose music moves the most dramatically of all.

To Tovey, furthermore, and I think many naive listeners follow him here, Beethoven's music more than any other suggested links with life experience. Darkness, mystery, fierceness, ghostliness: Beethoven puts words like these into the critic's mouth in a way that Bach and even Haydn and Brahms do not. Beethoven also suggests psychological states of mind. It is striking that at the beginning of the Beethoven book, when Tovey announces that he will avoid "vulgar entanglements between the art and the artist's private or public life," he also goes out of his way to commend the influential little book by J. W. N. Sullivan, *Beethoven: His Spiritual Development,* first published in 1927. Sullivan explicitly traced Beethoven's music to his psyche. He was writing in reaction to the "pure music" view which was to reach its most distinguished formulation in the study by Walter Riezler, though also in reaction to the romantic sentimentality of such writers as Bekker; with infinite caution, Sullivan traced in one work after another the expressions of Beethoven's developing response to experience. It was this that must have impressed Tovey, though his own estimation of the composer's heroic inner life was expressed in rather different terms. We should not, I think, judge that this was a light matter for Tovey simply because he talked about it only sporadically: Beethoven was a great penitent, he had made up his mind about his responsibilities, and his duty was to preach and to edify. One gets an idea of what Tovey meant by the "soundness" of Beethoven, or of those musical minds in which Beethoven occupies a central place.

Significantly, perhaps, Sullivan distinguished between several kinds of music: music which "exists in isolation" and appeals only to our strictly musical perceptions, music which communicates spiritual states of mind, and music with an actual program. He offered no examples of music in his first category; Beethoven, of course, was his paradigm for the second. I have often wondered whether Tovey accepted this distinction as equivalent to his own distinction between "architectural" and "dramatic" styles of music. Though he wrote luminously and copiously about Bach, what he was able to say about him was of a different order from his discourse on Beethoven and the other composers in the sonata style. In reference to Bach, Tovey's musicological insights are sharpest and most frequent, but the impression he gives of the actual flux of time and of aesthetic particularity is much less specific. A statement such as the following, referring to the *Clavierübung* chorale preludes, would never have been made about Beethoven: "I do not advise the listener to expect more from the music than what would engage my own attention—that is, a flow of noble fugue texture dominated by the chorale tune."[11] Tovey always insisted that fugue was to be regarded as a texture, not a form. But he likened the aesthetics of the sonata fugue to that of the play-within-a-play, such as *The Murder of Gonzago* in *Hamlet*. Plays have form—dramatic form.

It is interesting, incidentally, to see the term "dramatic"—hardly a favorite of the Victorians—emerge as a criterion in Tovey. One does not get the impression that he was much of a theatergoer; most of his ideas about drama appear to have been derived from reading Shakespeare and the Greek tragedians. It seems surprising, even so, not that he considered Baroque opera to be "a limbo of vanity," but that he found so little to say about the operas of Mozart, or Verdi's *Falstaff*. Only one opera kept springing to his mind as he reflected upon music, Beethoven's *Fidelio*. He often used this to make the point that the overtures were of necessity more truly dramatic than the numbers actually involved with the action. But Tovey quite genuinely found the dramatic action of *Fidelio* edifying; it could engage his full sympathies in a way that the operas of Wagner, Handel, most of Verdi (and some of Mozart?) could not.

v ·    Tovey's busiest period as a writer was in 1927–31, when he issued his two "Companion" books and his annotated editions, revised his *Britannica* articles for the fourteenth edition, and wrote major essays on Gluck, Haydn, Beethoven, Schubert, and Brahms as well as heaven knows how many program notes. The major Beethoven piece, "Some Aspects of Beethoven's Art Forms,"[12] was written for a magazine issue commemorating the centennial of the composer's death in 1927. The occasion seems to have inspired Tovey to work through two of his chief critical preoccupations—one theoretical, one practical—more fully here than anywhere else in his writings.

The theoretical one was his belief that every true work of art takes its unique form from its own material, irrespective of its strictness or freedom according to the superficial (or "jelly-mold") view of musical form. Tovey set out to demonstrate the freedom (or "uniqueness") of one of Beethoven's strictest (or "most normal") compositions, the Sonata in B Flat, op. 22, and then the fundamental "normality" of his most "unique" work, the Quartet in C-Sharp Minor, op. 131.

Dealing with works in sonata style by Beethoven, rather than with chorale preludes by Bach, Tovey had much more refined critical tools at hand, and he deployed them at leisure. The result is as brilliant in realization as it is original in concept. We may not be quite persuaded that op. 131 approximates to "that Bach-like condition in which the place of every note can be deduced from the scheme," but we can never hear the piece again as in any sense "aberrant" in form. The freshness extracted from op. 22 ought to serve as an object lesson to jelly-molders of all ages. If this is formalist criticism, it is of a kind that finds more life in the work of art than does most people's impressionism.

The other, more practical preoccupation which Tovey aired thoroughly in the centennial article is his notorious skepticism about the "thematic process in music," as we have learned to call it from Rudolph Réti. Tovey insistently posed this as a polemical issue between himself and earlier, unnamed, but mainly German critics, and it has become a polemical issue again with post-Réti critics in England, such as Keller. His essential point was that musical form—which for him was equivalent to aesthetic content—does not depend on thematic relationships, even when these are unmistakable and overt. "Themes have no closer connexion with larger musical proportions than the colours of animals have with their skeletons." Therefore musical analysis built on thematic relationships which are less than unmistakable, on covert relationships, is as futile as literary analysis based on puns ("there is a B in both"). Music depends on tensions and arrivals, balances and resolutions, and these may or may not be reinforced by themes; in recapitulations, for example, the thematic return serves to reinforce the tonal return, which is primary, rather than the other way around. Tovey did not like to think that music existed in which various motives, themes, transitions, figurations, and cadences might all be indiscriminately related. For some critics, a texture permeated with thematic relationships is richly unified. For him, such a texture was otiose and directionless. This must have been one of the main grounds for his antipathy toward Wagner, and one of many things that repelled him in Schoenberg.

In the article at hand, Tovey carefully explains just how far he will go with Beethoven in the matter of "thematic process." When, in the first movement of the "Archduke" Trio, a remote passage of trills and scales is derived step by step from the main theme, Tovey accepts this as a lucid process articulating the development, itself a part of the larger articulation of time. In the finale of op. 131, a brief stretto answer to the "mournful theme" first heard in bars 22–29 becomes ultimately, in bars 291–92,

an emphatic and unmistakable allusion to the first four notes of the fugue. For reasons already discussed, I am generally sceptical about such long-distance resemblances, where the composer has no means of enforcing his point; for instance, I shall never believe that Beethoven intended the transition passage to B flat in the first movement of the Ninth Symphony to fore-shadow the choral finale which comes three-quarters of an hour afterwards. If he had meant anything by the resemblance, he could have made his meaning clear in the introduction to his finale, where he calls up the ghosts of the previous movements. But here, in the C sharp minor Quartet, he goes out of his way to accentuate his point; the point refers to the very beginning of the work, and not to some transitional passage heard only twice in its course; and not only is the point thus explicable but it has no other explanation. The other matter is the reappearance of the flat supertonic in a shuddering cadential passage that breaks in upon the height of the passion; having no connexion of theme with its surroundings, and requiring no such connexion.[13]

The themeless cadential passage which recalls other flat supertonic effects caused Tovey no problem, of course. But almost incredibly, he did not recognize a connection with the fugue subject the *first* time the "mournful theme" occurs, in bars 22–29. Nor did he recognize, in the Adagio of the Sonata in D Minor, op. 31 no. 2, a thematic connection between the ending six bars and any previous passage in the movement; "palmistry is not more debilitating to the mind" than efforts to trace such things. In *The Classical Style* Charles Rosen has only to quote the two passages in question to make the relationship—a relationship of harmonic progression and melodic contour—self-evident.[14] Rosen's analysis does not negate Tovey's point that the essence of the ending consists in its newness and its relative proportions. The ending is new and also not new, both at the same time, because the relationship is, exactly, a little obscure.

It seems clear that in this whole matter Tovey's ideology was getting in the way of his ear, that his remarkable musical sensibility was inhibited by deeply ingrained instincts hardened into aesthetic dogma. Perhaps he feared that he would not keep the naive listener with him if he taxed him with special subtleties. (But *themes* are what the *really* naive listener likes best of all.) One does not have to reject Tovey's scale of priorities, only the rigidity of his own rejection of thematic relationships. What basically disturbed him in situations such as that in the D-minor Sonata was, I am inclined to think, their ambiguity. He admired subtleties, but only subtleties which admitted of due resolution into the clear world of Victorian certainties; genuine ambiguities were not consonant with his image of Beethovenian soundness. Ambiguities disturbed him in the music of Romanticism, too, about which he was never entirely easy. His attitude toward Chopin, Schumann, and Mendelssohn was chivalrous rather than affectionate; Berlioz aroused in him feelings of exasperation, amusement, and contempt; and Liszt aroused something closer to fury. Toward Wagner his attitude was equivocal in the extreme. He was quite aware that throughout the nineteenth century, emphasis on thematic relationships—overt and covert—went along with a decay of the musical values established by the

Viennese Classical masters. It is as though for Tovey Beethoven was holding the line—the same line that Brahms, glumly, was still holding half a century later. That is another measure of Beethoven's centrality in Tovey's mind. It is not accidental that by far the greatest number of the attacks on thematic analysis which come up again and again in his writings come up in response to (or in defense of) music by Beethoven.

VI ·    So in his analysis of the *Eroica* Symphony Tovey definitely did *not* trace a derivation of the E-minor development theme from the opening theme, as Schenker, Riezler, Rosen, and others have done. The triadic figures in bars 24 and 109 are "new," too. But he writes unforgettably about a major crux in the movement, as he heard it—the reinterpretation of the C♯ in the opening theme as D♭ in the recapitulation, the ensuing brief modulation to F major with its quality of "strange exaltation," the "swing of the pendulum" to the balancing key of D flat, and the immense scope that these digressions confirm or maintain in a movement of already unimaginable range and power.[15] Do not matters of this sort, Tovey asked, mean more than thematic relationships, to naive *and* sophisticated listeners? The issue can be expressed, perhaps, as one between background unity and surface coherence. "Where are my favorite passages?", Schoenberg is said to have exclaimed on seeing a Schenker diagram of the *Eroica*. "Ah, there they are, in those tiny notes." But neither in the prose sections of Schenker's exhaustive monograph on the *Eroica*, nor in the notes in the diagrams, however tiny, is there to be found any reference whatsoever to those crucial modulations.[16]

Another very fine piece of criticism is the long essay on Beethoven's "Ninth Symphony in D Minor, Op. 125—Its Place in Musical Art."[17] This work touched Tovey very deeply, for at least two reasons. First, it was the decisive testing ground for his belief that absolute music could absorb non-musical contents; in this respect, what the Ninth Symphony meant to Tovey was just about the opposite of what it meant to Wagner. Second, this symphony expresses more emphatically than any other work those non-musical qualities of mind that Tovey admired in Beethoven. He never wrote better about basic musical movement than in reference to the introduction, development, and recapitulation of the first movement, and he wrote with uncanny sympathy for Beethoven's overriding philosophical idea, both in the "Ode to Joy" and in the symphony as a whole. On *Fidelio*, another work with strong non-musical content, he wrote most trenchantly in a very original essay on the *Leonore* Overtures nos. 2 and 3. Discussing them in tandem gave him an opportunity to analyze two works of art in which the same content grew into two different "unique" forms. This is a more than usually close and subtle study of the implications of musical proportions and the articulation of the flux of time. Incidentally, Tovey never paid any attention to arguments that the *Leonore* Overture no. 1 was in fact the first written—a theory still upheld by Joseph Schmidt-Görg, Director of the Bonn Beethovenhaus, in 1970 and only finally laid to rest by Alan Tyson, on documentary evidence, since that time.[18] Tovey accepted Nottebohm's date of 1807 because it fitted the stylistic evidence, as he saw it, and because it fitted his own theory of Beethoven's maturing understanding of the function of an opera overture. Since symphonic "drama" is more potent than drama on the stage, the action of *Leonore* was undercut by Beethoven's first two overtures; the simpler *Leonore* Overture no. 1 suited the opera better, and the blander *Fidelio* Overture of 1814 suited it best of all.

Some of Tovey's more penetrating critical lances were broken on behalf of certain Cinderellas and Ugly Ducklings: the Triple Concerto, the *Namensfeier* Overture, the Sonata in E Flat, op. 27 no. 1, and even the Fantasy, op. 77. As he remarked in the general introduction to the *Essays in Musical Analysis,* the writer of program notes necessarily assumes the stance of counsel for the defense. This attitude ran deeply in his criticism, in fact. Knocking music was not something Tovey enjoyed; what he felt he had to say about Liszt, Saint-Saëns, the "Interesting Historical Figures," and the moderns was said, usually, in hasty asides. But he was adept at selective statement, faint praise, and expressive silence, as well as more kittenish forms of veiled disapproval. He seldom criticized Beethoven as directly as in the famous essay on the C-minor Concerto, and one feels he did so there only because Beethoven's momentary miscalculation of concerto form (as Tovey explains it) was set right in the nick of time. As he himself said, he did not regard Beethoven as infallible, though probably it is only after getting to know Tovey's work well that one is actually ready to believe him.

It is a pity, perhaps, that the projected Beethoven book was not taken as an opportunity to discuss more thoroughly categories of music that Tovey did not ordinarily encounter when writing program notes. It is a thousand pities that Vincent d'Indy, and not Tovey, wrote the Beethoven article in Cobbett's *Cyclopaedic Survey of Chamber Music* (to which Tovey contributed the remarkable essays on Haydn and Brahms). But of course he was never that systematic, and the book remained a torso when drafted before 1910[19] and again when revised in 1936. Certain chapters were never executed beyond a few pages, and other, longer ones were left obviously unfinished. The most striking thing about the book, no doubt, is its very concept: a book on Beethoven which "covers" neither the life nor the works, but deals step by step with basic technical means and then with musical "art-forms." The plan was to start off with "The Three Dimensions of Music," rhythm, melody, and harmony; typically enough, the draft as left by the author included three chapters dealing broadly with tonality, two (of which one is only a sketch) on rhythm, and none at all on melody. Then, after two illuminating chapters on sonata form, the energy flags: six pages on "The Rondo and Other Sectional Forms," twelve on variations, and a one-page stab at fugue.

*Beethoven* contains analyses and insights not found elsewhere in Tovey's work, as well as familiar ones in new and always newly interesting reformulations, such as we encounter again and again throughout his writings. As a whole, however, the *Companion to Beethoven's Pianoforte Sonatas* is a more satisfactory book, despite an unaccustomed dryness brought about by the routine tabulation of analytical descriptions (Keller's "eminently professional tautology"). It is the one large study that Tovey really worked out systematically, and the rigorous format had a good side-effect in restraining his prose style—that brilliant, donnish, discursive, epigrammatic, self-indulgent prose style which is utterly winning and also, too often, plain confusing. No one would read Tovey if not for that prose, but it does not always hold to Beethovenian standards of normality and responsibility. Discipline is a welcome feature of the *Companion,* which has in any case its luminous pages as well as its dry ones.

VII ·  "Beethoven is a complete artist," Tovey wrote at the very start of his draft of the Beethoven book. "If the term is rightly understood, he is one of the completest that ever lived."[20] Like so many of the terms thrown at the reader with Tovey's aggressively commonsensical spin, this one is hard to field; but in some sense he himself was also one of the completest musicians who ever lived. Our latest musical dictionary calls him a "musical historian, pianist, composer and conductor,"[21] a list which is obviously only half as long as it should be: he was also a legendary teacher, a musical analyst, theorist, music critic, and aesthetician. (This last designation, like that of musical historian, would have surprised Tovey, but if used informally it seems perfectly just.) If the term "criticism" is taken as he himself took it, to denote a synoptic activity encompassing aesthetic judgment and technical analysis, it is as a critic that Tovey is now chiefly remembered. Not many musicians can still remember him as a performer, though no doubt the piano always remained his first love.

But one is struck, still, by the wholeness of his musical activity and experience. His endless stream of program notes grew directly out of his work as pianist and as conductor of the Reid Symphony Orchestra in Edinburgh; besides analytical and critical comments, they contain many astute practical remarks about performance. The composition of his opera *The Bride of Dionysus* helped him understand certain important points of musical aesthetics, as he never tired of pointing out. His occasional and occasionally brilliant musicological *aperçus* were arrived at in reference to music that he was performing and writing about in consequence. At this distance in time, what is most admirable in Tovey's writing is the steady interpenetration in it of aesthetic ideas, critical judgments, analytical descriptions, and (sometimes) historical insights. They are inseparable in Tovey's work because he wanted them so, because he had a fundamental commitment to wholeness.

This, surely, is the real basis for the continuing interest in Tovey's writing. We may admit that his aesthetic ideas do not hold together so very well, that his criticism is to an extent simplistic, and that his analysis has clear limitations. We must also forgo his closed world of Victorian certainties—his unswerving faith in the sensibilities of the naive listener, his vision of Classical music that is crystal-clear and without ambiguities, his circumscribed body of "perfect" works of art focused on the oeuvre of Beethoven. But there is a continuing need for a criticism that pays attention both to technique and to aesthetic results. We read Tovey because (one last quotation) "All's not false that's taught in public school"—and because basic education is a less secure business today than it was in his time. His emphasis on the rhythmic surface of music is not dated, either, and will never date. Tovey would have shut his mind to modern musical analysis, but it is a notable fact that some of the most promising strains of it are now dealing essentially with rhythm.

And with whatever old-fashioned or defective tools, Tovey fashioned a portrait of Beethoven that lives, as other portraits do not live, because it takes account of so many of the essential sides of that protean personality. The composer of the "Ode to Joy," the "Hammerklavier" fugue, op. 22, and op. 131 will not yield very far to a populist criticism that hesitates to broach difficult matters, to an impressionist criticism that evades technical analysis, or to a formalist criticism that disdains incorrigibilities. Tovey's grasp was, if not "complete," a great deal more complete than that of most critics. This is not to say that he was equally effective over the entire range of his art. Beethoven, as we have seen, brought out the best in him, and for richness, consistency, and completeness, Tovey's Beethoven stands out as the most impressive achievement, perhaps, yet produced by the art of music criticism.

## Notes

1. Mary Grierson, *Donald Francis Tovey: A Biography Based on Letters* (London, 1952), 108. Biographical information in this essay is taken from this source.
2. Donald Francis Tovey, *The Main Stream of Music and Other Essays* (New York, 1949), 160. [Tovey's commanding influence on my work will be obvious to any reader of this book. My first attempt to come to terms with him was a review of his posthumously collected writings, published in Britain as *Essays and Lectures on Music* and in America as *The Main Stream of Music and Other Essays*: "Counsel for the Defense," *Hudson Review* 3 (1950): 438–46.]
3. *Main Stream of Music*, 164–65. (Unless otherwise indicated, Tovey is the author of all works cited in this chapter's notes.)
4. *Beethoven* (London, 1944), 16–17.
5. *Main Stream*, 159.
6. Ibid., 373.
7. *Beethoven*, 17.

8.  *A Companion to Beethoven's Pianoforte Sonatas (Bar-to-Bar Analysis)* (London, 1931), 1.

9.  Hans Keller, "K. 503: The Unity of Contrasting Themes and Movements," *Music Review* 17 (1956): 49 and 54, reprinted in *Mozart: Piano Concerto in C Major, K. 503,* ed. Joseph Kerman (Norton Critical Scores; New York, 1970), 178 and 185.

10. *Encyclopaedia Britannica,* 11th ed., s.v. "Beethoven."

11. *Essays in Musical Analysis: Chamber Music* (London, 1944), 26.

12. "Some Aspects of Beethoven's Art Forms," in *Main Stream,* 271–97.

13. Ibid., 296.

14. Charles Rosen, *The Classical Style: Haydn, Mozart, Beethoven,* rev. ed. (New York, 1972), 38–39.

15. See *Essays in Musical Analysis,* vol. 1, *Symphonies* (London, 1935), 30–31; *Main Stream,* 153; and *Musical Articles from the Encyclopaedia Britannica* (London, 1944), 219–28.

16. Heinrich Schenker, "Beethovens dritte Sinfonie zum erstenmal in ihrem wahren Inhalt dargestellt," *Das Meisterwerk in der Musik* 3 (1930): 15–101. The Schoenberg story is told in Rosen, *The Classical Style,* 35.

17. *Essays in Musical Analysis,* vol. 2, *Symphonies (II), Variations, and Orchestral Polyphony* (London, 1935), 1–45.

18. See Alan Tyson, "The Problem of Beethoven's 'First' *Leonore* Overture," *Journal of the American Musicological Society* 28 (1975): 292–334.

19. See Grierson, *Donald Francis Tovey,* 117–18.

20. *Beethoven,* 1.

21. *Collins Music Encyclopedia* (London and Glasgow, 1959); [and by 1980 this had shrunk to "musical scholar, conductor and pianist" in *The New Grove Dictionary of Music and Musicians.* See "The Grove of Academe," *19th-Century Music* 5 (1981): 168–69.]

# An die ferne Geliebte

An afterthought by Anton Schindler tells us how Beethoven esteemed the poets of some of his songs. To the shadowy Count Haugwitz, author of the song "Resignation," Beethoven conveyed or sought to convey "his gratitude for giving him such a 'happy inspiration.' He had honored only a few poets in this way before: Matthisson for 'Adelaide,' Tiedge for 'An die Hoffnung,' and Jeitteles for his song cycle."[1] Beyond this, nothing is known of Beethoven's relations with Alois Isidor Jeitteles, the poet of *An die ferne Geliebte*. Jeitteles was a young Jewish medical student who achieved some prominence in Vienna around 1815 to 1820. "A brilliant youth," according to Thayer, he later became a noted physician in Brno, his home. His literary career was encouraged by Beethoven's friend Ignaz Castelli, who published several poems by Jeitteles—one of them thirty-two pages long—in his almanac *Selam* for 1815, 1816, and 1817, and collaborated with him in writing a highly successful parodistic play called *Der Schicksalsstrumpf* in 1818. In spite of statements that have sometimes been made to the contrary, it does not appear that the poems of *An die ferne Geliebte* were ever published apart from the music, so the composer must have obtained them from the poet. It is a natural inference that the two men were brought together by Castelli.

The literary text, never having been published separately, exists only in musical sources. The transcript below follows Beethoven's careful orthography in the autograph.[2]

From *Beethoven Studies,* ed. Alan Tyson (New York: Norton, 1973), 123–57.

An die entfernte Geliebte.
Sechs Lieder von
Aloys Jeitteles
in Musik gesezt
Von L. v. Beethowen

1.  Auf dem Hügel si[t]z ich spähend
    In das blaue Nebelland
    Nach den fernen Triften sehend,
    Wo ich dich Geliebte fand[.]

    Weit bin ich von dir geschieden,
    Trennend liegen Berg u. Thal
    Zwischen unß u. unserm Frieden,
    Unserm Glück u. unsrer Quaal.

    Ach den Blick kannst du nicht sehen,
    Der zu dir so glühend eilt,
    Und die Seufzer, sie verwehen
    In dem Raume, der unß theilt.

    Will denn nichts mehr zu dir dringen,
    Nichts der Liebe Bothe sejn?—
    Singen will ich Lieder singen,
    Die dir klagen meine Pein!

    Denn vor Liedesklang entweichet
    Jeder Raum u. jede Zeit,
    Und ein liebend Herz erreichet,
    Was ein Liebend Herz geweiht!

2.  Wo die Berge so blau
    Aus dem nebligen grau
    Schauen herein,
    Wo die Sonne verglüht,
    Wo die Wolke umzieht,
    Möchte ich sejn!

    Dort im ruhigen Thal
    Schweigen Schmerzen u. Quaal
    Wo im Gestein
    Still die Primel dort sinnt,
    Weht so leise der Wind,
    Möchte ich sejn!

    Hin zum sinnigen Wald
    Drängt mich Liebes Gewalt
    Innere Pein.
    Ach mich zög's nicht von hier,
    Könnt ich, Traute! bej dir
    Ewiglich sejn!

I sit on the hillside, peering out
into the blue land of mists,
toward the distant meadows
where, beloved, I found you.

Far from you am I parted,
mountain and valley stand
between us and our contentment,
our happiness and our pain.

Ah, you cannot see the look
that hastens so warmly toward you
and the sighs—they are blown away
in the space that separates us.

Will nothing, then, reach you now,
nothing be a messenger of love?
I will sing, sing songs
of lamenting that tell you my distress!

For at the sound of songs
all time and space recede,
and a loving heart will attain
what a loving heart has blessed!

Where the mountains so blue
look in
through the misty grey,
where the sunshine dims,
where the clouds gather—
could I only be there!

Down in the peaceful valley
sorrow and anguish are stilled;
where among the stones
the silent primrose broods,
the breeze wafts so softly—
could I only be there!

Away to the mindful wood
I am driven by love's force,
by inner pain.
Ah, I would not be drawn from here
could I only be, dearest,
with you for all time!

3. Leichte Segler in den Höhen,
Und du Bächlein klein u. schmal
Könnt mein Liebchen ihr erspähen,
Grüßt sie mir viel Tausendmal!

Seht ihr Wolken sie dann gehen
Sinnend in dem Stillen Thal,
Laßt mein Bild vor ihr entstehen
In dem Luftgen Hiṁelssaal.

Wird sie an den Büschen stehen,
Die nun Herbstlich falb u. kahl
Klagt ihr wie mir ist geschehen
Klagt ihr, Vöglein! meine Quaal.

Stille Weste bringt im Wehen
Hin zu meiner Herzenswahl
Meine seufzer, die vergehen
Wie der Sonne le[t]zter Strahl.

Flüstr' ihr zu mein Liebesflehen
Laß sie Bächlein klein u. schmal,
treu in deinen Wogen sehen
Meine Thränen ohne Zahl[.]

4. Diese Wolken in den Höhen,
Dieser Vöglein muntrer Zug
Werden dich, o Huldin! sehen—
"Nehmt mich mit im leichten Flug!"

Diese Weste werden spielen
Scherzend dir um Wang und Brust
In den seidnen Locken wühlen—
"Theilt ich mit euch diese Lust!"

Hin zu dir von jenen Hügeln
Aemsig dieses Bächlein eilt
Wird ihr Bild sich in dir spiegeln—
"Fließ zurück dann unverweilt!"

5. Es kehret der Majen, es blühet
   die Au
Die Lüfte sie wehen so milde, so lau,
Geschwätzig die Bäche nun rinnen;
Die schwalbe die kehret zum
   wirthlichen Dach,
Sie baut sich so Aemsig ihr bräutlich
   Gemach,
Die Liebe soll wohnen da Drinnen.

Light-scudding clouds on high,
and you, little winding brook,
if you can spy my love
greet her for me a thousand times!

If then you see her, clouds, walking
lost in thought, in the quiet valley,
make my likeness appear to her
in the lofty hall of heaven.

Should she stand by the bushes—
autumn-yellow now, and bare—
tell her, lamenting!, how I am,
tell her, little birds, of my anguish.

Quiet westwinds, gently blow
to my sweetheart
these sighs of mine, which fade
like the sun's last rays.

Whisper to her my entreaties,
little winding brook, and let her
clearly see in your ripples
my numberless tears.

These clouds on high,
this gay flock of little birds
will see you, fair goddess:
Take me along on your gentle flight!

These westwinds will play
and jostle you on cheek and breast,
ruffling your silken curls:
Let me share that joy with you!

Hurrying to you from those hills
comes this busy little brook:
if her image is mirrored in you,
Flow back to me forthwith!

May returns, the meadow blooms,
the breezes blow so gentle and mild,
the brooks run chattering.
The swallow who returns to the friendly roof
so busily builds herself her bridal chamber;
love will dwell within it.

Sie bringt sich geschäftig von Kreuz
u. von queer
Manch weicheres Stück zu dem
Brautbett hieher,
Manch wärmendes Stück für die
Kleinen.
Nun wohnen die Gatten bejsammen
so treu,
Was winter geschieden verband nun
der Maj,
Was liebet das weiß er zu einen.

From here and there she nimbly brings herself
many soft bits for the bridal bed,
many warm bits for the little ones.
Now the pair live faithfully together;
what winter parted, May now conjoins:
he can unite all who love.

Es kehret der Majen, es blühet die Au,
Die Lüfte sie wehen so milde so lau,
Nur ich kann nicht ziehen von
Hinnen;
Wenn alles was liebet der Frühling
vereint,
Nur unserer Liebe Kein Frühling
erscheint,
Und Thränen sind all ihr Gewinnen.

May returns, the meadow blooms,
the breezes blow so gentle and mild—
I alone cannot stir from this place.
When spring is uniting all those who love,
for our love alone no spring comes about,
and tears are its only earnings.

6.  Nim[m] sie hin denn diese Lieder
Die ich dir, Geliebte sang,
Singe sie dann Abends wieder
Zu der Laute süßem Klang.

Accept them, then, these songs
that I sang for you, beloved;
sing them again at twilight
to the lute's sweet sound.

Wenn das Dämmrungsroth dann
ziehet
Nach dem Stillen blauen See,
Und sein le[t]zter strahl verglühet
Hinter jener Bergeshöh;

When evening's red glow is drawn
toward the still blue of the lake,
and its last beam fades
behind that mountain peak,

Und du singst was ich gesungen
Was mir aus der vollen Brust
Ohne Kun[st]gepräng erklungen
Nur der sehnsucht sich bewußt:

And you sing what I sang,
from a full heart,
sounding without the adornments of art,
conscious only of love's longing:

Dann vor diesen Liedern weichet,
Was geschieden unß so weit,
Und ein liebend Herz erreichet
Was ein Liebend Herz geweiht!

Then, thanks to these songs,
what so far parts us will recede,
and a loving heart will attain
what a loving heart has blessed!

The last stanza of song no. 1, which is so similar to the last stanza of no. 6, was almost certainly an addition by the composer. Beethoven is known to have tampered with his original literary material in other cases,[3] and there are several reasons for thinking that he did so here. A fifth stanza in no. 1 breaks the rigid symmetry established by Jeitteles in the stanza count and general layout of the poems (see

**TABLE I**     Prosody of *An die ferne Geliebte:* Synopsis

| Song no. | 1 | 2 | 3 | 4 | 5 | 6 |
|---|---|---|---|---|---|---|
| Number of Stanzas | 4(+1) | 3 | 5 ⎰⎱ 3 (8) | | 3 | 4 |
| Meter | trochaic | anapestic | trochaic | | anapestic | trochaic |
| Number of Lines Per Stanza | 4 | 6 | 4 | | 6 | 4 |

table 1): the first, middle, and last poems contain four, eight, and four stanzas of four trochaic lines each,[4] and the intervening poems contain three stanzas of six anapestic lines. This symmetry appears if we treat nos. 3 and 4 as a unit—as Beethoven did by setting them to music both in the same key; and indeed, although in its poetic content no. 4 moves in a somewhat new direction, it shares verse structure, imagery, and even an interlocking rhyme with no. 3. It is even possible that Jeitteles wrote this pair of poems as a single entity and Beethoven split it at a logical point because eight stanzas were too many for a strophic setting. Ludwig Nohl actually printed the two poems as a single number as though he were following some independent text, but without offering a word of explanation.[5]

Apart from the question of symmetry, the fifth stanza in song no. 1 has a false sound. Jeitteles was quite sensitive to half rhymes, arranging them systematically between all the stanzas of the early songs; he placed them *within* stanzas only at the end of the final song, presumably as a means of achieving climax.[6] In song no. 1 he would not have wanted the surfeit of *ei* sounds produced by the rhymes *entweichet/erreichet* and *Zeit/geweiht* (stanza V) right after *eilt/teilt* (stanza III) and *sein/Pein* (stanza IV). Moreover, if the cycle is read closely, I think it will appear that the thought introduced in this stanza belongs logically in song no. 6, not in song no. 1.

In no. 1, read as a four-stanza poem, the poet sets the stage: separated from his beloved, the lover will sing songs to tell her of his pain. Then in the set songs that follow, an obvious sense of continuity is established by images carried over systematically from one to the next. The "Berg" and "Thal" of no. 1 carry over into no. 2, and the "Wolke" and "Wind" of no. 2 turn into three of the five insistent images of no. 3 (one per stanza) and no. 4: "Wolken," "Segler," "Weste," "Vöglein," and "Bächlein." These are still present in no. 5, where the "Weste" reappears as "Lüfte," the "Bächlein" as "Bäche," the "Büschen" as "Au," and—most startlingly—the "Vöglein" as a "Schwalbe" with a complete family. Besides continuity, there is a crescendo in feeling and fantasy-making as the songs proceed. First the lover dwells nostalgically (but realistically) on the spaces separating him from his beloved, spaces filled by mountain, valley, and wood (no. 2). Next he begins to dream of agents that will bridge space for him. In no. 3, these agents are to convey to the beloved *his* greetings, *his* image, *his* sorrows, sighs, and numberless tears; in the markedly warmer no. 4, he wishes to be taken to *her* (by the bird), to fondle *her* (with the wind), and to see *her* image (in the brook).[7] Fantasy runs riot in the picture of the Biedermeier love nest, no. 5, with its heady anapestic meter. The relentless way in which Jeitteles pursues his images repels, but perhaps he earns a few points by contriving to combine the sense of continuity with crescendo throughout the cycle of poems. He achieves a fairly genuine effect of spontaneous emotional outpouring.

Number 5 is a lyric of a standard category, in which the lover's distress is placed in sharp relief against the general burgeoning of springtime. One famous prototype familiar to musicians is Petrarch's "Zefiro torna"; the pathetic turning point "Ma per me, lasso" becomes "Nur ich kann nicht ziehen von hinnen," the fantasy collapses with a bump, and the lover returns to the realization that only songs can bridge space on his behalf, not birds or brooks. And no. 6—a poem of the "Gitene canzonette" category—introduces a new thought. The songs are now sung not to convey the lover's pain but in order to be sung back by the beloved; the "logical" conclusion is drawn in the final stanza—separation will be eased by songs experienced in common. This small fresh insight has emerged from the modest drama of fantasy and sublimation played out in nos. 2 to 6. By adding a near-duplicate of this climactic stanza to song no. 1, Beethoven achieved an obvious tightening of the "cyclic" effect: a stanza sung at the beginning is sung again at the end to the same music. But he lost something in the way of a logical unfolding of ideas.

Jeitteles also devoted considerable care to the modulation of spatial and temporal imagery in the cycle. The first two poems concentrate on the space between the lovers and the next two on agents that bridge space. However, nos. 3 and 4 also include some temporal images ("den Büschen . . . Die nun herbstlich falb und kahl . . . Wie der Sonne letzter Strahl"), and such imagery dominates nos. 5 and 6. Number 5 is about May, winter, and spring, and in no. 6 the singing of songs takes place at evening, "Abends":

> Wenn das Dämm'rungsrot dann ziehet
> Nach dem stillen blauen See,
> Und sein letzter Strahl verglühet
> Hinter jenen Bergeshöh' . . .

This rather surprising emphasis on evening imagery, consuming an entire stanza—a stanza set by Beethoven in a rather surprising way, too—is to be explained as the climax of a tendency gradually increasing through the six poems. There is only one clearly spatial image left in the whole of no. 6, "Bergeshöh'."

It is easy to get impatient with the young man on the hill. If his beloved is really within "spying" distance, or close to it, he might well set about crossing the intervening landscape rather than making up mawkish songs. We can perhaps take the cycle a little more seriously if we are prepared to regard space-distance as a metaphor, gradually clarified by the poet, for time-distance. The poet is celebrating a past love affair. And this would accord better with Beethoven's own situation in April 1816, when the cycle was composed. To Beethoven, if I am right, we owe the one line that frankly brings together space and time:

Denn vor Liedesklang entweichet
Jeder Raum und jede Zeit . . .

This brings us to the delicate question of Beethoven's own identification with the lover of Jeitteles's poems, and the identification of "The Distant Beloved" with "The Immortal Beloved" or some other one of his actual amours.

II ·
The figure of a Distant Beloved, adored from afar, is not exactly rare in lyric poetry. Still, it turns up in what would appear to be more than a statistically fair share of Beethoven's song poems.[8] In broad terms, this may be seen as reflecting the quality of Beethoven's actual relationships with women all through his life—or at least, what little he has allowed us to piece together about those relationships. The construction by Editha and Richard Sterba in *Beethoven and His Nephew* has influenced most recent biographers in their treatment of this matter. Martin Cooper writes:

> [Beethoven's] attitude to women was always ambiguous, as is shown by the conflicting accounts of his contemporaries and his known abortive relationships with a series of generally aristocratic girls. . . . The attraction that he felt towards his aristocratic pupils—among the most famous Therese von Brunsvik, Josephine von Deym, and Giulietta Guicciardi—often seems to have thrived in proportion as it was unrealisable in fact and the letters to the Immortal Beloved, even if they were ever sent and were not simply a literary effusion, show him retreating behind vague excuses and finding reasons in advance why his passion could never be consummated.[9]

Beethoven was attracted to many women, but so far as we know he withdrew from a full commitment to any of them. He either chose his women at a safe distance or, when necessary, placed them there.

Other features of the poems would have invited identification on Beethoven's part. The aptness of the lover who makes songs, in nos. 1 and 6, is obvious. The domestic bliss recorded in no. 5 corresponds to a nostalgic wish that he often voiced.

Indeed, it is hard not to go one step further and surmise that *An die ferne Geliebte* refers to a specific woman. Even Thayer remarked that the piece was composed shortly before Beethoven wrote to Ries, "I found only one, whom I shall doubtless never possess" (8 May 1816), and not long before he told Giannatasio del Rio that he had been in love, hopelessly, for five years.[10] No one can hear the songs "adequately sung," added Thayer in a rare burst of innuendo, "without feeling that there is something more in that music than the mere inspiration of poetry." The conversation with Giannatasio is reported by his daughter Fanny, in her diary entry for 16 September 1816:

> My father asked him if he did not know anyone, etc. I listened with the
> utmost attention, at some distance, and learned something which threw my
> inmost soul into turmoil, which confirmed a long foreboding—he was un-
> happy in love! Five years ago he had become acquainted with a lady, a more
> intimate union with whom he would have considered the greatest happiness
> of his life. It was not to be thought of, almost impossible, a chimera. Never-
> theless, it is now as on the first day. I have still not been able to get it out of
> my mind, were the words which affected me so painfully.[11]

The phrase "five years ago" rings a bell for anyone who knows of the letter to "The Immortal Beloved" of July 1812. Fanny did not, of course. Thayer misdated it. But now that the 1812 dating is accepted, most biographers conclude that the letter and the song cycle were addressed to the same lady.

There is something else striking about the conversation reported by Fanny. Beethoven says that he cannot get the five-year-old affair out of his mind ("noch nicht aus dem Gemüth bringen können"), but the signs are that he was trying to accomplish exactly that. Always a poor judge of his own feelings and motives, Beethoven tells Giannatasio "it is now as on the first day" and he may very well have thought so; but from his actions of the time I think we can infer otherwise. For the first time in five years (so far as we know) he now begins to talk about his secret love, to a relative stranger such as Giannatasio. He drops hints about it to the Giannatasio girls in another conversation recorded in Fanny's diary.[12] He writes about it, albeit cryptically, in a letter to Ries. He composes songs about it which will be dedicated to Prince Lobkowitz, sold to Steiner, and broadcast to the world at large. We also know that a decisive new turn was taking place in Beethoven's emotional life at exactly this period. As was clear to sensitive observers of the time—such as Fanny[13]—his affections were converging intensely on his nephew

Karl, whose guardianship he had assumed a few months earlier, following the death of his brother in November 1815.

Music had often provided Beethoven with a field for the working out of emotional conflicts. A brief but impressive article by Alan Tyson has traced this mechanism in reference to the crisis memorialized by the "Heiligenstadt Testament."[14] It seems probable that something of the same kind was happening now in reference to a crisis of another kind, recorded by another famous document, the letter to "The Immortal Beloved." By bringing his feelings into the open, Beethoven was renouncing or abandoning them. Projecting himself into Jeitteles's poems, he was saying that love was removed from him in time as much as in space: distant from him, and also well behind him.

If we read *An die ferne Geliebte* in this way, it may throw more light on Beethoven's inner life than if we join the hunt for the particular lady to whom it was secretly (and hypothetically) dedicated. Possibly it served as a literal love offering; more probably it served as a nostalgic hymn to past love in general. On the other hand, I believe that in another respect a literal reading can be more illuminating than a general one. Beethoven, through Jeitteles's lover, seems to be saying that only through art could he achieve loving communication; the beloved is unreachable except through songs. There is therefore some justification for regarding the cycle as an act of renewed dedication to music, to the artist's mission in general.[15] But we would also do well to recall what, quite literally, Beethoven and his time understood by "Lieder / . . . aus den vollen Brust / Ohne Kunstgepräng' erklungen, / Nur der Sehnsucht sich bewusst." The renewed dedication to art turns out to be a dedication to a new artistic ideal—new, and not altogether expected.

III ·     Our term "art song" is miserably confusing as far as the modern German song in its early years is concerned.[16] The lied grew up in reaction to the "art music" of Italian opera, cantata, and canzonet, and also in reaction to the artifices of mid-eighteenth-century poetry. Simple, direct verses were to be kept in balance with simple, direct melodies. Goethe, in his review of *Des Knaben Wunderhorn,* conceived of no distinction between a Volkslied and a newly composed song:

> But best of all, may this volume rest upon the piano of the musical amateur
> or the professional, so that the songs contained within it may either be done
> justice to by means of familiar traditional melodies, or may be matched to
> their individual proper tunes, or—God willing—may elicit notable new
> melodies.[17]

As for Goethe's own activity as a lyricist, Frederick Sternfeld has put his finger on one of its most significant aspects by showing how frequently the lyrics were "parodies," written out of enthusiasm for some simple melody that the poet heard and felt impelled to provide with verses of his own.[18] A man who writes poetry from this standpoint will have little patience with complex musical settings; Goethe's well-known championship of strophic as against through-composed songs stemmed inevitably from his devotion to the *Volksweise* ideal. In this he was seconded by his "house composers" Johann Reichardt and Carl Friedrich Zelter. By his emphatic support of this ideal, Goethe lent it prestige at the very time it was being questioned by a new generation of composers, and by writing his own superb lyrics with this ideal firmly in mind, he raised it to a level of artistic dignity that they could not easily brush aside.

Beethoven seems to have been caught between an innate allegiance to *Kunstgepränge* on the one hand and a growing sensitivity to the attractions of *Volksweise* and strophic setting on the other. In the best songs of his early years, he tried to inject musical complication of the same order as that of his instrumental music. "Adelaide" has something like a whole tiny sonata squeezed into its four Sapphic stanzas; "Neue Liebe, neues Leben" and "Mailied" employ aria forms; the Gellert "Busslied" does much violence to the stanza structure before changing mode, tempo, and style halfway through. But in the eight years prior to the composition of his song cycle Beethoven had repeatedly been brought face to face with the contrary aesthetic of song composition. He had been setting many Goethe poems, including "Sehnsucht" (Nur wer die Sehnsucht kennt) four times, in a spirit of experiment. He had associated with people close to the great man, and in 1812 had actually met him. Goethe the poet he admired unequivocally—we have no reason to doubt his statements to this effect—and somewhat more equivocally, he admired Goethe the man: a dominating, revered figure in the world of letters such as Beethoven wished to become (and soon did become) in the world of music.[19] Furthermore, in the years in question Beethoven was spending a lot of time on George Thomson's behalf making folk song arrangements. A folk song melody is written out on one of the sketch pages for *An die ferne Geliebte*.[20] A few months later he composed "Ruf vom Berge," WoO 147, modeled on a folk song.

Beethoven's ambivalence on the question of simple or complex song setting appears in his two versions of Tiedge's "An die Hoffnung," works that he put considerable store by even though they are never sung today. Opus 32 (1805) is strophic, with three stanzas sung to a single carefully fashioned melody. Opus 94 (1813?) is through-composed, with five new lines of recitative proceeding to an intense, highly inflected, furiously modulating treatment of the same three stanzas. The only way Beethoven could get the piece on an even keel was to make a literal da capo of stanza I, words and music, at the end. This action, and the resulting musical form, both have their parallels in *An die ferne Geliebte*.

What Beethoven saw about the Jeitteles poems was that they gave him the opportunity to have his cake and eat it too. The issue of musical complication, which in "Adelaide" and the second "An die Hoffnung" had been worked out on the level of the relationship among stanzas, could be shifted onto a higher level, the level of the relationship among the six songs. The individual songs could be treated very simply while a plan of some subtlety and power was put into operation for the cycle as a whole. Perhaps Beethoven also realized that this was a "special" solution of the problem of strophic versus through-composing, a solution that was not likely to bear issue. Still, those were lean years, and he was interested enough to try the notion out. Work went swiftly, to judge from the sketches.

Schlesinger in Berlin and the Bureau des Arts et d'Industrie in Vienna published Zelter's songs in four volumes between 1810 and 1816. Did Beethoven have the idea of beating Zelter at his own, or rather Goethe's, game? It is possible, though if this had been a major incentive he would presumably have used poems by Goethe, not Jeitteles. However this may be, *An die ferne Geliebte* really ought to have mollified the old poet, for many aspects of the piece seem tailor-made to validate his own theories of song writing. The melodies are simple, direct, *volkstümlich*. The piano accompaniment is held down to a most unobtrusive role; the figuration becomes only slightly agitated to reflect increasing agitation in successive strophic stanzas, as Goethe allowed and, indeed, encouraged. Beethoven marked numerous ritardandos, fermate, and the like in order to bend the melodies to match successive stanzas, just as Goethe had recommended to the singer Eduard Genast in their famous session on the song "Jägers Abendlied" in 1814. Changing mode for certain lines or stanzas—as in songs nos. 2, 3, and 5—was also a resource that Goethe and Zelter admitted.[21] Singing a stanza on a monotone while the piano plays the tune, as happens in Beethoven's no. 2, was an admired (and imitated) feature of Reichardt's "Erlkönig."[22] "Erlkönig" was probably Beethoven's model, in fact, for his own song.

Technical matters apart, what was central for listeners of the time was the elusive folklike quality of the tunes. And this was not something they would have expected to find in the latest new Beethoven opus. Power, complexity, overwhelming feats of construction and development, motivic unity, high drama—these, rather than artless strains, were qualities associated then (as now) with the composer of the *Eroica* Symphony. His contemporaries can be forgiven, too, if they viewed the turn toward simplicity in the song cycle as a sport in the composer's output. He did not continue writing such songs, and the great sensation of the next opuses—opp. 101, 102, and 106—was a turn toward fugue of a particularly gritty kind. Today we can hear in the music of Beethoven's late period not only new complexities but also a new and determined effort toward simple, direct expression. I have spoken of this tendency elsewhere[23] and shall return to it briefly later in this essay. Beethoven's dedication to songs "without the adornment of Art" had lasting consequences for his artistic development in his last decade.

In 1823 Marianne von Willemer seems to have sent Goethe a copy of *An die ferne Geliebte:*

> Ask someone with a beautiful, gentle voice to sing you Beethoven's song to
> *die Entfernte;* the music seems to me unexcelled, comparable only with that
> to *Egmont,* and the words correspond very well to a loving, youthful-feeling
> spirit; however, it must be sung simply and calmly and must be played very
> well. How I should like to know that it has given you pleasure, and what
> you think of it.[24]

Goethe was, of course, at least as equivocal in his attitude toward Beethoven as the
other way around. His admiration for the *Egmont* music is well known (to Marianne
as well as to us), and so is his sharp objection to the setting of "Kennst du das Land"
in op. 75. In the present instance the old poet found it expedient to fall back on
silence, as was not infrequently his way. He would not have agreed about the
Jeitteles poems, and the operatic ending of the cycle was just the sort of thing he
had always disliked about Beethoven's songs. As Frau von Willemer must have
seen, *An die ferne Geliebte* represents a large step toward Goethe, whether or not
this entered at all into Beethoven's calculations. Goethe, one suspects, was not
really disposed to meet him halfway.

IV · Both content and form of Jeitteles's cycle of poems would have interested Beethoven, then: the subject matter, with its yearning for a distant love blending into
nostalgia for past love, and the poetic structure consisting of six separate but closely
linked lyrics. On the level of structure, it was very likely the hint of "cyclic"
form—the plain invitation in poem no. 6 to make a da capo of song no. 1—that
started him thinking. This was the thread around which the large-scale musical
form of the song cycle would rapidly crystallize. It is not surprising that Beethoven's idea of how to handle this da capo can be seen to have been refined through
several stages in the process of composition.

The sketches for *An die ferne Geliebte* known today are the same as those described
by Nottebohm.[25] An isolated early sheet is bound into a sketch miscellany at the
British Library, Add. MS 29997, fol. 9. Written in pencil, doubly folded, and
scribbled with street addresses, this was one of those casual sheets that Beethoven
carried around on his walks. Then there is a compact set of six pages in what is
now the "Scheide" sketchbook at Princeton, pages 68–73. Here, sketches cover
the essential work on the first five songs. Two sketches also appear in the autograph, which has been published in facsimile.[26] They are found on the last (back)
page, page 28, and refer to the concluding piano passage of the cycle on page 27.

In the sketchbook, as Nottebohm did not fail to point out, the tune we now know for song no. 6 is entirely absent while stanza I of poem no. 6 appears with the tune of no. 1.[27] So evidently the original plan for the last song was to bring back the old tune for all four stanzas. At some later point Beethoven decided to restrict the da capo to the final stanza only, stanza IV. To begin the song he wrote a new tune which recalls the original one in a rather subtle way; we shall return to this point presently. It was now, presumably, that he also decided to reinforce the musical da capo with a textual da capo, and "planted" that final stanza (or something very much like it) at the end of song no. 1. Restricting the tune to a single stanza at the end was doubtless good insurance against overexposure. It also provided the final stanza with the emphasis and freshness it needed if it was going to provide an effective concluding stretta.

(A problem of declamation that Beethoven seems to have overlooked in the sketch stages may now have started him off in modifying his original plan. In poem no. 1, the first syllable is weak in most of the lines, including—and this was crucial—the very first one, "Auf dem Hügel sitz' ich spähend." The scansion ◡ ◡ – ◡ – ◡ – ◡ fell into patterns in 3/4 time beginning on beat 2 or 3. But in poem no. 6, although most of the first syllables are still weak, there are awkward exceptions: the first line "Nimm sie hin denn, diese Lieder," and another line which I believe interested Beethoven particularly, "Ohne Kunstgepräng' erklungen." The triple-meter patterns of song no. 1 would not do for "Nimm sie hin" and would sound flabby on the word "Ohne." In a situation like this a composer is well advised to hedge his bets. After choosing a basic 2/4 meter with each line beginning on beat 1, Beethoven also leads the first melodic phrase up to an agogic accent on the third syllable, so that lines such as "Und du singst was ich gesungen" would work as well as "Nimm sie hin denn, diese Lieder.")

A second refinement in the da capo plan was made after the autograph had ostensibly been completed. In fact, this refinement counts as the most significant addition to the autograph, which is a very clean one, by Beethoven's standards, incorporating relatively few additions or major corrections. But in the final song the quiet, tentative-sounding piano recollection of the single line "Auf dem Hügel sitz' ich spähend," just before the voice brings back the whole of the tune, was a last-minute inspiration. The two bars in question were squeezed into the space originally occupied by the following one bar. It is even possible Beethoven had a momentary temptation to mirror this piano statement at the very beginning of the cycle; at bar 1, song no. 1, there is the relic of an erased "caret" (⊗).

This little piano passage has interesting parallels in two instrumental compositions written within months of the song cycle, the Cello Sonata in C, op. 102 no. 1, and the Piano Sonata in A, op. 101. These sonatas are twins, standing together and apart from other pieces by Beethoven in a number of ways. They both open with an unusually gentle lyric statement, followed by a forceful vivace movement in one of the submediant keys. Then comes an adagio in the original tonic key (tonic minor in op. 101); this turns out to be an extended introduction to the coming finale. In both sonatas the transition to the finale is a sort of meditative miniature cadenza centering on a return of the first bars of the opening movement. Such returns are, of course, rare in Beethoven, and here they have a surprisingly Romantic cast, seeming much more like momentary nostalgic recollections than like recapitulations in the approved Classical style. The effect stems from the subtle tonal placement of these returns. Coming within cadenzalike passages, they sound as if they are hovering on the dominant, even though in op. 102 no. 1 the music looks as though it is in the tonic and, in fact, no dominant pedal is present. A few years earlier Beethoven had achieved a similar effect in a true cadenza (or what starts out like a true cadenza), with the return of the horn theme in the cadenza of the first movement of the Piano Concerto No. 5. In all these passages, actual tonic arrival or establishment waits for a later juncture—in the concerto, for the final ritornello, and in the sonatas, for the first downbeat of the finale themes.

The parallel passages in the sonatas and the song cycle illuminate one another, at least to my way of thinking or apprehending the music. The returns in the sonatas help us hear the piano return in *An die ferne Geliebte* as a tiny cadenza or fermata, introduced by an arpeggio and perched over a dominant which Beethoven takes care not to clarify too rapidly. The slowly reiterated B♭ at the beginning of the tune is directly to the purpose here; the arpeggio is also a slow one, surely; tonic arrival waits for the vocal statement of the complete tune, with its cadence. Furthermore, the fact that the return in the song cycle is directly symbolic—the beloved echoing the songs sung by the lover—conveys something about the quality or the mood of the sonata passages. They, too, are distant half-visions, unexpected, muted, nostalgic in effect. And like the echo of the lover's song in *An die ferne Geliebte,* they seem to inspire directly the forthright, affirmative music that follows.

Then at the very end of the cycle, the last two bars of the piano postlude contain the melody of "Auf dem Hügel" once again, played in a compressed version an octave higher, this time *forte*. The passage appears in the autograph, but as a correction; something has been scratched out under certain of the notes. Thanks to the sketches on the back of the autograph, we can see that this thematic return, too, was an afterthought (example 1). Beethoven must have thought of this final piano statement of "Auf dem Hügel" in conjunction with the earlier one, though the autograph does not make it clear whether or not they were both done at the same sitting.

What the piano does as its final gesture here is to interpret the first fragment or motif of a longer melody as a self-contained cadential unit. This device, with its inherent quality of paradox, had been used occasionally by all the Classic composers: by Haydn in the Quartet in G, op. 17 no. 5 (the earliest example?), and in

EXAMPLE I

EXAMPLE 2

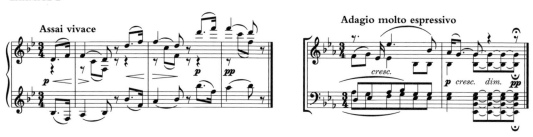

the op. 33 quartets; by Mozart in the Overture to *La finta giardiniera* and in Symphony No. 39 in E Flat; by Beethoven in the op. 12 violin sonatas and recently in the Eighth Symphony.[28] In most earlier cases the melodic outline of the motif is what one would expect—a descending fifth from dominant to tonic (*5* to *1*). The situation in *An die ferne Geliebte* is richer in that the fragment arches from *5* up to *1* down to *3* and leaves ambiguous which interval is "functional," *5–1* or *1–3* or *5–3*. The result is more aphoristic and arresting in effect than paradoxical or witty.[29] The scherzo of the *Hammerklavier* Sonata is interesting to consider in this context, and so is the cavatina from the Quartet in B Flat, op. 130 (example 2).

v · We have seen how the "cyclic" idea in *An die ferne Geliebte* grew from a simple da capo of the opening tune in the final song to a recapitulation of considerable subtlety. For the intervening songs, Beethoven followed a relatively simple plan.

EXAMPLE 3

On the evidence of the sketches, he hit upon this at once in almost all particulars. The songs are set in different keys, except for nos. 3 and 4, which Beethoven treated as a unit in this respect: the keys are E flat, G, A flat, A flat, C, and E flat. Between them come short, sometimes abrupt piano transitions which take care *not* to establish the new keys with the force of a true modulation. Internally, too, most of the songs shun modulation. Exceptions are no. 2, in which the second stanza shifts to the subdominant, C, and no. 6, in which the second stanza modulates to the dominant, B flat.

Two striking things about this key scheme are the strength of the mediant, G, shadowed by the submediant, and the weakness—almost the nonexistence—of the dominant. The subdominant, though it is the key of two songs, nos. 3 and 4, is also weakened. In no. 3, the cadence to each stanza comes on one of Beethoven's characteristically quirky six-four chords, root-position triads occurring only at the beginnings of the following stanzas. In no. 4, the beginning of the tune is over a dominant pedal, and although the end of it does cadence on a root-position tonic triad, this is undercut by a preceding *échappée* figure supported once again by a six-four chord. All this confirms the feeling that in large structural terms the subdominant, A flat, is an upper neighbor to the important mediant degree, G.

The prominence of the mediant appears more clearly yet from a consideration of the tessitura of the six songs. In example 3 small notes indicate the initial notes of the various tunes, stemless "chords" their overall vocal ranges, and circled notes their cadential tonics.[30] The tessitura rises steadily, mirroring the emotional crescendo we have noted (and Beethoven noted) in the poems. While the songs in E flat and A flat remain, in general, within the E♭–E♭ octave and those in G and C remain within the G–G octave, the cadence notes themselves rise from low E♭ to C. Then, after the da capo, the coda makes a cadence for the cycle as a whole on high E♭, within the G–G octave. Both the last cadence in the voice and the last cadence in the piano stress the note G strikingly: the voice by means of the *échappée* figure G–F–G–E♭,[31] and the piano by means of the recollection of "Auf dem Hügel" (B♭–C–D–E♭–E♭–G) discussed above. The last treble note heard is G.

Example 4 attempts to summarize the articulation of Beethoven's key scheme and the role played in this by the piano transitions. The large notes represent the tonic keys of the various songs and the small ones reproduce the transitions, in complete or in skeleton form. In song no. 6 subsidiary bass notes within the piece are also shown. It will be seen that there are several threads running through these

EXAMPLE 4

1. Auf dem Hügel    2. Wo die Berge so blau    3. Leichte Segler

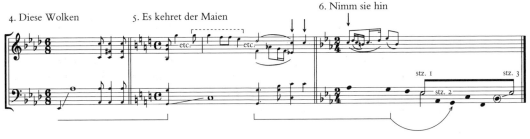

4. Diese Wolken    5. Es kehret der Maien    6. Nimm sie hin

transitions: a pattern of three reiterated notes derived from "Auf dem Hü(gel)"; semitone steps E♭–D/D–E♭ and especially G–A♭/A♭–G (which places A♭ in a neighbor relationship to G); and a descending-third motif ("Ewiglich dein!"; "Es kehret der Maien"), which, as we shall see, has some larger importance for the cycle as a whole. It is significant, perhaps, that Beethoven pulled none of these threads very tight.

However, he definitely had the piano transitions very much in mind from the start. This is one thing that is not clear from Nottebohm's extensive and otherwise fairly effective display of the Scheide sketches in *Zweite Beethoveniana.* The following sketch(es), for example, which record an early idea for song no. 2, may show a transition from nos. 1 to 2 and perhaps also the germ of a transition from nos. 2 to 3:

EXAMPLE 5

An even earlier notation for no. 2 hints at a different sort of transition:

EXAMPLE 6

The next idea for this transition was a passage of up-and-down triplet scales—as Nottebohm should have shown but did not at the beginning of his transcription of a large-scale ink draft of no. 3; he did, however, show the scales as they recur to form the interlude between stanzas, and they can be inspected in *Zweite Beethoveniana,* page 338, lines 10–11. Another sketch suggests cloudily how these scales were going to hook in with the end of no. 2:

EXAMPLE 7

To return to the transition between nos. 1 and 2: an obscure, different idea for this precedes a large-scale draft of no. 2:

EXAMPLE 8

On the previous page, but seemingly written later, is a corrected sketch approaching the final version. The bass semitone is there and also some kind of reiteration:

EXAMPLE 9

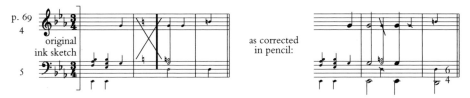

The absence of transition between nos. 3 and 4 was decided on at the start, as is indicated by an early sketch for no. 3 (this sketch precedes the large-scale draft mentioned above):

EXAMPLE 10

Next, a large-scale ink draft of no. 4 is followed by pencil squiggles, which can be interpreted (with hindsight) as gestures toward the long piano introduction to no. 5:

EXAMPLE 11

Pencil sketches for this transition on the previous page were, again, evidently written later:

EXAMPLE 12

Number 5 is sketched less than the earlier songs. There does not seem to be any indication of a piano transition (or retransition) after it.

It should be said that the transcriptions in examples 5–12 are, to a considerable extent, conjectural; these sketches are, for the most part, hard or impossible to read exactly. Indeed, that was one reason why Nottebohm skipped them.

VI ·  The Insel Verlag in 1924 brought out an elegant little 12ᵐᵒ edition of *An die ferne Geliebte,* edited by the great lied scholar Max Friedlaender. Friedlaender's presentation copy to Dr. and Mrs. Alfred Einstein, now in the library of the University of California at Berkeley, has on the flyleaf an obvious-enough quotation from Jeitteles: "Nehmt sie hin denn, diese Lieder." Less obvious is the music written above this, a conflation of tunes nos. 1 and 6 that is definitely *not* a quotation from Beethoven:

EXAMPLE 13

Nehmt sie hin denn, die - se Lied-er

This was a slip stemming from a deeper wisdom, perhaps. It was probably many, many years previous to this that similarities between the two tunes had lodged in some corner of Friedlaender's brain.[32]

The last song of the cycle is the most interesting, and one feels more than one twinge of regret that sketches for it are not present in the Scheide group. Its melody

EXAMPLE 14

Auf dem Hü - gel...

*stanza 3 only:*

*Stanza 1:* Nimm sie hin denn . . .
*Stanza 3:* Und du singst, und du singst . . .

*stanza 1: piano introduction*

*stanza 3: voice*

*piano*

*piano*

*cancellation
in the autograph,
stanzas 1 and 3*

is modeled on tune no. 1, which emerges in its final form only at the end of the extensive series of sketches in the sketchbook. The richest feature of tune no. 1 is the memorable drop of a sixth, E♭–G, on the word "spähend"; harmony comes into play as well as melody, for within the stylistic limits of this music the C-minor chord is striking in itself and the more so for being approached by a leap in both outer voices.[33] All this conspires to stress the note G, the importance of which in the cycle as a whole has already been indicated. Also important is the interval of a descending third, B♭–G, between dominant and mediant degrees (5 and 3). This interval encloses both phrases 1 and 3; in one case the path from 5 to 3 is arpeggiation of the tonic triad, in the other chromatic step motion, but the echo is still clear (even without listening to the rhymes in the verses). Things become even clearer in song no. 6, where the same interval reappears as a direct echo between the cadences of phrases 1 and 4.

The descending third 5–3 is also prominent in the two mediant-submediant songs, nos. 2 and 5. Number 2 ends with this interval in the voice on the words "Ewiglich dein!"

The relationship of tunes nos. 1 and 6, and the role of the descending third in this relationship, can be seen from a composite example (example 14). Phrases 1, 2, and 4 of the later song mirror phrases 1, 2, and 3 of the earlier one in terms of initial, final, and peak notes. The "spähend" minor sixth is still there, though by being filled in it is made quieter (this can be said also of the other phrases). The cadences of phrases 1 and 4, which are identical, consist of the descending third B♭–G filled in diatonically. Ending on 3, the tune does not come to a thorough cadence; resolution waits for the da capo and the coda.

Beethoven was sufficiently interested in the interval 5–3 to echo it in the piano after stanzas I and III—doubtless as a *Nachklang* of "der Laute süssem Klang" mentioned rather gratuitously by Jeitteles in stanza I (but the publisher gratefully seized on this lute as the subject of his title-page vignette). As late as at the time of writing the autograph, Beethoven actually contemplated multiplying these piano echoes: there are extra, canceled bars in the autograph after stanzas I and III and after the piano introduction, too (see example 14). They would certainly have sounded saccharine and flabby. The double echo in stanza III, in particular, would have spoiled the effect of the vocal echo on the words "Nur, nur der Sehn(sucht)," which carries the voice up to high F.

The one phrase of the new tune that is not modeled on the old one, phrase 3, consists of the eight notes F–F–F–F–F–G–G–F. Beethoven seems to have been playing a dangerous game of quiet here. One can adduce some mitigating circumstances—the ostinato F points toward the dominant, B flat, soon to be introduced for the first time in the cycle; the phrase comes on F no more than twice; the other time it comes, in the piano introduction, it sounds less dull because it is transposed up to B flat and provides a springboard for a melodic climax on high F in the phrase that follows. (This climax would not have been good to bring into the song itself; as we have just noted, high F was being saved for the words "Nur der Sehnsucht sich bewusst.") Another explanation for the brute simplicity of this fragment of music may perhaps be found in the words ultimately joined to it in stanza III, "Ohne Kunstgepräng' erklungen." Did Beethoven take this statement so seriously that he fashioned a musical line for it that would sound almost pre-artistic? It is a remarkable fact that he also "simplified" the word "Kunstgepräng'" when he copied the Jeitteles poems in the autograph—the sole word that is garbled in his careful transcript (see page 176.)

Stanza II, "Wenn das Dämm'rungsrot dann ziehet," is the only through-composed stanza in the cycle. One reason for this special treatment was the text, obviously; Beethoven may have been moved by the idea of temporal distance suggested by the rich evening imagery in this stanza, or he may have been responding to the richness for its own sake. The throbbing triplet chords are in his best pantheistic vein. Another reason was probably a desire to find a position, at last, for a clear dominant in the total key scheme of the cycle. We can refer back to example 4 on page 189. By beginning song no. 6 on the subdominant, Beethoven was doing a number of rather elegant things. He was making possible a common-tone link between songs nos. 5 and 6; he was referring for the last time to the key of nos. 3 and 4 and to the large-scale semitone pattern G–A♭–G enclosing them; and he was placing the dominant, which is finally to emerge, in maximum—though, at the same time, very delicate—relief. After stanza I ends on G in the voice, stanza II heads back to a major triad on G; G is everywhere in evidence in

EXAMPLE 15

molto adagio

Und    du  singst,

*An die ferne Geliebte,* and perhaps the "Berge so blau" of no. 2 are now finding their reflection in the "stillen blauen See." From here a circle of fifths produces a clear but peaceful modulation to the dominant, B flat.

Beethoven gets out of the dominant by means of one of those extraordinary compressed gestures that become more and more frequent in the third period (example 15). The hollow, molto adagio B♭ evokes the slowly reiterated B♭s of "Auf dem Hü(gel)"; then the solemn two-part counterpoint in octaves gingerly picks out the chords of E flat, G major, A flat, even A-flat minor, as well as the semitone G–A♭ which had joined (or, rather, disjoined) the earlier songs. This bar seems to hold the entire tonal dynamic of the composition in a nutshell. It also stresses the key words "und du singst," words which record the psychological turning point of the poem, and it associates tune no. 6 more closely than ever with tune no. 1 (see examples 13 and 14).

Without much doubt the expressive climax of the song cycle comes at the through-composed stanza of the last song and the molto adagio bar following it. The discharge of tension represented by this climax—the full resolution of the dominant—is delayed for quite a considerable length of time. The next stanza, stanza III, returns to the tune, which begins on the subdominant and which never comes to a thorough cadence (when coming to cadences with the tonic in the bass, the voice always settles not on *1* but on *3*, via the descending-third figure we have just been discussing). At the end of the stanza the voice repeats the last line, "Nur der Sehnsucht sich bewusst," and the music hovers, cadenzalike, as the piano tentatively recalls "Auf dem Hügel," half in the tonic and half over the dominant. Resolution is accomplished only at the end of the vocal da capo of this tune, at the end of stanza IV.

Thereafter, in the coda or stretta, the voice and the piano concentrate on the phrase of tune no. 1 in which the descending third B♭–G is filled in chromatically. The cadence zone resounds with thirds hinging on G. After the voice ends with the *échappée* figure G–F–G–E♭, the piano plays the chromatic motif from B♭ to G one more time before ending with the last recollection of "Auf dem Hügel" and the descending sixth E♭–G.

# VII

It may be of interest to take up a few more points about the sketches and the autograph.

The early sheet of pencil sketches in London is only minimally informative. Seven of the total ten lines on one side contain some music, roughly written and faded, about twenty bars in all, and it is not clear that more than four of these bars are consecutive at any one point. For instance, example 16a shows the complete line from which Nottebohm took his transcription. It is perhaps safe to infer from this that the unfortunate "up the hill" beginning of the tune, still present in the Scheide sketches, was one of the original notions, and that Beethoven had not yet seen that the climax of the first phrase should be on "spähend" rather than "Hügel." A somewhat clearer line of sketches suggests that the last phrase of the tune was the earliest fixed into something like its present state (example 16b). This impression is confirmed by the Scheide sketches. There are no identifiable sketches for any of the other songs on this early sheet.

In the Scheide sketchbook, the six pages devoted to *An die ferne Geliebte* follow closely on another six-page unit for the song "Sehnsucht" (Die stille Nacht umdunkelt), WoO 146. There is a detailed study of these sketches by Lewis Lockwood.[34] As with the "Sehnsucht" sketches, the first page opening for *An die ferne Geliebte* (pages 68–69) consists mainly of dense work on a single tune, "Auf dem Hügel."[35] Then the remaining four pages are used essentially for large-scale drafts—though not drafts for the same piece, as is the case with "Sehnsucht," but drafts of the other songs in the cycle.[36] All three stanzas of song no. 2 are drafted consecutively on page 70. Number 3 is mapped out in full on page 71 and runs into the first bars of no. 4, which continues (on two staffs) overleaf, page 72. Page 73 has full drafts of the tunes of nos. 5 and 6, the latter being simply the tune of "Auf dem Hügel" with an indication of the new words. In short, a different method of sketching was used for the later songs; they could be roughed out swiftly and surely, without the careful work of melodic modeling that the first song seems to have required from the start. It also required later attention, and it is not an easy matter to see exactly what was written at any one sitting. Peppered over the pages are notions for the piano transitions, as shown in examples 5–12 above.

Nottebohm printed almost as many sketches for the "Auf dem Hügel" tune (twelve) as he did for "Sehnsucht." Consequently the former song has formed the basis for cloudy or plainly erroneous statements about Beethoven's compositional process as frequently as has the latter. Here, Lockwood's comments on the situation with "Sehnsucht" are exactly apposite. The aspect of the pages devoted to "Auf dem Hügel" does not suggest long, tedious labor so much as "the rapid tumbling-out of ideas," and the process of melodic formation can be seen to have been less a matter of random exploration than of trying out options around certain firmly fixed constants. One such constant was the high note on "spähend," another was the general form of the last phrase.

(cf. N II, p. 334)

f. 9r
6

pencil    weichet    Auf dem

f. 9r
4, end

What was not fixed was that descending sixth on "spähend" and the resulting low note G. Even though as we listen to the piece today this leap down to G sounds like the direct impetus for the move to G major in the next song, the choice of G major was certainly made first and the descending sixth decided on only later. It is worth noting that in both "Sehnsucht" and "Auf dem Hügel" a significant part of the problem was the balance of 5 and 3 degrees; Beethoven can hardly have been unaware of the parallel, for he sketched both songs for a time in the same key, E flat.

Sketches for the second song, "Wo die Berge so blau," are in some ways the most interesting. After two preliminary sketches, given in examples 5 and 6, there comes a series of superimposed drafts that pose a pretty problem for the transcriber. It seems that on lines 2–6 of page 70 (figure 1) Beethoven first wrote a hasty pencil draft covering all three stanzas, but with some passages skipped over with "etc." indications. Then he came back with pen in hand and wrote over this draft, trying two alternative versions one above the other—lines 1, 3, and 5 aligned (and barred) with lines 2, 4, and 6 respectively. He ran out of space and continued after a *Vi-de* mark on lines 15–16. The original pencil draft and the ink revisions are shown separately in example 17.

The third of these transcriptions is unproblematic, but the second is conjectural and the first is speculative. I have ventured to set down all three because, for all their uncertainties, they do establish certain points. Beethoven had the descending-third figure D–C–B in mind quite early, although he dropped it momentarily in the second draft (compare also example 7). He contemplated an ostinato for stanza II on F♯ rather than on G(!). And taken with the preliminary sketches, the drafts show Beethoven's changing ideas about the declamation appropriate to this poem. Vacillation continued until the autograph stage, where the beginning of the

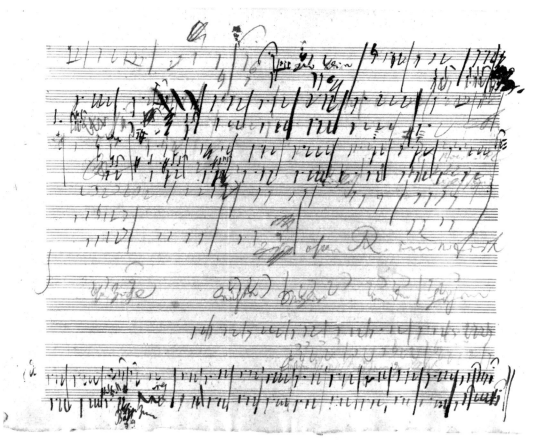

FIGURE I "Scheide" sketchbook (Scheide Library, Princeton, New Jersey), p. 70.

song was first written as shown in example 18 in small notes, then corrected as shown in full-size ones.

The main points of alteration in the autograph have already been discussed in the pages above. Hubert Unverricht, in his valuable study of problems of textual criticism in Beethoven, mentions and illustrates another interesting point, in the piano postlude six bars from the end of the composition, where the autograph reflects the composer's "inner aural conception while the first edition offers a notation that can be realized technically."[37] Since the paper is ruled with twelve staves and they are all filled by four systems of music, Beethoven did not have any space at hand for the composing or recomposing he always found necessary at the autograph stage. As a result, he made many of his smaller corrections by scratching out the original and writing the new version on top; the original is often impossible

EXAMPLE 17

EXAMPLE 18

to reconstruct with confidence. Larger corrections had to be made on separate sheets, a recourse that seems to have been needed only once, in the introduction to song no. 5 (page 16). The idea of including two bars of the tune in the piano, just before the voice enters, was either an afterthought or something that slipped Beethoven's mind as he wrote the autograph. These two bars do not appear there, but from a "caret" (⊗) one can infer that Beethoven was sending along an insert sheet to the copyist. To be precise, the insert (which is now lost) must have covered the last bar prior to the two-bar passage as well; that last bar does appear in the autograph, but it is canceled and the left-hand chords were never put in.

VIII ·    In the total span of Beethoven's output we can see *An die ferne Geliebte* as a quiet herald of the third-period style. Of the various features discussed in the paragraphs above, two in particular encourage such a view—the surprising assimilation of the *Volksweise* ideal and the treatment of tonality. As I have remarked before, a tendency toward means of immediate communication on the most basic level is very marked in the late music. The tune for the "Ode to Joy" is the famous paradigm for this tendency. But it is also manifested in other works and in other ways: in the late bagatelles, in the songlike sonata and quartet movements entitled "arietta," "arioso," and "cavatina," in the instrumental recitatives which seem to break down controlled discourse in favor of direct communion, and in those naïve country-dance scherzos—movements so different in mood from the scherzos of earlier years. *An die ferne Geliebte* was Beethoven's first emphatic essay in this new genre. It was also the first of his two all-but-explicit ideological statements about it, the other being, of course, the "Ode to Joy." Songs without the adornments of art can achieve loving communication and brotherhood.

To be sure, the ambivalence in respect to simple and complex utterance that we noted in Beethoven's earlier song writing is still much in evidence in the later music. Even the "Ode to Joy," starting as an unprecedented, unaccompanied, and utterly unpretentious tune, works its way up through ornamental variations to a double fugue. More quietly, *An die ferne Geliebte,* too, shows that Beethoven could not accept the *Volksweise* ideal in its strong form. Indicative here is the way the piano almost imperceptibly assumes more and more importance as the piece proceeds. In song no. 1, all that the piano provides is accompaniment, an introductory chord to give the singer his note, and small self-effacing interludes between the stanzas. In the next three numbers the piano also plays two bars of the vocal melody before the voice sings it. A twelve-bar piano passage of nature illustration begins no. 5—bolstered at the last minute, as we have just seen, by a two-bar forecast of the melody as in the earlier songs. In no. 6 the piano plays the entire tune before the voice enters, and, what is more, plays it in a somewhat different and more emphatic version. During the middle, through-composed stanza of this song it is really the piano that guides the voice, and the da capo of tune no. 1 is initiated (and, in symbolic terms, impelled) by the piano. The excited coda sees the voice swept along by the piano, which behaves like the orchestra in a miniature cantata or opera finale. Small wonder that the wording of Beethoven's original title page in the edition, "Ein Liederkreis . . . mit Begleitung des Piano-Forte in Musik gesetzt," did not satisfy him and came to be changed in the second issue to the less invidious rubric "für Gesang und Piano-Forte."[38]

It is also the piano that, by carrying through the transitions illustrated in example 4, controls the unusual tonal dynamic in the song cycle. These transitions are arranged so as *not* to make convincing, stable modulations. The new keys G, A flat, and C are simply asserted or, as it were, placed in apposition to the original tonic, E flat; the original tonic is never erased from the listener's memory. It has already been mentioned (page 188) how the cadences in the two middle songs weaken any impression that they have an independent tonality of their own. At the end of the cycle, there is no need for tonic reestablishment by means of anything like a customary Beethovenian retransition passage, with extended dominant preparation and all the rest (it is significant that the tonal return in this composition comes well ahead of the thematic return). As a result of this treatment of tonality, there is a distinct feeling of instability or tension in the way the middle songs "set"; nothing arises to dispel this feeling, since the songs are so utterly simple in themselves. It can be interpreted as a feeling of unreality, perhaps, corresponding to the fantasy-making indulged in by Jeitteles's lover in these middle songs. His reality, in this interpretation, is the E flat tonic of songs nos. 1 and 6.

The interconnection of all the songs in *An die ferne Geliebte,* accomplished by the piano transitions, is always mentioned by writers on this history of the lied. This feature distinguishes Beethoven's song cycle, the first serious example of the genre, from almost all later ones. What is less frequently mentioned is that this feature makes the inner songs dependent—much more so than the songs of *Die schöne Müllerin* or *Die Winterreise,* or even those of *Dichterliebe,* for all of Schumann's anxious tonality-plotting. Indeed, Beethoven's inner songs hardly have enough lyrical distinction—and they certainly do not have musical distinction of any other kind—to sustain them simply on their own terms. They live by their special tonal placement in the total composition; unlike "Die Post" or "Ich grolle nicht" they would be unthinkable as separate numbers. This was what Hans Boettcher was saying when he described the cycle, in his monograph on Beethoven's songs, as "gleichsam *ein* ungeheuer erweitertes Lied."[39]

Something of the same tonal poise between large musical sections is encountered in certain of Beethoven's last compositions, such as the *Grosse Fuge* and the Quartet in C-Sharp Minor, op. 131. We may not wish to describe the quartet as "a single dreadfully extended movement, so to speak," but manifestly Beethoven went further here than ever before in the direction of unifying the members of the cyclic sonata, quartet, or symphony form into a single unit. There are no stops between movements, but instead curt musical transitions which are interesting to compare with those in *An die ferne Geliebte.* Again, the simplicity of certain movements— simplicity, at least, relative to Beethoven's ordinary musical style in quartets—contributes to a sense of tension in the way these movements "set" vis-à-vis the opening tonality of C-sharp minor. The famous Neapolitan position of the second movement contributes a great deal to its strange ephemeral quality and is still sufficiently vivid in the listener's memory to validate the Neapolitan echo at the end of the finale. Of another movement, the presto following the A-major variations, Robert Simpson has recently observed that it actually sounds on the dominant of A all the way through, rather than in its own ostensible key of E.[40] And Joachim von Hecker, studying the sketches for the C-sharp-minor Quartet, came across a startling analogy to *An die ferne Geliebte:* in place of the G-sharp-minor adagio prior to the finale, Beethoven once planned a return of the opening fugue theme.[41] Even after dropping this idea, he still made one of the finale themes echo the fugue theme in an unusually direct way, as is well known.

Whether or not the specific analogies drawn above seem convincing or prove to be suggestive, there will probably be little argument on the general proposition that a new quality of tonality emerges in Beethoven's late music. This quality is not easy to characterize, but perhaps one can say that tonality is now treated less as a process and more as a kind of absolute. Movement from one tonality to another, with its concomitant psychological sense of sequence, or direction, or achievement, or whatever—this interests Beethoven less at this stage than tonality as a framework, an orientation, a system. To venture a metaphor from electricity, he is no longer taking tonality as the potential to drive musical currents of all kinds in all directions, but rather as an electrostatic field. It is in the light of this new attitude that we can best understand his well-known reticence toward the dominant tonality during his late years. The dominant is employed less often, and when it is employed it is handled in a notably quiet, undynamic way. This feature, too, is adumbrated in *An die ferne Geliebte*—more strikingly, I should say, than in any of the earlier music.

After the small burst of song writing in 1815–16 that produced "Sehnsucht" and *An die ferne Geliebte,* Beethoven in effect abandoned song composition. There are only two more significant songs: "Resignation" (1817) and "Abendlied" (1820). Yet the incorporation of song into his large-scale instrumental works became more and more important to him as a compositional impetus. And somewhat paradoxically, these works assimilated certain formal and tonal procedures pioneered in his most ambitious song composition, procedures that evolved in direct response to the quite special conditions imposed by Jeitteles's cycle of poems and the compositional choices open to Beethoven as he approached them specifically as a song writer. In the annals of musicology *An die ferne Geliebte* has a safe place only, it seems, in the history of the lied, and even this place is not always conceded with good grace or good sense. It is also important for its role in Beethoven's own development—in his musical development as well as what J. W. N. Sullivan called his "spiritual development," the musical record of his changing response to life experience. It deserves study in the context of the musical style of his third period, the music of the last decade.

## Notes

1. Anton Schindler, *Beethoven As I Knew Him,* tr. Donald McArdle (London, 1966), 337.
2. Beethoven's erratic capitalization is preserved. A few emendations have been made: no. 3, line 5, Beethoven writes "denn"—the first edition reads "dann"; no. 4, line 12, Beethoven puts the quotation mark at the start of the previous line (this is followed in all early editions); no. 6, Beethoven writes the numeral erroneously as IV; no. 6, line 8, Beethoven writes "jenen" (this is followed by the first edition but changed to "jener" in the second issue). For other such corrections in the second issue—many of them involving the capitalization, which obviously worried Beethoven—see Alan Tyson, "Beethoven in Steiner's Shop," *Music Review* 23 (1962): 120–21.
3. Hans Boettcher, *Beethoven als Liederkomponist* (Augsburg, 1928), 50.
4. This "vierfüssige Trochäus" was a favorite line with Jeitteles, according to Castelli, who considered it to be a verse form of Spanish origin: see his *Memoiren meines Lebens,* ed. Josef Bindtner (Munich, 1913), 2:278.
5. Ludwig Nohl, *Eine stille Liebe zu Beethoven* (1875), 2d ed. (Leipzig, 1902), 128–29. There are so many plain errors of wording in Nohl's transcript (which includes the fifth stanza of song no. 1) that one dare not take it seriously as an authority. Yet lumping two poems together is not the sort of thing that happens through an error nor, one would think, through editorial whim. As for the "Six Songs" mentioned in Beethoven's title, I do not think that

constitutes evidence one way or another. He could have been following Jeitteles or he could have been pointedly recording a new numeration of his own.

The term *Liederkreis* first appears in the first edition, probably at Beethoven's instigation and certainly with his approval.

6. Half rhymes between stanzas: in no. 1, *spähend/sehend, sehen/verwehen; Nebelland/fand, Tal/Qual; eilt/teilt, sein/Pein.* In no. 2, *Tal/Qual; Wald/Liebesgewalt; verglüht/umzieht, hier/dir.* In no. 4, *Zug/Flug, Brust/Lust; spielen/wühlen, Hügeln/spiegeln.* In no. 5, *rinnen/drinnen, hinnen/Gewinnen; Kleinen/einen, vereint/erscheint.* In no. 6, *Lieder/wieder, ziehet/verglühet,* and within stanzas (the two final stanzas) *gesungen/erklungen, Brust/bewusst, weichet/erreichet, weit/geweiht.* In no. 3 half rhymes do not come into consideration because there are true rhymes between all stanzas.

7. This conceit, with its erotic or voyeuristic overtones, occurs in other Beethoven song poems: "Sehnsucht" (Was zieht mir das Herz so?) and "Ruf vom Berge."

8. "Adelaide," "An den fernen Geliebten" (Einst wohnten süsse Ruh), "Sehnsucht" (Was zicht mir das Herz so?), "Lied aus der Ferne," "Andenken," "Der Jüngling in der Fremde," "Ruf vom Berge," "Gedenke mein." For Paul Bekker, "Beethoven's whole lyric output might almost be regarded as a series of variations upon the *An die ferne Geliebte* theme" (*Beethoven,* tr. M. M. Bozman [London, 1925], 256).

9. Martin Cooper, *Beethoven: The Last Decade, 1817–1827* (London, 1970), 13, 32.

10. *Thayer's Life of Beethoven,* ed. Elliott Forbes, rev. ed. (Princeton, 1967), 2:647. The version of the letter given by Emily Anderson in *The Letters of Beethoven* (London, 1961), no. 632 (footnoted "This is a literal translation of the original German"!), renders "Ich fand" as "I have found," a little twist that manages to strengthen the impression that Beethoven was still in love.

11. Nohl, *Eine stille Liebe,* 86; compare *Thayer's Life of Beethoven,* 2:646. One hesitates, perhaps, before a report of a conversation overheard as precisely as this. But although Fanny was more than half in love with Beethoven, her diary entries in general seem accurate, sensitively observed, and transparently honest, and they are generally credited. It has been suggested by some popular biographers that Beethoven was deliberately exaggerating his feelings as a way of scotching matchmaking overtures on Giannatasio's part; but this does not feel like Beethoven's style.

12. *Thayer's Life of Beethoven,* 2:539.

13. Ibid., 2:532.

14. Alan Tyson, "Beethoven's Heroic Phase," *Musical Times* 110 (1969): 139–41.

15. Bekker calls the last song *Widmungsgesang* (*Beethoven,* 364).

16. For an introduction to the vast literature on the lied, see the *Musik in Geschichte und Gegenwart* articles "Lied," by Kurt Gudewill, and "Goethe," by Friedrich Blume.

17. Johann Wolfgang von Goethe, Review of *Des Knaben Wunderhorn, Deutscher Taschenbuch Verlag Gesamtausgabe,* 22, no. 21 (January 1806).

18. Frederick W. Sternfeld, *Goethe and Music* (New York, 1954).

19. How characteristic is Beethoven's inscription on the autograph of the fourfold "Sehnsucht" setting—"Sehnsucht von Göthe und Beethoven"!; see Georg Kinsky and Hans Halm, *Das Werk Beethovens: Thematisches-bibliographisches Verzeichnis* (Munich-Duisberg, 1955), 598.

20. See Gustav Nottebohm, *Zweite Beethoveniana,* ed. Eusebius Mandyczewski (Leipzig, 1887), 340.

21. Though, in fact, Zelter does not appear to have employed the resource often in his own songs. Among those available in modern editions, only the Schiller "Bergleid" and "Kennst

du das Land" involve mode changes (*Fünfzig Lieder*, ed. Ludwig Landshoff [Mainz, 1932]). From the dissertation on Zelter by Gertraud Wittmann one can infer that this also happens in "Künstlers Abendlied" and Schiller's "Der Taucher" ("Das klavierbegleitete Sololied C. F. Zelters" [Ph.D. diss., University of Giessen, 1936], 44, 56).

22. His best-known song today; see Donald Jay Grout and Claude V. Palisca, *A History of Western Music,* 4th ed. (New York, 1988), 579.

23. Joseph Kerman, *The Beethoven Quartets* (New York, 1967), ch. 7, "Voice."

24. *Marianne und Johann Jakob Willemer: Briefwechsel mit Goethe,* ed. Hans J. Weitz (Frankfurt, 1965), no. 123. Weitz takes it for granted that this letter was accompanied by a copy of the work as a gift.

25. Nottebohm, *Zweite Beethoveniana,* 334–39. Though Nottebohm speaks of early sketches found on "single sheets" ("auf einzelnen Blättern"), only one such sheet is known today—the very one from which his (single) example is taken. He may have seen others, which have since disappeared from view; but I do not think we can quite certain that he did.

26. *Beethoven. An die ferne Geliebte: Faksimile nach dem im Besitz des Bonner Beethovenhauses befindlichen Original* (Munich-Duisburg, 1970). The autograph is described in Hans Schmidt, "Die Beethoven Handschriften des Beethovenhauses in Bonn," *Beethoven-Jahrbuch* 7 (1971): 561.

27. Two sketches show this (Nottebohm, *Zweite Beethoveniana,* 336–37, 339). The first is found among sketches for song no. 1 (p. 69) and is headed "Nim̃ sie hin lezter Vers." This heading might admit of two interpretations, but Beethoven's meaning is clarified when text words from stanza I appear: "die ich dir Geliebte sang ~~Zu der Laute~~ Sin[ge]." "Nim̃ sie" are the sole words accompanying the second sketch, which appears with the sparse sketches for song no. 5 and the coda (p. 72).

28. Incidentally, the idea of ending the first movement of the Eighth Symphony in this way was, again, a last-minute refinement of Beethoven's original plan; compare the early version in *Beethoven: Supplemente zur Gesamtausgabe,* ed. Willy Hess (Wiesbaden, 1961), 4:70. In considering this device in general, a distinction is worth making between those cases in which the truncated figure is played several times to make the cadence, and the more unexpected cases in which it is played just once.

29. In his article "Kleine Beiträge zur Beethovens Liedern und Bühnenwerken," *Neues Beethoven-Jahrbuch* 2 (1925): 55–56, Hans Joachim Moser noted a special "Schlussdevise" in Beethoven's songs "Andenken," "Adelaide," "Wonne der Wehmut," "An die Hoffnung," op. 94, and *An die ferne Geliebte.* For Moser the effect was "like a dreamlike echo." However this may be, I find fewer similarities between the end of *An die ferne Geliebte* and those other songs than differences—in thematic content, dynamics, phrasing, even scoring (voice or piano), and certainly in the overall quality of the gesture. On the other hand, the ending of the cavatina in op. 130 (ex. 2) seems to me close in spirit to that of the songs.

30. Song no. 2 and the first part of no. 6 have no circles because the music remains unresolved melodically, the voice cadencing not on *1* but on *3* in both cases (on B and G respectively). The chord in parentheses in no. 2 refers to the range of the tune when it is played a fourth (actually an eleventh) higher by the piano while the voice sings the words of stanza II on a monotone—the monotone being G.

31. Compare the *échappée* cadence to tune no. 4, mentioned above.

32. Few commentators seem to have noticed these similarities, an exception being Romain Rolland in *Beethoven: Les grandes époques créatrices* (Paris, 1937), 3:197. But, in fact, I know of only two serious or extensive studies of *An die ferne Geliebte*—Rolland's and that of Moser,

in *Das deutsche Lied seit Mozart* (Berlin, 1937), 2:16–24. It is beyond belief how much musicologists can write—the most recent of the *Beethoven-Jahrbuch*'s five-year Beethoven bibliographies has 504 entries—without looking hard at important compositions.

33. An improvement over the most advanced sketch, in which the space between E♭ and C in the bass is dutifully filled in by a D. Nottebohm's transcript of this sketch (*Zweite Beethoveniana,* 337, line 8) omits the D.

34. Lewis Lockwood, "Beethoven's Sketches for *Sehnsucht* (WoO 146)," in *Beethoven Studies,* ed. Alan Tyson (New York, 1973), 97–122.

35. The page opening was not quite clean when Beethoven started the song. Line 1 of p. 68 has a two-bar sketch in A major, and lines 1–2 of p. 69 have a copy of the folk song "Es ritten drei Reiter" (cf. n. 20).

36. These drafts can be found in Nottebohm, *Zweite Beethoveniana,* as follows: no. 2, p. 338 (incomplete, cf. ex. 18); nos. 3–4, pp. 338–39 (incomplete); no. 5, p. 339; no. 6, p. 339.

37. Hubert Unverricht, *Die Eigenschriften und die Originalausgaben von Werke Beethovens in ihrer Bedeutung für die moderne Textkritik* (Cassel, 1960). In bar 6 of Unverricht's transcription from the autograph, p. 26, I believe that the second and third notes should be A (natural assumed) and A♭ (the flat is written in under the cancel line); compare with the first sketch in example 1.

38. Pointed out by Tyson, "Beethoven in Steiner's Shop," 121.

39. Boettcher, *Beethoven als Liederkomponist,* 67.

40. Robert Simpson, "The Chamber Music for Strings," in *The Beethoven Reader,* ed. Denis Arnold and Nigel Fortune (New York, 1971), 274.

41. Joachim von Hecker, "Untersuchungen an den Skizzen zum Streichquartett cis-moll op. 131 von Beethoven" (Ph.D. diss., University of Freiburg, 1956). [See also Robert Winter, *Compositional Origins of Beethoven's Opus 131* (Ann Arbor, 1982).]

12

# Taking the Fifth

*For Carl Dahlhaus*

At the beginning of one of his major essays, "Issues in Composition," Carl Dahlhaus draws attention to the brevity of characteristic themes favored by late nineteenth-century composers.[1] Themes in their pieces tend to be shorter than in the compositional models they admired. In Beethoven's Fifth Symphony, for example—that paradigmatic "musical work of art" for their time and ours—the opening theme is now understood as consisting of four pitches, articulated by eight notes, initially presented in five measures including two fermatas. Before Schenker's long analytical essay of 1921–23, however, only the first four notes were generally analyzed as "theme," and the following four notes as a sequential extension. The historical significance of this misreading, Dahlhaus observes, lies in its embodiment of typical late nineteenth-century attitudes. "What to Beethoven was a part, a component, was understood later in the nineteenth century to be an independent, self-sufficient musical idea, because the composers of the day looked for and found in Beethoven what they themselves practiced."[2]

We can also draw a historical moral from the great impression that was made by Schenker's analysis. Within a few years it was being cited by mainstream scholars such as Arnold Schmitz and Walter Riezler, and today it has achieved the status of orthodoxy. Schenker's insight about the true extent of the theme was irrevocably bound up with a polemic, one which evidently struck a responsive note at the time: he sought to minimize two "surface" features of the music, both of which obscure

From *Das musikalische Kunstwerk [The Musical Work of Art]. Geschichte. Ästhetik. Theorie. Festschrift Carl Dahlhaus zum 60. Geburtstag,* ed. Hermann Danuser, Helga de la Motte-Haber, Silke Leopold, and Norbert Miller (Laaber: Laaber Verlag, 1988), 483–91.

the theme's purely melodic form. These features are the repercussions (of the notes G and F) and the fermatas (on E♭ and D). The repeated notes are to be reduced away, says Schenker, because they evoke the *Beiklang* of one or more spoken words—a "rhetorical" effect inappropriate to pure instrumental music.[3] As for the fermatas, strictly speaking they could be omitted; and Wagner's famous tribute to them in "On Conducting" ("But now suppose Beethoven's voice were heard from the grave calling to our conductors: 'Hold that fermata of mine! Cling to it! I was not making a joke; I was not waiting to decide what to do next. . . . I was dividing the seas in order to behold the abyss beneath. I was parting the clouds in order to behold the shining sun and the blue sky,'" etc.)[4] provided a springboard for Schenker's ready sarcasm.

The repercussions and fermatas are, of course, the first features that give the Fifth Symphony its immediate shock value. They release primal, unmediated emotional energies, energies that were as thoroughly buried in traditional Viennese Classical music as Florestan in Pizarro's *oubliette*. What Thomas Mann described as "the naked human voice" sounds with particular urgency in the Fifth Symphony. Hence for Wagner, surveying Beethoven's output, the Fifth was the crux where lyrical pathos stands ready to transmute into ideal drama;[5] and despite Wagner's warning against the attempt to reduce this ideal drama to anything specific, the chthonic violence of the piece as much as its thematic, tonal, and rhythmic dynamic makes it, probably more than any other piece lacking an actual program, *suggest* a program. Its free-floating signification is positively overloaded, its implied narrative line—whether fatal or imperial—virtually palpable. This too was something for Schenker to rail against.

If, however, the Fifth was indeed the paradigmatic "work of musical art" for the nineteenth century, its violence and its signification must have been a good part of the reason. No one has ever doubted any of this, surely. But—to add platitude to platitude—what was severely in doubt in the early twentieth century was the propriety of acknowledging any of it in academic discourse. For this reason, it may be suspected that of all Beethoven's symphonies, the Fifth has been the hardest for analysts, musicologists, and serious critics to take. We have conducted elaborate analyses of, especially, the first movement, following upon Schenker's meticulous essay (and if in 1978 Peter Gülke could list eight different interpretations of the metrical anomaly in the development section, at least two more can now be added).[6] On the other hand, serious interpretations of the Fifth as an expressive entity have been in short supply. Critics have not wanted to leave themselves open to self-incrimination. Gülke is a brave exception.

II ·  The first mention of Beethoven's Fifth in Wagner's "On Conducting" occurs in a remarkable passage:

In my case the clue to the right tempo and expression in Beethoven was provided years ago by the inspired delivery of the great Schröder-Devrient. Take that passage for solo oboe in the first movement of the C minor Symphony just after the beginning of the recapitulation: [music example]. I could no longer bear hearing that moving passage thrown away as it invariably was. Furthermore my handling of it made me realize the importance of the first violins' fermata in the corresponding passage of the exposition: [music] and the powerful impression I drew from these two apparently insignificant details led to a fresh understanding of the movement as a whole.[7]

Wagner says that, in effect, he read the symphony backwards from one particularly celebrated fermata—a fermata that Schenker's exhaustive discussion passes over with studied velocity.

It appears that the composer had a little more trouble reading the symphony forwards. In public, he more than once balanced praise for the finale with praise for the *Eroica* finale: one had greater richness, the other greater concision. In private, he once said jokingly to Cosima that the finale of the Fifth was a lot of celebrating over nothing. Something else he said may also be echoed in Cosima's remark that only someone who could sway the public—i.e., R.—was able to perform the Fifth convincingly.[8] In the twentieth century the finale has often received a bad press. A memorable article of 1947 by Virgil Thomson, to cite an extreme but not atypical example, proposed a genre called "the editorial symphony" and at once traced the misuse of this genre to the finale of the Fifth.[9]

The Andante con moto, on the other hand, Wagner would appear to have admired unqualifiedly—he had done so at least since the time of his C-major Symphony of 1832—as did Hoffmann, Lenz, Grove, and Tovey, to mention only a few famous names. Only occasionally does one come across in the literature quietly phrased expressions of reserve. Thus while Grove found the movement "beautiful to hear," he also found it "wanting in the *spur*—the personal purpose or idea which inspires the preceding movement and gives the present work its high position in Beethoven's music."[10] Grove then went on to lament that Beethoven did not leave us a programmatic clue to this wanting "spur." Clearly something about the expressive profile of the movement disturbed him.

III ·

First E. T. A. Hoffmann, and then virtually every other writer on the Fifth Symphony, has associated the Andante con moto with Haydn's characteristic "double variation" procedure. To think of Haydn, however, one does not have to wait for variations. The opening texture—low strings in two-part harmony—recalls the "Drumroll" Symphony and the last String Quartet, op. 77 no. 2, and the thematic process is close enough to Haydn's spirit: a lyrical theme ($A^1$) maps out the world of Classical harmony in a deft and "logical" way. For eight—six—bars, the theme sounds, if not like Haydn, like Beethoven trying to sound like Haydn.

After the disruptive unfamiliarities of the first movement, then, the beginning of the second soothes not only through its dynamics, tempo, key, and so on, but also through its sheer familiarity.

Yet defamiliarization sets in almost at once. The C-major triad in bar 4 coincides with a strong, even harsh change of accent in the opening motive ♩♪ , and the change back in bars 7–8 is stronger yet—strong enough to derail the musical process: in A² the double echo of the 5–3 cadence seems less lyrical than schematic, a stratagem to open up new octave regions. And despite the expressive appoggiaturas, there is also something schematic about the resolution of 5–3 to 5–1 in a direct linear descent. An added bar brings about a masculine cadence followed by heavy closure that is bound to sound disruptive so early in the movement.

As for the second element (B), that is clearly so loaded with inchoate signification that it can only be understood quasi-programmatically, as Grove sensed. (The structure of Beethoven's earliest sketch for B,[11] a balanced pair of repeated phrases marked "quasi Trio," has been so thoroughly superseded in the final version that no sense of balance remains; this is not a case where knowledge of the genesis of a work of art helps its understanding.) A conservative new melody—deliberate in its accompaniment figuration, cautious and retrospective in its melody and rhythm—commences, moves up, aspires; then, after two motivic statements, the melody is overtaken by events. A change in practically every musical parameter destroys its sense of identity, if not its sense of direction. For the second time in the piece, the opening motive appears with its accents harshly reversed at the appearance of a C-major triad; but now, instead of appearing to continue, the melody seems to be preempted by an unexpected very great force:

> This theme, blaring out raucously in trumpets, horns, oboes, and drums, has been described . . . as parading forth a "triumphant" C major, but I would imagine that most listeners have always been shocked and disturbed, even frightened by it, even on repeated hearings. It is sudden, aggressive, and deliberately overwrought as a gesture.[12]

Another Haydn symphony comes to mind, parodied with real malice—the "Surprise." What is especially shocking, perhaps, is that aggression wears the face of conservatism.

Whether triumphant or frightening, this vision fades in such a way as to show the unsettling hollowness of the great force—only to replace it by an equally unsettling mystery made out of attenuated voice leading and harmony. There can be no doubt in the listener's mind that the lurid story (which is no less lurid for

EXAMPLE 1

being inarticulate) follows from the story of the first movement. "It is as though the awful phantom that seized our hearts in the Allegro threatens at every moment to emerge from the storm-cloud into which it disappeared, so that the comforting figures around us rapidly flee from its sight"[13]—that is how Hoffmann expressed the link. In an essay remarkable for its emphasis on Beethoven's *Besonnenheit,* this is one of the few points where Hoffmann was tempted to suggest, if not a program, programmatic images such as clouds, waves, flames, night and day: here, storm-clouds. Speaking technically, Peter Gülke rightly describes the reference to the original ♩♫ ♩ rhythm in the B theme as cogent, if less than manifest;[14] and in the famous chromatic passage at bars 39–48, various features refer to bars 83–94 in the Allegro con brio—the new diminished seventh chord, the motivic repetition, the momentary minor tonic chord, and the emphatic resolution to the dominant (example 1). In the second appearance of B, these references are knit together by the telltale added bass rhythm ♪♫♫ , as is well known.[15]

IV ·    The return of A, in variation, may be thought to presage a return to normal, a return to Haydnesque form and spirit. The gesture is disorienting, however. For the material so far does not sound at all like a subject for variations, in Haydn's manner or anyone else's (of course B is never treated in variation, and never could be). The juxtaposition of these two sections constitutes a stark demonstration of Beethoven's developing concept of musical form. A is a closed—indeed, an ex-aggeratedly closed—structure, whereas B is one of those themes-in-process that Dahlhaus has singled out as decisive for Beethoven's "new path" of the early 1800s.[16]

 The sense of disorientation is forced by the very device through which Beethoven offers to smooth over his transition: the sustained solo clarinet line above the violas and cellos. Emerging at the end of B from an enormously energetic upward sweep of E♭s, this line becomes a weirdly dissonant superior pedal. Lawrence Kramer relates this clarinet line to the symphony's two prominent oboe solos (Wagner's rhetorical cadenza in the Allegro con brio, bars 254ff., and bars 172ff. of the final Allegro); the variations, Kramer remarks,

> are simply old-fashioned "doubles" that do nothing to transform the thematic material; one could argue, especially in view of the transformations introduced later on, that the doubles are present to retard the transformation of thematic material. In this role, they create a sense of suspension or repose which is underscored by the fact that they coincide with a long-breathed phrase on the woodwind. . . . It is this phrase . . . that stands out during the variations, the neutrality of which highlights it sharply.[17]

It is as though the first variation has started too soon, while the clarinet is holding an unmarked fermata. Yet between the violins' highly directed line in bars 40–48 (example 1) and the clarinet's wavering line in bars 49–57 there is a suggestion of an echo, even of an antecedent–consequent relationship, which makes for a tenuous bridge between Beethoven's unlikely pair of double-variation themes (example 2). The step E♮–E♭ in bars 42–43 (itself echoed by F♭–E♭ in bars 45–46) makes the functional move away from the menacing C-major outburst back to A flat. Recalling this, the step E♭–E♮ in bars 52–53 reminds us (by means of a doubled third!) that the outburst itself reflected a C-major chord in the original tune. The variation is looking back uneasily over its shoulder.

In the present variation, A² returns *without* variation—a circumstance that underlines its distinction from A¹ despite their close linkage in linear terms. To Berlioz, the return of A² without variation was a particularly moving feature of the work. The return of B without variation (save in figuration) may seem a particularly shocking and frightening feature, like a precisely recurring nightmare.

We may find the next variation in some ways easier to "read," even though the sections are broadly expanded in increasingly imaginative ways. A¹, repeated twice, builds such momentum that A² starts with a fermata and traces its *5–3* progression in a written-out cadenza (example 3). In B the motivic elements of the C-major outburst are drawn out and multiplied, and the hint of A-flat minor in the retransition is expanded into a fragmentary *minore* variation. Schenker did not hear this *minore* as a variation at all, because it traces the *Urlinie* ♭*3–2* (part of a larger *5–2*) rather than *3–5–1*. The B♭ reached at the end of the *minore* certainly stands out, the strongest dominant sound in the entire movement.

After the last, climactic variation of A¹, A² returns unchanged once again. In the coda, the line E♭–D♭–C–C♭–B♭ that Schenker traced in the expanded variation *3* is echoed by G♭–F–F♭–E♭ of the Più mosso. Finally, an apotheosis of the *5–3/5–1* complex reveals this as a linear epitome of the tonal crux A-flat major/C major; the very end of the movement is one of those points in Beethoven where, as Charles

EXAMPLE 2

EXAMPLE 3

Rosen has remarked, the composer attempts "to strip away . . . all decorative and even expressive elements from the musical material—so that part of the structure of tonality is made to appear for a moment naked and immediate, and its presence in the rest of the work as a dynamic and temporal force suddenly becomes radiant."[18] The striking melodic expansion in bar 225 (G–F–E♭), which may be seen as an ornamentation of the fifth degree, E♭, coincides with the strongest subdominant sound in a movement containing remarkably few subdominant or dominant sonorities. It also provides the most expressive moment in an otherwise singularly cold movement. Immoderately expressive, perhaps. Kramer could rightly describe this gesture, too, as overwrought.

v ·     The repercussions and fermatas of the opening theme of the Allegro con brio penetrate all four movements of the symphony, of course. The movements are bound together not only by a silent program—to borrow a term from Constantin Floros—and not only by common motivic shapes, rhythmic configurations, and harmonic processes. They are also unified by similar basic, subthematic gestures— gestures about time and articulateness, about stability and coherence.

Thus time notoriously refuses to move through this work in a steady metrical flow—refuses more truculently, perhaps, than in any other work by Beethoven prior to his last years. The impression made on Wagner by the first-movement fermatas has already been noted. We have also noted the curious temporal effect of the superior pedal E♭ in the Andante con moto, where the clarinet gives the impression of starting a *ritardando* without the cellos noticing. This movement also contains one actual fermata, at bar 123. The passage following it is best understood as a long cadenza *in tempo* for the wind instruments emerging from that powerful fermata. The shorter wind-instrument passage after the *minore* can be understood

EXAMPLE 4

EXAMPLE 5

similarly, as another, albeit less radical, suspension of temporal stability. The elongations of the motive in the final appearance of the C-major passage can also be experienced as a series of written-out fermatas.

As for repercussion, that produces some of the symphony's most famous effects: in the first movement, the proliferation of the motive's upbeat notes after its collapse from a third to a unison, and in the third movement, the sequence from the already repercussive horn theme to continuous drumbeats and then to a drumroll. Here repercussion becomes reduction and ultimately inarticulateness. In the Andante con moto, various passages might be described as repercussive in a weaker sense: bars 6–11, 26–28, 35–37, 38–40, 97, 160–165, 232–242. Perhaps the clearest analogy to the instances in the fast movements comes with the reiteration of sixteenth-note Gs in bars 145–47 (example 4). Does this sound like a powerful summons to the C-major episode, replacing the sudden preemptions that happened before? Or do the instruments seem to stammer?

In each of the other movements, too, there are passages in which the end result of repercussion is an almost incoherent stammer (example 5). As Hoffmann remarked dryly in reference to example 5b, "To many people this may seem playful, but for the reviewer a sinister feeling was awakened." Words such as *ängstlich, fremd, furchtbar, Geheimnisvolle, schauerlich, Schmerz, Unbekannte, unheimlich,* and *Unruhe* abound in his great essay, culminating in his reference to an *Angst* "which tightly constricts the breast" prior to the transition to the finale. Hoffmann attributes these feelings to *Geisterfurcht,* which could mean among other things terror of the unknown, the inchoate, and the inarticulate.

To attempt to exorcise the primal and the subartistic in the Fifth Symphony is to engage in a coverup. Hoffmann made no such mistake. The analytical project to mute Beethoven's insistent evocations of "the naked human voice" memorializes a bizarre moment in the recent academic history of Beethoven reception.

### Notes

1. Carl Dahlhaus, "Issues in Composition," in *Between Romanticism and Modernism: Four Studies in the Music of the Later Nineteenth Century,* tr. Mary Whittall (California Studies in 19th-Century Music, ed. Joseph Kerman, no. 1; Berkeley and Los Angeles, 1980), 40–78. Originally "Zur Problemgeschichte des Komponierens," in *Zwischen Romantik und Moderne* (Berlin musikwissenschaftliche Arbeiten 7; Munich, 1974).
2. Dahlhaus, "Issues in Composition," 41–42.
3. Heinrich Schenker, *Beethovens V. Symphonie* (Vienna, 1925), 7; see also Heinrich Schenker, *Counterpoint: A Translation of "Kontrapunkt,"* tr. John Rothgeb and Jürgen Thym, ed. John Rothgeb (New York, 1987), 1:42. Elliott Forbes, in his very useful casebook, made Schenker's analysis of the first movement widely available to English readers, adding valuable explanatory notes (but—like other American editors—omitting Schenker's disagreeable excursus, in this case a sixteen-page assault on the previous literature): *Beethoven, Symphony No. 5 in C Minor* (Norton Critical Scores; New York, 1971).
[An Austrian friend has provided me with a gloss on Schenker's word *Beiklang*—which is not in the dictionary—by analogy with *Beigeschmack* or *Beischmack:* "the taste of something extraneous to the thing itself," as in "this grapefruit juice has a metallic *Beischmack.*"]
4. Richard Wagner, *Three Wagner Essays,* tr. Robert L. Jacobs (London, 1979), 63.
5. Richard Wagner, *Beethoven,* tr. Edward Dannreuther (London, 1890), 75. "Hier betritt das lyrische Pathos fast schon den Boden einer idealen Dramatik im bestimmteren Sinn."
6. In *Zur Neuausgabe der Sinfonie Nr. V von Ludwig von Beethoven* (Leipzig, 1978), p. 56, Peter Gülke mentions contributions by E. Tetzel, Th. Wiehmayer, M. Frey, R. Hammer, Müller-Reuter, Weingartner, Schenker, and Andrew Imbrie; see also Lionel Pike, *Beethoven, Sibelius, and the Profound Logic* (London, 1978), 146–55, and Charles Rosen, *Sonata Forms,* rev. ed. (New York, 1988), 193–96.
7. Wagner, *Three Wagner Essays,* 53–54. [A conductor known for his restrained treatment of the fermatas in Beethoven's Fifth had been Mendelssohn.]
8. Relevant references to the Fifth Symphony in Cosima's diaries appear under the dates 1879: 15 July; 1880: 11 Jan., 3 Feb., 13 July ("I realize that this symphony in particular can only make its effect when played by R.; it is quite deliberately aimed at rousing the audience, there is something oratorical about it . . .") and 14 July; and 1881: 22 Feb. ("this

cheerful rejoicing about nothing, he adds gaily") and 28 Feb. *Cosima Wagner's Diaries,* ed. Martin Gregor-Dallin and Dietrich Mack, tr. Geoffrey Skelton, vol. 2, *1878–83* (New York, 1980).

9. Virgil Thomson, *The Art of Judging Music* (New York, 1948), 303.

10. George Grove, *Beethoven and His Nine Symphonies* (London, 1896), 157–58.

11. Gustav Nottebohm, *Beethoveniana* (Leipzig, 1872), 14–15. To the discerning remarks on this sketch made by Peter Gülke (*Zur Neuausgabe der Sinfonie Nr. V,* 28–30), it may be added that the "quasi Trio" is already asymmetrical (like the final version) in its phrase lengths, and already contains the characteristic climactic transference of the opening upbeat figure to a strong beat.

12. Lawrence Kramer, *Music and Poetry: The Nineteenth Century and After* (Berkeley and Los Angeles, 1984), 235.

13. *E. T. A. Hoffmann's Musical Writings,* ed. David Charlton, tr. Martyn Clarke (Cambridge, 1989), 99, 245.

14. Gülke, *Zur Neuausgabe der Sinfonie Nr. V,* 58.

15. In the first movement the motive is accented on the weak bar, in the second movement on the weak beat of the bar.

16. Carl Dahlhaus, "Beethoven's 'New Way,'" in *Ludwig van Beethoven: Approaches to His Music,* tr. Mary Whittall (Oxford, 1991), 166–81. Originally "Beethoven's 'Neuer Weg,'" *Jahrbuch des Staatlichen Instituts für Musikforschung Preussischer Kulturbesitz* 7 (1974): 46–61.

17. Lawrence Kramer, "The Shape of Post-Classical Music," *Critical Inquiry* 6 (1979): 149.

18. Charles Rosen, *The Classical Style: Haydn, Mozart, Beethoven,* rev. ed. (New York, 1972), 435.

# Beethoven's Minority

*For Alan Tyson*

This is not a biographical essay on Beethoven's early years in Bonn, the years before he had to take charge of his family as a result of his father's incapacity. It is, rather, a somewhat speculative investigation into his use of the minor mode. Beethoven's usages in this area are more distinctive, I venture to say, than is generally recognized. To be sure, his proclivity for one particular minor key, C minor, is often remarked upon, and has been discussed by Alan Tyson in one of his most dazzling essays, "The Problem of Beethoven's 'First' *Leonore* Overture."[1] Tyson arrived at this question by way of a rich nexus of sketches, brought together and analyzed with his usual virtuosity—sketches from the years 1806 and 1807, the period when the C-minor syndrome becomes, in Tyson's words, "something of an obsession."

There may be something more to find out by looking at the question from a more comprehensive standpoint. The point of departure for the present essay is an analysis of the key relations that Beethoven chose for all of his minor-mode sonatas, orchestral works, and chamber music. Later, I make a number of moves that broaden the inquiry and, I hope, thicken the explanatory context for Beethoven's idiosyncratic minority.

II · Let us take the plunge and start with a compendium of Beethoven's compositions in the minor mode, showing their primary key relations in a diagrammatic form. Table I consists of two chronological lists, the first for C-minor works and the

---

◄— To appear in *Haydn, Mozart and Beethoven: Studies in the Music of the Classical Period Presented to Alan Tyson,* ed. Sieghard Brandenburg (Oxford: Clarendon Press, forthcoming).

TABLE I — Beethoven: Key Relations in the Minor Mode
(first and last movements of cyclic works)

*a. Works in C Minor*

| | FIRST MOVEMENT | | | | | | FINALE | | | |
|---|---|---|---|---|---|---|---|---|---|---|
| | *Exposition* | | *Recapitulation* | | | | *Exposition* | *Recapitulation* | | |
| | 2nd group 2nd theme | End | 1st group | 2nd group | End | Coda | 2nd group 2nd theme | 1st group | 2nd group | End |
| Piano Trio op. 1 no. 3 | III ——— | | i+I | i ——— | | | III ——— | | I–i— | I: tierce |
| String Trio op. 9 no. 3 | III ——— | | i ——— | | | | iii–III | i–I | v–i— | I: tierce |
| Sonata op. 10 no. 1 | III ——— | | IV+i — | | | | III ——— | | I–i— | I: tierce |
| Sonata op. 13 | iii | III | iv | i — | | | III ——— | | I–i— | |
| String Quartet op. 18 no. 4 | III ——— | | I ——— | | | i | rondo | | | I: tierce |
| Violin Sonata op. 30 no. 2 | III–iii | III | I–i —— | | | | sonata rondo† | | | |
| Concerto No. 3, op. 37 | III ——— | | I ——— | | | i | sonata rondo: III ——— | | I–(i) | I: coda: Presto |
| Overture Coriolan | III+iv+v — | | iv | I+ii+iii | i | I–i | | | | |
| Symphony No. 5, op. 67 | III ——— | | I ——— | | | i | *whole finale is in the major* | | | |
| ★Sonata op. 111 | VI ——— | | I–iv | | i | I tierce | *whole finale is in the major* | | | |

| | *Exposition* | *1st theme* | *Development* | *Recapitulation* |
|---|---|---|---|---|
| †Violin Sonata, op. 30 no. 2 finale (sonata rondo): | i  III+iii  III | i–I | | i  i+i — |

★ = two-movement sonata
i+I = theme comes twice, in i and then in I
I–i = theme changes mode en route

TABLE I (continued)

### b. Works in minor keys other than C Minor

| | FIRST MOVEMENT | | | FINALE | | |
|---|---|---|---|---|---|---|
| | *Exposition* | *Recapitulation* | | *Exposition* | *Recapitulation* | |
| | *2nd group* | *2nd group* | *Coda* | *2nd group* | *2nd group* | *End* |
| Sonata in F Minor WoO 47 | III —— | i —— | | III —— | i —— | |
| Piano Quartet in E♭ Minor WoO 36 no. 1 (second movement) | v —— | i —— | | *whole finale is in the major mode* | | |
| Sonata in F minor op. 2 no. 1 | III —— | i —— | | v —— | i —— | |
| ★Cello Sonata in G Minor op. 5 no. 2 | III–iii  III | I–i —— | I: tierce | *whole finale is in the major mode* | | |
| ★Sonata in G Minor op. 49 no. 1 | III —— | i —— | I: tierce | *whole finale is in the major mode* | | |
| Violin Sonata in A Minor op. 23 | v —— | i —— | | v —— | i —— | |
| Sonata in C♯ Minor op. 27 no. 2 | | | | v —— | i —— | |
| Sonata in D Minor op. 31 no. 2 | v —— | i —— | | v —— | i —— | |
| Violin Sonata in A Minor op. 47 | v —— | i —— | | *whole finale is in the major mode* | | |
| Sonata in F Minor op. 57 | III–iii —— | I–i —— | | v —— | i —— | |
| Quartet in E Minor op. 59 no. 2 | III —— | I —— | i | v —— | i —— | |
| Overture, *Egmont* | III —— | VI — | (via i) . . . . . . . . . . . . . . . . . . | | | I: coda: Allegro |
| Quartet in F Minor op. 95 | VI —— | VI + I - | i | v —— | iv–i— | I: coda: Allegro |
| ★Sonata in E Minor op. 90 | v —— | i —— | | *whole finale is in the major mode* | | |
| Symphony No. 9 op. 125 | VI —— | I–i —— | | *after introduction, finale is major* | | |
| Quartet in A Minor op. 132 | VI —— | III / I–i | | v —— | iv–i— | I: coda: Presto |
| Quartet in C♯ Minor op. 131 | | | | III —— | ♭II + i | I: tierce *(early idea* I: coda: Largo*)* |

★ = two-movement sonata
i + I = theme comes twice, in i and then in I
I–i = theme changes mode en route

second for works in other minor keys. At issue are the first movements, all but two of which are in sonata form, and the finales, which are in sonata, rondo, or sonata-rondo form.

For the C-minor works, table 1a indicates first of all the key of the second group of the exposition—generally a single key, though the first movement of the *Pathétique* Sonata, to take a rare example, brings its lyric "second theme" in the minor mediant (iii) and the following cadential material in the major (III). Then the table shows the key for the first group in the recapitulation when, exceptionally, this is anything other than the minor tonic; for the second group in the recapitulation; and for the coda, if this shows a significant change. When a theme is repeated directly one or more times in different keys or modes, this is shown by plus signs: I + ii + iii or I + i. When a theme changes mode halfway through, this is shown by a dash: I–i. A somewhat simpler scheme is adopted for the second category of works, works in keys other than C minor (table 1b).

Most diagrams strike their compilers as paradigms of clarity and elegance; and most diagrams confuse and repel those who are enjoined to learn from them. But even those disinclined to puzzle through table 1 can catch my main drift if they will simply scan the facing pages and compare them for the amount of upper-case Roman numerals. Upper-case appears much more in category a than in category b. In b, the majority of movements have their second group in the minor dominant (v); with the earlier works, and with finales at any period, the preponderance of this arrangement is striking. In category a, on the other hand, not only does a major key—nearly always the mediant (III)—invariably appear in the second group, but the tonic major (I), too, is always represented somewhere. This is quite rare in category b, at least until the time of the F-minor Quartet, op. 95, and the music for *Egmont*.

Both of these Beethovenian syndromes—the hankering of C minor for its parallel major, and the tropism of other minor keys toward their minor dominants—are aberrant according to the norms of the Classic period. They are certainly not characteristic of Haydn and Mozart, Count Waldstein's anointed models for the young prodigy. Nor, on the basis of an admittedly incomplete search, are they at all common in the works of C. P. E. Bach and Franz Sterkel, composers who are said to have influenced the young prodigy. But they developed early in Beethoven's career. Prior to any of the Vienna works, his 1785 Piano Quartet in E Flat, WoO 36 no. 1, contains a stormy sonata movement in E-flat minor which moves to B-flat minor for its second group. The choice of this key could even be considered willful: this quartet was shown long ago to be modeled on Mozart's Violin Sonata in G Major/Minor, K. 396, and of course Mozart's minor-mode movement moves to the mediant.

Beethoven declined, then, to follow the standard procedure of the older masters. Could he have been following the example of one particular, aberrant composition?

In Mozart's oeuvre, practically the only minor-mode movement with the minor dominant as its subsidiary key is the finale of the Sonata in A Minor, K. 310. (Beethoven would presumably have known the Paris publication of 1782.) Before bringing the second theme in v, Mozart's unusual rondo also brings a bit of the first theme in iii, C minor, just beforehand. This might have provided Beethoven with encouragement for his minor-mediant forays in op. 9 no. 3 and op. 13, if by that time he required any encouraging.

There is also one unusual (but famous) work by Haydn that comes to mind. During the period 1767–74, for which it seems impossible to retire the term "Storm and Stress," Haydn wrote a dozen or so symphonies, sonatas, and string quartets in the minor mode, but only one movement among them modulates to the dominant, rather than the mediant. This is the first movement of Symphony No. 45, the "Farewell." After Beethoven's early piano quartet, the next composition by him in which the exposition moves from i to v is the finale of the Piano Sonata in F Minor, op. 2 no. 1. It will be remembered that this finale eschews a development section in favor of a placid, regular binary melody—complete with repeats and written-out ornamentation—in the mediant, A flat. In this it is unlike any other Beethoven composition, but not entirely unlike the first movement of Haydn's "Farewell" Symphony.

Certainly Haydn's stormy movement was calculated to impress the young Beethoven; and an incomplete symphony draft from the Bonn years, Hess 298, appears to show clear signs of its impact. Preserved in the "Kafka Sketchbook," this draft was duly noted by Nottebohm and first published in the *Sammelbände* of the International Musicological Society in 1912. I give a rather extensive music example (example 1) to support my impression that Beethoven's reliance goes past the urgent mood and the thematic configuration; the way the rhythmic acceleration is managed also seems influenced by Haydn.

It would be pleasant to be able to say that Beethoven also followed Haydn's aberrant tonal scheme for his budding symphony and used the minor dominant for the second theme. But the draft is in C minor, and the second theme is in E-flat major. After the modulation, the draft grows more and more conventional. The second theme, a meandering rococo melody, shows no sign of concluding when the draft breaks off.[2]

III ·   As early as the Bonn piano quartet, Beethoven had achieved a sort of minor-mode saturation in a single movement; it is an effect he may have learned to admire from Haydn's "Farewell" Symphony. Table 1b reminds us of other dark movements—the finale of op. 59 no. 2, despite its repeated gesturing toward C major, and the finale of op. 95, despite its improbable last-minute rescue. In the Sonata op. 31 no. 2 Beethoven surrounded the Adagio in B-flat major by two resolutely D-minor

EXAMPLE I

movements, movements in which a consolatory major-mode sound is scarcely ever to be heard. (The finale contains twelve bars or so of B-flat major.) Minor-mode saturation clearly appealed to Beethoven, in one of his moods, and bringing the second theme in the minor dominant, rather than the mediant, was the way to bring it about.

On one occasion Beethoven went so far as to experiment with minor-mode inflection for the second group of a minor-mode composition that does *not* move

EXAMPLE 2

to the minor dominant. In the opening Allegro of the Sonata in F Minor, op. 2 no. 1, both the second theme and the cadence theme are in A-flat major—at least, they are both harmonized in A-flat major. Both melodies, however, avoid the mode-defining degrees *3* and *6,* while also incorporating some clear minor-mode articulation—F♭ and C♭ respectively (example 2). Hence, when recapitulated in the minor, the themes do not require any melodic alteration at all (until bar 6 of theme 2). Just a few left-hand chords changed from major to minor does the trick.

IV ·  The tendency of works in C minor to break into C major is something we take for granted, perhaps, because of the Fifth Symphony. It is still rather remarkable to see this tendency played out on one level or another in every single one of Beethoven's many works in this key. It is doubly remarkable when the other minor-mode works are also brought into consideration. Looking at table 1a, we can almost imagine the composer experimenting with all kinds of schemes to incorporate some *maggiore* sonority before going all out, as he did in the Fifth.

Occasionally it is the first group of the recapitulation that admits a major-mode episode (in the first movement of op. 1 no. 3 and the finales of op. 9 no. 3 and op. 30 no. 2). More often, it is the second group. In either case, the mode soon returns to the minor. Listening to the finale of the C-minor Trio, op. 1 no. 3, for example, one expects to hear the second theme recapitulated with its mode switched to minor, but it appears in the tonic major, changing back to the minor during the course of the theme. The theme is extended from twenty-one bars to twenty-five to allow for this mode change (example 3); then the movement continues in the minor mode, but ends with a tierce de Picardie. Tierces de Picardie end four of Beethoven's early C-minor works, but none of his minor-mode works in other keys, until op. 131.

This scheme—the "major-minor" recapitulation pattern, as we may call it—proved to be something Beethoven could use for second groups again and again. There are nine more instances, five from the early repertory, if one counts in this category the Allegro con brio of the Sonata op. 10 no. 1, where the second theme returns in the major of the subdominant key, F (the tonic major having already put in an unexpected appearance at the beginning of the development section). The finale of this sonata and the finale of the *Pathétique* follow the same scheme as the

EXAMPLE 3

Op. 1/3

Piano Trio finale. And what may be considered a smoother version of it occurs in the first movements of the C-minor Violin Sonata, op. 30 no. 2, and the G-minor Cello Sonata, op. 5 no. 2: in the expositions of these movements, the second theme in its original, mediant-major version already moves to the minor one or two bars from the end. For purposes of exposition this move is immediately negated, of course, but when Beethoven comes to the recapitulation, he can transpose the theme literally and now maintain the minor mode up to the final cadence.

Another scheme that Beethoven was able to use many times makes its debut with the op. 18 string quartets. The Allegro ma non tanto of the C-minor Quartet, op. 18 no. 4, makes room for more tonic major within the tonal scheme than do any of the works discussed so far. The exposition brings the second group in the mediant E flat, as expected, and the recapitulated second theme comes in C major; but then instead of switching back at once to the minor mode, Beethoven maintains the major tonic throughout the rest of the second group—an extensive section of music featuring two distinct new themes. It remains for the coda to restore the minor mode, which it does by way of a violent progression involving a Neapolitan chord.[3]

This "major recapitulation/minor coda" pattern becomes a feature of several important middle-period works, in C minor and other keys. Upon their codas much more structural weight devolves than on the codas of earlier minor-mode compositions. The first movement of the C-minor Concerto is a case in point,[4] as is also the celebrated and unusually concise first movement of the Fifth Symphony. After the bassoons in the recapitulation take over the French horn tattoo—which is modally ambiguous, of course—the second group annexes C major and holds on to it until the coda, a section of music which is just about as long as the recapitulation and nearly as eventful. Like the coda of the C-minor Quartet, this coda also begins with an abrupt move featuring Neapolitan harmony.

Other examples of the "major recapitulation/minor coda" pattern are the first movements of the String Quartets op. 59 no. 2 and op. 95, and the Overture to *Egmont*. The way the coda begins in op. 95 recalls the C-minor Quartet and the Fifth Symphony.

v ·     If we try to find models for Beethoven's treatment of C minor, with its *maggiore* admixture, a scan of the minor-mode compositions by Haydn and Mozart provides even slimmer pickings than for his "saturated" treatment of other minor keys. With the exception of one important group of works, Haydn and Mozart in their minor-mode sonata movements avoid tonic major sonorities. They avoid them, indeed, in what certainly seems like a conscious and purposeful manner.

And the exception? I refer, of course, to Haydn's later works in the minor mode, which regularly switch mode once and for all at the second group of the recapitulation, the entire sonata movement ending in the major.

Such a work is Symphony No. 95 in C Minor, dating from 1791, which Douglas Johnson has proposed as a model for the thematic structure of Beethoven's Piano Trio, op. 1 no. 3, of 1795.[5] Yet I would register strong resistance to any claim for Haydn as a model for Beethoven's C-minor syndrome. Both composers bring C major into C-minor works, but from the standpoint of musical effect the ways they do this are diametrically opposed. Haydn introduces C major so as to erase minor-mode tensions and end a moody, brusque movement jovially; Beethoven introduces C major only to contradict it, to restore minor-mode tensions made all the more intense by the temporary contrast. Haydn's essential dynamic is minor-to-major, Beethoven's is major-to-minor. Even Beethoven's tierce de Picardie endings, one feels, depend on an unsounded minor *Nachklang*.

Indeed, the way Beethoven deals with C minor seems to me closer in its essentials to Mozart than to Haydn. In the unforgettable minor-mode compositions of Mozart's Vienna years, the move to major at the end of a piece is very rare, and never carried out in Haydn's manner. One thinks of the G-minor String Quintet, the D-minor Piano Concerto, and *Don Giovanni;* but one also thinks of many more works which hold fast to the minor mode until the end. The recapitulation is a point of stability, and for Mozart that entailed stability of mode. Mozart's minor-mode sonata movements invariably stay minor: in the G-minor Symphony, the C-minor Concerto, the C-minor Sonata, and other works.

And when the lyric major-mode second theme comes back with the mode changed, it comes infused with new pathos. Many critics have marveled at Mozart's special ability to devise melodies that will return in the minor with special poignancy. An example that must have impressed Beethoven (must impress, in fact, any musician), from a Mozart work he drew on for his Piano Concerto No. 3, op. 37,[6] is shown in example 4. Mozart's recapitulated themes move us because

EXAMPLE 4

we remember them from the last time we heard them, in the exposition, when they were major.

This is not an effect that Beethoven seems ever to have sought. Presumably he never cared for it, and indeed as a young man he may have felt he lacked the technique to carry it off. He also evidently did not care about the modal stability of recapitulations; at least when in C minor, he was prepared to forgo this in favor of something else. He switches the mode to major at the beginning of the second theme, and switches back at some point later.

The first shift, which destroys the minor-mode stability of the recapitulation, can however be said to maintain "stability of mood," in that the theme returns with its mode unchanged. The second shift, however, parallels Mozart's effect of pathos, though in a more immediate and, no doubt, a less subtle guise. The listener need not remember the theme in its major-mode version, heard several minutes before. The major-mode theme dissolves into the minor on the spot, before the theme is over.

It is of course impossible to know whether Beethoven actually had the idea that his major-minor shifts would achieve some kind of Mozartian pathos (we do not know about Mozart either). And it is not always easy to empathize with the early Beethoven C-minor recapitulations. That pathos was his idea does seem to be borne out, however, by the most accomplished and beautiful case, that in the finale of the *Pathétique* Sonata (example 5). Here Beethoven went out of his way to destroy the minor-mode stability of his recapitulation by means of a lengthy major-mode preparation for the second theme. Such preparation was needed, perhaps, because the theme will change mode after only four bars; the major-minor shift sets in unusually early, and is underscored by a long extension, running into a *calando*. The fact that this extension crowds out the busy cadential material that we heard

EXAMPLE 5

the first time around may be thought to add to the pathos. Even the last return of
the rondo melody, which follows, has a newly pathetic cast at its beginning, thanks
to a well-known anomaly in its *Gestalt* at this point—the excision of the original
upbeat figure to bar 1.

Beethoven wanted pathos, then, but he wanted pathos on his own terms. Mozart's pathos is a long-term effect, Beethoven's is a short-term effect. The two
procedures can be displayed and contrasted as follows:

MOZART  tonic minor  mediant (major)  ‖  tonic minor  tonic minor

BEETHOVEN  tonic minor  mediant (major)  ‖  tonic minor  tonic major—tonic minor

In the first movement of the *Appassionata* Sonata, Beethoven actually transferred
the effect of major-minor pathos back to the exposition:

tonic minor  mediant major—mediant minor  ‖  tonic minor  tonic major—tonic minor

The situation elicited an extended gloss from Tovey, who claimed that the *Appassionata* as a whole is a work that transcends pathos:

> No other work by Beethoven maintains a tragic solemnity throughout all
> its movements. . . . The conception [of the Andante con moto] is sublime,
> and may be taken as representing the ultimate faith underlying the tragic
> emotion. At the opposite end of the emotional scale, the realization of that
> which was feared, comes the entirely new theme of the *Presto* at the end of
> the finale.

As for the first movement, both the exposition and the recapitulation bring the second theme in the major mode and then turn to the minor, as shown in the diagram; it remains for the coda to present a frenetically abbreviated version of the second theme at last in the tonic minor. Sketches for the exposition show that originally the entire second group was planned in the minor mediant—a plan which reminded Tovey of the D-minor Sonata, op. 31 no. 2—but Beethoven changed his mind and put the lyric second subject (only) in the major. This "glorious afterthought converted the whole movement from the gloom of storm to the active passions of tragedy."[7]

VI ·

Pathos, poignancy, tragedy: with a little help from Tovey the discussion has moved past technical and historical concerns—tallying key relations, searching for models—to the analysis of musical effects. There has been a change in the mode, we might say, of the discourse. Another critical move seems mandated, toward the consideration of extramusical referentiality. We need to look beyond symphonies, sonatas, and chamber music to music with texts.

It may be surprising (the first time we notice) to find Beethoven favoring C minor so much over other minor keys for his instrumental works, and to find C minor always implicated with C major. With his texted works the situation is even more singular. Beethoven wrote four large-scale vocal works between 1802 and 1808, and all of them turn on the crux of C minor and C major. Let us take up these works in reverse chronological order.[8]

1. Choral Fantasy, op. 80. After the solo piano "improvisation" starting (and ending) in C minor, the orchestra enters with a menacing (mock-menacing?) fugato in the same key. This is resolved by the C-major "Gegenliebe" theme and its variations, first played and then sung: "Schmeichelnd hold und lieblich klingen unsers Lebens Harmonien." It could be argued (though I would not press the argument too hard) that the move from C minor to major is the Fantasy's most salient harmonic feature.

2. Mass in C, op. 86. After three movements in C major, the Sanctus is in A, and the Agnus Dei moves from C minor ("Agnus Dei," Poco andante) to C major ("Dona nobis pacem," Allegro ma non troppo).

    As we know also from the *Missa solemnis,* Beethoven read the phrase "Dona nobis pacem" as a promise of relief after the considerable anguish registered by the preceding *Misereres.* The simple, almost childlike quality of his setting of that phrase in the later Mass is forecast by the earlier setting. Also forecast is the dramatic recollection of distress that interrupts the "Dona" of op. 123—the famous battle music and recitatives. In the

Mass in C, Beethoven brings the words "Agnus Dei . . . miserere nobis" back within the "Dona" for a distressful sixteen-bar passage in C minor. The transition back to C major is made with solo woodwinds, as at the end of the previous section, the Agnus Dei (Poco andante, C minor).

Beethoven went further, "planting" a somewhat similar C-minor–major progression at the earlier point in the Mass at which some of the same words appear. The Qui tollis in the Gloria starts in F minor, Andante mosso, turning to C minor for the third appeal, "Qui sedes ad dexteram Patris, miserere nobis"; the supplicatory C minor then resolves into a triumphant chorale-like passage in C major, Allegro ma non troppo, for the Quoniam. The transition is worked by solo woodwind utterances, similar to those of the Agnus Dei.

3. *Leonore,* op. 72. The opera's massive reliance on the crux of C minor–C major did not survive the 1814 revision, of course. At the beginning of the original Act III finale, Leonore and Florestan hear what they take to be a threatening crowd singing "Zur Rache" in C minor. This resolves through several stages—via A major and F major—to the final chorus of celebration in C major.

And Marzelline's aria, which originally came first, right after the C-major overture, forecasts the conclusion by encapsulating the same C-minor–major progression. One can doubt that this long-range effect would have made much of an effect in the theater, without in the least doubting Beethoven's intention.[9]

4. *Christus am Oelberge,* op. 85. As in *Leonore,* the progress from despair to triumph is rendered by the progression from C minor (Christ's aria, no. 2) to C major (the final Alleluia Chorus, no. 8).

*Christus* begins with a slow, disturbed *Trauermusik* in E-flat minor, running into the opening recitative in C minor. This incorporates a citation from Haydn's *Creation* which must have raised eyebrows at the time: a mention of chaos—"noch eh die Welt auf dein Geheiss dem Chaos sich entwand"—is set to music which resolves to a blaring C-major fanfare in the orchestra, marked Maestoso. "Ich höre deines Seraphs Donnerstimme," remarks Jesus. C minor to C major paints light after darkness (even though Beethoven's C major soon turns toward G); this can be thought to forecast and encapsulate the tonal dynamic of the total oratorio.

The aria "Meine Seele ist erschüttert," a binary structure in C minor, brings its second main theme (for the words "Vater! Tief gebeugt und kläglich") in the mediant, E flat, and recapitulates it in C major, changing back to the minor mode for the concluding cadential section. We recognize this "major-minor" recapitulation pattern from instrumental works of a slightly earlier period.[10]

How do these resolutely affirmative vocal works connect, or entwine, with the minor-mode instrumental works we have traced before? It is time for the discussion to change mode once again, this time in the direction of synthesis—a move that makes me uneasy, not only because of some diffidence as regards my own mobility, but also because there are major gaps and obscurities remaining in the territory itself. My best scenario goes something like this.

Young Beethoven, I have suggested, was especially impressed by a few unusual (if famous) minor-mode works in the Classical pantheon. He resolved to keep his own minor-mode works as minor as could be. Haydn's "Farewell" Symphony ended its stormy first movement in the minor mode, only to dissipate the effect in a jesting major-mode finale; Beethoven's first piano sonata would end stormily in the minor. Mozart's A-minor Sonata reached for the minor dominant as its subsidiary key, in a rondo finale mollified by a *maggiore* episode; Beethoven's D-minor Sonata would celebrate the minor dominant in its first movement *and* in its finale. The D-minor Sonata would keep both movements fanatically free of major-mode sonorities.

But at some point, early on, Beethoven had a contrary vision, that of troubled C minor ceding to serene C major. The vision haunted him. He dashed off a silly bagatelle marked Lustig (C major) and Traurig (C minor). He kept mapping out instrumental works in C minor that cope with the issue in one way or another. They had to be resolutely minor, yet they somehow had to hint at major-mode resolution. Sometimes he ended them with a quizzical tierce de Picardie. More often, he recapitulated the lyric second theme in its original major mode (rather than in the minor, as Mozart had done and as he himself invariably did in works in minor keys other than C minor) before returning to the minor at the end of the second group. The result—to make one more critical move, this one from personal scenario to personal reaction—was often uncertain in its emotional effect. Haydn's advice to Beethoven, as teacher to student, was hopelessly wrong, of course; the C-minor Piano Trio had to be published. But it is possible to feel some sympathy for the teacher in this case.

Later C-minor works were more accomplished. And I believe that a slow process of clarification set in when Beethoven began to deal with large-scale texts. (This happened after the premiere of a very, very important work that moves from C minor to C major, the *Creation*.)[11] Fortuitously or not, it turned out that the librettos Beethoven set always involved the ultimate resolution of some sort of tension; and Beethoven always found himself thinking about C minor resolving to C major. This resolution traced the sequence from despair to faith, with a subsidiary move from chaos to angelic order. It also traced the unwinding of an actual plot, the plot of an extended rescue drama culminating in the psychological journey of hero and heroine from peril to relief and rapture. The ascent from guilt-ridden supplication to confidence in God's grace—C minor to C major, once again. Likewise the progress from unspecified anxieties to the joyous contemplation of cosmic harmony. That Beethoven found an object of personal identification in each of these works is now, thanks to a small but influential article by Alan Tyson, widely accepted.[12]

I have suggested that a process of clarification began when Beethoven found himself setting large-scale texts. Tyson's study of the *Leonore* overtures documents this slow, even tortuous process. The C-minor symphony begun in 1804 was four years a-borning, and numerous other C-minor sketches were aborted. These include some apparently intended for the *Leonore* Overture no. 1, and for a minor-mode finale to the String Quartet, op. 59 no. 3. Tyson has argued powerfully that works as substantial as the *Coriolan* Overture and the C-minor Variations for Piano were forced into existence, as it were, without commission or occasion by Beethoven's "obsession." Both of these works still conclude in the minor mode; the Variations include a mellow major-mode episode, and *Coriolan* brings the C-major glint that seems obligatory in the recapitulations of C-minor works among an astonishing array of minor keys (ii, iii, iv, and v are all represented). Indeed C major glints a second time: for when the recapitulation closes abruptly on a Neapolitan sixth, the second theme starts again in C major, turning back to the minor after four bars.

Finally, in 1807, the Fifth Symphony was completed. The first movement, as we have already seen, makes stirring use of the "major recapitulation/minor coda" pattern, one of Beethoven's devices to approach or approximate Mozartian major-to-minor pathos. But of course the Fifth traces a C-minor–major drama not only in the first of its movements but through all four. This work transcends pathos as thoroughly as does the *Appassionata* Sonata—in the other direction. Mozart's major-to-minor dynamic has yielded to a famously exultant, and very un-Haydnish, minor-to-major.

VIII ·    But as has already been intimated, one piece of the puzzle is rather conspicuously missing. Why was it C minor that took on this special role for Beethoven? Why did other keys not enter into consideration? I feel sure that the piece must be the Cantata on the Death of Emperor Joseph II, WoO 87, of 1790 . . . though I am not at all sure just how it fits into the puzzle.

The cantata is generally regarded as Beethoven's most impressive accomplishment before his departure for Vienna. Once again, it would be pleasant to be able to report that his first important C-minor essay, the chorus "Tot!" from this cantata, includes an arresting episode in the tonic major. But it does not. Neither the first appearance of this chorus at the beginning of the obsequies, which moves to E flat, nor its second appearance at the end, which remains in C minor, includes so much as a hint of consolatory C major.

One can speculate: did the saturated minority which he was able to indulge in this work finally strike the composer as *too* saturated? And had he perhaps mishandled the matter of resolution? Halfway through the middle of the cantata comes a famous consoling aria with chorus, "Da stiegen die Menschen an's Licht," in the major mode—in F major. But the libretto demanded a return to lamentation and C minor for the conclusion.[13] Perhaps Beethoven was left with a feeling of dissatisfaction about the way his first effort to cope with a large text had turned out. The project must certainly have left him frustrated for another reason: though the cantata was clearly the young composer's most prestigious commission, it never was performed—the premiere planned for the memorial service in March 1790 was scrubbed for reasons unknown, and a later performance was given up because the music was found to be too difficult.

One can speculate further, about inchoate fears that might have been stirred in Beethoven by the cantata's crass text:

| | |
|---|---|
| Tot! stöhnt es durch die öde Nacht | Death! echoes through the empty night; |
| Felsen, weinet es wieder! | Mountain crags, weep it again! |
| Und ihr Wogen des Meeres, heulet | And ye waves of the sea, howl |
| es durch eure Tiefen: | It through your depths! |
| Joseph der grosse ist tot! | Joseph the Great is dead! |
| Joseph, der Vater unsterblicher Taten, | Joseph, the father of undying deeds, |
| ist tot, ach tot. | Is dead, alas, dead. |

It is hard to estimate how deeply involved Beethoven felt with the Austrian Enlightenment's principal father figure. It is easier—only too easy—to think of deaths in his own family that he had heard about, endured, or was anticipating.

But by now I have made all the moves I am comfortable with in this situation. We cannot trap Beethoven, only maneuver our way into a position from which, as we study it, some of the many gambits and strategies he was juggling become clearer. To change the metaphor, we cannot "explain" Beethoven's fixation on C minor (what would that be like?); we can assemble technical, historical, and aesthetic strands that seem germane, but past a certain point it is not possible to weave, tease, or even sort them with confidence. Another strand is that of the mysterious, chromatic, slow C-minor introduction resolving to diatonic major—a strand first spun by Mozart in his "Dissonance" Quartet, K. 467, twisted and twined by Haydn in the *Creation,* and knotted by Beethoven in the third "Razumovsky" quartet, op. 59 no. 3 (Beethoven brings C minor back a second time, after the Minuet, so as to work a double resolution). Yet another is the circumstance that of the few Beethoven slow movements with programmatic titles, two are in C minor—his only two slow movements in this key: the Marcia funebre of op. 55 and "Abwesenheit-L'absence" in op. 81a.

EXAMPLE 6

WoO 87: No. 1

Op. 72: No. 11

To return to the "Joseph" Cantata: Beethoven surely thought well of this precocious undertaking, if he was ready to cannibalize it so many years later for *Leonore,* another work in (or around) C minor. The cantata's flanking C-minor chorus was echoed in F minor at the beginning of the dungeon scene, and its F-major aria was cited at the opera's denouement. So this time the *maggiore* consolation follows in the correct key, eventually—though that key is no longer C (example 6). In the revised opera, we do not have to wait so long for the F-minor–major resolution that symbolizes darkness dispelled by a heroic rescue; in *Fidelio,* resolution comes during the aria which directly follows the F-minor recitative. This aria now ends not with an Andante un poco agitato in that same dark key, as it did originally, but with the familiar Poco allegro in F major, depicting Florestan's vision of that very rescue, still in the future ("Ich seh . . . ein Engel, Leonoren, der Gattin so gleich, der führt mich zur Freiheit"). Other new elements, besides the key of F major, link the beginning of Act II of *Fidelio* with the denouement in the finale: a hallucinatory obbligato oboe threading through the new aria section, and a pair of *sforzato* woodwind chords added to the finale (shown bracketed in example 6). The minor-major resolution could be said to be overdetermined, and, as is characteristic of the new version of the opera, there is less real tension than in the original. Yet the resolution itself is stronger and clearer. All in all, the resolution that was withheld in 1790 was supplied in 1805, and strengthened in 1814.

Once alerted to the possibility of multiple long-range resolutions in *Leonore,* we may be inclined to experience the A-major section of the finale, in which Rocco unravels the plot to the accompaniment of a fidgety bass motif, as a laying-to-rest of the grave-digging duet, "Nun hurtig fort, nun frisch gegraben," another of the opera's minor-mode numbers (example 7). This would also be a case of over-determination, since the next number after that A-minor duet is the A-major terzetto "Euch werde Lohn in bessern Welten." Overdetermined or not, *Leonore–*

EXAMPLE 7

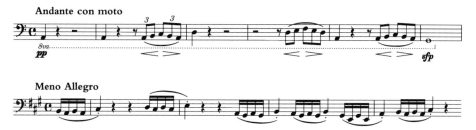

*Fidelio* begins to look like Beethoven's most exhaustive study in minor-major resolution.

IX ·

Beethoven's affair with C minor reached a terminus in 1808, when he saw how the C-major triumph that he kept projecting in his vocal works could be used to conclude and consummate a great instrumental work. That is one measure of the importance of the Fifth Symphony. The symphony has no text, nor does it have a program; yet as I have argued elsewhere, the Fifth not only suggests but positively flaunts a "secret program," as Constantin Floros would put it, and the endless efforts to unravel it by nineteenth-century listeners and critics answer to the essential content of the piece better than our own century's more surgical approach.[14] That one strand of its origins runs back to texted works may help resolve the paradox whereby Beethoven's Fifth—not his Sixth—became the inspiration and model for the nineteenth-century program symphony.

After the Fifth, it was thirteen years or so before Beethoven returned to C minor for the main key of a major composition. This was the Sonata, op. 111, of 1822. As we will have noticed from table 1, Beethoven's regular procedure with two-movement sonatas in the minor mode—there are four of them—was to make the finale entirely major. Only in op. 111 is the resolution fully expressive and consequential; and I have to feel that Beethoven returned to C minor only because he had conceived of a quite new quality of resolution, as different from that of the Fifth Symphony as from those of *Fidelio* or any other of his works.

And if *Fidelio* counts as Beethoven's most exhaustive study in minor-major resolution, op. 111 must count as his most single-minded. There is (to my ear, at least) a strangely unsubstantial quality to the C-minor gestures and alarums of the opening movement; if the Congress of Vienna works represent a "pastiche of the heroic manner,"[15] in Maynard Solomon's memorable phrase, perhaps this movement can be seen as an example of the higher pastiche, a reflection upon a C-minor syndrome that goes all the way back to Bonn. Among the retrospective features here is the obsession with diminished seventh chords, albeit in a newly systematic

EXAMPLE 8

way, as Charles Rosen has remarked.[16] The minor-mode inflection of the cadence theme allows it to be recapitulated with minimal melodic alteration, as in the F-minor Sonata, op. 2 no. 1 (example 8). The subdominant cast of the recapitulation recalls several earlier C-minor compositions (see table 1a), and so does the tierce de Picardie; as in the early two-movement sonatas, the tierce here points directly to the mode change to come. Both the form and the figuration of the finale celebrate C major, the quintessence of majority. Opus 111 is Beethoven's radiant essay in minor-major modality.

The present essay, meanwhile, has been suffering for some time from plagal sprawl, the result of repeated moves to the subdominant; the last thing it needs, one would think, is Neapolitan inflection *am Ende*. Yet an investigation into Beethoven's minority cannot end—cannot be allowed to end—without some reference to Robert Winter's discovery about the Quartet in C-Sharp Minor, op. 131.[17] At an advanced stage of the sketching, this work was going to include an extra, eighth movement in D-flat major, using the theme we now know from the Largo of op. 135. Objectively considered, this must be one of the most extraordinary data ever uncovered by Beethoven sketch studies, and I have wondered a number of times since Winter divulged it why it has elicited so little response in the Beethoven literature. Perhaps the reason may be that no one knows what to do with it, because no one can conceive imaginatively of the resolution that Beethoven was plotting here. As with op. 111, he had some really new idea; and the fact that it miscarried in op. 131 does not mean that if Beethoven had lived he would have failed to carry it off another time.

The terminus of the Fifth Symphony was not a final one. New perspectives on the minor mode were opening up in Beethoven's visionary last works.

*Notes*

1. Alan Tyson, "The Problem of Beethoven's 'First' *Leonore* Overture," *Journal of the American Musicological Society* 28 (1975): 292–334, especially sections 7–9.
2. James Webster, who enters large claims for the importance of the "Farewell" Symphony for the later music of the Viennese Classicists, does not discuss the immediate influence of the piece on Beethoven, Mozart, or other major composers. See his *Haydn's "Farewell" Symphony and the Idea of Classical Style: Through-composition and Cyclic Integration in His Instrumental Music* (Cambridge, 1991).

3. The same general layout can be observed in the Adagio affettuoso ed appassionato of the Quartet in F. A sonata movement in D minor, this impressive Adagio brings the second group in F major and recapitulates all of it in D major; D minor reappears in the wrenching, highly gestural coda. These may be the two first Beethoven codas which can be said to be truly "functional" from a harmonic standpoint, in that they complete a harmonic process left open at the end of the recapitulation.

4. Robert Simpson has recently argued that the extended tonic major area in the recapitulation of this movement must be understood in relation to a well-known anomaly in the initial orchestral ritornello, its departure from the one-key norm of the Mozart concertos (and of Beethoven's own later examples). The eight-bar second theme appears in E flat, followed by a second appearance in C major, whereupon the mode changes to minor for the cadential material. A diagram for this ritornello would be i III + I i.

Tovey considered that the ritornello move to the mediant was a mistake (this was part of a broader argument, which Simpson attacks root and branch). While Simpson does not really refute Tovey's claim that the ritornello of op. 37 is too "symphonic," he is surely right to point out that a stronger C-major area in the ritornello would have killed the C-major appearance of the second theme in the recapitulation. As the ritornello stands, the "C-majorness" of the theme is suitably clouded by E flat beforehand as well as by C minor afterwards. The theme begins with the major-defining note E♮—an especially sensitive note in this work, as Simpson also observes. See Simpson, "Beethoven and the Concerto," in *A Companion to the Concerto,* ed. Robert Layton (New York, 1989), 118.

5. Douglas Johnson, "1794–1795: Decisive Years in Beethoven's Early Development," in *Beethoven Studies 3,* ed. Alan Tyson (London, 1982), 18–22.

6. The finale tune in op. 37 is one of the few Beethoven constructions in C minor that modulates to G minor, as in the Mozart finale which it echoes.

7. Donald Francis Tovey, *A Companion to Beethoven's Pianoforte Sonatas (Bar-to-Bar Analysis)* (London, 1931), 177–78. "Das Stürmische und Düstere herrscht," writes Nottebohm. "Das Milde fehlt und mit ihm der Contrast" (*Zweite Beethoveniana* [Leipzig, 1887], 438).

8. Tyson does not fail to draw Beethoven's vocal works into his discussion of Beethoven's C-minor syndrome ("The Problem of Beethoven's 'First' *Leonore* Overture," 325n. and 329). I allow myself some amplification here.

9. My reading of the tonal situation in *Leonore* was influenced by Philip Gossett's study of the different versions of Marzelline's aria, presented at the American Musicological Society annual meeting in Minneapolis in November 1978, and I should like to acknowledge this even though, as I read the printed version of his paper, I sense that he would not wish to define the situation in just the way I do. See "The Arias of Marzelline: Beethoven as a Composer of Opera," in *Beethoven-Jahrbuch* 10 (1978–81): 141–84.

10. Alan Tyson discovered that Beethoven rewrote this aria after the first performance ("The 1803 Version of Beethoven's *Christus am Oelberge,*" *Musical Quarterly* 61 [1970]: 551–85). Although the first version cannot be reconstructed from the surviving sources, it is clear that the revision did not extend to the *maggiore* recapitulation.

Incidentally, "Meine Seele ist erschüttert" seems to owe something to the tenor aria "Tradito, schernito" in *Così fan tutte.* (I do not know if this has been observed before; that Beethoven had "Per pietà" in mind when he composed "Komm, Hoffnung" for Leonore has long been accepted.) Ferrando's cavatina has a rather characteristic early-Beethoven feel to it, with its brusque, gestural opening and its fulsomely lyric second theme (compare the minor-major place in the finale of op. 30 no. 2). To be sure, "Meine Seele" is very different from "Tradito, schernito" in scale and feeling, and it returns to the minor mode after the tonic major intervention, unlike Mozart's aria. Yet the two second themes themselves are not so dissimilar; and in both arias, before the second theme is sung it is anticipated by the *Harmonie* (see example below). Mozart provides his own gloss on Beethoven's C-minor-major paradigm: after first responding to his desertion and humiliation in C minor, Ferrando ends up in C major, caught up in the boundlessness of his love. "Ancora quest'alma l'adora; io sento per essa le voci d'amor."

11. Part I, from the Representation of Chaos to "The Heavens Are Telling." Beethoven borrowed from the latter chorus in his Second Symphony (see Donald Francis Tovey, *Essays in Musical Analysis,* vol. 1, *Symphonies* [London, 1935], 27).

12. Alan Tyson, "Beethoven's Heroic Phase," *Musical Times* 110 (1969): 139–41.

13. There is really no warrant for Schiedermair's suggestion that the return of the "Tot!" chorus at the end of the cantata was due to Beethoven (*Der junge Beethoven,* 3rd ed. [Bonn, 1951], 313).

14. See "Taking the Fifth," pp. 207–16.

15. Maynard Solomon, *Beethoven* (New York, 1977), 222.

16. Charles Rosen, *The Classical Style: Haydn, Mozart, Beethoven,* rev. ed. (New York, 1972), 141–44.

17. Robert Winter, "Plans for the Structure of the String Quartet in C Sharp Minor, Opus 131," in *Beethoven Studies 2,* ed. Alan Tyson (London, 1977), 124–25.

OPERA AND CONCERTO

# Translating *The Magic Flute*

*For Jonathan Kerman*

W. H. Auden and Chester Kallman have taken the bold, right tack and say so at the very start: "Probably no other opera calls more for translation than *Die Zauber-flöte,* and for a translation that is also an interpretation."[1] Their version of *The Magic Flute* is at once a superb job of translation for music and a striking, intimate critique of the opera as drama. It was commissioned by the NBC Opera Theater for the two-hundredth anniversary of Mozart's birth, give or take a fortnight; at the moment it looks like one of the main contributions of the *Mozartjahr* to Mozart, also one of the best things yet to come out of the television industry. The production was lavish, earnest, and as artistic as a 24-inch opera stage would let it be.[2]

The printed text includes several indifferent poems not intended for the stage, or perhaps we should say, the tube. There is a Proem, and a long Metalogue which has Sarastro discourse in genial heroic couplets about Mozart and the modern age. Then in a Postscript addressed to the Translators, the Queen of the Night damns their point of view, rejects a number of their prized innovations, ridicules their diction, and questions their very motives. Indifferent or not, this written-in review has given the present reviewer a depressing sense of superfluity, making it impossible for him to proceed except in a circuitous, hangdog fashion.

So he will first have a stab at *The Sea and the Mirror,* Auden's "Commentary on Shakespeare's *The Tempest,*"[3] remarking on the evident analogies between *The Tempest* and *The Magic Flute.* Each play combines metaphysics and low comedy in

From *Hudson Review* 10 (1957): 309–16; the original title was "Auden's *Magic Flute:* Postscript to a Bicentennial." The Addendum has been excerpted from "Translation for Music," in *The Craft and Context of Translation,* ed. William Arrowsmith and Roger Shattuck (New York: Anchor Books, 1965), 147–64.

a fairyland inhabited by disembodied Spirits and informed with the particular magic of music. In each the Princes are led through educational trials while the Princesses progress out of naïveté, under the guidance of a good magician. Monostatos, though a lay figure, is quite parallel to Caliban; paternal Sarastro is sufficiently close to Prospero; especially the lovers are strangely alike in their relationship, although Mozart develops his more fully. Masque and Masonic ritual interrupt the more conventional dramatic flow as "musical" elements in structure. More seriously yet, something of the permeating poetic mood seems common to these two late, last dramas.

Auden's commentary, however, is not Shakespeare's play, and for Auden dramatic criticism is secondary to a critique of all the world that's a stage; Prospero the mage, Shakespeare the poet, and God the Creator are all under review. In Caliban's magnificent speech Auden plunges to the heart of the problem in his most articulate, not to say loquacious, analysis of the nexus of Night and Day, art and life, mirror and sea, superego and id. Caliban is "the distorted parody" of the unconscious, son of the Queen of Love, art's enemy "who does not rule but defiantly is the unrectored chaos"; Ariel is the spirit of reflection in the mirror held up to nature. Caliban worries this brilliantly. He specifies the existentialist dilemma prefigured earlier in the poem by Antonio; he suggests the Christian solution which lies behind Auden's existentialism, and which finds more central affirmation in the companion poem *For the Time Being: A Christmas Oratorio.* Prospero as he returns to Mantua finds himself unable to reconcile to Caliban or Ariel. But as a Postscript the two of them come together in a sad echoing lyric, which incidentally is placed in the poem as a whole with a perfect sense of musico-dramatic form.

Auden draws another, more novel dualism: between Prospero the learned manipulator, enormously conscious of himself and of his ultimate failure, and Antonio the simple doer, unanalytical, unsympathetic, with the plain strength of awareness of his condition which is his aloneness. Prospero is necessarily presented by means of a lengthy self-analysis, Antonio by means of two pages of shrewd observation, plus a series of sardonic refrains. This second dualism is perhaps the finest element of this fine poem—perhaps because it is less purely metaphysical than the other, and is set forth more dramatically, in terms of persons rather than harangues. Certainly we have not seen the last of Antonio the existential man; Auden's latest libretti with Chester Kallman, however, bring back particularly the crux of Caliban and Ariel.

*The Sea and the Mirror* is not much concerned with the lovers, with Ferdinand's quest or Miranda's maturing. The dramatic form appropriate to such themes was provided by *The Rake's Progress,* and indeed Hogarth's framework, which is said to have been suggested by Stravinsky, encouraged Auden to devote himself to the quest more whole-heartedly than in any work since *The Dog Beneath the Skin.* The

*Rake* has doubtless been sufficiently hashed over in this magazine. In an illuminating essay George McFadden has shown, in effect, how Auden here turns toward orthodox existentialism;[4] while for my part I continue to regard the conclusion of the opera as unfulfilled dramatically, however consistent philosophically. Perhaps this failure has to do with the fact that in *The Rake* Auden practically let lie his preoccupation with Night and Day and the saving Christian hope—this in spite of the presence of the Devil and of Baba, who represents "the it," in Sellem's words (Mr. McFadden brings this out). As will be evident in a moment, for Auden the conflict of Night and Day has to form the metaphysical matrix for the quest.

The themes come together in a second opera libretto by Auden and Kallman, *Delia, or A Masque of Night,*[5] which so far has not been set to music. This once again is a derivative work, a complicated rewriting of George Peele's *The Old Wives' Tale*. Peele's play is a marvelous little confusion of romance material, riddles, rustics, and grand guignol. As a setting, Gammer Madge is made to tell the tale to some sophisticated peasants, between sunset and sunup. Delia has been bewitched by the magician Sacrapant, who requires her for the maintenance of his youth and power, symbolized by a light in a glass which may be broken only by "one that's neither wife, widow, nor maid." Delia is sought by a succession of questers: her two brothers, a pair of comic knights parodied from Ariosto, and Eumenides, whose good deeds to the rustics gain him the fantastic support of Jack's Ghost. All are assisted by Erestus, who has some prophetic power—no doubt as compensation for his enchantment by Sacrapant into a bear by night, an old man by day. It is finally Erestus's fiancée who breaks the glass. Eumenides's supreme test comes when Jack's Ghost, who has been promised half of all that Eumenides gains, demands his fair share of Delia. But he stays Eumenides's sword, and all ends well.

Auden makes this over to be as much like *The Magic Flute* as possible. There is now only one suitor, Orlando, the enamored, who gains Delia only after a fairly arduous educational journey. Half of Erestus lives in Bungay, a comic bear-man who bears a strong resemblance to Papageno the bird-man—at least to Auden's Papageno, at least to Auden's Papageno with a Xantippe wife. The other half of Erestus lives in a new character, a Crone "gathering hips and haws" to whom Orlando gives alms. She guides him to Delia with good counsel which he cannot quite follow; it is then she who makes the supreme demand of Orlando, that he marry her instead of Delia. But when he kisses her, the Crone releases him from the vow, revealing herself as

> The Lady of the Green
> Of Night and Elfland the high Queen
> Whom some Diana, some Dame Nature call,
> Of all that live wise Mother original.

She engages in several central agons with Sacrapant, a much more conscious person than Peele's figure, or than Sarastro. By an elaborate riddle proposed by the Crone and solved by Orlando, Bungay, and Xantippe, the mage's light is extinguished. But as Bungay steps out of his bear-skin and returns to Xantippe, as Orlando goes off with Delia, the Crone relights the lamp with a kiss:

> Child of my sorrow, through this day
> Take your rest while rest you may;
> Soon, too soon, will set the sun
> And our wars be rebegun.

The libretto closes with a morning chorus for woodland animals ("Day breaks for joy and sorrow") exactly parallel to their sunset chorus near the start. One can practically hear the musical echo, the repetition, the daily renewal of wars.

The themes come together, as I have said, but do not really engage. While cosmic forces clash around them, Orlando and Delia work out their limited destinies without understanding Sacrapant or the Crone. Unlike Tom Rakewell, Orlando does not "go it alone," and from the libretto one might be tempted to judge him a somewhat indefinite hero. Delia seems duller yet. But of course no judgment can be made until the libretto is set to music; this is an important point. So far we have only an incomplete work, and it is precisely in the area of the consciousness of the leading characters that the music is going to be most powerful and decisive. All that can be said now is that the librettists have provided enough incident and enough occasions for self-expression; so harmless a line as Delia's "I begin to understand . . .", placed as it is, might become as extraordinary as Anne Trulove's "He loves me still" or Pamina's "Tamino mein, o welch' ein Glück!" It is apparent, in any case, that *Delia* is a virtuoso piece even by Auden's standards, the verse exuberantly intricate and archaizing (referring to the century from Ariosto to Peele), and the structure fantastic in its ingenuity, demanding a rapid succession of very many small musical numbers. Echo songs, rounds, and so on are wittily imported from Peele. How well this could be set by Stravinsky.

*Delia* has been worth describing at some length because it makes so clear Auden's intention with *The Magic Flute*. Like *Delia, The Magic Flute* "combines two themes, both of great interest. The first and most basic of these is the story of the change in relation between the Dionysian principle and the Apollonian, Night and Day. . . . The second theme is an educational one: how does a person discover his vocation and what does the discovery entail?"[6] These two themes are indeed of great interest to Auden. Only their presence, one imagines, made the poet willing to submit to the shackling incumbent on an opera translator, even if he is to be something of an "interpreter" too. For in an opera that is already made, the dramatic articulation is fixed in the music and inviolable. To alter the musical expression is to distort the opera; with the musical numbers all that can be allowed is to shade the effect slightly by modifying the meaning of verses substituted for the German. To be sure, with the sections of spoken dialogue between the musical numbers, which exist on an altogether different imaginative level, Auden and Kallman may legitimately (and do) change Schikaneder's libretto as radically as Peele's play. Precisely because the imaginative level in these sections is so low relatively, modifications do not make an essential difference.

In *The Magic Flute,* as in *Delia,* the dichotomy of Ariel and Caliban is dramatized for the stage as the conflict between magician and queen. The Princess abducted by Sarastro is actually the daughter of the Queen of the Night, who has therefore an added interest in guiding the Prince to rescue her. But whereas in *Delia* we see a fairly benign Queen gain control, in *The Magic Flute* we come in at another stage of the unending cycle. *Delia* is a Masque of Night, *The Magic Flute* an opera of sunlight and day. The good Sarastro is in ascendency, and it is he, not the Crone, who abdicates to necessity—at least according to a spoken addition of the translators:

> Now my task is almost done:
> When tomorrow's rising sun
> Sees the Queen of Night's defeat
> Shall my mission be complete,
> And in that victorious hour
> I must also lose my power.

The words, of course, are nearly Prospero's. "Though the Queen must be defeated in order that the New Age may come, her defeat completes Sarastro's task: he must now hand on the crown to Tamino and pass away like Prospero in *The Tempest*."[7]

Sarastro and the Queen are seen to be indissolubly bound together, opposed but also interdependent in a cyclic relationship. This explains the easy commerce between their respective kingdoms, and accounts for many well-known "inconsistencies" of the libretto: that the Kingdom of Light and Truth should harbor a Monostatos—whom Auden's Sarastro addresses quite as Prospero addresses Caliban; that the Three Spirits seem equally at home in the realms of Night and Day; and that the audience is asked to switch sympathies from the Queen to Sarastro between Acts I and II. Without any question the metaphysical basis of *The Magic Flute* is much clarified in this version, perhaps fully rationalized for the first time.

But in what sense is this theme "first and most basic"? The point, I take it, is not what Auden thinks or what one of his reviewers happens to think, but what we can tell of Mozart's opinion. And Mozart was more attracted to the "educational theme," to the progress of Tamino and more particularly to the progress of Pamina.

Probably he found this better suited to music, as well as personally more congenial; in any case he made his position plain by involving the music more crucially with the lovers' journey than with the wars between Night and Day. Musical involvement defines the central action of an opera. Unfortunately the translators have managed to modify this central action by changing the order of certain musical numbers.

Not that one doesn't sympathize with their concern about the illogical arrangement of the second act. Something is clearly wrong with the plotting, and various revisions have been proposed since Ernst Lert's interesting book *Mozart auf dem Theater* of 1918, if not earlier—either in order to restore Mozart's "true intention" or else more frankly to patch things up. In Mozart the sequence of events is as follows:

- Pamina is attacked by Monostatos ("Alles fühlt der Liebe Freuden," no. 13)
- she is saved by her mother the Queen, who gives her a dagger and threatens her with a curse unless she uses it on Sarastro ("Der Hölle Rache," no. 14)
- she wavers, but Sarastro kindly comforts her ("In diesen heil'gen Hallen," no. 15)
- she is rejected by Tamino, and grief-stricken ("Ach ich fühl's," no. 17)
- she is comforted again by Sarastro, this time in company with Tamino ("Soll ich dich, Teurer! nicht mehr sehn?," no. 19)
- she tries to kill herself with the dagger, but is saved by the Three Spirits (Finale, no. 21)
- the final epiphany as she joins Tamino for the Ordeals


Auden's rearrangement:

- Pamina is rejected by Tamino, grief-stricken ("Ach ich fühl's," no. 17)
- she is comforted by Sarastro, in company with Tamino (no. 19)
- she is attacked by Monostatos (no. 13)
- she is saved by her mother, who gives her the dagger, etc. (no. 14)
- she wavers, but Sarastro kindly comforts her (no. 15)
- she tries suicide (no. 21)
- the final epiphany

It does not seem natural that, having seen Pamina fall into Tamino's arms at the end of Act One, she should appear, when we see her next, to have forgotten his existence. Secondly, the effect of Monostatos and her mother upon her would be a much greater temptation to suicidal despair if she had to endure them after she imagines her lover has deserted her rather than before, when she could console herself with the thought of him and even call on him for help and guidance. Thirdly, we wished to make her appearance in the Finale with a dagger more plausible and more dramatic.[8]

But there is a decisive argument against the rearrangement—much more decisive than the one objection to it raised and dismissed a little facilely by Auden, namely the disturbance of Mozart's system of key relationships. The change spoils the essential dramatic rhythm of Pamina's progress. Her trials must increase: from frightening advances by Monostatos, to vicious behavior by her mother, to rejection by Tamino, to despair, to suicide attempt. This rhythm has been pre-defined *musically* by Mozart. If anything is musically certain, it is that Pamina's great aria "Ach ich fühl's," so striking in its expressivity by contrast with the rest of the opera, comes as a late climactic ordeal for Pamina, not as a first one. The rather silly girl whom we see fall into Tamino's arms at the end of Act I could never summon up that kind of feeling; after her preliminary sufferings, yes. We need not doubt that Mozart was perfectly aware of the confusion in the libretto, and we need not suppose that he was cynical enough to set just anything, however rushed he may have been. The libretto did allow Pamina's trials to increase, however, and as this was central to the play that Mozart wanted, he composed it accordingly, and did not worry about inconsistencies.

The gloomy truth is that Auden's rearrangement of the musical numbers is going to militate against the practical use of his version of *The Magic Flute,* a version so admirable in other respects. The whole record of Pamina's development has been weakened, and weakened in a way that is rather disquieting. At approximately the place where Mozart has a lyric, emotional climax, Pamina's aria, Auden substitutes a verbal, mental climax—Sarastro's final clarification of the nature of his relationship with the Queen. The Prosperan speech comes here; the aria is shifted back out of the way. To replace musical effects by literary ones is to distort Mozart's piece and to go against the nature of opera. It is exactly at this point, and only at this point, that Auden's very free treatment of his original material becomes inadmissible.

It is idle to speculate, I suppose, but I cannot help wondering how much was deliberate policy. Enthusiasm for the metaphysical theme may very well have made the translators careless of the human theme, and made them miss the force of what Mozart was actually doing. Moreover, the undercutting of Pamina is rather characteristic; there has been something unsatisfactory about all Auden's heroines within the framework of the quest. Rosetta of *The Age of Anxiety,* who seeks alone, is the best realized, but both Anne Trulove and Delia suffer from their treatment as symbols of their male's quest rather than as people in themselves. This is not the way Mozart treated Pamina. (A composer may help Delia, but Stravinsky could not altogether save Anne.)

Missed what Mozart was doing, or mistrusted it? Years ago Auden asked in the name of Orpheus

> What does the song hope for? And his moved hands
> A little way from the birds, the shy, the delightful?
>   To be bewildered and happy,
>   Or most of all the knowledge of life?[9]

The answer was no hope on either count. More recently faith in the Quest Musical still wavers in "The Proof," a poem included (with exact propriety) in the section "In Sunshine and in Shade" of *The Shield of Achilles:*

> But Tamino and Pamina
> Walked past its rage,
> Sighing O, sighing O,
> In timeless fermatas of awe and delight
> (Innocent? Yes. Ignorant? No.)
> Down the grim passage. . . .

and they

> . . . opposed its spite,
> With his worship, with her sweetness—
> O look now! See how they emerge from the cleft
> (Frightened? No. Happy? Yes.)
> Out into sunlight.[10]

What is most of all lacking is any sense of Mozart's knowledge of life; the poetic music, to my ear, proves nothing. Yet even Antonio, self-certain and alone, tough, cynical, un-lyrical, knows

>           given a few
> Incomplete objects and a nice warm day,
> What a lot a little music can do.[11]

Some such trust, surely, however flecked with doubt, has to support any serious work with opera, whether in composition, performance or production, libretto writing, translation, or critique.

A word in appreciation, finally, for this version of *The Magic Flute* as verse for music. So much about it is *benissimo trovato* that one might never guess that operatic translation is the world's most frustrating business. Above all the tone of quiet elegance is so simple and right, so simply right. Of the complete arias and other musical numbers, "Ach ich fühl's" is to my mind the weakest in translation, which is interesting; but on the other hand a passage that always seems awkward in the German, Pamina's suicide attempt, comes warmly to life and into character. Tamino was no doubt the easiest role to handle, and Papageno the hardest, but Papageno as here imaginatively transformed is the most individual and consistently successful conception of the whole opera. Sarastro, Monostatos, the Three Spirits, and the Armed Men all sing as though the English language were naturally theirs. On the page all the verses may not be immediately striking, perhaps, but sing them to Mozart's music, or listen to them sung, and the integrity of the entire effect commands as much admiration as the ingenuity of solution of many very difficult details.

*Addendum*   The axiom is devastating; Auden and Kallman put it in words of one syllable: "The goal of the translator, however unattainable, must be to make audiences believe that the words they are hearing are the words which the composer actually set."[12] I should separate out three requirements for this belief:

1.   Plausibility of language: if other criteria are to be given weight, you cannot hope for elegance, lucidity, or force of language; merely for plausibility. This is of course a function of the poetic convention that is established. But this must be a live convention, not some preposterous poetic license invoked tacitly to support lines like "Oh, how to see her I am yearning! / Oh, how to free her I am burning!" or "I know not if 'tis joy or pain / That overwhelms my reeling brain." If Auden's version were merely plausible—but it is a great deal more—it would already stand nearly alone in a field which poets have, understandably, avoided. But if this work is to be done, poets are needed, precisely because their craft allows them to create infinitely wider ranges of plausibility than the rest of us know about. This range provides a reserve—which should be spent not first of all in refining literary quality, but in the precarious service of further demands.

2.   Plausibility of declamation: again, no more than plausibility can be hoped for. Hope to persuade the audience that the composer might reasonably

have set your words, not that he set them beautifully. And again, plausible declamation is a relative matter depending on the musical convention, for musical styles set up their own imaginative consistencies of verbal treatment, even unlikely ones (as we know from *The Rake's Progress*). Once the convention is grasped, however, the translator ought to bind himself to it fanatically. For an audience, nothing destroys the illusion that "the words they are hearing are the words which the composer actually set" so instantly as clumsy declamation at a sensitive juncture. One bad slip and the whole convention totters. The idea of having words sung instead of spoken seems suddenly monstrous.

3.   Momentary meanings, syntax, verse form, and so on should be kept or simulated when (and only when) they are important to the musical conception. I crowd all these considerations together because admittedly none is a sine qua non, as I consider plausible language and plausible declamation to be. Yet unless they are honored in translation, musicians will always complain. To illustrate for the moment generally and simply: suppose a sudden rich harmony occurs in the music, prompted by and joined to an emotional phrase like "Ich fühl" in the original language. I wish the English phrase to be not only decent in itself and well declaimed, but also roughly parallel in meaning. "Heart" or "rich," "marvel" or "enchant" will do as well as "feel," often enough (and luckily enough); but unless the word is somehow emotional, the harmony will seem limp because unmotivated. Or to take a syntactical example: where a musical climax is spurred or supported by mounting tension in the sentence structure, something parallel should occur in the translation. To bring a preposition at the climax will be weak in itself and false to the composer's total gesture. As to verse form, rhymes are never important intrinsically, but only in situations where they have been used in a significant way, such as for example to cement parallel cadence structures. It is obvious that a crowd of possibilities as vast as a composer's imagination can turn into necessities here.

Auden has not often felt himself committed to considerations of this kind. But ideally the translator should penetrate into the musical conception, take a position on just what is and what isn't important in the total complex of word and tone, and then struggle to keep or simulate factors that he finds important. He is free to scrap the rest even if it means changing notes or rhythms. "A too-literal translation of the original text may sometimes prove a falsification," said Auden, and then later: "it is often better, once [the translator] has grasped its emotional mood and general tenor, to put the actual words out of his mind and concentrate upon writing as good an English lyric as possible."[13] It will be better only in cases where the setting is so neutral that the sense of individual words and word order has only a superficial relationship to the music. Papageno's strophic songs are such cases. But where Mozart is writing at full tilt, melody, harmony, phraseology, accompaniment, and all the rest are bound in with momentary verbal meanings. If falsification is to be avoided, a good deal of careful respect for the original words is required after all.

The two poets have gone at *The Magic Flute* like literary translators. I scarcely blame them; that is the only way to do it with any joy. Unfortunately, or fortunately, the music remains as a rigid control. A literary translation is made for someone who does not read the original, or else (in the grimmest case imaginable) for someone who reads the original and the translation a piece at a time, successively. But in a musical translation, the music is steadily in your ears, not merely in the back of your mind. Imagine reading Pope's *Iliad* while Homer is chanting the original hexameters synchronized exactly with the English, line by line.

Let me give just a few notes on how my three requirements confront the translator in one specific instance, Tamino's Air in *The Magic Flute* (example 1).

| | |
|---|---|
| Dies Bildnis ist bezaubernd schön, | True image of enchanting grace! |
| Wie noch kein Auge je gesehn! | O rare perfection's dwelling-place |
| Ich fühl es, wie dies Götterbild | Where beauty is with virtue shown |
| Mein Herz mit neuer Regung füllt. | More noble than itself alone. |
| | |
| Dies Etwas kann ich zwar nicht nennen, | Is she the dream to which I waken, |
| Doch fühl' ich's hier wie Feuer brennen; | The pursuit where I am overtaken, |
| Soll dies Empfindung Liebe sein? | Body and mind and heart and soul? |
| Ja, ja! die Liebe ist's allein. | She is! To love her is my goal. |
| | |
| O wenn ich sie nur finden könnte! | How do I speak as though I knew her, |
| O wenn sie doch schon vor mir stände! | When I must find her first and woo her? |
| Ich würde—würde—warm und rein— | O tell me, image, grant a sign— |
| Was würde ich? [ich würde] sie voll |     Am I her choice? |
|   Entzücken | She will be won—O sweet occasion!— |
| An diesen heissen Busen drücken, | By gentle force and warm persuasion, |
| Und ewig wäre sie dann mein. | And with her love will answer mine. |

Mozart's poem is wretched (in case you hadn't known). As poetry Auden's is immensely better. Obviously, he determined to take a strong line about sentimentality: "Herz," "Busen," "fühl," "Entzücken" and even much of the first-person singular have been neatly paraphrased away. But the question is, what has the poetic tone to do with the music? A great deal, and the translator ought not to remove the offending mush, but keep it—refined, if he wishes, to a seemly emotionalism such as Mozart presumably read through the mush. What Auden has done is write

EXAMPLE I

the lyric that we should have preferred Mozart to have set. But if Mozart had had Auden's lyric—O sweet occasion!—the music would have come out differently; and the music is *there,* as a rigid control. The music can be "interpreted," but it can no more be translated than a cathedral.

So I would have to start over:

> Sweet vision, image of true grace,
> O rare perfection's dwelling-place!
> Enchanted by this heavenly sight
> My heart is moved to strange delight.

EXAMPLE I    *(continued)*

love her,    I    love ___ her:    that    I ⌣ know.
*Lie- be,    die Lie   -   be    ist's    al - lein.*

How may I seek her to con- fess   my love?    How may she answer when I   tell   my love?
*O wenn ich sie nur fin-den könn   -   te!    O  wenn sie doch schon vor mir stän   -   de!*

I'll seek her,    seek her    far and near—but how, in-deed?    I'll  seek her
*Ich wür- de,    wür - de    warm und rein—was wür- de ich?    ich  wür- de*

hand,    I will be - hold her,    And in my  arms  with joy  en - fold her;    So
*sie ___    voll⌣ Ent - zü - cken,    An dies-en  hei - ssen  Bu-sen ⌣ drü - cken,    Und*

dear - ly won she will be   mine,    So dear  - - ly  won she will be   mine,
*e - wig wä - re  sie dann mein,    Und e - -  wig  wä - re sie dann mein, etc.*

This nameless feeling quite evades me,
But a sweet contentedness pervades me;
Why does this new affection wake in me?
I know! I love her: that I know.

How may I seek her to confess my love?
How may she answer when I tell my love?
I'll seek her—seek her—far and near—
    but how, indeed?
I'll seek her hand; I will behold her;
And in my arms with joy enfold her;
So dearly won, she will be mine.

Such literary refinement as this can claim it can thank Auden for; the elegance and simplicity of his first couplet seems to me reproachless, and I very much wished to keep it. The word "image," however, falsely convicts Mozart of false declamation—and in a sufficiently conspicuous context. "Image" is a pyrrhic word, which quantitatively might stretch to a spondee, but not to a trochee; "picture" or "portrait" or "vision" are examples of roughly spondaic words which might be stretched either to iambs or trochees. The first two seem drab for Mozart's ecstatic leap of a sixth. "True vision" would make no particular sense; "sweet vision" injects a little warmth right away, and also matches the spitting "s B" of "Dies Bildnis." A subtle detail, perhaps: in Mozart the clash of consonants plays in to the breathless exclamation, and in a curious way justifies the panting thirty-second-note upbeats of the orchestral preface.[14]

Auden's equally elegant second couplet is unfortunately far too cold. Tamino cannot speculate, he must register strange emotional stirrings. Not to speak of the German verse, why else would the music indulge those exquisite inverting chromatic inflections, the surprising seventh leap, the cadential appoggiaturas, and the diminished seventh interrupting the cadence? At the start, the repetition of words on the musical sequence should not only be kept, but if possible also motivated: Tamino half stammers, something he would not be expected to do expatiating upon aesthetic value. He stammers because the unexpected chromatics overwhelm him; they should be linked, if not to "feel," at least to something like my sense of enchantment. At the end, likewise, an affective word such as "delight" makes sense of the romantic cadence; Auden's "alone" does not. Like it or not, "heart" or something as obviously sentimental ought to be preserved here. For "heavenly sight" there is less excuse; but it does pick up the high note, and the musical contour masks some of the triteness.

In the next stanza, Auden's Tamino talks like Tom Rakewell; the music, to be sure, is rather neutral and courtly. I too allowed myself a slightly dandified "quite" and the double rhyme "evades me"—"pervades me." The recurrence of "sweet" seems blameless; "sweet contentedness," while considerably cooler than "Feuer brennen," keeps a modicum of warmth in the verse. Auden's run-on line 7 goes against Mozart's Zwischenspiele, the first of which acts as strong punctuation, and the second of which comments serenely on the fresh insight: "Liebe."

Faced with a sloppy final stanza, Mozart paid little or no attention to poetic form. Anyhow, his hero is getting excited. But faced with the first "couplet" of this stanza, translators have always improved upon him by supplying a rhyme. This seems to me undesirably pat; I myself ran into a half rhyme which I like well enough. With line 11 in view, "how" was deliberately reiterated, and "seek" deliberately planted, in spite of the double "k" sounded with "confess." The extra syllables at the end of these lines seemed no violation, here as elsewhere.

Now, this line 11 is the only one in the piece which declamation actually controls. For once the line has no melodic integrity. There is a particular urgency, then, in the declamation sounding entirely natural; if not, the listener won't even be left with purely musical consolations. Auden had the charming (and scenically useful) idea of making Tamino question the portrait at this point, and then receive a silent answer in the evocative *Generalpause*. However, his climactic question "am I her choice" could never conceivably be declaimed to the notes that Mozart molded to "was würde ich." "Her choice" comes out gobbled, "choice" so weak as to provoke a mirthful denial. A case could be made out for altering Mozart's notes here—only I should not care to do so, not with Mozart. Instead, my attempt, which also changes the original sense somewhat, contrives to keep the original conceit of an unexplained stammer word ("würde") answered by itself in the next line, after the *Generalpause*. "I'll seek her / I'll seek her hand" is trickier than the German, and admittedly "but how, indeed" makes only the most approximate sense. But hopefully it sounds like an involuntary interruption, as does the music, and echoes appropriately the "how"s in the previous lines, and declaims itself tolerably well (unlike "am I her choice," or "what would I then," "ah, what would I," or "what would I do," as variously translated before).

The stammer ("würde" / "seek her") should be repeated when the melodic fourth figure recurs a step lower. Especially in declamatory writing of this kind, such a sequence makes no sense except as the outcome of verbal repetition. "Far and near" is fitted to Mozart's G♭; "far" sets up overtones of distress to match a diminished-seventh harmony that is the most intense and disturbed in the entire composition.

A foolish non sequitur, "I will behold her," goes by more smoothly than you might expect, and is correct at least to this extent: it provides verbal intensification to the musical repetition, which is what Mozart needed in this case and what he achieved with "Entzücken." The climax of thought and music develops surprisingly fast here; one should avoid the temptation to let Tamino's fantasy blossom too early. For once, at the line "And in my arms with joy enfold her," the inversion strikes me as plausible and right, because ostensibly forced on the verse by the emotional crescendo both of the music and of the word sequence culminating in "enfold her" ("drücken": the most vivid, physical word on Mozart's V/IV chord). Auden depersonalizes the fantasy while still artfully managing the climactic surge. But, however squeamish, I did feel a need at least for "arms," "joy," "enfold." . . .

The final line cools again, more than in the German. Mozart's first musical setting of the line seems to me to emanate a curious and affecting stillness; "so dearly won," I venture to hope, may be heard in support of this sense, which is more precious than the subsequent coarser tone of the cadential repetitions (where "dearly won" may sometimes be replaced by "always." In Auden's final line, "with" cannot really bear the responsibility of one and a half beats plus a turn.) My last and least of concerns, at this point, was the rhyme, which Mozart pretty well obscured by his free handling of line 11. Naturally I should have preferred to rhyme the very last word with "near," or perhaps with "know" or "delight," or even half-rhymed it with "enfold her"—but I could not. It seemed a small loss.

— *Notes*

1. W. H. Auden and Chester Kallman, preface to W. A. Mozart, *The Magic Flute,* English version by W. H. Auden and Chester Kallman (New York, 1956), reprinted in W. H. Auden and Chester Kallman, *Libretti and Other Dramatic Writings, 1939–1973,* ed. Edward Mendelson (Princeton, 1993), 129.

2. This production, which has not been preserved on videotape, was directed by Lincoln Kirstein, with designs by Rouben Ter-Arutunian and choreography by George Balanchine. The singers included Laurel Hurley, Yi-Kwei Sze, and the young Leontyne Price.

3. W. H. Auden, *The Sea and the Mirror,* in *Collected Poems,* ed. Edward Mendelson (New York, 1976), part 8.

4. George McFadden, "*The Rake's Progress:* A Note on the Libretto," *Hudson Review* 8 (1955): 105–12.

5. W. H. Auden and Chester Kallman, *Delia, or A Masque of Night,* in *Libretti and Other Dramatic Writings,* 95–126.

6. Auden and Kallman, preface to Mozart, *The Magic Flute,* in *Libretti and Other Dramatic Writings,* 129, 130.

7. Ibid., 130.

8. Ibid., 131. [Auden is referring, of course, to the fact that in nos. 13–15 Pamina does not mention Tamino, let alone "call on him for help and guidance." Her behavior does not seem so unnatural if no. 19, the Trio "Soll ich dir, Teurer! nicht mehr sehn?," is transposed all the way back to follow no. 10, Sarastro's aria "O Isis und Osiris." In that case Pamina has indeed seen Tamino again and knows he is undergoing mysterious trials. This transposition is common in productions today.]

9. Auden, "Orpheus," in *Collected Poems,* 132.

10. W. H. Auden, "The Proof," in *The Shield of Achilles* (New York, 1955), 43, reprinted as the fourth of "Five Songs," in *Collected Poems,* 439–40.

11. Auden, *The Sea and the Mirror,* in *Collected Poems,* 317.

12. Auden and Kallman, preface to Mozart, *The Magic Flute,* in *Libretti and Other Dramatic Writings,* 131. They also wrote elsewhere on the subject: Chester Kallman, "Opera in Translation," *Center* 1 (1954): 11–13, and W. H. Auden in collaboration with Chester Kallman, "Translating Opera Libretti," in W. H. Auden, *The Dyer's Hand* (New York, 1962), 483–99.

13. Auden and Kallman, preface to *The Magic Flute,* in *Libretti and Other Dramatic Writings,* 133.

14. [I was able to keep the word "image" after all, on the second beat, where the accented preposition "of" was not very attractive. I was, at least, when I came back to this translation in 1992 and made some improvements: in lines 1, 3, and 7–8.

For the poets' defense of their version of line 1, see "The Magic Flute: Auden–Kallman vs. Cross," in *Libretti and Other Dramatic Writings,* 642–43.]

# 15

# Wagner: Thoughts in Season

When Wagner died in 1883 he left, as everyone does, full memories to his friends and to his enemies. His great legacy to the European consciousness was an ideology, and to the world of music a polarization, an alignment on either side of a split forced by confrontation with his scores. More tangibly, he left operas, music-dramas, and a set of *Gesammelte Schriften* running to ten gold-embossed volumes in the second edition, revised and augmented by the author. Wagner left, inevitably, debts, which (again inevitably) were to be taken care of by somebody else. The question I wish to raise is, to what extent are we still paying off these debts? For of course, over the years we have had to pay, and we have had to reckon in everything: *Das Judenthum in der Musik* as well as *Tristan und Isolde,* the split as well as the *Gesamtkunstwerk,* the dross of Wagnerism as well as whatever metal may be in Wagner's art.

By 1959 the friends and enemies have all been depersonalized into history; an obvious point, perhaps, but one that is worth noting. For so long as they lived, they extracted bitter interest in every transaction concerning the great man. Wagner was, to put it shortly, something of a monster in private life; and as that private life was well broadcast, the Victorians could not consider any aspect of the Wagner complex without considering the moral man. This is not the place to debate how, if at all, such consideration should weigh with a modern historian or critic. I note

⬥ Delivered at a conference on "A Century of Revolution and Counter-Revolution, 1859–1959" at the Ohio State University in 1959; published in *Hudson Review* 13 (1960): 329–49 and *The Score* 28 (1961): 9–24, and, under the title "Debts Paid and Debts Neglected," in *Darwin, Marx, Wagner: A Symposium,* ed. Henry L. Plaine (Columbus: Ohio State University Press, 1962), 139–65.

simply that as vivid personal memories fade, Wagner's conduct can take its place in our customary uncomfortable historical perspective, along with that of Tasso, Caravaggio, Rousseau, and other unpleasant great men.

The ideology of Wagnerism is now also essentially a matter of history, but it is a history that must detain us. The very term gives pause; word forms of this order are rather rare and suspect, especially so within the arts. There are no such isms as Bachism or Mozartism or Schoenbergism, but there are Wagnerism, Orphism, Petrarchism, Darwinism, Marxism: all denoting frames of mind that go far beyond personal influence or personal propaganda, far beyond the strictly artistic, scientific, or social-scientific into the ideological realm. As soon as ideology begins by its very nature to transcend the local realities of the originating figure, it attracts the suspicion of professionals—musicians, scientists, or social scientists who see the fatal distorting appeal made in one direction to the dilettante, and in another direction to the mass. So as Wagnerism moved beyond music it moved with a good deal of hostility from the trade. And, paradoxically, although Wagnerism had begun with an idea about art, one did not need to be a musician to be a Wagnerian. The ideology could flourish divested of any essential artistic import.

If, as may happen, an ism were to grow up around a man posthumously or during his lifetime but without his active interest, it might possibly be passed over as irrelevant to his actual contribution. But of course this was not so with Wagnerism. The apologists are wrong when they claim that the ideology was manufactured only after Wagner's death, in the unscrupulous Bayreuth press mill run by Cosima Wagner, Houston Stewart Chamberlain, Glasenapp, Wolzogen, and the rest. Wagner invented Wagnerism, fostered it with the greatest care, and was for some years the first and only Wagnerian. Moreover—and this touches at once the fundamental artistic problem—Wagner has always been suspected of caring more about Wagnerism than about art, of writing his music-dramas less as works of art than as evidence for Wagnerism. If there is any truth at all in this, it follows (paradoxically again) that we have to know Wagnerism before we can know Wagner. Or looking at it the other way, if there is no truth here, but only prejudice, we have to know Wagnerism in order to confront the prejudice. In any case, the debt to Wagnerism must be retired before we can begin collecting royalties on Wagner's art. Examination of the ideology, then, is important not only per se as a study of European culture of the last hundred years, but also as a step to an appreciation of Wagner as artist.

Wagner's whole career may be scanned from the standpoint of his development of Wagnerism. He first attracted mild attention in the 1840s, a provincial conductor and composer of operas in which such careful observers as Spohr, Liszt, and Hanslick already appreciated qualities of restless novelty. Actually, though the world was not yet loudly informed of the fact, Wagner was growing increasingly dissatisfied with the artistic situation as he knew it, and with the state of society as a whole. This dissatisfaction, symbolized by great debts, made him eagerly join Bakunin in the Dresden aftermath of the 1848 revolution, and participate actively enough to make it necessary for him to flee to Switzerland. Thus more than he could ever have wished, Wagner found himself forced into a quixotic rupture with society, a break that he was hardy enough to turn into a heroic, pathetic—but in any case prominent—stance. Exile also interrupted Wagner's career as a musician. Instead, he wrote voluminously for several years: tracts, pamphlets, polemics, treatises, and hundreds of letters in which ideas that had been in his head for some time settled into Wagnerism.

That this ideology, Wagnerism, absorbed into itself much of the thought of the time is a commonplace; obviously it did, or it could not have succeeded so well. It may even be true that every important element of Wagnerism had been enunciated separately before Wagner. His role was to make a brilliant synthetic formulation, and this is perhaps most simply approached not from its origins in intellectual history, but from the rather practical standpoint taken by Wagner himself. Wagner was first an artist. Basic to his thought was a special high calling for art, a high calling that may be succinctly characterized as "magical."

R. G. Collingwood makes much of this term in his *Principles of Art*. A "magical art," as he defines it, "evokes of set purpose some emotions rather than others in order to discharge them into the affairs of practical life." Magical art is to be distinguished from "entertainment art" which evokes emotions simply to gratify the audience, and from "art proper" which does not set out to *evoke* emotion at all but instead to *express* emotion. Under magical we can readily group medieval art, religious art, patriotic art, and such various lowbrow arts as weddings, balls, banquets, and so on. Even lowbrow magical arts have an urgency in society that Wagner coveted; and as for the highbrow ones, he dreamed avidly of their dignity or dominance in the world of affairs. Greek drama was Wagner's favorite archetype, a festivity expressing not any personal vision but the very life-soul of the city-state, and channeling the powers of feeling to the common good. Had not Plato insisted that certain modes of music produce virtue, while others should be banished from the republic? "Art as expression," in Collingwood's sense, was altogether too private a concept for Wagner's aesthetic, as was Hanslick's notion of music as *tönend bewegte Formen*. "Art as entertainment," however, Wagner knew well and reviled, and "Art as magic," on the highest of highbrow levels and with Wagner as the grand wizard, was his ideal.

A basic commitment to magic is naturally a basic commitment to unreason. In best romantic tradition, Wagnerism always claimed that music-drama appealed to instinct rather than to reason. Many of Wagner's techniques bear this out, such as his opulent harmonic and orchestral sound and his use of repetition sometimes to a soporific degree. "Don't argue, repeat" might stand as Wagner's motto both in prose and in tone—the characteristic tactic of the demagogue. Considered as a group, furthermore, the heroes of Wagner's mature works provide an exhaustive study of unintellectuality in all its subtle shades: Siegfried the joyful savage, Parsifal the pure fool, Tristan whose intensity of will transcends law and life, Walther the spontaneous singer inspired by nature's birds and by the eternal Eve. (Walther does have his *Doppelgänger* to teach him form in addition to content. But even Sachs says of Walther's song: "Ich fühl's, und kann's nicht versteh'n"—which is enough for Sachs; as a good Wagnerian, he does his all for the hero.) Critical discrimination, on the other hand, was anathema to Wagner, and unscrupulously he pilloried criticism as pedantry and malice, making Beckmesser a personal caricature and a Jewish caricature for good measure. Wagner even opposed vivisection, an essentially analytical process which does indeed do violence to the *élan vital*.

But we are attempting to vivisect the ideology of magical art. In 1850, the ideal required two things: a new kind of art and something to be magical about. To a nineteenth-century German, the latter lay easily at hand in the gathering concept of the *Volk*, inchoate but free, impersonal but vital, true, and German. Thus Wagnerism plunged headlong into German *Kultur* mystique, with its corollaries of racial purity and anti-French sentiment. Art should discharge emotion to the purpose of driving the communal national consciousness along its dynamic march into the future. All this Wagner upheld emphatically, not only in the writings of his exile, but also later in the manual of statehood that he drew up for Ludwig II, *Was ist deutsch?*, and in the runic meditations of his last years. His *Gesammelte Schriften* formed a rich mine for later generations of mystic nationalists.

As for the former requisite, the new kind of art: Wagner invented this, and it remains one of the remarkable intellectual achievements of the century (in spite of his anti-intellectual stance, which was not without an element of sham, as we shall suggest later). Since Wagner's new art is to stir the *Volk*, it must reach a hitherto unreached audience. Only some sort of theater, with its well-known appeal and its well-known mystique, can serve—an idea already fundamental for Schiller, as Carlyle had observed. Since communion is achieved not by reason but by feeling, and since music is the art closest to unbounded emotion, the new art must be some sort of musical theater. Not, of course, conventional opera—Franco-Jewish entertainment music at its most degenerate—but a new organic combination, a *Gesamtkunstwerk*. The idea of synthesis, so dear to the romantic spirit, guarantees a super-art combining the virtues of all: drama served by music, poetry, gesture, and scene. The subjects must stem from national myth, which presents eternal if cryptic truths in ideal concentrated form. Since feeling, not reason, can reach the *Volk*, once again, a whole new armory of technical stratagems is required. Limitation of dramatic "business," relentless piling up of repetitions, new breadth of time-scale, a new steady pitch of intensity, *Stabreim,* leitmotiv, orchestral continuity, transformation scenes, "endless melody," eight horns and four tubas—all these were developed for the new magic.

Add to this the historistic dynamic interpreting this art as the chosen art of the future, and add to it the organic fallacy in aggravated form, and you have the main components of Wagnerian ideology. The orthodox felt not only that each Wagner music-drama was a perfectly integrated work of art in itself, but also that the seven of them formed a single coherent corpus, sprung mystically from a basic seed. This far, at least, the organic ideal holds good: irrationality and *Volk* mystique cannot be dissociated from Wagner's concept of art or from his highly individual artistic techniques. The ideal of art as magic is comprehensible only in view of the mystique; the techniques are comprehensible only in view of the intended function of the art.

The entire structure, to repeat, was worked out in Wagner's head after his exile in 1849. For six years he wrote no music at all, but instead bombarded an astonished world with an ideology that seemed to many dangerous visionary nonsense—as did *Mein Kampf* in 1925. In 1853, however, Wagner published privately the libretto for a gigantic *Gesamtkunstwerk, Der Ring des Nibelungen,* showing that he certainly meant business; and it soon became known that he had composed the first two parts of the *Ring,* as well as (in 1859) another mythical drama, *Tristan und Isolde.* Meanwhile, all that one actually heard was his early music, which could be pressed into the cause of Wagnerism only by means of outrageous special pleading. This was not lacking, and in 1860, Brahms, then aged twenty-seven, felt constrained to sign an unfortunate antimodernist manifesto, thereby formalizing the corrosive rift in late nineteenth-century musical life. The manifesto served to magnify the Wagner myth. So did two famous fiascoes of this period: the 1861 Paris scandal over *Tannhäuser* and the retraction of *Tristan und Isolde* from its intended premiere in Vienna after seventy-seven fruitless rehearsals.

For years Wagner had little prospect for the performance of his three extraordinary music-dramas. Then, as is well known, luck changed. The new king of Bavaria, though only eighteen, was already a rabid Wagnerian, and under his aegis Munich saw the first performances of *Tristan, Die Meistersinger, Das Rheingold,* and *Die Walküre* from 1865 to 1870. Incredible as it seemed, Wagner had succeeded; and the nineteenth century was fairly hypnotized by this success. Fascinating also was Wagner's ruthless personal life: his success with other men's wives, in his search for a mate who was also a Wagnerian, symbolized mastery not only for Wagner but also for his contemporaries—Siegfried the superman, after all, is rewarded by Brünnhilde. Wagner celebrated the War of 1870 quite unmystically by sending, unsolicited, a triumphant *Kaisermarsch* to the Kaiser, and by circulating under a pseudonym and then actually publishing a wretched skit mocking the fall of Paris, *Eine Kapitulation.* Wagnerism, he publicly suggested, should become the official ideology of a resurgent Germany now set on its historic mission. Bismarck was contemptuous, but Wagner had his way; and fifty years later, Hitler was not contemptuous.

Wagner's way was the most formidable move in the history of Wagnerism: Bayreuth. The time was right, with German nationalism at the height, with five Wagner music-dramas newly before the public, and with the most impressive intellectual tribute to Wagner in the making: Nietzsche's first book, *Die Geburt der Tragödie aus dem Geiste der Musik*. In 1872, the cornerstone was laid for the Bayreuth Festival Theater, a temple specially constructed in a special idyllic Mecca for special celebratory performances of works specially to be created by the master. For the opening rite (1876) nothing less impressive would serve than the great tetralogy (or, to follow Wagner's anxious analogy with Greek drama, the great trilogy with an introduction) based on the myth of the German *Volk*, *Der Ring des Nibelungen*. As Bernard Shaw and others have pointed out, Wagner's final implementation of his twenty-year-old plan did more credit to his Wagnerism than to his artistic integrity. To make the next festival (1882) more awe-inspiring yet, art as magic was carried to its logical conclusion. *Parsifal*—a gigantic communion service, a static drama of priesthood—absorbs Christianity into Wagnerism as blandly as Arthurian romance had absorbed pagan grail rites into Christianity. *Parsifal,* too, looks back twenty years to *Tristan und Isolde* in a subtle, very interesting, and yet curiously reactionary way.

As the festivals at Bayreuth followed more frequently, their importance for the Wagner myth grew. Wagner had not only written, composed, fought, borrowed money, and stolen women—all prodigiously—but also he had *built;* and to the nineteenth century, the tangible symbol of the *Bühnenfestspielhaus* and the Villa *Wahnfried,* where Wagner's body rests, confirmed Wagner as the superman for whom it had yearned since Carlyle. That Bayreuth instantly became not an ideal, pure shrine but a somewhat vulgar commercial enterprise made no difference. This fact may have depressed Wagner—though not deeply enough to hinder work on *Parsifal*—and it may have disgusted confirmed enemies like Nietzsche, who now saw in Wagner every abomination of nineteenth-century German culture. But confirmed friends, the pilgrim Wagnerians, the crowned heads, and the humble members of *Wagner-Vereine*—these responded not to the realization but to the ideal. Art had risen up and forced the world of affairs to make it a home and a temple. The artist was acknowledged legislator of mankind.

More than 10,000 articles and books had been written about Wagner by the time of his death, and the climax of Wagnerism was still to come. The 1880s saw the French Wagnerian movement, inspired essentially by Wagner's writings (hard as that may be to believe today). Eduard Dujardin and Theodor Wyzewa of the *Revue wagnérienne* were the standard bearers; Villiers de l'Isle-Adam and Mallarmé lent their authority; Catulle Mendès, Verlaine, Huysmans, René Ghil, and Maurice Barrès served as the younger contingent. What fired the symbolists was the Wagnerian cult of feeling rather than reason. For this they were prepared to ignore

Germanism so thoroughly as to rationalize *Eine Kapitulation* as a parody on German glee at the fall of Paris; they were prepared to conclude that neither music nor the combination of arts was necessary to essential Wagnerism. Of such paradoxes any mystique is capable. In England, true-blue Wagnerians (the adjective is Ernest Newman's) were issuing a magazine with the highly unlikely title of *The Meister*. The late 1880s also produced Nietzsche's devastating critique. To counter this, the Bayreuth publicists found an even better tactic than their usual ones of ignoring, distorting, or villifying opponents. Piously they commiserated with mad Nietzsche, and pressed him to their breasts as a brother Wagnerian on the basis of his early books.

The final, violent stage of Wagnerism was a political one, or perhaps we should employ the term coined by the Wagnerians themselves: a "metapolitical" one. For Peter Viereck, who developed this thesis in a furious book called *Metapolitics*, Wagnerism stands to Nazi ideology as the most important single fountainhead. That a political leader liked to relax at the opera has in this case unusual and ominous significance: Hitler's well-known devotion to *Lohengrin* and *Siegfried* was not merely a matter of affection, but a complete spiritual commitment. The line runs directly from the Bayreuth circle of Cosima Wagner and Houston Stewart Chamberlain to Alfred Rosenberg, Dietrich Eckart, and Adolf Hitler, who was introduced to Bayreuth in 1923. *Mein Kampf* is Wagnerian in style and content, and much later Hitler was to say, quite simply, that anyone who wishes to understand Nazi Germany must know Wagner. Much in Wagnerism the Nazis chose to ignore. But the nineteenth-century ideology provided soil and seed for all their key ideas: the communal spirit of the *Volk,* the relentless march into the future (*Lebensraum*), the goal of racial purity, the cult of might, the appeal to the irrational, the demagogic technique of "the big lie," and the mystic idea of the Führer.

This is not to say that Wagner could be claimed as a Nazi by retrospect, even if the Nazis did celebrate their victory at the polls in 1933 by a ceremonial performance of *Die Meistersinger*. They could not even make a Nazi opera out of what is, in actual fact and in spite of what everybody says, not even a very nationalistic piece. However, they could manipulate it as symbol and as magic; and they were right in seeing the precursor of the Führer in the Wagnerian hero. By the same token, Beethoven could not be claimed as a Wagnerian, however frequently Wagner extolled and conducted the Ninth Symphony to herald the Dresden uprising or to celebrate the laying of the cornerstone at Bayreuth. But again, the Wagnerians were right in seeing the precursor of Siegfried in Beethoven's ideal of the hero—if not perhaps in the *Eroica* Symphony, at least in the Schilleresque *Held* of the B-flat Alla marcia in the Ninth. The romanticism of the early nineteenth century became Wagnerism in a later stage, and Wagnerism became the ideology of Nazism, transcending the world of art altogether.

II ·   No further stage is evident. As was observed at the beginning of this long excursus, the ideology of Wagnerism is by now essentially a matter of history. The present has its own up-to-date mystiques, but these can scarcely be traced to Bayreuth. Every once in a while, to be sure, we catch the true Wagnerian *Nachklang*. I caught it last year at a lecture by Karlheinz Stockhausen, as he explained how the music of instruments and human expression shall give way to the music of machines, and how a new concept of composition and a new type of concert hall shall come into existence—not *should* or *may* or even *will,* but *shall* according to an unnamed but all-compelling historistic necessity. Still, it was just an echo. This one of Wagner's debts has been squared, at the price of the Nazi *Götterdämmerung*—or *Götzendämmerung,* Nietzsche would have said. And today, while Nietzsche remains in our intellectual heritage, Wagner seems to be in danger of becoming a forgotten man. Our debt *to* Wagner, that is to say, is for the most part neglected.

It was not always so. In the decades around 1900, when Wagnerism was a living issue, the tremendous artistic impact of Wagner's scores was likewise fresh and unavoidable. Only now have we allowed this impact to dim with time, wrongly I am sure. In those decades, indeed, Wagner as a composer was the main issue in the musical revolution dividing what is now called contemporary music from the nineteenth century. Half of the composers tried to encompass Wagner and carry through the implications of his work, while the other half tried to contradict him. Then as now, the complex relationship between Wagner-as-composer and Wagnerism was a source of confusion, harassment, and depression. Yet, on the whole, Wagnerism *as ideology* had less influence in music than in certain other areas.

That is not strange: according to the musician's limited, professional, matter-of-fact way of looking at things, Wagner was simply another musician. Ideology commenced only as Wagner moved away from music. So while composers could be swept away by Wagner's technical innovations, they never quite cottoned on to the ideology. For one thing, Bayreuth saw not the slightest need for a successor to the Meister. Richard Strauss, one musician who was able to take over Wagner lock, stock, and barrel, and with amazing facility, turned the whole apparatus away from magic toward entertainment, so that in a certain sense he may be said to have betrayed Wagnerism more profoundly than anyone else. Scriabin, who would have added Indian mysticism, color, and scent to the already bulging *Gesamt* of Wagnerian orthodoxy, came to nothing. On the other hand, Bruckner and Hugo Wolf composed lasting symphonies and songs under the influence of certain of Wagner's techniques. So decisive, indeed, were these techniques at the historical juncture, that it was a follower of Wagner in this technical sense—not a follower of Brahms or Verdi or Rimsky-Korsakov—who became the key figure of the twentieth-century musical revolution.

Around Arnold Schoenberg and his school there still exists a split in musical life as jagged as that of Wagner's own time. This item of the Wagner *Nachlass* has not been paid off; if anything, we appear to have taken on a heavy second mortgage. Is it the same split, or some kind of modified continuation of the old one, or something altogether fresh? The question is, I think, definitely worth pursuing. In the contemporary musical consciousness, the importance of the twelve-tone phenomenon and serialism would be hard to overemphasize.

Actually, two schools should be distinguished: the original Viennese twelve-tone group formed around Schoenberg and the recent international serial group formed around the memory of Anton Webern, Schoenberg's radical pupil. Between both of these schools and musical Wagnerism, striking parallels appear at once—on the surface, at any rate: the same apparatus of composers, favorite conductors and performers always ready to present their work, devotees and hangers-on, intellectuals and publicists, magazines, societies, little festivals. Though the modern movement has always been much humbler in scope than Wagnerism, it has recently achieved a certain analogous chic. A little below the surface, the movements have in common the mode of polemic, the mood of an elite, and the adherence to a historicist view of musical progress. Like the Wagnerians, the serialists are marching along the one truly modern path, which has evolved inexorably from the past, in face of a reactionary opposition that is as powerful as it is underhanded. Equally scornful are the members of this opposition, armed with arguments very similar indeed to those of the anti-Wagnerians: twelve-tone music is too dissonant and chromatic for man or beast, too complicated, unsingable. It consists not exactly of "endless melody," but certainly of an endless unarticulated flux. The steady high level of intensity frays the nerves (Hanslick complained of "continuous nervous unrest" even in *Die Meistersinger*). According to a somewhat more elegant criticism, twelve-tone music is feeble rhythmically (Nietzsche on Wagner: "the complete degeneration of the feeling for rhythm, *chaos* in the place of rhythm . . ."). Below specific objections lies once again a blind conviction that the music is being composed less for its own sake than to justify an abstract, extramusical system. What is more—and this turns the historicist argument back on itself—twelve-tone music is considered decadent on account of its roots. Wagner was accused of vulgarity *à la* Meyerbeer; Schoenberg is accused of tawdry romanticism *à la* Wagner. The twelve-tone school has to live with *Verklärte Nacht* and the Alban Berg Sonata, just as Wagnerism had to live with the prelude to the third act of *Lohengrin*.

Now even if there were no more connection than this, I should think it a matter of likely significance that the *form* of the Wagnerian quarrel is so clearly echoed in the twelve-tone quarrel—even if the *content* were not. This whole way of thinking about music was unknown before Wagner, or at any rate before Wagner crystallized the growing conflict in nineteenth-century music. Though we take this way very much for granted today, it has its own peculiar modernity. However, the connection surely lies deeper than the form of controversy alone; and with all due care and with all due sympathy in both directions, I should like to examine analogies in content. As we have seen, the essence of Wagnerism was a partly extramusical structure and a mystique. But is not the very same true of serial music? Obviously, the old structure and the old mystique differ enormously from the new ones in their actual natures. Equally obvious, to me, is the similarity between the two schools simply on the basis of their essential orientations around *a* structure and *a* mystique.

Structure for the Wagnerians was a relentless multiplication of musical, poetic, dramatic, philosophical, and ideological details to create the magical *Gesamtkunstwerk*. Structure for the original twelve-tone school was a systematic application of a special method in composing a musical work of art. Starting with what has been called his "precompositional assumption," the composer selects a set or row, a fixed ordering of the twelve available notes of the scale. Then, as raw material he uses pitches only in the sequence of the row or of certain derivatives of the row (transposition, inversion, retrograde, and combinations of these). From these origins, the later serial school has developed methods requiring much more complex operations on the row, and controlling musical elements other than pitch—rhythm, timbre, dynamics, and so on—by means of analogous "precompositional assumptions."

To describe all this as structure will cause no difficulty, but to call a structure "extramusical," or half-extramusical, which is so directly involved with the act of musical composition, may appear mistaken and prejudicial. I grant and stress that the term as used here means something quite different from Wagnerian extramusicality. Nevertheless, in the very concept of the row, exhaustive and rigorous as it is; in the frankly mathematical nature of the derivations and operations, notably with the latest serialists; and in the speculative quality of "precompositional assumption" itself—in all these I think we can hardly fail to see something extramusical at work. That vaguely similar things can be seen in some great composers of the past, too, in Josquin and Bach and Mozart and Wagner, proves merely that extramusical ideas have been affecting music for a long while.

What will cause more difficulty is reference to a twelve-tone or serial mystique. The fact is that serialism is felt—not thought, *felt*—to offer a key to the musically good. It provides control by formula over the raw material of music; it solves problems of logic and organization; and most important of all, it beards that great chimera of modern music, organicism. Indeed, the mystique is essentially one of organicism. To the most superficial twelve-tone sympathizers, application of mathematical technique guarantees an organic whole, which is to them tantamount to success.

The fantastic apparatus of mathematical set theory and acoustical formulas, the shibboleth of "total organization," so called—these belong to the most extreme new serialists, not to Webern or Schoenberg. Nevertheless, in a quieter form the idea of artistic success through increasingly rigorous control undoubtedly played its part with the original twelve-tone composers. The classic statement of this mystique has been made in artistic form in Thomas Mann's panoramic novel *Doctor Faustus,* whose hero is a mythical first twelve-tone composer. The modern Faust achieves a "break-through to the subjective"—an equivocal redemption—through a diabolic pact whereby he renounces humanity and even reason and suffers a cold bond to the mathematical and the occult in order to gain the strictest objective mastery over artistic resources. This excruciated dialectic Mann presents unforgettably, with the greatest imaginative penetration and sympathy. Mann was also able to see Wagner more steadily than most observers.

Schoenberg, however, publicly repudiated the book; with half of his strange being he fought against mystique, which is certainly more than can be said of our advanced serialists. To Schoenberg and his most intelligent sympathizers, serialism is just a technique, a "method of composing with the twelve notes," and true artistic problems come only after the "precompositional assumption" and all the manipulations of the rows. The historical "necessity" of Schoenberg's development is always insisted on. But the trouble with this nonmystical explanation is that serialism, viewed merely as a working method, seems to everybody else artistically (if not perhaps historically) arbitrary, imposed from the outside, and, above all, labored. Why this method rather than another? Why the passion for rigorous application, which could bring Schoenberg himself in his late years to incorporate dogmatic members of his row in unheard grace-note chords? Conversely, what justification can be found for so-called free twelve-tone composers—composers who are, as it were, just a little bit pregnant? Viewed as a mystique, however, the twelve-tone system presents no problems at all. Number mystiques have nourished the arts since the time of Pythagoras, with good results as well as bad. It is certainly not remarkable that in this scientific, uncertain age, musicians and artists should seek a talisman.

Let there be no misunderstanding about the manifest differences between Wagnerism and serialism. The new mystique is a compositional mystique, not a world view. The new structure is a technical structure, and even its extramusical quality may be said to be technical rather than philosophical. The twelve-tone and the serial schools eschew magic, demagogy, aesthetic-politico-racial superstructure, and even personality. The very names are not "Schoenbergism" but terms severely expressive of technique; the literature comes in magazines called not *The Meister, La Revue wagnérienne, Bayreuther Blätter,* but *The Score, Polyphonie, Die Reihe.* Most (not all) of this literature is highly professional, beginning with Schoenberg's written contribution, a *Harmonielehre*—and Schoenberg was a great teacher, unlike Wagner and unlike every other great composer since Bach. Personality is not the issue here; if it were, we might reflect on the ironic, indeed tragic, contrast between Wagner and Schoenberg in the outward course of their careers, to say nothing of their conduct. In serialism the Führer concept is totally absent, as irrelevant to a technical movement as it was essential to Wagner's all-embracing ideology. Consequently, serialism has more than one single master and is exerting a more profound, more flexible influence on the course of music than Wagnerism ever did, for all its pride in romantic dynamism.

All this is true; yet there is one more bond, and it is, of course, the deepest one, between Wagner and the twelve-tone system. In the historical moment, Schoenberg did not proceed illogically. He was meeting the great problem in musical style that was his debt inherited from Wagner—the problem stated emblematically in a famous book title *Romantische Harmonik und ihre Krise in Wagners Tristan,* a study by Ernst Kurth (1920). Romantic music, seeking to mirror the inner life of feeling, had instinctively clouded clear forms wherever possible. Most serious of all, it clouded the traditional framework of harmony and tonality. Seeking intense expressivity, Romantic music leaned toward more and more chromaticism—a tendency that weakened the tonal system very specifically by drawing attention away from harmony and toward linear impulsion.

All this came to a head in 1859 in the extraordinary score to *Tristan und Isolde,* which for most critics remains Wagner's finest work, as well as the most important musical work of the later nineteenth century. *Tristan* challenged the very postulates of music as it was known: the centrality of a tonic note, triad, or key; the accepted hierarchy of other notes, triads, or keys in relation to the tonic; the standard rhetoric of tendencies and relationships between one sound and another. For fifty years music hovered anxiously around this challenge, which Wagner took care to aggravate by many vexed, beautiful passages in his later operas. Schoenberg wrestled with musical organization first of all quite in Wagner's spirit; but as he followed through the implications of *Tristan,* the question of musical repetition, in particular, grew more and more problematic. Schoenberg's solution was to leave tonality altogether and to organize music in a radically different way. As a frame of reference for the "rightness" of sounds, he developed the serial principle, self-defined by a private "precompositional assumption" rather than accepted according to the tacit tradition of tonality.

The analogy with perspective may perhaps be helpful here. By Wagner's time, tonality as the fundamental binding force of music was thoroughly weakened under the stress of expressive linear chromaticism. Schoenberg's abandonment of tonality was as drastic a step as the abandonment of perspective in painting—as drastic and, some would say, as necessary.

It was obvious that Wagner had brought music to a breaking point. What caused the crisis, it is hardly necessary to add, was not simply the interest of his searching experiments, but rather the authority, that is to say, the integrity, of his operas as works of art. The situation was desperate enough; all serious composers in the early part of the century were trying to erect some kind of structure from the fallen bricks of Classical tonality. That Schoenberg and Webern should have attempted a drastic solution is much less remarkable than the character of that solution: the rigid systematization with its strong leanings toward a mathematical mystique. The interesting fact is that analogues to this rigid systematization—the way they arranged the bricks—are already evident in the Wagner operas.

This seems a paradox; Wagnerism is dogged by paradox. What has Wagner's cult of irrationality and his endless, vague, emotional trance to do with a technique that has been accused of being cold and mathematical and which, it must be said, has never properly nullified the accusation? The paradox runs all through Romanticism, starting before 1800 with Novalis's maxim of *Systemlösigkeit in ein System*—"systemlessness as system." Seen from one side, this idea glorifies irrationality. Seen from the other side, it sets up a system. And so it must be for the artist; Romanticism might seek to imitate life in its elusive, self-contradictory chaos, but the artist if he wanted to do anything at all—whether to express his soul or to influence others magically—had to come to a point. Art has to assert form on content. Perhaps, indeed, the more the artist wishes to give the impression of formlessness, the firmer must he draw the secret bonds of artistic form. The slice of life, the stream of consciousness, the impressionist haze, and the expressionist nightmare are far from formless in artistic realization. The paradox is evident in Maurice Maeterlinck's *Pelléas et Mélisande,* for instance, a play dear to musicians on account of the beautiful (and curiously Wagnerian) musical setting by a leading anti-Wagnerian, Debussy. The action appears to revolve around moody non sequiturs and aimless people drifting in and out; but just below the surface lies the chromium grid of the well-made play. The paradox comes in *Ulysses,* a dreamlike evocation organized more minutely than any other major work of literature since the *Divine Comedy.* It comes in Alban Berg's *Wozzeck,* whose subject is crack-up, and whose form is an odd anthology of tight purely musical structures.

In the music of the nineteenth century, it was Wagner who reflected the paradox of Novalis most strongly. He worked and schemed and plotted for his magic. The ancient Egyptian priesthood is said to have made a great secret scientific discovery, steam power, in order to rig miracles. A later age unmasked them; and though Wagner's *Gesammelte Schriften* are conspicuously silent on the subject of intellectual structures, these have become more and more apparent as analysts vivisect the scores themselves.

Intellectual organization for Wagner was first a matter of leitmotiv structure, as was well understood at the time. The function of the leitmotiv is manifold: to work an elaborate cross-reference system for presumptive dramatic good, as well as to explain the action to an audience which is by design half-unmusical, but which as communing body must not be left in doubt. Another function is technical: as the musical continuity grows larger and more tenuous, the time-scale expands and tonality becomes more vague; therefore, it is urgent to have as many organizing themes as possible—to have plenty of foci, as it were, around which the fog can precipitate. Sometimes Wagner handled leitmotivs in a drab, mechanical way. With this in mind, Jacques Barzun interprets Wagner less as a Romantic than as a "mechanist"; the insight is important, though the conclusion does not necessarily follow.

In addition to leitmotiv structure, Wagner used minute organization by phrase, period, and key; the "endless melody" is structured down to the bone. Guido Adler seems to have understood this first, around the turn of the century, and his ideas were exaggerated in the Wagner analyses of Alfred Lorenz, which are notorious in musicology as the *locus classicus* for Procrustean lopping. Nevertheless, although half of what Lorenz saw in Wagner existed only on his own drawing board, the other half was true, important, and something of a revelation. For instance, it had often been said that in spite of his claim to be following Beethoven, Wagner worked his themes less by development than by repetition and sequence; what had not been realized was how rigorously this work proceeded—"mechanistically" indeed. Furthermore, very remarkable long-range structures came to light. To take an example from *Die Meistersinger:* the overture is built around four keys (C, E, E flat, and C again); then four hours later, and at ten times the length, the final scene of the opera is built around exactly the same keys. Another example, from *Tristan:* the piece begins in A minor and ends in B major; the key directly between them, E, is somehow avoided in all the hundreds of modulations contained in the opera—avoided and saved for one appearance: the beautiful passage in Act III where Tristan attains his maximum serene consciousness ("Wie sie selig, hehr und milde wandelt . . ."). An example from *Parsifal:* to conclude the piece on a note of huge serenity, Wagner selected the sound of a plagal cadence, already at hand in his "Grail" leitmotiv, the so-called Dresden Amen. After moving from the Neapolitan key of D plagally up a fifth to A, he moves up another fifth to E, up another, and another, and another, and another—six times in all, exactly half way around the full tonal circle.

This type of organization is far from twelve-tone organization; but the two have in common a mood, a quality, and that is their schematic quality. An artist who would go so far toward systematization as to multiply a progression six times might go the rest of the way and group all twelve notes of the scale in a set pattern. An artist so hypersensitive to the key of E major in the five-hour flux of *Tristan und Isolde* might develop similar concern for the very note E, and once he had sounded it, might not want it again until all the eleven other notes had intervened. The parallelism of keys in *Die Meistersinger* brings up a crucial question at once: Has this structure any aesthetic import or is it purely speculative? Is it *heard* or is it an instance of "paper" organization? Something similar is asked about *Ulysses* and the Pound *Cantos.* The very same question is asked all the time about serial music, not only in reference to its formation around the row on a small scale, but also to its modes of coherence on a larger scale. In contemporary criticism this question is central, and the analogy with Wagner should serve as a tool in the answering, or vice versa.

Analogy only; analogy in spirit but not of course in actual detail. With this reservation clear, the link between Wagner and contemporary music may be seen to be more than historical. Wagner's musical organization prefigures in a certain respect Schoenberg's twelve-tone technique and also the fantasy of "total organization" developed by Stockhausen and others. That a technical, even hermetic, aspect of Wagnerism should survive in modern music while more blatant aspects are discredited is, once again, characteristic of the resolute technical limitation of the serialists. The new technical mystique depends even more critically than the Wagnerian on the illusion of organism, on the indestructibility of works that must be judged according to their own "precompositional assumption," on their technical virtuosity, on their logic and economy. And while "economy" is probably the last word that anyone would think of applying to Wagner, it does finally explain itself as the back of the coin of Wagner's insistence on organic synthesis.

III ·      Recently, I spent an afternoon looking through the literature on Schoenberg's unfinished opera *Moses und Aron*. Much of this literature is by twelve-tone adherents, and some of it is pretty impressive stuff; yet the name of Wagner is contained in it hardly once. In its fundamental dramatic conception, however, *Moses und Aron* is the most egregiously Wagnerian piece since *Parsifal*. (N.B.—I am not saying that the piece sounds like Wagner, or that Schoenberg's philosophy is as shabby as Wagner's, or that his rhetoric resembles Wagner's; I say simply that in its fundamental dramatic conception, *Moses und Aron* is the most egregiously Wagnerian piece since *Parsifal*.) The work is a didactic racial epic of momentous import. The concept of the *Volk,* indeed the very term, occurs more prominently than ever in Wagner, even in *Die Meistersinger.* The libretto, gauche as only a homemade libretto can be, treats in symbolic terms of universal ethical and political problems; and if George Bernard Shaw could see Bakunin and contemporary socialist doctrine in the *Ring,* I can certainly see in *Moses und Aron* the idealistic Zionism of Theodor Herzl and Rabbi Magnes pitted against the political Zionism of Ben-Gurion. The action consists of static dialogues arranged in a stiff dialectic plan—with the exception of the famous Golden Calf Scene, where stage directions out-Wagner Wagner's vanishing castles, swimming Rhinemaidens, and magic fires: four Naked Virgins are stabbed and their blood caught in cups, after which rapacious stripping of the chorus is the order of the day. There is blood, sex, *Liebestod,* even the quintessential *Schlange.* There is a direct parallel to, and derivative of, *Stabreim.* There is the by now customary rigorous construction and the enormous complexity of the score. Close to four hundred rehearsals were required for the first performance—shades of *Tristan!*—and that first performance came twenty years after the work was composed, facts which the enthusiasts have greeted with the customary cries of martyrdom and panegyric.

*Moses und Aron* belongs in this discussion for several reasons. First of all, it bears witness to an almost unbelievable survival of Wagnerian dramatic conception in the work of the central, inescapable, brooding figure of twentieth-century music. Second, it shows how skittishly Wagner is handled today even by the elite (for so the twelve-tone adherents regard themselves). Wagner stands for Romanticism; Wagner stands in some obscure way for bogus; his name would taint the modern masterwork. And if this elite shies from Wagner, so much the more does the opera-going public, which sees Wagner less and less; so much the more does the new, important mass audience made up of phonograph listeners, who have been able to buy twelve different recordings of *La Bohème* but not a single complete *Siegfried*. This is the age of Mozart, Webern, perhaps Puccini, maybe Vivaldi, certainly not Wagner. If courses on the forgotten man are still offered by certain colleges, that is no doubt a sign of their characteristic archaism.

However, a third reason to bring up *Moses und Aron* is the serious one. Here is Schoenberg's largest and most ambitious work, and according to many critics, his greatest. It is a work that ought to be in our ears right now, for the posthumous first performance was only in 1954, the first stage performance came three years later, the record was issued and reviewed in 1958, and the third performance recently took place in Berlin, to the accompaniment of mild riots. *Moses und Aron* has the authentic aura of a masterpiece. What is to be made of this piece, with its new problematic dimensions added to the standard difficulty of any Schoenberg score?

The question, which is scarcely to be met by marching along with any school or ism, may be helped by Wagner. Wagner is needed today, if for no other reason than to clarify *Moses und Aron*. Every element in the latter that calls for clarification—the mystique, the complication, the innocence, the impact, the aura—has its analogous element (not identical, but analogous) in the Wagner canon. It should be as unthinkable to deny the defects of *Moses* as to deny those of *Parsifal;* it should be unthinkable to deny the transcendent artistic power of one work or the other on account of defects. Of course, nothing will be settled by speculative analogy; what counts always is the critical ear. But the old work can help define a stance for the new. The same applies *pari passu* to twelve-tone music in general, as has been suggested, though there, obviously, the relationship is a good deal more complex.

In short, we have to settle Wagner's debts, and then we have to settle our own debt to Wagner if our credit is to be really good for contemporary music. One might even suppose that close study of Wagner would be necessary for anyone engaging in modern musical composition. However this may be, it is certainly true that a fresh effort to encompass Wagner is necessary for an adequate critical or historical grasp of the music of the present. Answers are needed to the questions about bogus, vulgarity, insincerity, magic, overextension, overcomplication, paper organization, organicism, and the unquestionable incandescence that the operas still attain. This is not the time for such an effort, which I have adumbrated elsewhere. I suggest only one preliminary axiom: resist all pressure to regard the oeuvre as an inviolable, necessary, superbly constructed organic whole. There is no such artistic entity as "Wagner"; only four fantastic works of art—*Tristan, Parsifal,* the *Ring, Die Meistersinger*—with their successful and unsuccessful aspects, with their great beauties and their *bêtises.* Organicism is not the issue. Even this much, perhaps, hints at an attitude for more recent music, and indicates the importance of the half-historical, half-critical study that Wagner seems to require, a hundred years after *Tristan.*[1]

## Note

1. [The decision to publish this paper without footnotes—it originated as a symposium lecture—was entirely unselfconscious, as best I remember, but the same cannot be said about reprinting it the same way, and I would certainly not wish the lack of references to suggest that the piece exists in a contextual vacuum.

On the contrary, probably no essay in this book needs to be read with a more strenuous application of historical reserve. "Wagner: Thoughts in Season" was a product of a particular moment in time, an intersection of trajectories in what we now call the "reception" of Wagner and Schoenberg. In the 1950s Wagner performances had fallen off; Flagstad and Furtwängler were listened to with a slightly bad conscience, and the impact and import of Wieland Wagner's work was not yet understood by many. There was a parallel lull in Wagner studies. Neither Robert Gutman's biography nor Robert Donington's *Wagner's "Ring" and Its Symbols* had yet appeared, and the work of Robert Bailey, Deryck Cooke (on Wagner), Carl Dahlhaus, John Deathridge, Bryan Magee, and Anthony Newcomb was still far in the future. Probably the one study of Wagner in English that was most influential in the 1950s, besides those of Ernest Newman, was Jacques Barzun's *Darwin, Marx, Wagner,* the study that inspired the Ohio State symposium. It did not seem so strange to find oneself reintroducing Wagner, in 1959.

With Schoenberg the situation was very different. If Wagner's fortunes were in decline, those of Schoenberg and especially the Schoenberg school were in the ascendancy. Books by René Leibowitz, Hans Stuckenschmidt, and Josef Rufer had all been published in translation, to say nothing of *Die Reihe* (also issued in translation). The first staged performance and the first publication of *Moses und Aron* took place in 1957, and I was responding immediately to the recording issued at that time, with its famous essay on the opera by Milton Babbitt.]

# 16

# Verdi's Use of Recurring Themes

*For Oliver Strunk*

In the last act of *Otello,* at Otello's entrance *di una porta segreta* and again at his suicide, the orchestra plays music that was first heard at the high point of his love duet with Desdemona in Act I. It is a famous dramatic stroke; many listeners, I believe, would have to search hard in their memory of Verdi's operas or of anyone else's to match its extraordinary feeling of summation, poignancy, and catharsis. One's sense of this masterstroke can be clarified by study of the "interior context," analyzing the musical and dramatic structure of *Otello;* it can also be clarified by study of the "exterior context," tracing outside the work the tradition to which the device belongs. For manifestly the idea of recalling earlier music in an opera did not come new to Verdi's mind in 1887. Everyone will think of thematic recurrences in many of the earlier operas—in *Rigoletto* and in *Aida*—without perhaps realizing how widely, indeed how indiscriminately, Verdi employed this means throughout his career. This essay will trace some aspects of Verdi's use of recurring themes, or recurring passages, with special attention to the type that reaches its culmination in *Otello.*

This type has been given the name of *Erinnerungsmotiv,* or "reminiscence theme": "the introduction of a previously heard theme when there is in the action an obvious reminiscence of the earlier situation with which the theme is associated."[1] I think we would do a little better with the term "recalling theme," since opera is a form of drama, and of all memory verbs "to reminisce" seems the most undramatic. Notice that the above definition speaks of recalling a dramatic situation, not a

From *Studies in Music History: Essays for Oliver Strunk,* ed. Harold Powers (Princeton: Princeton University Press, 1968), 495–510.

person or a notion. It is both possible and helpful to discriminate between "recalling themes" and "identifying themes"—the latter being associated in a general way with groups of people (armies and priests in *Nabucco,* monks in *Don Carlos*), or with persons (Aida, Tom and Sam), or with ideas (the force of destiny). Identifying themes are sung or played when the group, person, or idea is strongly in evidence, like a sonorous or "hermeneutic" extension of its physical or psychological presence. They are not used to link one stage of the drama to another, but simply to identify or make vivid. They serve to remind the audience rather than to remind the people in the play.

That the greatest subtleties are possible in the use of such themes we know from Wagner's practice, within which it would certainly be reckless to try to draw a hard line between functions of identification and recall. But, surprisingly or not, with Verdi the distinction can be drawn rather cleanly. His use of identifying themes is with a few exceptions very uncomplicated. As an artistic device, the recalling theme interested him much more.

And in this area, a number of types are worth distinguishing, roughly graded on a scale of dramatic usage running from literalness to imaginativeness. Sometimes a libretto furnishes occasion for what may be termed "literal recall": a character is reminded in so many words of something said at an earlier juncture in the opera. In *Ernani,* Silva taunts Ernani in Act IV by quoting to his face the words and music of his pledge in Act II. In *Rigoletto,* however, when Rigoletto remembers Monterone's curse, he does so without Monterone talking to him; the musical recollection is motivated psychologically, not literally. To be sure, the librettist still pointed the way by having Rigoletto say to himself, out loud, "Quel vecchio maledivami!" In the last act of *La Traviata,* a more imaginative stage yet is reached. When Violetta is reading Germont's letter, and then again later when she expires, the orchestra plays the music of Alfredo's original declaration of love in Act I even though no words in the libretto specifically refer to that act or that occasion. The composer has taken it on himself to interpret her memory.

An interesting and historically not unimportant middle stage between literal recall and more imaginative types comes up with persons in abnormal states of consciousness. When someone is mad, or dreaming, or in prophetic fervor, he may be supposed to "hear things." So recurring music for such a character really amounts to a literal representation of his abnormal state. The *gran scena* of *delirio* or *sogno* or *sonnambulismo* or *profezia* emerges as a regular cliché from the time of Bellini and Donizetti on. Often the character hears music from earlier in the opera—preferably from an earlier love duet; and he or she may very well be restored to sanity by the right tune. The popularity of these scenes must have been due in part to the opportunities provided for musical recall.

When Verdi began writing for La Scala, around 1840, the thematic recurrences in the operas he heard were almost all of the literal kinds.[2] Identifying marches, choruses of priests, and so on formed a part of every composer's stock in trade. "Recalling themes" tended to be concentrated in dream scenes and mad scenes—literal representations of unusual states of mind. Thus Bellini in *La Sonnambula* and *I Puritani,* and Donizetti in *Lucia di Lammermoor, Maria Padilla,* and *Linda di Chamounix,* to mention some of the more important works. *Linda* (1842), an especially extreme case, scored a particular success at La Scala at the time of *Ernani,* right after *Nabucco* and *I Lombardi.* Abandoned in Act II, Linda goes mad, singing part of the cabaletta of her previous love duet (later we are informed that in her madness she sings it all the time). When the repentant Carlo returns to her, she refuses to credit him until *he* sings the cabaletta, which done, she regains her wits and all ends happily. In addition there are several appearances of a melancholy ballata (descended from Rossini's *La Cenerentola*) having to do with a girl who was unable to follow her mother's good advice about sexual prudence. Thus the two recurring themes symbolize the central dramatic conflict of the opera, such as it is.

On the other hand, some important works managed perfectly well without recurring themes. Mercadante's *Il Giuramento* and *Il Bravo,* the great successes at La Scala just prior to Verdi's run with *Nabucco, Lombardi,* and *Ernani,* involve none at all.

In French opera, recurring themes had a considerable tradition. Meyerbeer made the most of this with the repetitions of Rimbault's ballade in *Robert le diable,* and of "Ein' feste Burg" in *Les Huguénots;* the fashion seems to be reflected in the Parisian work of Bellini and Donizetti—scattered thematic recurrences of one sort or another may be noted in *I Puritani, Le Duc d'Albe, La Favorite, Les Martyrs,* and *Dom Sébastien,* as well as in Verdi's French undertakings. Most interesting in this respect is *Le Prophète,* the toast of Paris while Verdi was there with Giuseppina in 1849. In this opera—it has been characterized as "hysterical and disheveled"[3]—Meyerbeer seems to have cast around for musical repetitions of all kinds and descriptions. The most obvious, the recurring *prêche* of the Anabaptists, will be cited later. The hero Jean's first major piece, in which he relates his prophetic dream, looks forward thematically not only to the famous Coronation March—see example 1—but also to the big chorus on the occasion of his investiture in Act IV. Prior to this, when on two separate occasions he has qualms about joining the Anabaptists, the orchestra cites arias associated with his mother Fidès or his sweetheart Berthe. And at the start of the prison scene in Act V, Fidès almost absent-mindedly recalls a few bars of the cabaletta that ended Act IV.

Abramo Basevi, a Florentine physician, opera composer, and music critic who wrote a detailed study of Verdi's early operas in 1859—a study that is still better than most—considered that recurring themes in opera were first introduced and best used by Meyerbeer, run into the ground by Wagner, and not too well handled by Verdi: "Il *Verdi* veramente non fu mai molto felice nella ripresa dei *motivi;* nella quale industria il *Meyerbeer* fu tanto eccellente, e forse unico."[4] With which we

EXAMPLE I

cannot agree. However, it is clear that Verdi's heritage in this matter can be traced quite simply to Donizetti and Meyerbeer. (Wagner is, of course, not in the picture.) That a real tradition existed in Italy until shortly prior to Verdi's career is not so clear, though the reader may amuse himself by thinking of recurring themes in considerably older operas.

II · For the first dozen years of Verdi's career, his operas contain many recurring themes, used in a thoroughly haphazard fashion. So it was with his contemporaries. Only rarely in the 1840s does Verdi go beyond what is called for—shouted for—in the libretto. Identifying choruses and marches recur in *Nabucco* (1842), *I Lombardi* (1843), *I due Foscari* (1844), *Stiffelio* (1850), and especially in *La Battaglia di Legnano* (1848), which displays something of the grim system of *Les Huguénots*. In *I due Foscari*, Verdi experimented rather surprisingly with a full network of identifying themes for each of the three principals, the Council of Ten, and even the people of Venice; each has a musical "calling card," which serves not to recall previous dramatic situations but simply to identify. I am unable to say whether Verdi copied this scheme from any other opera. In any case he did not follow it again until *Aida*.

As for "recalling themes," an instance occurs as early as *Oberto* (1839), Verdi's rather unassuming first work for the stage. At the beginning of Act II, the *seconda donna* recalls some music from her earlier love duet with the hero: "Riccardo! . . . Oh! soavi memorie! . . ." In *Nabucco* (1842), the monologue of the mad King Nebuchadnezzar involves several past themes as well as a future funeral march; when he repents, prays to the God of Israel, and is miraculously cured, the distinctive solo cello is heard from the previous *preghiera* of the Israelite High Priest. The heroine of *Giovanna d'Arco* (1845), as an "inspired" character, hears a recurring chorus of angels and also one of devils. She also hears, in Act I, six bars of what is to be an important military march in Act III (this is oddly prophetic of the prophetic *rêve* in *Le Prophète*). In *Attila* (1846), the vision which presently becomes a reality was specifically set up in the libretto, like the repetition of the pledge in *Ernani* (1844).

In these years there is little consistency and little art in Verdi's use of recurring themes. A third of the early operas do not employ the means at all. We are doubtless sufficiently grateful for not having to suffer a procession of tired recalling themes during the *gran scena di sonnambulismo* for Lady Macbeth (or during the *sogno* for Francesco in *I Masnadieri*). Verdi too may have felt that the evocative dream or mad scene had seen its day.

Musical recall on a more imaginative level, however, was another proposition. It was in the course of composing *Rigoletto*, in 1850–51, that Verdi seems to have been struck by the immediate theatrical force of this device, and perhaps also by its congeniality to his personality, musical style, and conception of drama.

Thanks to the full-length composition draft of *Rigoletto* published in facsimile by Carlo Gatti, we are able to see something of the evolution of Verdi's idea here.[5] As is well known, the original title was to have been *La Maledizione,* and from the first, Verdi followed the obvious course of providing parallel music for Rigoletto's parallel exclamations at the end of Acts I and III, "Ah! la maledizione!!" At the time of the draft, however, he did not yet intend to use a single musical setting for the recurring words "Quel vecchio maledivami!" in Act I, scene 2—even though the librettist Piave set them up for him, almost literally, no fewer than four times during the scene. In the draft, the four remarks are set to different declamatory patterns, the first three (evidently) to be sung unaccompanied, *cupo voce,* and the last to be supported by a diminished seventh chord (example 2). Within the next months, Verdi changed this to the greatly superior German sixth that we know, altered the other three places to agree with it, and then composed the Prelude to the opera out of this material. (The draft contains no indications for a prelude. In *Ernani,* too, the recurring pledge music appears in the Prelude.) It is noteworthy that the figure for "Quel vecchio maledivami!" is not precisely equivalent to any of the actual curse music of Monterone, similar as it may be on account of the monotone C and the rhythmic profile. The non-identity is a relic of Verdi's original reluctance, as it seems, to provide obvious relationships.

In any case, the recollection of Monterone's curse is suitably gripping—one is tempted to think, the more so for not consisting of a precise quotation. As for "La donna è mobile," that was an item handed on a silver platter from Hugo to Piave to Verdi. One might attempt to describe it as an "identifying canzone" handled ironically and climactically, but the piece seems safely *hors de classification*.

And after *Rigoletto,* Verdi would appear to have tried to work recalling themes of the imaginative variety into all or almost all his operas. To be sure, in *Il Trovatore* (1853), a retrospective work, the character who does the remembering is again half-mad: Azucena twice recalls the burning of her mother through the spectral canzone "Stride la vampa!" It will be granted that this refines the treatment of people "hearing things" past the stage represented by *Nabucco.* In his next forward-looking work, *La Traviata* (1853), Verdi used imaginative recall even more extensively than in *Rigoletto*. As mentioned above, Alfredo's declaration from Act I, "Di quell' amor," reappears in the orchestra two acts later as Violetta reads the letter,

EXAMPLE 2

RIGOLETTO: Quel vec - chio ma-le-di - va-mi!

Quel vec-chio ma - le - di - va-mi!

Quel vec - chio ma-le-di - va-mi!

Ah    da quel vec-chio fui  ma-le - det - to!

and again as she dies; on the latter occasion the theme is developed simply, but movingly, by means of a modulating sequential extension. But this theme of Alfredo's had already been sung by Violetta during the aria "Ah, fors' è lui," at the end of Act I, when she is debating whether to devote herself to *amor* or to *gioia*. Then, in order to dramatize her conflict, Verdi actually has "Di quell' amor" sung again by Alfredo off stage during her cabaletta "Sempre libera." Alfredo is said to be serenading outside *sotto al balcone,* but it is possible that the whole thing is a figment of Violetta's excellently fertile dramatic imagination.[6]

In *Rigoletto* and *La Traviata,* the recalling theme becomes what Gino Roncaglia calls a "tema-cardine," a recurring theme around which the entire drama is made to hinge.[7] It spans the total action, from the first act to the last, and it is contrived so as to touch on the central dramatic idea: Monterone's curse, the love of Alfredo. Viewing Verdi's oeuvre as a whole, I could not quite agree that the "tema-cardine" functions as systematically, as consciously, or always as artistically as Roncaglia implies, but his point is certainly well taken in reference to *Rigoletto* and *La Traviata.* These recurring themes do more than recall or identify: they provide, in a single musical gesture, a compelling particular focus for the dramatic action.

# III

Between *La Traviata* and *Otello,* Verdi experimented restlessly with recurring music of all varieties. The results are never as convincing as in *Rigoletto* and *La Traviata,* and indeed, by comparison with those works on the one hand and *Otello* on the other, none of the middle operas makes a satisfactory dramatic totality (not even *Aida,* in the present writer's judgment, for all its ostentatious smoothness of technique). In *Simon Boccanegra* (1857), Verdi repeated music only along the most conventional lines: for the chorus and for the fevered dream or *sogno* of the Doge. In *Un Ballo in maschera* (1859), a number of fragments recur. Amelia arrives on the heath in Act II to the strains of her prayer from Act I; Riccardo, preparing to renounce Amelia, recalls his earlier love song about her;[8] Tom and Sam are identified by a rather unfortunate recurring theme in fugato. *La Forza del destino* (1862, 1869) features an even more unfortunate identifying theme for the force of destiny, which pries its way into many arias and other numbers. Then Leonora's prayer from the beginning of the Monastery Scene is sounded just before her formal induction into the hermitage at the end of the scene. (Music and treatment are modeled on those of Amelia in *Ballo.*) *Don Carlos* contains a large number of recollections—too many, even in the original version for Paris (1867). The cabaletta in which Carlos and Rodrigue pledge friendship, "Dieu, tu semas dans nos âmes," is recalled several times, generally with pathetic overtones. Elisabeth brings to memory during her great last-act aria excerpts from her love duets with Carlos in Act I (Fontainebleau) and Act II. The Fontainebleau love-duet theme also occurs to Carlos in prison (Act IV, scene 2). An identifying monks' chorus links Acts I and V.

Rather curiously, *Aida* (1871) works with a regular scheme of identifying themes for persons and groups, like *I due Foscari* of thirty years before. While in general the dramatic use of these themes is stiff and uninteresting, there are some highly imaginative exceptions: notably the bleak development of the Priests' fugato during Aida's reply to Amonasro's tongue-lashing ("Padre! a costoro schiava non sono," Act III; see example 3). Once again the most emphatic recalling theme is a prayer, Aida's "Numi, pietà."

For fifteen years following *Aida,* Verdi composed no new operas, but he did revise *Simon Boccanegra* and *Don Carlos* for La Scala (1881 and 1884). The revisions show little solicitude for the recurring themes. In *Simon,* some melodic details were improved in the cabaletta "Figlia! al tal nome io palpito" (Act II), but when during his *sogno* Simon dreams this piece, the orchestra coolly recalls something very much like the earlier, inferior version (Act III; see example 4). In *Don Carlo,* that Fontainebleau love-duet theme which is recalled twice in later acts was in real jeopardy, for Verdi's decision was to cut out the Fontainebleau episode altogether. The new version salvages no more than six bars of music from the duet, played cryptically by the orchestra during the course of Carlo's opening scene in the new Act I, some time before Elisabetta makes her first entrance (example 5). Still, in Act IV Elisa-

EXAMPLE 3

EXAMPLE 4

SOGNO (1857 = 1881)

EXAMPLE 5

betta remembers a full *ten* bars of the tune—which in the new version of the opera she had never even heard. As though to make up for this, Verdi threw in recollections of two more love themes, bringing the total number of these to four. The effect is rather disheveled. One thinks of *Le Prophète*.

# IV

With *Otello,* however, nothing is careless and nothing is diffuse. As impressive as the force and centrality of the recalling themes in this opera is the economy with which they are handled, especially by contrast with *Don Carlos* and *Aida.* There are only two such themes. The lesser of them, Iago's unctuous phrase warning Otello of the "green-ey'd monster," forms the substance of the Prelude to Act III—a phrase which, as Francis Toye observed, "fortunately did not become a 'jealousy-motif.'"[9] In the Prelude the general *Stimmung* somewhat resembles that of the passage cited above from *Aida* and also resembles the opening of Act V of *Le Prophète* (example 6). The modal *unisono* theme that appears here in the bass recurs several times in the course of the opera. It is the Anabaptists' sermon "Ad nos, ad salutarem undam" (known also as the subject of Liszt's fugue).

The differences between the two act-openings doubtless interest us more than their similarities. Verdi builds an appreciable piece of music out of the theme, as against Meyerbeer's single period; he also furthers the drama very subtly by seeming to conclude with a deceptive cadence and then returning to it and completing it after the first recitative, the Herald's speech. What the Prelude records is the relentless working of the *veleno* of jealousy in Otello's mind between the acts—something that Shakespeare indicates in a quite different way by opening his Act IV in the midst of a shattering exchange:

*Iago.*  Will you think so?
*Oth.*              Think so, Iago?
*Iago.*                     What,
        To kiss in private?
*Oth.*              An unauthoriz'd kiss.
*Iago.*  Or to be naked with her friend in bed
        An hour, or more, not meaning any harm?

The operatic Moor of Venice is distracted momentarily, by a deceptive cadence and a Herald announcing important affairs of the Signory. But only momentarily; Otello dismisses the Herald at once and returns to his obsession. Verdi's direction is exactly appropriate: *Come prima.* So is Otello's next word: "Continua"—to Iago, whose characteristic snarling trill has now invaded the cadence.

The other recurring theme, the orchestral music for the kiss at the height of the love duet in Act I, returns in Act IV when Otello enters to kill Desdemona and then again when he stabs himself. As in *La Traviata,* this deserves to be called a true "tema-cardine"; and now Verdi seems more conscious than ever of the full power latent in the device. The recalling theme spans the opera from first to last and touches on the fundamental tragic issue:

EXAMPLE 6

I kiss'd thee ere I kill'd thee. No way but this—
Killing myself, to die upon a kiss.


It can be argued that as a dramaturgical instrument, Verdi's recurring music does considerably more than Shakespeare's couplet. Otello's love for Desdemona, but particularly the crux of "kiss and kill," is central to Shakespeare's dramatic conception and also to Verdi's. Verdi's use of musical recall here reaches its ultimate dramatic refinement.

And in technical terms, this recalling of the kiss can be seen to follow a certain procedure developed in *Traviata, Ballo, Forza,* and *Aida:* reserving for purposes of recurrence the expansive *maggiore* conclusion to a composite piece of a kind that moves very emphatically from the minor to the major mode. Arias of this kind abound in Verdi's work: "Tacea la notte," "Il lacerato spirito," "Me pellegrina ed orfana," and others. After *La Traviata,* he had the good instinct to use the concluding *maggiore* part sometimes as a recurring theme. The paradigm in example 7 will perhaps make the point clear.

EXAMPLE 7

VIOLETTA: Ah for - s'è lui che l'a - ni - ma...

A quell'a - mor, quell'a - mor _____ che pal - pi - to

AMELIA: Con - sen - ti - mi, o Si - gno - re, vir - tù

LEONORA: Ma - dre, Madre pie - to - sa Ver - gi - ne...

deh! non m'abban - do - nar, pie - tà, pie - tà di me, Si - gno - re

AIDA: I sa - cri no - mi di pa - dre, d'amante...

Nu - mi, pie - tà del mio sof - frir! Spe - me non v'ha...

un bacio... un bacio ancora...

EXAMPLE 8

The novelty in *Otello* is, of course, that the recurring *maggiore* phrase is not a prayer or declaration but a purely orchestral fragment, to which Otello merely adds some broken words the first and last times. However, its emotional quality, and its surging appoggiaturas, six-four chords, and string tremolo show a definite kinship with the earlier compositions. (A primitive instance of the same technique may be pointed out in *Jérusalem,* the revision of *I Lombardi* for Paris in 1847. At the start of Act II, Roger [Pagano], as the repentant hermit, prays in a composite aria which comes directly from *Lombardi*—and which in *Lombardi* is heard this once and never again. But for Paris, Verdi made it recur. This happens after a starving pilgrim staggers in to tell of a group of his comrades in straits, and Roger, deciding to go to their aid, briefly sings the words "Fais ô mon Dieu que je sauve leurs jours" to the climax of the *maggiore* strain [example 8]. Ultimately Roger returns, and as the chorus whispers that this must indeed be the holy man, the *maggiore* phrase sounds again, now in the orchestra. The phrase serves, then, as a primitive and rather aimless identifying theme. It never turns up in the later acts.)

v · The expansive *maggiore* phrase used as a recurring theme—we have pursued it tenuously from Jerusalem to Cyprus, from Boston to Memphis—seems to come home to roost at last in Windsor. With just such a phrase, the merry wives read Sir John's outrageous twin love letters: "e il viso tuo su me risplenderà . . ."—and burst into laughter. Later on, after considerable byplay and scheming, they recall the letters, the music, and the laughter (example 9; the *minore* antecedent, already transformed in *Otello,* has entirely withered away). A love theme, again—but in a rather special light. It is beautifully characteristic of *Falstaff* that the case should involve parody, and a double parody at that: the merry wives mocking Falstaff's grandiloquence, and the old composer mocking his own emotionalism in one of his own favorite operatic devices.

EXAMPLE 9

But a discussion of *Falstaff* would have to move on to new ground: for whereas *Otello* can still be treated as a culmination (however astonishing) of the old tradition, this is not true of *Falstaff* in the matter of recurring themes or anything else. Recurring themes now serve as much for musical organization as for identification or recall, as witness the famous "Dalle due alle tre." Furthermore, thematic relationships on a much subtler level than simple recurrence seem to be constantly, and slyly, at work. These aspects of thematic treatment have been skirted in the present essay, because although they are not altogether absent from the early operas, they are less important there than blunter effects. But our rough scaffold of "recalling" and "identifying" themes is no longer adequate to support the "buon corpo di Sir John," the density and brilliance of Verdi's new musical technique in *Falstaff*.

The one completely straightforward use of recurring themes is the love music of Nannetta and Fenton, which shines luminously and clearly within each of the three acts. Its dramatic purpose would be to articulate or illuminate the dualism that grounds Verdi's conception here—as Edward T. Cone has pointed out:

> What is not usually mentioned is that the complete content involves a basic contrast. On the one hand is the world of fighting and clowning, of appetites and revulsions, of plots and counter-plots. Its depths are indicated by the darkness of Ford's jealousy; but its true representative is Falstaff himself. . . . But there is another world: that of Fenton and Nannetta, which they create for themselves. Its symbol is Nannetta's fairyland, and into its unreality the lovers are able, for a little while, to escape.[10]

The constancy and separateness of this charmed vision is determined in part by the constancy of the music that identifies it, and by the very simple way in which it recurs. So in addition to its numerous very amusing details of recollection—"Reverenza," "Va, vecchio John," "Caro Signor Fontana"—*Falstaff* has its real "tema-cardine," as Roncaglia would doubtless allow. The innocence of the technique itself, by contrast with the high style of thematic activity around it, reflects the contrast between fairyland and Windsor jungle.

The technique is not only innocent but old, old and blunt. Verdi had touched on it in *Oberto, Conte di San Bonifacio*. The study of a composer's development is often the study of his growing sensitivity to means known to him, but known imperfectly, from the beginning.

## Notes

1. Donald Jay Grout, *A Short History of Opera* (New York, 1947), 349.
2. Repertory is listed in Pompeo Cambiasi, *Teatro alla Scala, 1778–1881* (Milan, 1881), and Luigi Romani, *Teatro alla Scala: Cronologia* (Milan, 1862).
3. Wallace Brockway and Herbert Weinstock, *The World of Opera* (New York, 1962), 219.
4. Abramo Basevi, *Studio sulle opere di Giuseppe Verdi* (Florence, 1859), 71.
5. *L'Abbozzo del Rigoletto di Giuseppe Verdi,* with an introduction by Carlo Gatti (Milan, 1941).
6. Verdi, not Piave, must be responsible for this idea. It does not figure in the libretto.
7. Gino Roncaglia, "Il 'Tema-cardine' nell' opera di Giuseppe Verdi," *Rivista Musicale Italiana* 47 (1943): 220–22.
8. This case is interesting from another point of view. After Riccardo's meditative slow aria, the receipt of urgent news gives him every excuse to embark upon a cabaletta, but instead of this he simply sings an ecstatic epitome of his earlier piece. Did Verdi hope to achieve in this way something of the force of the traditional cabaletta without its tedium and banality? Ponchielli obtains a similar effect after the "Suicidio" aria in *La Gioconda*.
9. Francis Toye, *Giuseppe Verdi: His Life and Works* (New York, 1946), 371.
10. Edward T. Cone, *Music: A View from Delft,* ed. Robert P. Morgan (Chicago, 1989), 174.

# Two Early Verdi Operas; Two Famous Terzetti

They can be pretty hard to take, Verdi's early operas—hard for those who approach them from Verdi's own mature work, and hard for those coming the other way from Bellini and the mature Donizetti. The well-known robustness of style looks very much like crudeness. Verdi as a young composer had uncertain taste, faulty technique, and no more show-business scruples than the next man. What he did have was this extraordinary insight into dramatic essentials on the grandest level, and an iron determination to project drama in music that as often as not lacked the basic technical necessities for the job at hand. *Ernani,* his fifth opera, presents an object lesson in the disparity between artistic idea and realization. If we find it impossible to recapture the wild enthusiasm that *Ernani* evoked from audiences of the 1840s, we can perhaps still derive some interest and instruction from the lesson.

The first two acts do not contain much that is notable, I believe. The one moment of melodic distinction comes early, in the pretty Bellinian cantabile of the Prelude, part of which returns in the final act. Elvira's role throughout is supposed to be vigorous and sharply etched: witness her harsh upward-thrusting lines in "Ernani, Ernani, involami" and the stabbing rhythms in her *risposta* to the advances of Don Carlo ("Fiero sangue d'Aragona . . . ," "Aspirar non deggio al trono . . ."). Elvira emerges as a puppet character for all that, though one whose strings twitch more merrily than those of Ernani. Only a loose phrase or two stays in the memory from his entire role: perhaps "L'odio nullo che m'arde nel core / Tutto spegnere alfine

━ Combines "Notes on an Early Verdi Opera," *Soundings* 3 (1973): 56–65, and "*I Lombardi* in San Diego," *19th-Century Music* 3 (1980): 259–64.

potro" at the end of Act I, "Io sono il bandito Ernani" in the Act II terzetto, and "Vivi d'amarmi e vivere" at the very end.

Don Carlo already begins to come to life. The *declamato* beginning of the Act I terzetto, "Tu sei Ernani!", is well composed, and to my ear the best number in the early acts is the *Gran scena ed aria* in which Carlo threatens Silva for concealing Ernani. This is in Act II. The man is really angry in the opening recitative, the trumpet in the cantabile section ("Lo vedremo, veglio audace") certainly sounds savage, and for once the cadential section of this cantabile contributes something to the drama. Silva enters briefly—with no more than ten bars of singing—but most unexpectedly (example 1). According to the operatic norms of the time, Silva should either sing more or less—either engage in a full-scale duet with Carlo, or stay out of his aria altogether. But Silva's obstinate pride makes him dare to interrupt the king in order to insist glumly on his innocence. He is restricted to the range of a fifth, D–A (a muttery, not very effective range for a bass), and both his vocal line and the orchestral bass harp curiously on the fourth degree, D, which is repeatedly left unresolved. Silva does not presume to take part in the final cadenza, as he would in a true duet, for Carlo's raging song cuts him off on an unresolved D. What looks like a harmonic solecism makes a lively dramatic point. One almost thinks of the parallel fifths in the "Oro supplex" of the *Requiem*.

Interesting that the strongest number in the first two acts should come at the confrontation between Don Carlo and Silva. Although these two characters drift apart after this point in the action, the contrast between them develops into the crux of Hugo's (and Verdi's) dramatic conception. *Hernani,* written within a few months of the *Fantastic* Symphony, is a superbly dotty piece. It builds an outrageous romantic sexual fantasy, it expatiates dizzily on honor, and (most of all) it nurses a transparent allegory of youth and age. The three ages of man contend for—the sun, Doña Sol, Verdi's Elvira. Hernani is said to be twenty, Don Ruy Gomez de Silva sixty plus, and Don Carlos somewhere in the middle (a deliberate departure from history, for Charles V was nineteen at the date indicated for the play); Hugo himself when he wrote it was twenty-eight.

Sympathy must not waver for Hernani, and to keep sympathy stimulated Hugo crammed the first part of the play with intrigue. There are abductions, escapes, forced entries, secret passages, disguises, pledges, duels, ambushes, alarums, re-nunciations, reconciliations. And to add dimension, as it were, to this one-sided view of youth, Hugo changed sides (or crossed sides) in his attitude toward age and middle age. For three acts Don Carlos is a ruthless, suave villain, until he experiences a great change of heart causing him to spare Hernani's life and thrust him into the arms of Doña Sol. Early in the play, when Silva is the underdog, he earns our grudging sympathy in spite of his incredible rigidity; his painful longing for Doña Sol certainly strikes a more responsive chord than does Carlos's kingly

EXAMPLE I

lust. But at the end of the play Silva steps forward as a completely pitiless force, content to see Doña Sol die at his feet rather than cede her to Hernani.

Hugo's most extravagant move was the reversal in the role of Don Carlos. How did he carry this off? The conversion takes place when Carlos is waiting for news of his election as Holy Roman Emperor, a prospect that moves him deeply, the more so since he uncovers a conspiracy to assassinate him in the very hour of his vigil. The scene is romantically calculated to heighten his (and our) susceptibilities: the underground tomb of Charlemagne in the cathedral of Aix-la-Chapelle. Carlos reveres Charlemagne and hopes to emulate his greatness. (Carlos's veneration of his great ancestor, which ennobles him, contrasts with the quixotic ancestor-worship of Silva in the previous act—W. S. Gilbert's model for *Ruddigore*.) In particular, Carlos engages in a fantastically long soliloquy, five pages long without interruption, while awaiting the cannon shots announcing the electors' decision. He ponders governance, glory, mortality, and humanity, before concealing himself in Charlemagne's tomb to surprise the conspirators. When he emerges he is a new man—symbolically, Charlemagne reborn. "A Carlo Magno sia gloria e onor," he sings in Piave's libretto as he is acclaimed for his astounding act of clemency toward the conspirators. This was the number that Verdi's audiences read in a contemporary political context, substituting on at least one occasion the words "A Pio Nono sia gloria e onor."

Verdi could not, of course, follow Hugo in a five-page recitative. But he understood clearly that his crucial dramatic task was to do something analogous in order to validate Carlo's conversion, to make it credible. He labored mightily at this in the *Scena ed aria* that he wrote for the baritone at this point; no other Italian opera composer would have done so much. The solemn orchestration, first of all: in the *preludio* a bass clarinet solo, and during the main part of the recitative, only massed brass instruments playing piano or pianissimo. The aria itself is set apart (less happily) by harmonic figuration on a solo cello, but at the climax the brass returns. This aria, "Oh de' verd' anni miei," has a somewhat unusual musical form matched to the dramatic situation. Instead of following one of the stereotyped aria forms of the time, such as A A' b b A" or A A' b b C, Verdi made a kind of amalgam or, rather, an extension of the first of these patterns: A A' b b' A" C. The A" phrase seems all set to conclude the aria, for it brings back the opening melody in the tonic key; yet it lacks the obligatory melodic climax and at the last moment makes as though to modulate. There follows an emphatic new phrase in the tonic (C) for the last line of the text, "e vincitor de' secoli il nome mio faro." Carlo's name will echo down the centuries—the climactic thought. At last the melody surges up past E♭ for the first time, to F and even G♭; and instead of the mumbling cello, it now has the violins and woodwind doubling the irresistible vocal line.

Ordinarily an aria consists of two closed lyric sections, a slow cantabile and a fast cabaletta. The first section does not end with too solid a cadence, for the singer remains on stage and will presently launch into the cabaletta—which will have cadences to burn. This scene, however, is to include no cabaletta. Carlo does not remain on stage but moves solemnly into the crypt containing Charlemagne's tomb. So Verdi concludes the cantabile with a much more extended cadence than usual: after his cadenza, as Carlo conceals himself in the crypt, the melody of his memorable phrase "e vincitor de' secoli" echoes in the strings and sinks down to a pensive close.[1] One thinks of similar orchestral echoes after arias in *Simon Boccanegra* (after "Il lacerato spirito"), *Aida* ("O patria mia"), *Otello* (the Willow Song), and *Falstaff* (Ford's monologue—with a delicious parodistic twist). In early Verdi the device is much less usual.

In the terms of Verdi's dramaturgy, all this emphasis on the key words "e vincitor de' secoli" validates Carlo's conversion, which is manifested a little later in his act of Metastasian clemency. Or if it does not finally validate, at least it does the major work of psychological preparation. Verdi saw that the moment of clemency itself requires another jog, some "action" at the very moment; and this is provided (as in Hugo) by Elvira. When Carlo is swearing to execute the conspirators, including Ernani, and Elvira pleads passionately for them, Carlo suddenly recalls his new self-image and heeds her. The place is at once fascinating, heartening, and ludicrous, for it shows in a stroke how clearly Verdi understood what needed to be done, and how hopelessly inadequate his technique still was to do it (example 2).

Directly after the orchestral thunderclaps that end example 2, Carlo sinks to his knees to invoke the memory of Charlemagne, then rises ecstatically to free the conspirators.

> Je ne sais plus vos noms, messieurs!—Haine et fureur,
> Je veux tout oublier. Allez, je vous pardonne!
> C'est la leçon qu'au monde il convient que je donne.

The great concerted tableau at this point, the Act III finale, was the most admired number in the whole opera. A magnificent curtain for the baritone, it more than compensates for the fact that he does not appear at all in the last act, Act IV. When Liszt came to prepare his concert transcription of *Ernani,* the one theme he used was that of the *famosissimo* Act III finale.

II ·

Don Carlo's new nobility is projected in the Act III finale. Silva's deepening intransigence is projected in another of the celebrated numbers in *Ernani,* the terzetto finale of Act IV. As often happens in Verdi—we saw an example in the soliloquy aria for Carlo—this number derives its force from the way stereotyped lyric forms of the day are turned to account. The stereotypes are not broken but bent to suit dramatic exigencies.

EXAMPLE 2

ELVIRA: Ah, si - gnor, se t'è con-ces-so il mag-gio-re d'ogni trono, que - sta _ pol - ve-re ne-glet-ta or con-fon-di col per-do-no; sia lo sprez-zo tua ven - det - ta che il ri - mor-so com-pi-rà. Ta-ci, o don - na. Ah _ no, _ non _ si - a. Parlò il ciel _ per vo - ce _ mi - a: vir - tù au_gu_sta è _ la _ pie - tà.

The text consists of the following three stanzas (lower-case and Greek let-ters denote two-bar phrases, capitals four-bar phrases, and bold capitals six-bar phrases):

STA. I   *Elvira*

| | | | | |
|---|---|---|---|---|
| (to Ernani) | Ferma, crudele, estinguere | A | Hold, cruel one, why do you | |
| | Perchè vuoi tu due vite? | | Wish to end two lives? | |
| (to Silva) | Quale d'Averno demone | A' | What demon from hell | |
| | Ha tali trame ordite? | | Has woven these snares? | |
| | Presso al sepolcro mediti | B | Almost at the graveside, | |
| | Compisci tal vendetta! | | You rejoice to plan such a revenge! | |
| | La morte che t'aspetta, | B' | The death which you await, | |
| | O vecchio, affretterò. | | Old man, I shall hasten— | |

| | |  | |  |
|---|---|---|---|---|
| | | Ma che diss'io?<br>perdonami,<br>L'angoscia in me parlò. | p p<br>C | But what am I saying?<br>forgive me:<br>'Twas grief, not I, that spoke. |
| STA. II | *Silva* | E vano, o donna, il piangere,<br>E vano: io non perdono. | π<br>π | Vain, lady, is your weeping;<br>'Tis vain: I will not pardon. |
| | *Ernani* | (La furia è inesorabile.) | | (His fury is inexorable.) |
| | *Elvira* | Figlia d'un Silva io sono;<br>Io l'amo, indissolubile<br>Nodo mi stringe a lui. | | I am a daughter of the Silvas;<br>I love him, an indissoluble<br>Bond ties me to him. |
| | *Silva* | L'ami? morrà costui,<br>Per tale amor morrà. | | You love him? He shall die—<br>He dies for that same love! |
| | *Elvira* | Per queste amare lagrime<br>Di lui, di me pietà. | | For these bitter tears<br>Have pity on him, on me. |
| STA. III | *Ernani* | Quel pianto, Elvira, ascondimi<br>Ho d'uopo di costanza,<br>L'affano di quest'anima<br>Ogni dolor avanza.<br>Un giuramento orribile<br>Ora mi danna a morte,<br>Fu scherno della sorte<br>La mia felicità. | D<br><br>D'<br><br>E<br><br>E' | Cease this lament, Elvira;<br>I myself have need of courage.<br>The distress of this spirit<br>Is advanced by every grief.<br>A terrible oath<br>Now delivers me to my death;<br>A cruel jest of Fate—<br>Such was all my happiness. |
| | *Ernani* and<br>*Elvira* | Non ebbe di noi miseri<br>Non ebbe il ciel pietà! | p p<br>C | For us miserable ones<br>Heaven had no pity! |
| DA CAPO: | *Silva* | E vano . . . | π π **F** | 'Tis vain . . . |

Verdi composed this as a sort of double number; each section might be thought of as fairly conventional in itself, but not so the particular combination. The first cantabile, comprising stanza I of the poem, is sung by Elvira to a twenty-four–bar period in a form extended from the standard A A' b b C aria form mentioned previously. Silva roughly dismisses her plea with the first two lines of stanza II; the passage is arranged to sound exactly like the conventional *risposta* in a duet, but the rest of the stanza runs off into a short dialogue (of which more in a moment). Ernani now sings a new cantabile, stanza III, in the same key and meter and in the same ample twenty-four–bar form. This Verdi converted into another duet-like member by adding Silva's same *risposta* "E vano . . ." at the end—a da capo that is not specifically indicated in the libretto, though Piave would probably have expected any composer to supply it. It makes every kind of sense for Silva to reject pleas from Elvira and then from Ernani plus Elvira in the same implacable terms.

EXAMPLE 3

ELVIRA (p)                                    SILVA (π)

Ah!    Ma che diss' io, per-do-na-mi    E va - no, o don-na, il pian-ge-re, è va - no

|  | Stanza I | Stanza II | | | Stanza III | |
|---|---|---|---|---|---|---|
| SINGERS | Elvira | Silva | *dialogue:*<br>*13 bars* | Ernani | Elvira<br>Ernani<br>Silva | Elvira<br>Ernani<br>Silva |
| PHRASES | A A′ B B′ p p C | π π | ——— | D D′ E E′ | p p C | π π **F** π π **F**<br>+ *cadences* |
| KEYS | d (F)          D | D | b E A D d | D      (A) | D | D |

FIGURE 1  The Terzetto in *Ernani:* Form Diagram

Verdi went further and deepened the musical echo by his treatment of the ends of the three stanzas. These ends are, in each case, two lines set apart syntactically from the rest of the stanza, and these lines stress a common theme, the invocation of pity. The music for stanza III, lines 9–10, is the same as that for stanza I with an extra vocal line in octaves; the music for stanza II, lines 9–10, is gesturally similar; and all this music is similar to the music of Silva's twice-heard *risposta* (example 3). The latter similarity is indicated by the use of letters p and π on the text above and on figure 1.

Sheer length, simplicity of phrasing, and the many repeats of p and π are three features that give this terzetto its nagging, dragging quality. Other features that do so are the absolutely unvarying tempo and orchestral figuration—a "big guitar" in 9/8 eighth notes, andante assai mosso—and the tenacity of D-major harmony. As appears from the diagram, tonic centrality scarcely wavers, except in the fragment of dialogue in stanza II. Here a simple circle-of-fifths progression fits nicely with the situation. Ernani bursts out with a lament in the mediant-submediant region, Elvira proclaims her indissoluble love with a grand, warm swing to the dominant, and Silva sardonically uses her same bass (or something very like it) to thrust her back to the tonic. Which she accepts as a *minore*.

As for the drawn-out quality itself, that was something that Verdi found not in Piave's libretto but in Hugo's original play. The last scene of *Hernani* consists of an almost endless series of delays by the hero, evasions by the heroine, taunting demands for satisfaction from the villain, and convulsions all around as the result of slow poison. All this back and fill would have been confusing in the extreme on the operatic stage, as Piave understood. Verdi found his own way to invest Ernani's death with a musical quality that is analogous to Hugo's sense of pathetic excruciation.

It would not have been surprising if a composer at Verdi's level of technique in 1844 had botched this. Does this once-famous terzetto strike us as, simply, monotonous in phrasing, rhythm, accompaniment, key, and theme? It did not so strike Abramo Basevi, a contemporary critic who wrote a painstaking and by no means sycophantic study of Verdi's early operas in 1859:

> Next comes the final terzetto for Elvira, Ernani and Silva, which will surely be counted as one of the finest numbers, not least on account of a certain novelty of form. There are 95 bars of *andante mosso* in 3/4 time, which form 10 periods and a brief cadence passage; these periods, following one another and sometimes repeating themselves with or without some modification, are linked so effectively that they constitute a single musical thought with miraculous variety. The first melody alternates between soprano and tenor, then passes to the tenor, thence is continued by the bass. . . . To maintain a measure of unity in so much variety, Verdi has given the bass the phrase 'E vano o donna il piangere', which is repeated opportunely many times, and which stands out with much scenic effect. . . . It is a good idea to adopt a single musical thought which divided into many phrases and periods is applied to the different characters, but the idea must not be abused: for the musical memory of the listener is limited, and therefore one must not exhaust him by obliging him to retain more than comports to this faculty; furthermore the composer must not push beyond variety in this way to the point of rendering impossible the desired unity of the whole. Examples of variety analogous to that just noted are to be found among the ancients; and the great Sacchini, in his *Oedipe à Colone,* furnishes a notable example in the terzetto of the second act.[2]

Averting our eyes from Basevi's final display of operatic one-upmanship, which still has power to blind, we see that what he admired was exactly Verdi's lyric span, his ability to string out melody far beyond the confines of standard aria and duet forms. We too admire this ability—in pieces such as the love duet in Act I of *Otello*. So long as Ernani and Elvira can keep on singing, they are safe from the bitter realities of recitative; their unending lyric flow speaks for the growing intensity of their love as prospects wane for its consummation. Against the background of this pathos, Silva's *risposte* take on special vividness and terror.

This impressive terzetto is doubly or triply impressive because of its context, the manner in which it is placed in Act IV of the opera. The whole construction of the

| | No. 20, Festa da Ballo | No. 21, Gran Scena e Terzetto Finale | | | | | | | |
|---|---|---|---|---|---|---|---|---|---|
| PAGES | 267 | 276 | 277 | 278 | 281 | 282 | 284 | 295 | 296 |
| KEYS | E flat | C | G | e *(dec. cadence)* | b (oath) | c (arioso, Ernani) | d/D (terzetto) | b (e) (oath) | G *(dec. cadence)* |

FIGURE 2 *Ernani,* Act IV: Tonal Scheme

act is, in fact, a distinct forecast of architectural powers that we do not generally associate with Verdi until *Rigoletto,* Act III, at the very earliest. For purposes of reference it will be simplest to indicate the structure of the act by means of the main keys of its main sections (figure 2; page numbers in this figure refer to the Ricordi vocal score, brackets show musical repetitions, and dashed brackets show returns of music from previous acts). As in so many later operas, the climactic scene is also the densest locus of musical reminiscences, recapitulations, and the like.

The act opens in E-flat major with a footling wedding-ball scene, during which Silva stalks around silently *in maschera tutto chiusa in domino nero.* Left alone—one thinks of Act I of *La Traviata*—the lovers exchange tender words, resuming the Bellinian melody in C major first heard in the Act I prelude. This culminates in an ecstatic phrase in G major, sung in octaves to the following significant bit of doggerel:

Fino al sospiro estremo Till death's last sigh requites us,
Un solo core avremo. A single heart unites us.

But the phrase ends with a deceptive cadence, as Silva's horn interrupts from offstage with a solitary unaccompanied B (*un solo corno?*). Indeed, the whole remaining half of the act can be regarded as a huge interruption of this obligatory cadence, with its ambiguous coupling of love and death. The horn-call B seems to drive Ernani to his fate in E minor (the relative minor of G). After he manages to get Elvira out of the way for a moment, Silva enters and taunts Ernani by quoting to his face his own words pledging his life to Silva. This music was heard in Act II and also in the Act I prelude; Silva sings the phrase in B minor, so that its flex on the Neapolitan sixth comes out on a C-major triad. This Ernani picks up to plead with Silva in C minor. Elvira rushes on stage and, after a brief misunderstanding, joins the plea in the long-drawn-out D-major terzetto. C minor and D major serve as a prolonged cadential preparation for the key in which the opera is to end, G major.

Now the keys run symmetrically backwards. After grimly hearing out the terzetto, Silva contemptuously sings the pledge again in B minor; and at last Ernani submits to the force of this dominant and stabs himself in E minor. But now, miraculously, it is this fateful E-minor cadence that is made deceptive, by the same unaccompanied note, B—though instead of the ominous stopped-horn sound offstage, as before, it is now a transcendent shimmer of tremolo high strings. We recognize the effect from a later opera where Verdi used it again, *La Traviata,* at the death of Violetta. Sighing their last, the dying lovers repeat their ecstatic octave phrase in G major which this time, at last, receives proper resolution. A burst of triumphant orchestral noise on the G triad, regrettable but mercifully brief, rings down the final curtain.

I am not really entitled to say "the dying lovers"; Verdi's stage direction reads *Ernani spira ed Elvira sviene.* And Wagner's reads *Isolde sinkt, wie verklärt, in Brangänes Armen sanft auf Tristans Leiche. Grosse Rührung und Entrücktheit unter den Umstehenden. Marke segnet die Leichen.*[3] Once again, Verdi knew exactly what was required—a *Liebestod:* and he turned out a pretty fair example for 1844. Up in Dresden, the year before, was the one in *The Flying Dutchman* preferable? To be sure, Verdi lacked the technique to produce a really good *Liebestod* until the time of *Aida.*

In its ending, *Ernani* recalls *Traviata* and especially *La Forza del destino,* not *Aida.* There might have been a certain resemblance, however, if Verdi had accepted the disastrous plan he was originally offered. Here is a final footnote which I have from David Lawton, the young conductor and Verdi scholar who has found so much remarkable new material in the archives. (I also owe a sharpened awareness of Verdi's use of tonality to Professor Lawton's discussion of *Ernani* and other early Verdi operas in his doctoral dissertation.)[4] The first draft of the libretto that Piave prepared has the terzetto in Act IV followed by a "cabaletta finale a 2"! Of course Verdi would not touch it. In the composition of *Ernani,* this was only one of many decisions, interpretations, and inventions that show his precocious grasp of dramatic essentials.

III ·   The San Diego Opera Association, under its director Tito Capobianco, is engaged in a remarkable Verdi festival in which it is hoped "to present all twenty-eight [operatic] works of Verdi in an innovative and creative manner over a ten-year period." In 1978 they mounted *Falstaff,* in 1979 *La Traviata* and *I Lombardi alla prima crociata,* and for this year [1980] they have announced *Giovanna d'Arco* and *Il Trovatore* in the Paris version. *I Lombardi,* which played in New York in 1847, the first Verdi opera to reach America, has not been staged here since the nineteenth century.

One readily understands why: for there is no question that an appreciation of *I Lombardi* requires a strenuous exercise of the historical imagination. Produced in Austrian Milan in 1843, this opera must be taken first of all not as music, not as drama, but as a piece of carefully orchestrated political activism. Just how carefully, we shall have to wait to find out from the long-anticipated Verdi biography by Mary Jane Phillips Matz. In a typically spirited contribution to the San Diego program book, Ms. Matz depicts a Milan seething with revolution and musical intrigue, ready to pounce on any hint of patriotic leanings in Verdi's score. And by nature Verdi was not much of a hinter. He had strong medicine to administer for what ailed the body politic, and he had the backing of a political cabal to help him administer it. Donizetti, we have now learned, could be more vigorous in expression than used to be thought, and Mercadante could be vehement; but for uninhibited violence one had to turn to the young Bussetino. Many other qualities are already evident in Verdi's work, but it was the violence that made him the man of the hour.

The libretto of *I Lombardi* was derived tortuously from a then well-known verse epic, written twenty years earlier by the Milanese patriotic poet Tommaso Grossi. Presumably Grossi was present in the opening-night audience. The librettist was again the colorful Temistocle Solera, author of *Nabucco* the year before. As a focus for Milanese identification, *Nabucco*'s oppressed Hebrew slaves might seem more logical than *Lombardi*'s aggressive, aggrandizing Crusaders. But no doubt people felt more comfortable identifying with Lombards, and no doubt their patriotic enthusiasm was more akin to sentiments of aggression than of subjection. In any case Jerusalem was (and, as we well know, still is) a timeless and enormously potent symbol of human felicity, one that was bound to transcend the dramatic "logic"—the term is laughably inappropriate—of Solera's libretto. Thus when in Act II Giselda sings the following lines, in Lionel Salter's translation:

| | |
|---|---|
| I vinti sorgono, vendetta orrenda | The vanquished rise, and fearful vengeance |
| Sta nelle tenebre d'età vicina! | Lies in the shadow of the coming age! |
| A niuno sciogere fia dato l'alma | To none will it be granted to give up the ghost |
| Nel suol 've l'aure prime spirò! | Where he first drew breath! |
| L'empio olocausto d'umana salma | The impious holocaust of human bodies |
| Il Dio degl' uomini sempre sdegnò. | Was always offensive to the God of mankind. |

she is forecasting a *vendetta orrenda* on behalf of the Crusaders' victims and enemies. She thinks at that point that the Crusaders have slain her Saracen beloved, Oronte. But Verdi highlighted the passage and set it with the maximum *slancio*. Automatically its reference was transferred from the Lombard holocaust depicted on the stage to the Austrian one that was on everyone's mind.

There is a second scene in *I Lombardi* which ends with such a cabaletta for Giselda. Six other scenes feature stirring religio-patriotic choruses. No wonder the opera enjoyed an *esito di fanatismo,* as one La Scala archivist puts it, and that musical refinement and dramatic logic were altogether secondary considerations. In dramatic terms, the libretto suffers fatally from its derivation from an epic. Solera did not feel free to pick out a few seemly episodes, as Berlioz did with the *Aeneid,* nor to indulge in lengthy narrations, as Wagner did with the *Nibelungenlied*—and Solera had to get everything into one night. The opera completely lacks, as all commentators point out, the exemplary dramatic coherence and consistency of *Nabucco. Nabucco* looks forward to such coherent later works as *Macbeth* and *Rigoletto* and *Otello. I Lombardi* is a model for that other persistent strain in Verdi's output, the picaresque strain represented by *Il Trovatore, Simon Boccanegra,* and *La Forza del destino.*

In musical terms, much of *I Lombardi* is noxious; nevertheless, there are fine moments in it. On this latter point all Verdians close ranks: though as Andrew Porter points out, we do not always seem to agree on which those moments are.[5] I can venture some of my own favorites. Even Arvino's saber-rattling scene with the Crusaders, Act III, scene 2—one of the most noxious—comes to life as a result of a one-bar phrase overlap (Ricordi/Kalmus vocal score, page 251; compare the end of Act I, scene 1 of *Il Trovatore*). The "Salve Maria" sung by Giselda is, as Julian Budden says, astonishing, and the final scene seems to me Verdi's most impressive death prior to *Luisa Miller.* The famous patriotic unison chorus in the previous scene, "O Signore, dal tetto natio"—Matz says it is still taught to Italian schoolchildren—is by common consent sadly inferior to *Nabucco*'s "Va, pensiero," on which it was closely modeled. It is also inferior to the much simpler chorus in the final scene, "Te lodiamo, gran Dio di vittoria." This is the hymn heard by the dying Pagano (the Hermit) when the tent flaps are opened and he is shown Jerusalem with its walls "bedecked with the Crusaders' banners and illuminated by the first rays of the rising sun" (but not in the San Diego production). Pagano himself does not say too much, but Giselda's two speeches in this scene must be the earliest examples of Verdi transfixing a drama by means of short but enormously telling lyric phrases. (Elvira does something similar in Act III of *Ernani.*) The first speech by Giselda soothes the anguish of Pagano, and the second soothes the ire of her very choleric father, Arvino.

I was amazed at how moving this scene becomes on the stage, even with actors as indifferent as Paul Plishka and Cristina Deutekom. I wept, collecting myself only so far as to observe how the passing modulation to E flat at the end of this C-major chorus echoes the single half-remote passing modulation in the other C-major chorus, "O Signore, dal tetto natio," also to E flat, just a few minutes earlier, and how much better it is managed rhythmically. The sorts of long-range tonal phenomena that Siegmund Levarie has drawn attention to recently, occasioning responses from Guy A. Marco, myself, and others, are there to argue about in Verdi's work from the very start.[6]

Julian Budden's account of *I Lombardi* and the other early Verdi operas is as admirable for its critical sensibility as for its command of the historical background.[7] Budden seems to have been the first to pen a just appreciation of *Jérusalem,* the Paris version of *I Lombardi* made in 1847, showing the care with which Verdi went about the task and how considerably dramatic and musical matters were improved. Having "discovered" *Jérusalem,* as it were, Budden can certainly be forgiven a certain lack of warmth in the direction of *I Lombardi;* actually it is quite splendid how evenhandedly he deals with the two works. A note of reserve, though, can be detected in his treatment of the Act III terzetto, always the most applauded number in the opera, and the one that is best known today, thanks to a luminous broadcast which Toscanini made of it in the year of the opera's centennial, 1943, and which was still available on an inexpensive RCA record until quite recently. Budden is tight-lipped about the notorious solo violin in this terzetto; he is openly relieved to see it excised from *Jérusalem.* He admires the terzetto's "huge rhythmic span" and its "wealth of heartfelt melody," but finds the pressure to the dominant (from A to E and then to B) in the middle of the piece so strong as to make the final tonic return feel unmotivated.

I have written elsewhere about the other famous terzetto in Verdi's early corpus, that in *Ernani,* and commented on the composer's evident ambition to produce a long unbroken lyric sweep—Budden's "huge rhythmic span"—by means of a sort of interlocking multiplication of his standard A A B C lyric modules. In *I Lombardi* the technical means is not multiplication but expansion from within.[8] Figure 3 shows the form. Phrase B, in E major, closes *on* the dominant; phrase B' closes *in* the dominant, supported by a V-of-V chord. Yet to me the final tonic return (at phrases e e F) does not feel unmotivated, and I can suggest two reasons for this, the first of them linear. In the opening period (A A'), led off by the tenor Oronte, the line goes up only to F♯, which is touched by a characteristic motive of an upward fourth. (This motive is featured, remarkably, not only in this terzetto and in the recollection of it in the following Scene of the Vision, but also in Oronte's other main numbers, "La mia letizia infondere" and "Per dirupi e per foreste.") In the *risposta* by the soprano and bass (B B'), Giselda moves up firmly to G♯, a pitch which the tenor reaches shortly (in c') by way of the same motive. The soprano and bass stress G♯ further in the next section (d'). Then in the final section (e e F) all that remains is for the pitch A to be asserted powerfully in three octaves, initially by the Hermit, who now assumes leadership for the first time (example 4).

| SINGERS | Oronte | Giselda | Oronte | Giselda | Eremita |
| | | Eremita | Giselda | Eremita | Giselda |
| | | | | | Oronte |
| PHRASES | A  A′ | B  B′ | c  c′ | d  d′ | e e F   e e F + *cadences* |
| KEYS | A | E | g♯ | (c♯) | A |

FIGURE 3  The Terzetto in *I Lombardi:* Form Diagram

Verdi writes *tonante* over the bass part here—but he also writes a *subito pianissimo* for the orchestra. Toscanini manages this to perfection (and Samuel Chotzinoff plays the violin solo in a way to melt the heart). The climactic quality of the final section is underlined by an engagement between the voices that is new to the composition: the mutual rhythmic infection of the first two bass and soprano statements, then the imitation and the inversion.

A second reason why the terzetto does not feel harmonically unmotivated may stem from the characteristic *tinta* of the score as a whole. *I Lombardi* is shot through with prominent V-of-V sounds on the local level, and the terzetto can be heard to echo this on a larger scale. Frequent use of V-of-V or II chords is in fact only the tip of the harmonic iceberg, for Verdi at this time of his life had a strong propensity for what the Germans call *Stufenreichtum:* thus the climax of the "Salve Maria" is underpinned by the unmediated chord sequence I–aug.6–II⁷–V–♭III–(I)–III–VI⁷–II⁹–V⁷–I. Less drastically, local progressions featuring rather prominent V (V⁷, V⁹)-of-V chords occur in the vocal score on pages 2, 63, 88, 141, 193, 220, 232, 233, 259, 262, 270, 275, 277, 280, 284, 297, and 329. The progressions are sometimes pointed up by contrapuntal infelicities. (In the very last chorus, on p. 332, is the only example I spotted of the inversion that becomes so characteristic of Verdi later in life, $V_3^4/V$ or more precisely $V_{2-3}^4/V$—a chord which in *Jérusalem* is brutally destroyed, along with much else.) This dominant-inclined harmonic coloration, which one has no trouble associating with the Crusaders' ecstatic strivings toward Jerusalem, and its *ottocento* counterpart, is not characteristic of *Nabucco* or of *Ernani:* though interestingly enough, the progression I–V⁹/V–V comes up in the first strain of "Va, pensiero."

All this looks very deliberate, very calculated. It suggests that some accommodation is needed between our traditional picture of young Verdi the composer and the new picture that has been emerging for some time of the man. Thanks to the work of Frank Walker in the 1960s and more recently of Mary Jane Matz and Gerald Mendelsohn, among others, we are coming to see more and more signs of subtlety

EXAMPLE 4

and calculation in Verdi's personal relations, in his choice and treatment of dramatic themes, and in his political activism. His famous guarded manner concealed (from himself as well as from others) a personality full of complexities and conflicts. I am sure there is an important post-Budden study waiting to be done which will trace analogously cryptic qualities in Verdi's musical technique.

We know we have been too ready to take Verdi at his own preferred estimation as a warbler of native woodnotes wild, fancy's child, a sort of *italienische Volksgeist*. We have heard too much about the coarse sensibilities of nineteenth-century provincial bandmasters. George Ives should teach us caution. What if the violence which bore young Verdi on to his Jerusalem was not entirely the outcome of musical illiteracy, blind outbursts of patriotic fervor, and the like? Aspects of it may have been deliberately cultivated and assumed, while other sides of his musical personality were turned firmly aside. After Verdi's iron will and his chronic depression, nothing in his personal makeup seems more striking than his explosive emotional involvement with the public he worked for. He loathed the opera audience and it terrified him; the hissing of *Un Giorno di regno* became a trauma second only to the death of his first wife and children; a personal catastrophe which eventually, indeed, seems to have blended in Verdi's memory with the professional one. This young man, one feels, would do anything to succeed.

What is astonishing about the "Salve Maria" is not only that Verdi employed such sophisticated and delicate technical devices (leaving aside, to be sure, those harmonies at the climactic passage). What is also astonishing is that he shelved them for so long. People seriously compare this piece to the "Ave Maria" in *Otello*.

V ·   When Carlo Bergonzi was on stage as Oronte, the San Diego performance of *I Lombardi* reached a level of the greatest distinction. The role, "all tenderness and poetry," is the most grateful in the opera and very well suited to Bergonzi, who sang with a classic elegance of style and patrician musicality. He sang the entire terzetto on his knees. His rubati were of the kind recommended by Chopin. Such consistently beautiful tenor singing is seldom heard in Italian opera today, though the public may now cling to other heroes for vocalism pure and simple.

(After "La mia letizia infondere" Bergonzi sang the original, gentler cabaletta, not the *cabaletta nuova* heard on his remarkable comprehensive recording of arias from twenty-five Verdi operas on Philips 6747 193.)

Since 1972 Philips has been engaged in its own comprehensive Verdi project: the recording of all those Verdi operas that are not otherwise available on discs. *I Lombardi* was the first of seven rare works that have been issued to date, the others being *Un Giorno di regno, I due Foscari, Attila, Il Corsaro, I Masnadieri,* and most recently *La Battaglia di Legnano* (1979). Unfortunately, the series is vitiated by the slack conducting of Lamberto Gardelli, and although the singers are drawn from the greatest international stars, they are not always chosen intelligently. Placido Domingo, for example, was patently miscast by the Philips producer as Oronte. I also preferred the San Diego Pagano, Paul Plishka, to Ruggero Raimondi on Philips, who strikes me as too flexible and "psychological" for the role and, ultimately, cold. In any case, Plishka, to judge from the limited number of times I have heard him, is using his impressive basso more and more flexibly and impressively. I even preferred Cristina Deutekom's live performance at San Diego to her recorded one for Philips, though a wide vibrato which was generally under control when she made the recording is now generally out of control and *proprio brutto*. But whether Ms. Deutekom was carried away by the theatrical ambience or buoyed up by Maurizio Arena's brisk conducting, or both, she brought down the house with her cabalettas, which on the recording sound merely drab. The role is defined by these two violent numbers, because unlike Giselda's two quiet numbers they emerge powerfully out of the action.

The one lapse of taste in this performance, if I may so put it, came with Arena's efforts to sanitize young Verdi's orchestral sound. The stage *banda,* when it was not cut, was mellowed to a point where its distinction from the pit orchestra was blurred. Pagano's trombones sounded not like a lump of dull red-hot lead, but like a velvet drapery borrowed from the Prelude to Act III of *Die Meistersinger.*

Tito Capobianco deserves congratulations for the musical ensemble that he assembled for this occasion. The same cannot be said for his efforts on the dramatic side. He did not so much stage the opera as merely transfer it from the rehearsal floor to the main acting area. One can scarcely imagine an opera less suited to oratorio-like staging than *I Lombardi,* yet there is apparently some tradition for it; a Rome production in 1970 was criticized on this score, and the producer of the Philips recording speaks approvingly of the opera's "stylization." Instead of the vivid, furious milling around that so scared the Milanese censors, we were given a series of static tableaux. Verdi's intentions were flouted most egregiously, perhaps, in the great religious procession at the start of Act III, in which the chorus of Crusaders and pilgrims is heard offstage, enters, and goes off again (as in *Tannhäuser).* One had visions of *La Strada* and *The Seventh Seal,* of pardonably anachronistic flagellants and Knights Templar bearing the insignia of St. Michael, Our Lady of Mount Carmel, St. Ignatius of Antioch, San Ambrogio. . . . In San Diego the curtain rose to reveal the chorus already in place, facing half stage-right in a pose they would maintain, with but one concerted change, for their entire number. So rigid was this pose that it seems the men could not see the conductor, for they made a hash of the dotted rhythms in the middle section of their hymn at both performances I attended. Other scenes were burked in a similar way. Pagano died straining his eyes for the pennants of Jerusalem in the darkness of the balcony and the mezzanine.

To the director's sins of omission the scene designer added sins of commission (studied omission in the one case, I should say, and unstudied commission in the other). Things started out badly with a grimy projection unrecognizable as the ancient Church of San Ambrogio in Milan. They got worse in later scenes as back-drops for the unit set were made to resemble wall hangings with tasseled ropes. Were the former suggested by the kilims of Near Eastern interior decoration, and the latter by the rigging of Arvino's tent—the one setting used twice among the eleven scenes of this opera? The light, wispy quality of the decoration was utterly inappropriate to the eleventh-century setting and to the violence of Verdi's music, as was also the inexplicable, increasingly obtrusive neoclassical motive in the designs themselves. Nor were the costumes fortunate. The Crusaders were recognizable as such, but Oronte looked like a hidalgo, Giselda like nothing on earth, and the Hermit exactly like Pagano, since he did not put on his helmet and lower the visor to avoid recognition by his brother (nor to protect himself when twice leading the Christian attack). Disappointing, too, was the wardrobe of the Tyrant of Antioch's harem, at least to those of an historical frame of mind who might have been expecting something inspired by Delacroix or Bouguereau. The inspiration seems rather to have been Colonel Khadafi.

## Notes

1. In making stage designs for *Ernani,* one should elevate the tomb of Charlemagne or do something else to assure that Carlo's entrance into the tomb is as impressive visually as it is musically.

2. Abramo Basevi, *Studio sulle opere di Giuseppe Verdi* (Florence, 1859), 54–55.

3. From the printed editions of *Tristan;* the final sentence does not occur in Wagner's autograph score.

4. David Lawton, "Tonality and Drama in Verdi's Early Operas" (Ph.D. diss., University of California, Berkeley, 1973), ch. 1B.

5. Andrew Porter, liner notes to *I Lombardi alla prima crociata,* Cristina Deutekom, Placido Domingo, Ruggero Raimondi, Ambrosian Singers, Royal Philharmonic Orchestra, dir. Lamberto Gardelli, Philips LP Recording 6703 032 (1972), reissued as CD 422 470.

6. Siegmund Levarie, "Key Relations in Verdi's *Un Ballo in maschera*" and Joseph Kerman, "Viewpoint," *19th-Century Music* 2 (1978): 143–47, and 186–91, and Guy A. Marco and Siegmund Levarie, "On Key Relations in Opera," *19th-Century Music* 3 (1979): 83–89.

7. Julian Budden, *The Operas of Verdi,* vol. 1, *From "Oberto" to "Rigoletto"* (London, 1973), ch. 7.

8. [The distinction between an additive form and one expanded from within appears to have been prompted by a fundamental difference between the texts of the two terzetti. In *Ernani* the three stanzas (shown above) produce a narrative, albeit with a refrain, and Verdi sets them sequentially, as indicated by figure 1. The *Lombardi* terzetto—also consisting of three stanzas, of eight lines each—offers instead a static tableau, projecting the simultaneous thoughts of the three characters (Oronte in stanza I, Giselda in II, and the Hermit in III). Verdi does not set all three stanzas simultaneously, but he sets many segments simultaneously:

|          | A         | A' | B   | B' | c   | c' | d   | d' | e   | e | F   |
|----------|-----------|----|-----|----|-----|----|-----|----|-----|---|-----|
| stanza I | lines 1–4 |    |     |    | 5–6 |    |     |    |     |   | 7–8 |
| II       |           |    | 1–4 |    |     |    | 5–6 |    | 7–8 |   | 8   |
| III      |           |    | 1–4 |    |     |    | 5–6 |    | 7–8 |   | 8 ] |

# 18

# Reading Don Giovanni

Mozart's Don Giovanni—the man, not the opera—is one thing, and the Don Juan idea, myth, or archetype is another kind of thing altogether: though each is unthinkable without the other. Mozart himself and his poet, Lorenzo Da Ponte, would not have spoken of a myth, of course. But they were well aware of the long tradition of Don Juan depictions preceding their own; this anyone would assume, even without knowing that Da Ponte, in writing his text, helped himself liberally to another on the same subject, by the librettist Giovanni Bertati. Bertati, in turn, refers ironically to the myth in its essential stage tradition. (The prologue of his opus is about a theatrical company in financial straits, deciding reluctantly to mount a show that will appeal to the lowest common denominator—a Don Juan play. Bertati's version of this follows.) As sophisticated men of letters, Bertati and Da Ponte knew Don Juans by Molière, Goldoni, and others, which they drew upon in ways that scholars have traced with exemplary thoroughness. Da Ponte also knew that in the sophisticated Vienna of his own time, an improvised Don Juan play was mounted every year in the Octave of All Saints: a sort of Josephine Rocky Horror Show.

So much for Mozart's time; *our* own time offers myriad sources with which to expand or boggle one's mind about Mozart's Don Giovanni. There are Don Juans by Byron, Shaw, and John Berger, disquisitions on Don Juan by Kierkegaard, Reich, and Camus, as well as quite voluminous writings by musicologists and critics that are less brilliant, no doubt, but certainly not without insight. The

From *Don Giovanni: Myths of Seduction and Betrayal,* ed. Jonathan Miller (New York: Schocken Books, 1990), 108–25.

question is, perhaps, how much of this we need for whatever our purposes or interests may be. And if our primary interest is in Mozart's Don Giovanni, how much do we need to read into him? Why should we "read" Don Giovanni in any other way than by attending closely and deeply to the opera's text? Giovanni is marvelously molded by Mozart's music, even though he is also circumscribed by it (he is even circumscribed by Da Ponte's libretto). He would not seem to stand in need of support or sustenance from Don Juan.

In fact, Don Juan needs Don Giovanni more. As Bernard Williams points out in a devastatingly sensible recent article, modern thought about Don Juan has been dominated by Mozart's embodiment of the myth:

> This is not merely because the opera is by far the greatest work given to this theme. It is also because the opera is in various ways problematical, and that it raises in a challenging way the question of what the figure of Giovanni means. Hence, not only is the opera the historical starting-point of many modern thoughts on this subject, but some of those thoughts lead directly back to the problem of understanding the opera itself.[1]

Fair enough. But let us be clear about the concreteness and vitality of *Don Giovanni* at the present, in numerous productions by directors who refuse to be circumscribed. Don Juan, on the other hand, is now little more than an abstract idea left over from the past, awaiting an occasional new embodiment. Berger called his Don Juan novel *G,* not *J.*

This was perhaps already the situation in the time of Søren Kierkegaard, who, Williams reminds us, first brought together three central facts about *Don Giovanni:* "that the opera is of great and unsettling power, that a seducer is at the centre of it, and that the seducer is virtually characterless."[2] These facts provided Kierkegaard with a springboard for philosophizing about art and the erotic and the idea of Don Juan. Thinking about these same central facts in the light of Mozart's music can also help us read Don Giovanni.

II ·  There are two ways of viewing the picture that Mozart and Da Ponte have drawn of Don Giovanni as a seducer. One way takes the authors as ironists. This view is memorialized in a throwaway from Edward Dent's marvelous old book on Mozart's operas—a book which is probably still too influential on English Mozartians. "Busoni used to say that Don Giovanni was the man who gave every woman the supreme experience of happiness," wrote Dent, who was also a biographer and a great admirer of Busoni. Yet "if his adventures within the limited period of the opera are a fair sample, he has no success at all and is placed in a completely ridiculus situation every time."[3] The point that Giovanni's actions as set forth in the drama count and matter more than reportage by the envious, such as that in Leporello's Catalogue Aria, must be granted—an obvious point, perhaps, but one that it is just as well to have made.

The other way takes Mozart and Da Ponte as realists. Given the conditions of theatrical censorship at the time, it can be maintained that they have presented a picture of the seducer that is remarkably penetrating and unvarnished. *Bist du nicht willig, so brauch' ich Gewalt;* Don Giovanni as a seducer runs the gamut from persuasion to force. His first scene, which shapes our impression of him unforgettably, is an interrupted rape. His last seduction—his serenade to Elvira's maid—involves only suasion or cajolement. (This scene, however, besides being highly forgettable in dramatic terms, is conceptually bizarre. For in the deepest sense an opera character who does not sing does not exist, and this maid does not sing, nor even appear. No wonder the outcome of this mild seduction, or indeed anything else about it, remains unmentioned during the rest of the opera.)

The seduction of Zerlina—the only one that the opera treats at any length—shows explicitly how, in the seducer/rapist's transactions, violence is implicated with persuasion. On their first encounter, Don Giovanni does even less than cajole, in my apprehension of "Là ci darem la mano"; he is going through the motions knowing that he already has the green light. If we are encouraged to think of Zerlina's *sposo* Masetto as a premature *sansculotte,* we can hardly conceive of her as some kind of Arcadian shepherdess who believes Giovanni when he says he will marry her. She and Giovanni both have one thing in mind—an "innocente amor," as they call it later, innocent of violence or partiality.

So she tells him what he wants to hear, and he sings to her in the same spirit. Zerlina acknowledges Giovanni right away by singing his tune. All he has to do is set down the simplest of melodic building blocks; it is Zerlina who ornaments the famous melody, plays with it (and with Giovanni), extends it, and so on. Despite her show of tremulousness, she is fully in control. When Giovanni whispers "Andiam, andiam," moving gently higher and higher up through the scale degrees, Zerlina answers all by herself, on cue. When she sings "Andiam" on the dominant—that is, when the matter is officially decided—Giovanni doesn't even have to sing along.

Their second encounter is quite different, of course; Don Giovanni does not so much cajole Zerlina as push her. This is near the beginning of the Act I finale. Zerlina is upset because Masetto is watching, but a new plangency in the music indicates also that she now wants nothing to do with the seducer. Her chromatic appoggiaturas no longer sound pert, but painful; her tremulous semiquavers, if not quite frantic, are rushed and squeezed by comparison with "Là ci darem." Compare "non *son* più forte, non *son* più forte, non *son* più forte" in the earlier scene with "Ah, lasciatemi andar *vi*a!," "Se pietade avete in *co*re," and "far, so ben io, so ben

EXAMPLE I

ZERLINA: non son _ più _ for - te, non son _ più _ for - te, non son _ più _ for - te

Ah, la - scia - te-mi an-dar  vi - a . . .                    Se pie - ta - de a-ve-te in  co - re . . .

so    ben  io  quel che  può    far,_ so ben io,_  so ben io,_  so _  quel _ che  può   far

io" in the later one (example 1). As for the third encounter between Giovanni and Zerlina, that is recorded later in the finale by an offstage scream.

The history of this seduction, then, traces a sequence from play to pressure to assault. By extrapolation back to the Anna episode, and then forward to the end of the opera, the seducer's progress is shown to proceed from play to rape and murder, and from there to hellfire.

If with Zerlina what is developed in the opera is her actual seduction, with the other two women what is developed is the psychological damage occasioned by the seducer/rapist's ministrations. By the end of the opera, both Donna Anna and Donna Elvira are broken women. Many things are echoed twice in the dramatic structure of *Don Giovanni,* but only one thing happens, excruciatingly, three times: the humiliation of Elvira by Giovanni in front of his servant. On the last occasion, as Wye Jamison Allanbrook remarks, Giovanni's "dining-salon has become a private limbo in which all three characters are eternally joined in barren but immutable relation."[4] "Alone at the final curtain, she will have no future," writes Lawrence Lipking. "The violence done to her illusions has brought her to a sort of posthumous existence, in which she is conscious of the futility of her hopes even when acting them out."[5]

Donna Anna, in traumatized response to the opera's opening string of events, expresses herself in an accompanied recitative and a duet which are among the opera's most powerful, most radical, and greatest numbers. Still splendid as she sings "Or sai chi l'onore," she becomes a shadowed figure thereafter. The effect of her short entry speech in the Act III sextet, "Lascia almen alla mia pena," is of a single, piercing glimpse of anguish;[6] for better or for worse, it is Ottavio who is given the opportunity to dilate upon his feelings in this part of the opera (in the aria "Il mio tesoro"). Her own opportunity, near the end of the action, has received a sharply divided press. Anna's big aria "Non mi dir" impressed Berlioz for its "intense sadness, full of a heartbreaking sense of loss and sorrowing love," but Berlioz's outrage at Anna's coloratura later in the aria rankled till the end of his life ("one of the most odious and idiotic crimes against passion, taste, and common sense of which the history of art provides an example"). The piece has seemed "singularly cold and unemotional" to Dent, and—which is not the same thing— "chilling" to so sympathetic a recent commentator as Allanbrook.[7] Certainly Anna's final music—the little duet in which she puts off her wedding to Ottavio— is of stupendous vacuity.

We first see Donna Anna as a woman of formidable courage, pride, purpose, and, by the way, physical strength. When we last see and hear her she is a shell of her former self. She is Mozart's most cruel and painful portrait.

III · "An opera of great and unsettling power," says Bernard Williams. Unsettling, and powerfully so: because the work is manifestly problematic and tension-filled, and also because in some ways it can make a modern audience really uncomfortable. Lipking says as much in his discussion of the audience's enforced voyeurism of the *donna abbandonata,* and I have my own furtive list of things that perturb. George Bernard Shaw, who published his first dramas under the ironic title *Plays Pleasant and Unpleasant,* would not have applied the latter adjective to *Man and Superman,* his own contribution to the Don Juan–Don Giovanni crux. But I think of *Don Giovanni* itself as Mozart's unpleasant opera.

One reason is its repeated representation of cruelty: not only psychological cruelty, such as has been discussed to some extent above, but also low-level sadism. Leporello has to whistle with his mouth full as he waits on table, sidestep a rapier in the graveyard, and dodge a thrashing such as Masetto actually suffers. Even Zerlina figuratively bears her backside to Masetto (as well as her breast); and if we have read in Dent that "Batti, batti" refers to a then-recent scandal in which a Venetian doctor stripped a gentlewoman and flagellated her publicly on the Fondamenta della Tana, singing a vulgar song, the aria becomes distinctly unappetizing. Audiences have more or less cheerfully inured themselves to such staples of earthy humor. (They have drawn the line, thank heaven, at the Razor Duet, "Fra queste due mannine," which was added by Mozart to the second, Viennese performance but is seldom performed today—though there are directors who might enjoy Zerlina's symbolic castration of Leporello in his role as Giovanni-surrogate. The other additions to the second performance, Ottavio's "Dalla sua pace" and Elvira's "Quali eccessi, o numi"—"Mi tradì quell'alma ingrata," have entered the opera's canonic text.)

The opera is also unsettling because of its wild contrasts of tone and style. These stem from a much-debated generic crux. Da Ponte called *Don Giovanni* a "dramma giocoso," a recognized theatrical genre of the time which sought to fuse elements of *opera seria* and *opera buffa*. The same genre title was used by Bertati. Yet fusion seems to have been far from Mozart's mind. Donna Anna and Don Ottavio, the *opera seria* characters who promote so much of the action, nevertheless float above it, carrying out a desperate private inner action of their own. Tight-lipped, they sometimes allow Donna Elvira to come along—she is the so-called *mezza carattere* role, mediating between *seria* and *buffa*—but they cannot and never do acknowledge the existence of the *opera buffa* peasant pair. Although they occasionally address Masetto and Zerlina in *secco* recitative, their concerted music never engages. Ottavio's arias are notorious for their withdrawal from the opera's essential concerns, and this quality also explains why his confrontation with Giovanni in the Act I finale is so blank. It is not so much that Giovanni brazens the situation out, escapes, whatever. It is rather that he and Ottavio cannot engage within a single field of action.

There is one place of genuine engagement, to be sure, in the opera's indelible opening scene. Here Anna not only addresses Giovanni but engages with him physically, struggles with him. It is a problematic scene, as I shall suggest later, and the problem is compounded by the shock of generic violation. The genres do not fuse, they fight.

What is more, another genre is fighting to get out here—continuous opera: that is, opera in which the singing is continuously backed by fully developed orchestral music, rather than switching in and out of stretches of low-level talk presented in *secco* recitative. This was, as we know, the operatic wave of the future. Mozart must have known, too—from works he had encountered by Gluck—though the closest he himself had come to writing continuous opera was in the long sectional finales to Acts II and IV of *Le Nozze di Figaro*. All Mozartian opera is conducted on two sharply different imaginative levels, one defined by orchestral music and the other by a rudimentary, sub- or semi-musical framework of speech or *secco* recitative, accompanied only by harpsichord and a single cello. The great *Figaro* finales come at the end of scenes which begin in this "stop-and-go" mode, but which end as forecasts of continuous opera.

Before *Don Giovanni,* however, Mozart had never arranged for a long sectional finale actually to coincide with a whole scene, curtain to curtain. Now, when the curtain goes up on the opera's last scene, we hear continuous orchestral music and no *secco* recitative whatsoever until it goes down. The Act II finale is a virtuoso exercise in musical linkage involving nine distinct sections or "movements." The fact of continuity itself gives the scene an immediacy that was not available to any of the traditional eighteenth-century operatic genres—even apart from the particulars of Mozart's composition.

Something like this continuity, and this immediacy, exists across the opera's entire opening scene, too. The Overture leads directly (and consequentially) into the opera's first number, the sectional Act I Introduction; the end of this Introduction is not syntactically closed (has no final cadence) prior to a hasty *secco* recitative for Giovanni and Leporello; when Donna Anna returns, the same musical figure which ended the non-cadencing Introduction returns to initiate her accompanied recitative; and her duet with Ottavio emerges from that accompanied recitative seamlessly, again without punctuation. Technically speaking, the most radical feature here is the reactivation, in Anna's recitative, of the orchestra that had been suspended at the end of the Introduction. By this means Mozart contrived to include *secco* recitative within a compelling larger continuity, encompassing the entire scene.

This impressive and prescient essay in continuous opera is capped only by the opera's final scene, the giant continuous Act II finale mentioned above. It seems clear that these two special measures were taken in concert, because—in an unprecedented gesture—Mozart binds the two sections together musically. Segments of music from the Andante of the Overture and from the duel are recapitulated with a devastating effect for the Commendatore's arrival to supper and his browbeating of Don Giovanni, respectively. The Act I opening complex goes from D minor to D major to D minor; the Act II finale goes from D major to D minor to D major.

All this was done, surely, with the express intention of holding together a notoriously scrappy piece of dramatic construction. There is really no reason to doubt that Mozart, who was a dramatic genius as well as a musical genius, understood the problem that he was faced with by Da Ponte's cobbled-up libretto. He devised his own radical way of dealing with it, a strictly musical way. In opera, the dramatist is the composer.

It is late in this essay to say what everyone knows, that *Don Giovanni* is full of brilliant and beautiful music. It is also known that *Don Giovanni,* more than Mozart's other great operas, also contains patches that are less than brilliant or beautiful. One can tire of Leporello's Catalogue Aria; "Madamina" lacks the musical distinction of (say) the corresponding *basso buffo* aria in *Le Nozze di Figaro,* Bartolo's "La vendetta." Elvira's "Ah, fuggi il traditor," a puzzling and ineffective piece, in the last century was often cut. Anna's "Non mi dir" is problematic even for some of its admirers. There are dead spots in both the Act I and Act II finales. Though its ontological status is unclear—does it exact our attention as part of an "authentic" Viennese version of the opera?—there is also the exceptionally weak Razor Duet.

Of course the dead spot in the Act II finale comes only at the end, and "goes to show how drab life is without the Don."[8] Of course Mozart understood—and wanted us to know—that Leporello the cataloguer is a hollow man compared to Bartolo, who in the Act III sextet of *Figaro* positively (if momentarily) glows with humanity. "Non mi dir," I have said, is sung by a broken woman . . . and so on.

It is very uncomfortable for a critic, even nerve-wracking, to have to keep arguing in this way. One wants to say instead: obviously the dramatic construction is scrappy at many points; the piece is constantly threatening to fly apart, since Mozart did not always attempt to patch it on the spot. Instead he determined to bind the whole thing together on the highest level. The scrappiness of the plot and the binding created by the music—by the two continuous outer scenes with their musical echoes—go together.

This was an extraordinary conception, but also a scary one. Part of what makes *Don Giovanni* so unsettling is the sense—the teasing sense—that Mozart is going out of control. Actually this is not so: whether in spite of or because of its problematic nature, the piece always plays. But the tension in it between the dramatically centrifugal and the centripetal is practically palpable. *Don Giovanni* is a notoriously un-Classical piece.

IV ·   Three central facts about *Don Giovanni* are "that the opera is of great and unsettling power, that a seducer is at the centre of it, and that the seducer is virtually characterless." Although Giovanni "is in a deep way the life of the opera," as Bernard Williams puts it,

> such character as he has is not really as grand as that implies: he expresses more than he is. He seems to have no depth adequate to the work in which he plays the central role. He has, in a sense, a character—to a considerable extent a bad one. But we are not given any deep insight into what he really is, or what drives him on. We could not have been: it is not that there is something hidden in his soul. It is notable that he has no self-reflective aria— he never sings about himself, as Mozart's other central characters do.[9]

How are we to read this No-Man, as Wye Allanbrook persists in calling him? For "read" read "hear"—the caution is not redundant in this context.

We have to hear him in his famous Act I aria, the invincibly effective "Fin ch'han dal vino." If not self-reflective, this aria is certainly self-expressive, and deserves, perhaps, fairly close attention. The only possible trouble with the piece is its hectic velocity, its tendency to stun. It clocks in at just about eighty seconds; Don Giovanni sings at full tilt continuously, save for one two-bar rest which allows him a big gulp of air (or champagne) but which he manages to cede to the orchestra almost derisively, eight bars after it was their due.

Addressed to Leporello, the poem says, in a stanza-by-stanza précis: (1) Go prepare a party, (2) and bring some girls; (3) have them dance all kinds of uninhibited dances, (4) and I'll make love to many (5) and seduce/rape a dozen. (Da Ponte, using a four-line stanza, extended this deftly in stanza III to match the little

EXAMPLE 2

dance inventory which recalls Leporello's equally cosmopolitan catalogue: "Senza alcun ordine / la danza sia, / chi'l menuetto, / chi la folia, / chi l'allemana / farai ballar.") Whereas stanzas I and IV are sung only once, making little impact, especially at the presto tempo, stanza V is repeated again and again, so that the message comes across four times in all, plus some fractions. What Giovanni actually says is "you'll have to add *una decina* to my list."

Mozart also repeats stanzas II and III—not, I think, because we have any further need to hear these particular words, but because he wants us to hear them with new, and newly ferocious, music. A single motif, very heavily accented, is barked out ten times near the top of the baritone's tessitura to accommodate the ten lines in these stanzas (and Giovanni's *decina,* no doubt: example 2).

| | | |
|---|---|---|
| II | *Se* trovi in *piaz*za | Girls in the piazza, |
| | *qual*che ra*gaz*za, | Girls in the market, |
| | *teco* ancor *quel*la | Any you find there |
| | *cer*ca *me*nar . . . | Bring to the ball . . . |
| III | *Sen*za alcun *or*dine | Set them to dancing, |
| | *la* danza *sia,* | All out of order: |
| | *chi'l* menu*et*to, | This one the high dance, |
| | *chi* la fo*li*a, | That one the low dance, |
| | *chi* l'alle*ma*na | This one the mad dance, |
| | *fa*rai bal*lar.* | We'll have them all. |

This is a musical procedure of unusual violence. The motif that recurs so blankly again and again is merely incantatory in melodic contour and obsessive in rhythm. Indeed the rhythm—starting with a dactyl, – ⌣⌣ – – —which dominates this little section dominates the aria as a whole; we are assailed by it in every one of the poem's twenty-two lines, starting with "*Fin* ch'han dal *vino.*" (By no means all of the lines take kindly to dactylic declamation.) In this section, the accents come twice as fast and hard as before.

"A crude expression of the phallic," or "a feverish explosion of sheer sexual drive," according to some recent writers:[10] which is no doubt what earlier ones meant by the flesh incarnate or the life-force. However, Mozart had used fast driving rhythms of this kind before, in non-phallic contexts. He provided Figaro with such rhythms at the end of the minuet-like aria "Se vuol ballare," when Figaro suddenly speeds up to spit out the words "L'arte scher*mendo*, l'arte ado*prando*, / di qua pun*gendo*, di la scher*zando*" (Subtly outwitting, innocent seeming, Cleverly hitting, planning and scheming). He provided Osmin with something similar, in anapests, at the end of his big aria in *Die Entführung aus dem Serail,* when the goaded gaoler stutters his obscene, high-speed fantasy: "Erst ge*köpft,* dann ge*hangen,* / dann ge*spiesst* auf heisse *Stang*en, / dann ver*brannt,* dann ge*bunden,* / und ge*taucht,* geletzt ge*schund*en' (First beheaded, then hanged, Then roasted on a hot griddle, etc.).

The situation in both of these earlier arias is similar. They begin with the characters expressing anger, but anger that has been brought under temporary control. Then they abruptly break down into explosions of uncontained fury (Figaro, unlike Osmin, ultimately regaining his self-control). "Just as a man in such a towering rage oversteps all the bounds of order, so must the music too forget itself," writes Mozart in a much-quoted letter about *Entführung.*[11] Rage is presented in stages. In "Fin ch'han dal vino" the same *topos*—Monteverdi's *genere concitato*—is employed in isolation, without any warning; the special force, the menace of this aria comes from its projection of anger with precedent. This unmotivated anger (unmotivated by the dramatic action) is anger associated with, about, at, or in sex.

Jane Miller writes about an extended brutish trope in Richardson's *Clarissa*— where the brothel keeper Mrs. Sinclair is described as a "composite monster, dragon, hog, ferret and horse, distorted and curdled as it straddles and sputters." Miller's words about this seem apropos here: "The rape which is so bizarrely absent from the text itself has been displaced by the hatred it was intended both to express and discipline."[12]

How much angrier, by the way, "Fin ch'han dal vino" seems than Masetto's aria "Ho capito," where the singer is as funny as he is furious—distracted, confused, and tied up in knots by his aspirations to sarcasm.

v · To say that Don Giovanni's main aria is enraged may go some way toward explaining the aria's impact, but it does not do much to fill the void within the soul of No-Man. A negative quality of the piece also stands out, its lack of invention.

At one point Giovanni boasts about his "prolific talent" (*fertile talento*), but whatever talents he may possess, a talent for lyric fertility is not among them.

The "Fin ch'han dal vino" jingle is just that, a jingle which never evolves. The melody never even forms into an antecedent–consequent pair, and when it comes back for the new words of stanza V, it comes back unchanged. The music for the other stanzas does little more than thump, for the most part, and the cadencing, while unusually fierce, is as usual merely emphatic. Even one compensating rhythmic anomaly—the forceful cadential syncopation—is initiated by the orchestra, rather than by Giovanni's own invention.

It makes a critic uncomfortable, once again, to call a Mozart aria uninventive, let alone an entire Mozart role. Fortunately Mozart has left very many models of inventiveness in opera arias. One can try to compare "Fin ch'han dal vino" in this respect with Cherubino's "Non so più," Susanna's "Venite inginocchiatevi," the Countess's "Dove sono," Elvira's "Mi tradì quell'alma ingrata," Tamino's "Dies Bildnis ist bezaubernd schön," or the Queen of Night's "Die Hölle Rache." Some of these arias belong to Williams's "self-reflective" category, others not. But in all of them, people keep thinking up new musical ideas and developing them prodigiously as a reflection of their own fertile emotional energies.

(*Così fan tutte* yields fewer such arias. Don Giovanni's artful second-act aria "Metà di voi quà vadano" deserves a place in any such list; but while it may be diverting to speculate about a figure who can be creative only when disguised, presumably no one will be tempted to build a reading of Don Giovanni upon "Metà di voi." The key to his character cannot be found in a brilliant throwaway hidden in one of the plot's backwaters; it must be found in "Fin ch'han dal vino," "Là ci darem la mano," the Act I Introduction, the scene with the Commendatore—in the major scenes—or not at all.)

The Act I Introduction is another scene that does not show Giovanni in an inventive light. As remarked above, the scene does indeed present him with an unforgettable entrance, thanks to the stage action. But the music mutes this in a curious way which is not often remarked on, and which is worth pausing over for a moment. It seems Mozart and Da Ponte wanted explicitly to soft-pedal Giovanni's role in this episode.

This emerges with special clarity from the modeling situation. That Da Ponte copied much of the *Don Giovanni* libretto from a previous work, by Bertati, has already been mentioned. Set to music by Giuseppe Gazzaniga, an endlessly prolific but otherwise forgotten composer of the time, this opera held the stage for thirty years, playing in Paris and London as well as all over Italy.[13] Many of the scenes in *Don Giovanni* that we probably think of as among the most characteristic were modeled on Bertati: for example, the whole of the Act I Introduction, showing a grumbling man-servant who then comments on his master's struggle with a lady, a duel between the interloper and the lady's father, and the latter's death. Not the whole Introduction, but the episode with Anna is also a section of the opera where Mozart's music refers to Gazzaniga's (virtually the only such section). There are actual similarities of musical gesture.

Needless to say, in terms of musical detail the comparison is vastly to the advantage of Mozart; but this cannot be said so quickly of the comparison in terms of dramatic strategy. Mozart decided to play the scene for laughs, in effect—decided to play up Leporello's amused commentary on the action. Repeating himself much more than his opposite number in Gazzaniga, and in a much more unbuttoned fashion, the *buffo* bass ends up undercutting the struggle between the principals by nearly silencing them.

If Mozart bolstered Leporello's role, Da Ponte bolstered Anna's. Thus another difference from the Bertati–Gazzaniga opera is that Anna, not Giovanni, sings first. So the music Giovanni sings during their struggle is not of his own devising but echoed from Anna, as has often been observed. What is more, he also echoes her music later, when she has left, in the wonderful slow terzetto while he and Leporello watch the Commendatore die after the duel[14] (example 3; this terzetto, by the way, certainly does *not* have a precedent in Gazzaniga). The dramatic point of Giovanni's low musical profile is clear enough in the first instance, when he is trying to hide his identity. What about the second?

The only reason I can think of for Mozart to have used old music here, in a situation where it would have been much more natural to use new, was to show Giovanni at a loss for words, for music. While Giovanni does not exactly regret the killing of the Commendatore, he is taken aback by its suddenness and un-thinkingness; he might have wished for something else, if he ever took the trouble to think. Julian Rushton remarks with fine insight that Giovanni for once seems vulnerable. He is also revealed as lacking in musical, hence emotional, resource.

He is rather more resourceful in the wrenching scene with Donna Elvira in the second-act finale. Elvira bursts in on his dinner on the verge of breakdown, it seems—she can scarcely stay coherent long enough to beg him to save himself. Giovanni is at his most odious on this occasion, abandoning even the mask of civility. Toward the end of the scene, as he turns away from her with a blunt "Lascia ch'io mangi" (Leave me to my dinner), a piercing, mocking little tune emerges in the orchestra.

Giovanni has managed to generate music of his own; but the striking thing is that only halfway through this tune does he think of words for it, a true afterthought—"e se ti piace, mangia con me" (example 4). Inviting the humiliated Elvira to join him, at dinner or anything else, has to count as the acme of spontaneous cruelty. The tune finally accommodates itself to Giovanni's tribute to women and good wine as the sustaining glory of mankind—"Sostegno e gloria d'umanità." Perhaps in concept it is a musical quotation of an actual toast, like the quotes from popular opera hits that we have just been hearing from the little *Tafelmusik* band.

EXAMPLE 3

ANNA: Come Fu - rie _ dis - pe — ra - ta    GIOVANNI: Ah    già ca - de il scia - gu — ra-to

EXAMPLE 4

Allegro assai

GIOVANNI: e se ti pia - ce, mangia con  me.

The opera's seduction scenes, to be sure, resonate with Don Giovanni's music, music of his own invention. It is music that has been greatly and rightly admired. "Là ci darem" gave Chopin the subject for variations with which to launch his career, and gave Peter Shaffer the centerpiece for one of the better scenes in *Amadeus* (the movie). Giovanni's serenade struck Charles Gounod—the composer of *Faust*—as "a pearl of inspiration, alike in the elegance of its melody, harmony, and rhythm . . . a masterpiece of grace and gallantry" expressing "an intensity of longing and marvellous captivation."[15] One cannot hear this music and doubt for a moment the deep truth (if not the statistical particulars) of Leporello's account of his master's success as a seducer.

Yet the actual lyric *development* of his music counts as very modest. I have already made the point that in "Là ci darem" Giovanni issues the simplest of melodic units, and that it is Zerlina who invents the melody's adornments, extensions, diversions, and so on. In fact, Zerlina makes the piece her own. (She gets most of the opera's hit tunes.) As for Giovanni's later lovemaking, what is quite surprising about it is its repeated use of the same music. Giovanni sings approximately the same melody for his serenade to Elvira's maid, with strumming mandolin, as for his impromptu wooing of Elvira on behalf of the disguised Leporello. For all the difference of treatment, the similarity of melodic gesture is unmistakable.

There is a lesson here, no doubt, about the actual nature of improvisation. However this may be, we hear Giovanni fall back on a single formula, whether he finds himself in a formal situation or a spontaneous one. Why change, when success comes so automatically? Why invent?

EXAMPLE 5

GIOVANNI: Ho fer - mo in pet-to il co - re, Non ho ti-mor; ver - rò!

When the Commendatore issues his fateful invitation to dinner, Don Giovanni answers with four bars of music (example 5).

Ho fermo il core in petto       Stout-hearted,
Non ho timor. Verrò.           Unafraid: I'll come.

To say that this music will probably not strike us as "inventive" is not to deny its extraordinary impact (magnified by the awed response to it from the orchestra). These four bars could never have been predicted. Their unexpected features—stiff, pompous dotted rhythms and Baroque-sounding counterpoint, provided by the strings alone—are also features of Donna Elvira's Act I aria "Ah, fuggi il traditor," as Rushton has remarked:[16] one of those passing remarks that triggers (for me, at least) long unarticulated feelings about a work long known. They have nothing to do with Elvira, but everything to do with the antique quality of that strange aria of hers. Giovanni's language regresses to a hieratic mode of musical expression, as though to an archaic, frozen code of honor. Don Giovanni's finest moment is also, in a unique musical way, one of his most impersonal.

Perhaps it is laboring the obvious to say that what has been seen as a distinguishing feature of Don Giovanni since the time of Kierkegaard, namely his characterlessness, is compounded by uninventiveness. Bernard Williams, whose essay works to delimit idealistic accretions to Mozart's No-Man, nonetheless acknowledges Giovanni's sense of freedom and his recklessness, his

> single-minded determination to live life at the fullest energy, at the extreme edge of desire. . . . Those who survive Giovanni—not only the other characters, but, on each occasion that we have seen the opera, ourselves—are both more and less than he is: more, since, the conditions *on* humanity, which we accept, are also the conditions *of* humanity; and less, since one thing vitality needs is to keep the dream of being as free from conditions as his.

Yet Giovanni was "without love, compassion, and fairness, to mention only a few of the things he lacked."[17] Creativity was another of his chronic lacks. That is a big swatch of vitality to barter away for a dream.

## Notes

1. Bernard Williams, "Don Juan as an Idea," in *Mozart: Don Giovanni,* ed. Julian Rushton (Cambridge Opera Handbook; Cambridge, 1981), 81.
2. Ibid., 82.
3. Edward J. Dent, *Mozart's Operas,* 2d ed. (London, 1947), 185.
4. Wye Jamison Allanbrook, *Rhythmic Gesture in Mozart: "Le Nozze di Figaro" and "Don Giovanni"* (Chicago, 1983), 256.
5. Lawrence Lipking, "Donna Abbandonata," in *Don Giovanni: Myths of Seduction and Betrayal,* ed. Jonathan Miller (New York, 1990), 45.
6. See Daniel Heartz, "Goldoni, Don Giovanni, and the Dramma Giocoso," *Musical Times* 120 (1979): 993–98.
7. Hector Berlioz, *Memoirs,* tr. and ed. David Cairns (New York, 1969), 93; Dent, *Mozart's Operas,* 171; Allanbrook, *Rhythmic Gesture in Mozart,* 229.
8. [Joseph Kerman, *Opera as Drama,* rev. ed. (Berkeley and Los Angeles, 1988), 99. David Littlejohn, a persistent tracker of my work, has put down "Reading Don Giovanni" as a distended gloss on the picture of the Don first sketched in 1956, in *Opera as Drama.*]
9. Williams, "Don Juan as an Idea," 86.
10. John Stone in *Mozart-Jahrbuch 1984/85* (Cassel, 1986), 134; Charles Osborne in *The Complete Operas of Mozart* (London, 1978), 268.
11. *The Letters of Mozart and His Family,* ed. Emily Anderson (London, 1938), 3:1144.
12. Jane Miller, "The Seductions of Women," in *Don Giovanni: Myths of Seduction and Betrayal,* 53, 54.
13. Giuseppe Gazzaniga, *Don Giovanni o sia Il convitato di pietra,* ed. Stefan Kunze (Cassel, 1974).
14. [He is even unable to break away from her melodic structure: compare his "Ah già cade il sciagurato / affanosa e aggonizante" with her "Come furia disperata / te saprò perseguitar."]
15. Charles Gounod, *Mozart's Don Giovanni: A Commentary,* tr. Windeyer Clark and J. T. Hutchinson (London, 1895), 87. ["Smarmy" is how the serenade strikes a more recent commentator, however: Marian Smith, "'Poésie lyrique' and 'Chorégraphie' at the Opéra in the July Monarchy," *Cambridge Opera Journal* 4 (1992): 12.]
16. Julian Rushton, "The Music," in *Mozart: Don Giovanni,* 107.
17. Williams, "Don Juan as an Idea," 90–91.

# 19

# Mozart's Piano Concertos and Their Audience

In a well-known letter to his father Mozart explains why he should leave him, Leopold, and Salzburg and set himself up as an independent musician in Vienna. Leopold may think that life as a freelancer will be precarious; indeed Count Arco, the Archbishop's majordomo—he of the famous kick—has told Mozart that very thing. "At first you are overwhelmed with praises and make a great deal of money into the bargain—but how long does that last? After a few months the Viennese want something new." Mozart explains:

> It is perfectly true that the Viennese are apt to change their affections, *but only in the theater;* and my special line is too popular not to enable me to support myself. Vienna is certainly the land of the clavier! And, even granted that they do get tired of me, they will not do so for a few years, certainly not before then. In the meantime I shall have gained both honor and money.[1]

Months have grown into years. Leopold is not persuaded.

But in fact Mozart was right. After 1781 and *Die Entführung aus dem Serail* he had to wait eleven years for a comparable, indeed much greater triumph in the theater with *Die Zauberflöte;* none of the Da Ponte operas were successes in Vienna. But Mozart's popularity as a pianist continued unabated for five years. In the early part

Written originally for the symposium "Mozart and the Riddle of Creativity," sponsored by the Woodrow Wilson International Center for Scholars, Washington, D.C., 2–5 December 1991; reprinted with permission.

of his decade in Vienna, Mozart's career was essentially as a pianist—as a piano teacher, as a performer at aristocratic soirées, and as a concert pianist. He was able to set up *Akademien* centered on his performance of piano concertos, and he composed three or four new concertos for each of the four seasons from 1782–83 to 1785–86, starting with K. 414, 413, and 415 (in A, F, and C), and ending with K. 482, 488, and 491 (in E flat, A, and C minor).

At the end of the 1785–86 season, Mozart was finally able to produce an opera, *Le Nozze di Figaro;* the premiere was in May 1786. Thereafter opera replaces the piano concerto as Mozart's important public genre. After 1786 there were many fewer academies—and fewer new concertos. Perhaps the reason for this was that Mozart was just too busy in the theater. Or perhaps fickle Vienna had finally tired of him, as had been prophesied. Or both; these things can be overdetermined. By 1788, in any case, concert life fell off sharply because of the Turkish War. Heavy hints have been dropped by scholars, novelists, and playwrights about some mysterious personality change which may have had the effect of alienating his audience. Just lightly, I shall touch on this at the end of the present paper.

Before Mozart's time, concertos seldom figured in Viennese public concerts; regular concerts featuring concertos seem to have started with him.[2] This seems worth pondering. As we do so, I think it is more interesting to ask not why it happened, but rather, when it *did* happen, what it meant. At issue here is a situation that lasted for only a short, intense time and that has left, as its trace, some beautiful (and intense) music that we still listen to today. What is the meaning of the original *Zustand,* as Carl Dahlhaus would have called it, a situation, or a structure, as others would call it: the nexus of social occasions represented by Mozart's academies, involving just that audience and just this composer-performer, and these musical texts, all at a certain particular time and place?

We cannot get very far with this question by reading those texts in technical, strictly musical, "analytical" terms, certainly. We may get a little further by reading them metaphorically. The solo part and the orchestral part in a concerto and their relationship can be read as a composite metaphor for Mozart and his audience and *their* relationship. This hermeneutic avenue toward the Mozartian concerto is not, I think, unique or original; it is basically similar, for example, to that traveled a few years ago by Susan McClary, in a striking article which I shall return to later. To develop this type of reading, I shall need to go back to first principles, at least briefly, and I shall also need to touch on some technical matters after all.

II ·

What is at the basis of the aesthetic of the concerto? While we can of course peer back to Bottrigari, Viadana, and Praetorius for our starting point, as far as the modern concerto is concerned it may be more useful to glance ahead—to Tchaikovsky, let us say, who wrote to Madame von Meck about "a struggle [between] the powerful multicolored orchestra and its weak but high-spirited adversary."[3] This formulation is typical in its dialectic character. Tchaikovsky personifies the solo instrument and the orchestra as human agents. The orchestra is strong and multicolored, he said, the solo is light but agile, and he saw them locked in an adversarial relationship.

More fundamentally yet, the concerto agents or actors differ in their participation in certain basic musical activities, which I shall call *discourse* and *display*. I deliberately choose the word "discourse" over "logic," with its philosophical and mathematical implications, to refer in the broadest of terms to the ongoing play of musical material and rhetoric, musical process, music's illusion of movement and import. Theme, tonality, texture, dynamics, and contrast are some of the carriers of traditional musical discourse, which takes place quintessentially in the symphony, the orchestral genre par excellence. The musicological discourse that deals with musical discourse is analysis.

Display, on the other hand, is a primal quality of music making that can exist at low levels of discourse. Display is playing loud and fast and singing sexy; display can be extemporaneous, unpredictable, out of control, refractory to analysis (refractory, indeed, even to musicology). In certain genres of Western music, solo display is repressed, but the concerto is not among them. A concerto without bravura would not be worth the name—would probably be called a sinfonia concertante, in fact. Virtuosity as well as discourse is required of the concerto soloist, who is both discussion leader and acrobat, rhetorician and jock.

Listen to a Vivaldi concerto, and much of the time you will hear all this in a raw state. The orchestra discourses, the solo violin displays itself. There is not much "struggle"—a feature of the nineteenth-century concerto—in Vivaldi, and not much struggle in a Mozart concerto either. But Mozart added another element to the concerto that is of major importance. The two concerto actors, so dissimilar in some respects, nonetheless enter into dialogue. The relationship established between them is not adversarial but something much richer and more interesting, and the art of the concerto now devolves upon that relationship.

To say that Mozart "added" the element of dialogue to the concerto is to speak loosely; no doubt a better word would be "developed." No doubt there was dialogue of a sort in concertos before Mozart, just as there was dialogue of a sort in *opera buffa;* but Mozart is light years ahead of his predecessors and contemporaries in this regard. His dialogue technique in opera and concerto has been much studied and much admired. Without at all wishing to renounce the broader resonance of dialogue as a hermeneutic method, I also need to ground Mozart's practice in a mundane technical fact. Since dialogue transpires only when the principals speak the same language, in concerto dialogue the solo and the orchestra deal with one and the same musical material. In Mozart's concertos the solo and orchestra discuss with one another by, mainly, repeating each other's music. The art comes in the wonderful range of variation and nuance in the dialogic repetitions, repetitions that are experienced as responses.

Dialogue can take place on various levels. On the level of the immediate exchange of musical themes and other passages, we can speak of instantaneous response, rejoinder, repartee, and more generally of discursive *engagement*. In other contexts, however—for example, in the Socratic context—it is possible to think of beginning a dialogue one day and coming back to finish it the next. Dialogue over an extended time period is, in musical terms, dialogue on the level of musical form. Involved here are concepts like delayed response, recapitulation, and what may be called discursive *re-engagement*.

III · On the level of musical form, the global level, the subtlest and most powerful system of dialogic response was that codified for the first movements of classical concertos. This form was first explained by Donald Francis Tovey in an essay dating from 1903, which became famous after he reprinted it in the third volume of *Essays in Musical Analysis* (1936). Tovey called first-movement form "ritornello form," because he wanted to stress polemically that the opening orchestral passage was unlike a sonata-form exposition in its harmonic and rhythmic action. For Tovey, the concerto first movement was modeled on the aria. Since Tovey's time the form has been much studied—by Martha Feldman, C. M. Girdlestone, H. C. Robbins Landon, Charles Rosen (who calls it "concerto-sonata form"), David Rosen, Edwin J. Simon, Jane Stevens, and Hans Tischler. In music appreciation books the form is often called, *pace* Tovey, "double exposition form."[4]

Whatever we call it, the opening orchestral passage in a Classical concerto has as its function the presentation or exhibition of the movement's basic musical material. Put in another way, the opening ritornello lays down the basic conditions for the musical discourse. Then the solo makes its formal entrance, to initiate the first of two large solo sections, which I should like to call the "solo spans." Here the orchestral material is re-presented in a genial transformation. The solo, in close cooperation with the orchestra, re-engages with that material and edits it, subtracting some bits, adding new bits of its own, modulating, altering the pace, and so on. Both solo spans are terminated by shorter orchestral ritornellos, of which the second also sets up the cadenza, the soloist's supreme moment of athletic glory. The movement ends with another orchestral passage, ritornello 4.

The orchestral ritornellos serve among other things as a frame or container for the solo activity. The sequence goes: ritornello 1, first solo span, ritornello 2, second solo span, ritornello 3, solo cadenza, ritornello 4. The orchestra demarcates the various solo episodes, monitoring all the virtuoso flights and improvisational excursus, as well as offering the discursive material upon which the solo dilates. In an important sense, then, the orchestra can be said to control the form: and this was a situation that could not be maintained for long without challenge. I shall come back to this point later.

IV ·    First I want to draw attention to another level of activity in the Classical concerto first movement, apart from the level of engagement and re-engagement with the orchestra—apart from dialogue, apart from discourse itself. Much less is said about this by Tovey or other writers. In addition to joining the orchestra in a discursive drama, the solo conducts a private action of its own. What the solo does, twice, in the two solo spans, is to trace a progression away from dialogue toward virtuosity. It traverses a broad trajectory from discourse to display.

This action is obvious, even garish, and no doubt also regressive. We can probably remember how it goes in our and everybody else's favorite Mozart concerto, the C-major K. 467. First, the basic terms of discourse are laid down by the orchestra, in bar 1 and following: an *opera buffa* march, played *cupo voce* by the strings; an ingratiating answer; and an unexpected second answer from the woodwinds. The solo's dialogic response to this does not come until two-and-a-half minutes later, at the beginning of its first solo span. After a somewhat comical preparation process, the solo spins out an airy trill over the strings' march music, then melts the woodwind tattoos into gracious ornamentation.

The solo span has begun, then, with witty discourse. More dialogue ensues, at closer quarters; when the second subject is played by the woodwinds, the end of the second and fourth bars are echoed at once by the piano (example 1; Mozart often contrives concerto themes to allow for such short-range echoing). The solo span ends, however, with display. It ends with twenty-one bars of broken octaves, scales, arpeggios, and virtuoso fireworks such as occur in all Classical piano concertos. These solipsistic bravura passages end with a notorious concerto trademark, the climactic flashy cadential trill—a sort of high-five or pirouette which invites an admiring response to the solo in its role as athlete, not as dialogist. When the orchestra cuts in sharply at this point, we may hear the crowd roaring its approval; but we also hear the orchestra reasserting its hegemony over the formal process. The hegemony had been challenged by the passage of solo display.

In the second solo span, the trajectory from discourse to display is run through again in basically the same way, with this difference: that when the orchestra intervenes after the trill a second time, its task is less to cheer the soloist's bravura than to urge it on to more of the same, in the cadenza. This the orchestra does with an ostentatious formality that sometimes borders on the sardonic. The cadenza is occasion for increasingly uninhibited display, ending once again with a highly formal, flashy trill.

But after this, it is indicative that the movement's true cadence is accomplished not by the solo but by the orchestra, playing ritornello 4. After giving the solo its

EXAMPLE I

run in the cadenza, the orchestra briskly reasserts its authority. The orchestra opens the shop in the morning and closes it up at night.

As remarked above, critics and theorists of an earlier generation have not written in this way about the concerto. Display in the solo spans, improvisation in the cadenza (as we shall see later in this essay, cadenzas can play as important a part in a concerto as passages of cadential display)—in the age of formalism, these were seen as equally meretricious and suspect. The whole genre was deeply suspect, of course. Tovey, who struggled against this latter derogation, and whose insight into concerto discourse was pathbreaking, could simply not trust or appreciate concerto display. On the cadenza, for example, he wrote that "The saddest chapter in the story of the concerto is the classical custom of leaving all but the orchestral wind-up of the coda blank, and trusting to a display of the solo-player's powers of improvisation to fill up the blank with a cadenza." For Tovey, such improvisation was an aleatoric alibi for a crucial element in the formalist schema, namely the coda; hence his aphorism that cadenzas are "a form of appendicitis," and his lifelong hobby of writing out his own cadenzas for the great Classical concertos. When he published some of these, he explained that his intent was to supply the masterworks in question with plausible codas, modeled on Beethoven's symphonic codas.[5]

v ·   On the global level, the subtlest mode of dialogic response in the Classical concerto is that embodied in the first-movement form. The least subtle is that embodied in the concerto's main last-movement form, the concerto rondo. Musicologists and music theorists have paid relatively little attention to this form. I need to make just one point about it that I think important.

In the concerto rondo, it is typically the solo that commences, with a tune or the beginnings of a tune. Then the orchestra at once repeats what the solo has played. Unlike a long-term re-engagement, however, such as we have just been considering in the first movement of K. 467, the rondo repetition is without variation or nuance; it already feels less like a response or a rejoinder than like an acknowledgment, confirmation, or echo. There is something automatic, it seems to me, even empty about these repetitions. It also seems to me that this quality is independent of the syntactic function of the repeated phrases. Usually the repetitions are exact, as in themes that can be expressed diagrammatically as $a_I A_I b_I B'_I$ in K. 537, $a_V A_V$

$b_I\ B_I$ in K. 459, or simply $a_I\ A_I$ in several other opuses. (Lower- and upper-case letters refer to solo and orchestral presentation respectively; subscript numbers denote the scale degrees of cadences). But binary structure is also possible: $a_V\ A'_I$ in K. 450 and K. 456. As for the Piano Concerto in D Minor, K. 466, that feels entirely different from Mozart's other concerto rondos, for the opening solo theme is never repeated by the orchestra—though indeed the orchestra twice attempts, and egregiously fails, to accomplish this action.[6]

To return: the opening theme of the concerto rondo already contains these essentially formal (rather than dialogic) repetitions. Later in the piece there will be at least two, often three other occasions when the orchestra hears the solo tune again, and echoes it or parrots it again. What is significant about these places is the *readiness* and the *blankness* with which the repetitions come. This much reiteration fixes and formalizes the relationship in a decisive way, whatever else happens in between the repetitions. What happens in between is, of course, a good deal. Nonetheless, the pervading sense in concerto rondos from Bach's E-major Violin Concerto through Mozart all the way to Bartók and the Gershwin Piano Concerto in F is consensus, a consensus in aid of play, and a consensus in aid of a happy ending.

This relationship between solo and orchestra is very different from that in the first movement; the relationship has changed. To understand what may be behind this change, we should return to the historical situation.

VI ·

Mozart's piano concertos were not conceived in any spirit of abstract investigation of ideal relationship patterns. They were written for his academies, public concerts with which the young pianist-composer attempted to make the scene in music's capital city. The inner drama of concerto relationship can be viewed as the projection of an actual social dynamic.

Here too one can interpret on different levels. Most generally, one can identify the soloist with the individual and the orchestra with society, the evolving bourgeois or partly bourgeois society of the late eighteenth century. This is the line taken by Susan McClary, in an essay entitled, with a deep bow to Adorno, "A Musical Dialectic of the Enlightenment: Mozart's *Piano Concerto in G Major, K. 453*, Movement 2." The Classical concerto, says McClary, "enacts as a spectacle the dramatic tensions between individual and society, surely one of the major problematics of the emerging middle class,"[7] and although this interpretation may not be original, as has already been remarked, it has never been developed in any detail and would seem to offer much promise to a musicologist interested in postmodern critique. For McClary, who perhaps bows *too* deeply to Adorno, those tensions are still constrained by a simple dialectic between unyielding societal control on the one hand, and individual protest doomed to failure on the other. The adversarial scenario, in other words, or something like it. Even so, this hermeneutic framework empowers a critic of her sensitivity to read K. 453 in a fresh and impressive way (and incidentally, the results might be even better with the work that is to be discussed in a moment, K. 491). What seems strange is that in a long article including a detailed particularization of the musical tensions in a single movement, a critic of McClary's ambitions should spend so little time particularizing either the individual in question, Mozart, or the local form of emerging bourgeois society represented by Josephine Vienna.

We should work toward a view of this music less in broad general terms, more in its actual situation—Mozart's situation vis-à-vis his patrons as he worked to establish himself in the musical life of Vienna in 1781 to 1786. There exists a fascinating list of his concert subscribers in 1784, in a letter to Leopold. Though part of the letter is lost, the list still includes no fewer than 174 names; Landon compares it to the Almanach de Gotha, and Mozart remarks, "I have about 30 subscribers more than Richter and Fischer together."[8] Landon also provides us in *The Golden Years* with thumbnail profiles of many of these persons, some of whom were aristocrats, some bourgeois, and some upwardly mobile bourgeois of the type immortalized by Hoffmannsthal's Faninal. But a thick description of Viennese musical society in the 1780s has yet to be essayed, for all the flood of studies prompted by the 1991 bicentenary. And the other side of the equation, Mozart himself, remains an only-too-famous enigma.

Projected in the Mozart concertos, I suggest, is a single pervading myth. They follow a standard three-movement plan. In the first movement, with its elegantly articulated strategy of engagement and re-engagement, the concerto actors seem to enter into a collaborative test situation. The soloist presents himself to the orchestra and shows how he is able to cope with conditions they have laid down. Those conditions are not inflexible; in the process of dialogue, they can change considerably, for the orchestra allows and indeed encourages criticism, initiative, even spontaneous display and acrobatics on the part of the soloist.

Then comes a quiet slow interlude of some kind (there are several kinds, all of them beautiful). Then comes a rondo (usually); and here there is less at stake than in the opening encounter. For the slow movement has solemnized a ritual of mutual acceptance between the principals. The rondo finale, in consequence, feels less like a trial or a quest than a deal. The relationship between solo and orchestra feels less like collaboration than complicity, even collusion.

The three movements of a concerto trace a sequence from *interaction* to some sort of *respite* to *complicity,* from collaborative and creative exchange to accommodation. I associate this sequence with the underlying theme of comedy, the "myth of spring," as Northrop Frye expounded it many years ago. In this myth, the individual is incorporated into society and society is transformed. In one Mozartian comedic fiction, Tamino sues and wins entrance to the social order by playing on a magic flute. In seventeen others, Amadeus plays the fortepiano.

True, the Classical symphony or string quartet could be said to trace a similar course, without reference to actors or social formation, and the sequence could perhaps be traced in non-metaphorical, technical terms. What is different in the concerto is the way the myth is personified. That is what is so striking, so winning. Joan Crawford said it best, in a prewar movie few of us now remember. "I like some symphonies," said Joan, "but I like all concertos."

VII ·
The sharpest test for my interpretation of the Mozart concertos is the Piano Concerto in C Minor, K. 491, composed in March 1786. The first movement of this arresting work, as many have pointed out, departs in various ways from established norms, breaks free of tradition. The freedom results, I think, from a far-reaching response by the solo to its situation. The solo does not merely protest the hegemony of the orchestra, it seeks to wrest control of the discourse from that orchestra. In its equivocal effort to create or define the form, the solo is more assertive in this work—and also more vulnerable—than in any other Mozart concerto.

Several unusual features of K. 491 support this contention, I believe. First and most obvious, though the obvious implication is not always articulated or recognized, the solo does not begin its first solo span in the traditional way, with a version of the orchestra's main theme (as in K. 467). It begins with an expressive theme of its own invention. I take that as a clear bid to establish its own agenda. That agenda includes a new policy for the discourse-to-display trajectory that was identified above: in the first solo span, the trajectory is actually traced twice, in bars 100–200, then again in bars 211–65. The solo receives (or appropriates) not one but two extensive bravura passages, each ending with formal trills, lasting for eighty-four measures in all. Charles Rosen, who points out this innovation in *The Classical Style,*[9] is not concerned there to attribute it to the solo or the orchestra; and if I am to be scrupulous I will admit that there is no easy way to tell which of the two gets the credit for its inception. But certainly the solo is the one who capitalizes on it.

Judging from the sequel, one must also conclude that all this initiative on the part of the solo makes the orchestra restive; for the second solo span includes a rare example in Mozart of a real struggle between solo and orchestra. The passage in question begins with a series of familiar-sounding developmental modulations, after which the piano breaks free of the orchestra to make a vehement close, down in the low register. Too vehement, it seems, for the orchestra: the orchestra cuts in with a gesture that is elemental in facture and arresting because it is entirely new and entirely aggressive (example 2). The piano is swept away—horrified—as this

EXAMPLE 2

happens again and again. The fourth time it happens, just when the transaction is beginning to seem merciless, the orchestra relents and allows the piano to conclude its runs without further deflection.

After this humbling episode, the solo loses its form-defining impulse. From now on, in the section of re-engagement, the solo is distinctly subdued. When the solo is given a new theme to ornament, it doesn't do much of a job with it (bars 444–63). And it retains only a shadow of its two long bravura passages: to be precise, only twenty-eight bars are left out of an original total of eighty-four (and only one trill).

There is therefore special importance and special pathos to the solo's performance in the cadenza. In no other Mozart concerto first movement is the cadenza as important as in K. 491, even though we "have" that cadenza only in concept. Its ontological status is that of pure unspecified improvisation, but its function is urgent: the solo has been muted, and a redress is needed. And although Mozart, who wrote out cadenzas for most of his concertos, did not leave us one for K. 491, he did leave indication of a novel impulse that he had in mind. Even when he wrote out cadenzas, it was not Mozart's habit to write them out in the actual autograph scores; but in the autographs, he did write the ending cadenza trill as a sort of cue—and this cue is absent from the C-minor autograph.[10] Almost certainly this means that Mozart meant the cadenza to run directly into the coda without a trill.[11]

EXAMPLE 3

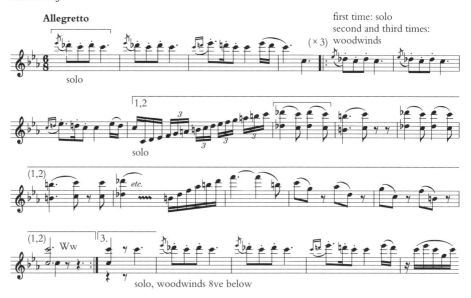

And Mozart being Mozart, the abandoned trill is part of a larger purpose. The solo not having closed itself off with a cadenza trill, it can continue with a wonderful effect to haunt the orchestra at the very end, in a famous passage, deeply influential upon Beethoven.[12] The smoky, glittery piano arpeggios that cloud the final orchestral ritornello—ritornello 4—challenge one more time the orchestra's authority. The issue of discourse versus display remains undecided. The power relations are in doubt.

VIII ·    As for the finale of the C-minor Concerto, that too breaks with tradition. It is a theme and variations, not a rondo, worked out in such a way that there is very little dialogue in it, whether collaborative/creative or complicitous/collusive. That in itself is not so significant; what is significant is the conclusion, consisting of the end of the last variation and the coda. Both segments are monopolized by the solo instrument. Instead of dialogue, Mozart is occupied with obsession here—with a single musical figure which, when the orchestra tries to play it, the solo takes back (example 3). This ostinato figure, articulating the step Neapolitan D♭–C in at least two different rhythms, comes no fewer than fourteen times: saturation of a most untraditional, un-Classical, un-Mozartian sort. The piece is in fact uncanny, *unheimlich* in the best early Romantic sense. Also uncanny is the similarity of this figure to the orchestra's angry, elemental interrupting motif in the first movement (example 2).

In this paper I have developed a view of Mozart's concertos as adhering to a general myth of comedy, and then I have spent a good deal of time purporting to show how one concerto, the C minor K. 491, does not follow the myth at all. K. 491 was the last piano concerto composed for the four-year run of academy concerts.

It was composed in April 1786 at the end of Mozart's fourth season, preceding the premiere of *Figaro* by just a few weeks. Mozart's first concerto composition for Vienna was a shamelessly popular display piece, the Rondo in D Major, K. 382, for the 1781–82 season; four years later he offered Vienna the disturbed, disturbing Concerto in C Minor. The next season yielded only one group of concerts, in December 1786, and Mozart wrote only one new concerto for them, K. 503 in C major. It is worth noting, too, that these concerts were the first for which he composed a special new symphony (this was the "Prague," K. 504). As Charles Rosen remarks, the C-major Concerto K. 503, though never a favorite with the public, is "one that many musicians (historians and pianists alike) single out with special affection."[13] But as compared to the other C-major concerto, K. 467, K. 503 is a monumental, rather forbiddingly magnificent work. It is not really much fun, and it is strangely cold: cold, despite the quality of melancholy which Rosen finely discerns in it. That Mozart did not write a fresh theme for the rondo finale, instead borrowing from an old composition that was a nostalgic favorite of his, *Idomeneo*— that too seems strange, disquieting. Austere and abstracted, K. 503 registers a clear change in mood in the sequence of Mozart concertos. It could be said to register a loss of heart.

Perhaps the Viennese audience tired of Mozart by 1786; that is not impossible. It is also possible that Mozart tired of the Viennese audience. More precisely, he may have grown weary of the consoling myth that he and they had enacted together, in concerto after concerto, year after year. With his C-minor concerto, he had put his tacit contract with them at risk; if any of his concert subscribers felt affronted and alienated by this deeply subversive work, we could hardly blame them. As Einstein remarked rather dryly, many years ago, "It is hard to imagine the expression on the faces of the Viennese public on 7 April 1786 when Mozart played this work at one of his subscription concerts."[14] As I imagine it, the whole communal exercise had begun to strike Mozart as hollow, irrelevant to his developing needs as man and artist. It was first Mozart, not his audience, who had begun to experience alienation.

## Notes

1. *The Letters of Mozart and His Family,* ed. Emily Anderson (London, 1938), 3:1099–1100 (2 June 1781).
2. H. C. Robbins Landon, *Mozart: The Golden Years, 1781–1791* (New York, 1989), 52.

3. Modeste Tchaikovsky, *The Life and Letters of Peter Ilich Tchaikovsky*, tr. Rosa Newmarch (London, 1906), 331.

4. See especially Donald Francis Tovey, "The Classical Concerto (1903)," in *Essays in Musical Analysis*, vol. 3, *Concertos* (London, 1936), 3–27, reprinted in *W. A. Mozart, Piano Concerto in C Major, K. 503*, ed. Joseph Kerman (Norton Critical Scores; New York, 1970), 137–63; also Charles Rosen, *The Classical Style: Haydn, Mozart, Beethoven*, rev. ed. (New York, 1972), ch. 5, sec. 1, and *Sonata Forms*, rev. ed. (New York, 1988), ch. 5.

5. See Tovey, *Essays in Musical Analysis*, 3:86; also Donald Francis Tovey, *Musical Articles from the Encyclopaedia Britannica* (London, 1944), 16; and Donald Francis Tovey, "Prefaces to Cadenzas for Classical Concertos," in *The Main Stream of Music and Other Essays* (New York, 1949), 315–24.

6. For a brief discussion of K. 466, see Joseph Kerman, "Mozart à la Mode," *New York Review of Books*, 18 May 1989, 51.

7. Susan McClary, "A Musical Dialectic of the Enlightenment: Mozart's *Piano Concerto in G Major, K. 453*, Movement 2," *Cultural Critique 4* (1986): 138.

8. Landon, *Mozart: The Golden Years*, 107; *Letters of Mozart*, 3:1297–1300 (20 March 1784).

9. Rosen, *Classical Style*, 245–48.

10. See p. 33 of the facsimile edition, *Mozart, Piano Concerto in C Minor, K. 491* (Washington, D.C., 1984).

11. A cadenza for K. 491 without a trill, by Saint-Saëns, may be heard on a famous old recording by Robert Casadesus.

12. For a brief discussion of this, see Joseph Kerman, "Notes on Beethoven's Codas," in *Beethoven Studies 3*, ed. Alan Tyson (Cambridge, 1982), 143–45.

13. Rosen, *Classical Style*, 251.

14. Alfred Einstein, *Mozart, His Character, His Work*, tr. Arthur Mendel and Nathan Broder (New York, 1945), 311.

# 20

# *Tristan und Isolde:* The Prelude and the Play

In the days of his ascendancy, Wagner was a figure to reckon with on the concert stage as well as in the opera house; his fame and his appeal arose from orchestral excerpts from his operas, as well as from the operas themselves. Today such excerpts are less popular on concert programs and recordings. A hardy survivor is the combination of the Prelude to *Tristan und Isolde* and Isolde's Transfiguration (the so-called "Liebestod"), the opera's final scene. This is sometimes performed with a singer, sometimes without.[1] "Bleeding chunks," Tovey exasperatedly called such concert items carved from the operas' capacious cadavers, and it must be granted that the Prelude and the Transfiguration one after another make a peculiar mixed grill. The opening pit music, before the curtain rises, joined to (sometimes) a wordless version of the concluding cantilena sung by Isolde after all of the action, conventionally considered, is over—this makes for a drastic short-circuit of Wagner's intricate music-drama.

Indeed, the perennial success of the Prelude and Transfiguration must seem startling, even ominous to the lover of *Tristan und Isolde: The Opera.* She can understand Wagner's promotion of this composite concert number in the 1860s, to broadcast excerpts of a work that had repeatedly defied efforts at production; and he can acknowledge the superior appeal of the gloomy Prelude joined to the rapturous Transfiguration as compared to the gloomy Prelude alone. But she also knows that to appreciate the Transfiguration truly, one must have lived through the great love scene in Act II of the opera, whose music it resumes in a spiritualized

To appear in *Richard Wagner: "Tristan und Isolde,"* ed. Carolyn Abbate (Cambridge Opera Handbooks; Cambridge: Cambridge University Press, forthcoming).

form. And the Prelude, as he knows, is just that—the initiation into a vastly greater experience in the course of which, among other things, the music of the Prelude achieves its full development and hence its true meaning, beauty, and force.

For concertgoers, there are clearly satisfactions to the Prelude and Transfiguration apart from such truths, apart from the opera at all. Similar satisfactions also seem to be available to music theorists. They have theorized so copiously about the Prelude (in particular) and the Transfiguration that it was possible for a leading Wagner authority, Robert Bailey, to issue a whole book of writings about these items. Included are essays or excerpts running to 200 densely packed pages by no fewer than seventeen authors.[2] What is startling, once again, is how little they find to say, or are allowed by the excerpting editor to say, about the opera itself.

Perhaps, though, it is not so startling. For even as regards the Prelude and Transfiguration, one observes that these writings limit themselves almost entirely to matters of melody and harmony, broadly defined. The present essay will address aspects of this music besides melody and harmony, and also seek to place the Prelude in the context of the total music-drama. This line is not taken purely in a polemic spirit, to redress what can only be seen as the anti-operatic bias of Bailey's collection. The larger point is that the music of the Prelude is essential to the music of the opera itself, more profoundly so than in the case of any earlier opera (or, at a guess, any later one). Wagner's dramatic vision hinges on the way the opera emerges from the Prelude, on the way the Prelude plays in to the opera. Arguably, an examination of this topic can provide the most effective short route to grasping the musical dramaturgy of *Tristan und Isolde*.

II ·  Much has been written about the linear and harmonic aspects of bars 1–17 of the Prelude to *Tristan und Isolde,* much more than can be summarized here. Let us bite the bullet and summarize none of it at all, for there are other important, even pressing points to make about this music—points about rhythm, dynamics, and affect. A single-staff reduction as in example 1 should suffice for illustration, even though this defangs the famous "Tristan" chords at the points where the equally famous chromatic motifs converge.

To speak first about rhythm: the phrases or cells formed as the two motifs converge are disjoined by silences which feel, at this slow tempo, unmeasured, though only the last of them is literally so (that is, marked with a fermata: ⌒). Even the Prelude's first downbeat is placed in time somewhat enigmatically; the five slow eighth notes of crescendo on the cello F in bar 1 are hard to count and construe. So are the rests in bars 3–4 and 7–8 (different rests in each case). After bar 11 the music falters palpably, as one fermata is followed by another. Only with the cello melody that emerges after the big deceptive cadence, in bar 18, does Wagner establish some kind of normal motion.

EXAMPLE I

The dark, mysterious, yearning quality of this opening passage is due not only to its chromatic lines and harmony, and to its orchestration, but also to its disjointed rhythm; this seems obvious. And however apt or inept it may seem to describe the Prelude's beginning as "dark, mysterious, and yearning," there can be little doubt that things begin to change in and around the fermatas of bars 11 and 13. The obsessive repetition of the naked appoggiatura E♯–F♯, grasping for resolution, grows intense and breathy to the point of harshness. The effect is heightened by the carefully differentiated dynamics at each of the appoggiatura's appearances. Then—when the bass E is supplied and resolves deceptively to F—the dynamic flares up to a momentary *fortissimo* as the music takes on its first explicitly sexual tinge. A spasm of desire, reinforced by vaulting French horns, is followed by a withdrawal exquisitely calculated in the anticipation of passionate renewal. It is the forward-moving cello melody that validates that anticipation.

Since the Prelude has interested theorists mainly on account of its chromaticism, they have not had a great deal to say about this cello melody. There is undeniably a sense of letdown when the rich, complex harmonies of the opening cede to a rather Lohengrinish march around standard secondary dominants and diminished sevenths skirting C major. Yet in the broadest sense the cello melody (which is genuinely "endless") coheres with bars 1–17 as an essential part of Wagner's idea. The linear connection (from A to A) is broken registrally, but this break is softened inasmuch as the same instrument that began the Prelude, the cello, resumes the pitch and the tessitura of the opening. And the diatonic cello melody seems in some deep sense to "resolve" the chromaticism of the opening bars (of course, this is only an interim resolution). Though itself resolutely open, the cello melody provisionally closes the chromatic drama of the opening.

For purposes of analysis, bars 1–17 of the Prelude are usually isolated. Bailey calls them the "opening unit." It is never easy to find the right terminology for music's unique structures, and in the present case "unit" suggests a fixity that seems unfortunate, even apart from the desirability of stretching the reference to cover the open-ended diatonic response from the cello. The term adopted here—for we do need a term to carry on the discussion—is "complex."

III ·   The end of the Prelude returns to the same "complex" as at the beginning—the chromatic motifs converging on the "Tristan" chord, the threefold upward sequence, the deceptive cadence, and the diatonic cello melody. But there are substantial differences, notably at the beginning of the passage. So far from emerging as a tentative *pianissimo,* the first motif rides the surge of a powerful climax and is blared out three times in succession by the French horns. On the first "Tristan" chord, the Prelude reaches its loudest *fortissimo,* only to back down again, to *piano,* in just a few seconds.

Then at the end of the passage, the cello melody is reharmonized. The chord change is simple, the effect wonderfully bleak (example 2). Wagner himself described the Prelude as "one long-articulated impulse" in which

> insatiable longing swell[s] up from the timidest avowal of the most delicate attraction, through anxious sighs, hopes and fears, laments and wishes, raptures and torments, to the mightiest onset and to the most powerful effort to find the breach that will reveal to the infinitely craving heart the path into the sea of love's endless rapture. In vain! Its power spent, the heart sinks back . . .

and on another occasion as the progression "from the timidest lament in inappeasable longing, the tenderest shudder, to the most terrible outpouring of an avowal of hopeless love."[3] He said nothing about the technical tour de force whereby the most terrible outpouring of hopeless love is set to the same music as the timidest avowal. As is often observed, Wagner the *Vielschreiber* wrote remarkably little about his specific compositional actions.

The same music—except for differences especially in dynamics, affect, and also rhythm. For the halting quality that was so striking at the beginning of the Prelude is arrested in this return. The gaps between the cells are equalized and filled in by a new motif (actually, the retrograde of an old one) played by the violins. This violin motif sounds rhetorical, even recitative-like; in any case, looking ahead to the opera itself, at later appearances of this music the pregnant gaps tend to be filled by declamatory singing, Wagner's equivalent of recitative. And with the benefit of hindsight, we can recognize that the music was composed with all those halts

EXAMPLE 2

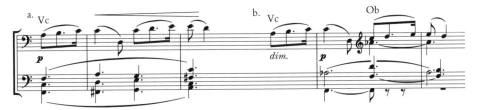

precisely so that they could be filled in in this way later. Put differently, the opening of the Prelude was designed not only to lay out the opera's unique musical language, but also to provide an elastic framework for recitatives, for actual verbal language.

Indeed, it is hard to see how Wagner could have proceeded differently if he meant to use the Prelude complex as a recurring unit (albeit a freely recurring unit) in the course of the drama. The point can be made most sharply by a comparison with the opera's other large recurring musical unit, which is the music of Isolde's Transfiguration. The Transfiguration music begins life as a twenty-four–bar rounded melody ("So stürben wir, um ungetrennt") introduced by Tristan within the Act II love duet, repeated by Isolde and Tristan, and then developed by the two of them in the duet's rapturous ending section. All of this music returns at length in the orchestra at the end of Act III, substantially unchanged up to some added cadential pages at the end; Isolde sings her new words ("Mild und leise") to new counterpoint set against what is now the orchestral melody. But whereas the Transfiguration music is lyrical in origin and vocal in concept, the Prelude complex is quintessentially orchestral. It is not music to be sung through, to one set of words or another. If the aggregate of orchestral ideas in the Prelude is to recur *en bloc,* it needs to accommodate words in the interstices, as it were. Through those words, of course, the recurring music interacts with and controls the developing dramatic action.

Themes with pregnant rhythmic halts in them are a well-known Beethovenian specialty. That great Romantic favorite the Sonata in D Minor, op. 31 no. 2, has fermatas in its opening theme which are unexpectedly filled by long, explicitly recitative-like passages when the theme returns at the recapitulation. Wagner prized another famous place of the same kind, the brief oboe cadenza in the first movement of the Fifth Symphony. After experiencing "the inspired delivery of the great Schroeder-Devrient," wrote Wagner in his essay "On Conducting,"

> I could no longer bear hearing that passage thrown away as it invariably
> was. Furthermore, my handling of it made me realize the importance of the

EXAMPLE 3

first violins' fermata in the corresponding passage in the exposition; and the powerful impression from those two apparently insignificant details led to a fresh understanding of the movement as a whole.[4]

Fresh understanding—and, it may be, fresh inspiration for work of his own. Indeed, the tremendous return of the opening music at the climax of the *Tristan* Prelude, discussed above, can be seen as Wagner's inspired misreading, as Harold Bloom would say, of the triumphant recapitulations so typical of Beethoven, exemplified by the Fifth Symphony. The insistent A♭–f–e–d♯ in the horns chromaticizes the even more insistent A♭–A♭–A♭–F in the horns and all the other instruments just before Beethoven's recapitulation. If it seems strange to think of Beethoven's Fifth as a model for certain aspects of the *Tristan* Prelude, consider (for certain other aspects) a passage from *Don Giovanni* (example 3).

IV ·  Each of the two versions of the Prelude complex heard within the Prelude—the "timidest avowal" version and the "terrible outpouring" version—is drawn upon in the course of the opera. Indeed, whereas the long melody comprising "So stürben wir" and its developments returns in the opera just once, at length, and substantially unchanged, the Prelude complex returns many times in many varied forms—varied in meter, rhythm, tempo, dynamics, orchestration, with the addition of counterpoints or other motifs, and so on. These variations supply new meanings to each of the dramatic situations they articulate, while at the same time drawing them all together. Interestingly, the Prelude complex usually remains unvaried in pitch and harmony. In theoretical parlance, pitch (pitch class) and harmony serve here as the basic referential parameters.

A final word about "So stürben wir": Wagner used the one return of this music to make a major dramatic point in *Tristan und Isolde*—indeed, *the* major point. Isolde's transfiguration is the action (or passion) that complements and fulfills Tristan's death in her arms a few minutes earlier. Likewise, returns of the Prelude complex in what we may call its "strong" form—a form in which all its elements are emphatically present—articulate other important dramatic junctures. Put more accurately, returns of the Prelude complex in its strong form allowed Wagner to define certain points in the drama as the principal ones.

One principal point is singled out in each act (the drama of *Tristan und Isolde* consists largely of psychological action that precipitates one momentous event in each of the three acts).[5] In Act I and Act III, the points in question are obvious enough: the drinking of the love potion in Act I, and the death of Tristan in Act III. In Act II, the point chosen is slightly less obvious, and will bear some discussion later in this essay: the Prelude complex returns not at the interruption of Tristan and Isolde's tryst by Marke and his hunting party, nor at the stabbing of Tristan by Melot, but rather at Tristan's response to Marke's extended reproach.

In Act I, what is recalled is the "terrible outpouring" from the end of the Prelude. The harmonic preparation is the same, the dynamic is *ff*, and Wagner contrives a *slancio* for the beginning that tops even the blaring horns of the Prelude . . . by the simple expedient of having Isolde actually sing the opening motif ("Ich trink' sie dir!"). There follows Wagner's most extreme distention of the gaps built in to the Prelude complex at its opening, "timidest avowal" appearance. After a new fermata on the first "Tristan" chord, the original rest of bars 3–4 (see example 1) expands to ten bars full of slow orchestral music. "Then [Isolde] throws away the goblet. They both shudder, and gaze into one another's eyes with the utmost emotion . . . their death-defiant expression changes to the glow of passion," reads the stage direction. Shuddering is registered by a *pianissimo* tremolo slide in the cellos, death-defiance by a portion of the impressive "Todgeweihtes Haupt! todgeweihtes Herz!" motif, and growing passion by the second sequential appearance of the opening motif. Trembling and tight heart-clutching, prescribed at a point corresponding to the rest in bars 7–8 of the Prelude, receive similar musical representations. The sequel includes the fermatas of bars 11 and 13 (heard here for the last time in the opera), the deceptive cadence, and the cello melody, the latter now doubled by dissociated gasps from the embracees—"Tristan!," "Isolde!," and so on (example 4).

The shenanigans in this scene, perhaps, have always been an embarrassment to Wagnerians. Ernest Newman, for one, averted his eyes while taking a mean swipe at the singers of *Tristan,* rather than the composer: "There follows the episode—generally an awkward one on the stage—that makes heavier demands on the singers as actors than any other situation in Wagner's works, demands which not one Tristan or Isolde in a hundred can meet."[6] Or perhaps Wagner's musical semaphor-

EXAMPLE 4

ing of onstage gestures is accepted by today's unembarrassable opera-goers as a matter of course, in much the same way they savor the dramatic values of accompanied recitatives in Handel. Let us hope so: for of course the drinking of the love potion must be understood and, if possible, experienced as the crucial moment in Act I. As the climactic resolution of fifty-odd minutes of psychological action, it is the most grandiose of all the many returns of the Prelude complex that Wagner planned for the opera as a whole.

So potent is this return that it produces a sort of aftershock a minute later, when a headlong version of the Prelude complex underpins the lovers' hasty little duet. We must call this a "weak" return, inasmuch as the opening motif—the one Isolde had sung to the words "Ich trink' sie dir!"—gets lost in all the excitement.

v ·

In Act III, at Tristan's death, the return of the Prelude complex in its "strong" form has clear points of contact with the Act I return discussed above. Again the opening rides the surge of a climax, and again the "Todgeweihtes Haupt" motif is present. Played by the trumpets *fortissimo,* this motif serves to introduce the Prelude complex, overlapping with it in a violent (and barely grammatical) fashion. While in a sense Wagner wanted to project the nexus of love and death at every moment of *Tristan und Isolde,* it was necessary first and foremost to draw the connection both at and between the climax points of Acts I and III, the drinking of the love potion and the death of Tristan.

After its crashing entrance, the music of the Prelude complex is compressed as never before; this is admirably matched to the urgency and agony of the dramatic situation (example 5; contrast this with the slow-motion effect in Act I). But the passage is marked with a long *allargando* and *diminuendo,* so that by the time the deceptive cadence arrives, it has completely lost its typical sexually tinged surge to

EXAMPLE 5

a *ff*. Delayed by long extensions of the cadential melody-notes B and A—in effect, written-out fermatas—the cello melody that promised the continuation of passion comes exceptionally late. It is also exceptionally slow ("Sehr langsam"). Again recalling Act I, Tristan gasps the one word "Isolde!" against the cello melody, which breaks off graphically, only too graphically at the precise moment of his decease. "Isolde!" is sung to the notes E and D marked with actual fermatas, echoing the written-out fermatas on B and A just beforehand.

It's been a long evening for Tristan, but he must try to extend those fermatas as long as he can:

> Hold that fermata of mine! Cling to it . . . as though you were wringing the
> last drop of life out of it. I was dividing the seas in order to behold the abyss
> below. I was parting the clouds in order to behold the shining sun and the
> blue sky.[7]

*Also sprach* Richard Wagner: though not, it is true, in connection with any of the fermatas in his opera. He was speaking in Beethoven's name about the fermata at the very beginning of the Fifth Symphony.

Over the full course of *Tristan und Isolde,* the rhythmic dynamic of the Prelude complex has been almost exactly inverted. Originally this music moves haltingly, with cryptic gaps and fermatas. It achieves its true stride only with the deceptive cadence and the cello melody, which surges forward confidently as though the emotion it portrays will never cease. When Isolde enters in Act III, the music flows with painful rapidity, gradually braking into the drawn-out deceptive cadence and the very slow, late-entering, fermata-studded cello melody. With Isolde's "Ha!" the music ceases entirely—and is sealed off from the sequel by one more fermata. Isolde should cling to that one, too.

VI ·  Act II of *Tristan und Isolde* has largely a different thematic vocabulary from Act I, though of course Wagner holds all the music of the opera together with the greatest art. Act II is about Night and Day, the latter representing everything the lovers must reject, and while there is still much talk about love and death, these ideas have acquired new meanings and new music. Death is now seen as transcendence and release, not as something ominous and to be feared—the clear message of "Todgeweihtes Haupt! todgeweihtes Herz!," a motif seldom heard in Act II. Nor is any of the Prelude music much in evidence. Hence the Prelude complex makes a particularly strong effect when it returns toward the end of the act.

This happens after the ten-minute reproach by King Marke, when Tristan speaks only cursorily to Marke before turning to Isolde: "O König, das — kann ich dir nicht sagen; und was du frägst, das kannst du nie erfahren." On one level—the level of everyday morality and etiquette—these words administer an intolerable snub, and no doubt that is how Melot takes them.[8] The audience, however, witnesses more than a breakdown of normal human relations. We experience a rupture of the opera's basic dramaturgical fabric. In Wagner, everybody always responds when they are addressed, usually at length; Tristan even takes the time to frame a rejoinder to Melot's challenge, at the end of the present act, and in the next one he mumbles a response to Kurvenal's expressions of solicitude when he is barely out of his coma. His refusal to engage with Marke articulates a moment of major importance to the drama. For although the lovers have talked a good deal about rejecting the world of Day, this is the moment when talk is crystallized into action.

The breach of the dramaturgical norm is enforced by the regressive music. It is as though Wagner has directed the conductor to close the score and turn back to page one. What returns is—for the first time—the "timidest avowal" version from the beginning of the Prelude: the dynamic is *pp*, once again, and the spare scoring is very similar (with the Prelude's unaccompanied cellos replaced by an unaccompanied English horn). The original rests in the model are filled by declamatory recitative, as Tristan stumbles through the 6/8 music in 4/8 time, his words dazed and faltering (example 6). Tristan is experiencing a trauma here that prefigures the plunge into *Urvergessen* taken when he falls upon Melot's sword. What occupies Tristan at this moment—and surely Isolde too—is not Marke's reproach, not the memory of love acknowledged with the drinking of the love potion, but rather an acceptance of that death-dedicated passion which existed between them long before the action of the opera began. Only on some such grounds can we rationalize the

EXAMPLE 6

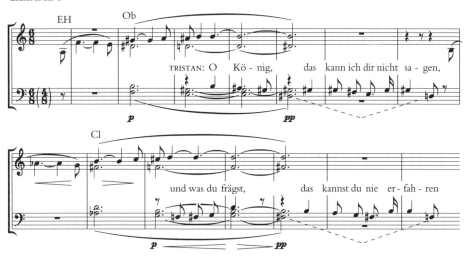

shock caused by the seeming inhumanity of Tristan's extraordinary snub. Tristan has dropped out of Act II; though his larynx may be on stage, his musical presence is back in the inchoate psychic wellspring of the drama before the curtain has even been lifted.

As a rule, the Prelude complex in its returns remains unvaried in pitch and harmony; but the Act II return is an exception that proves the rule. It does so with a little demonstration of Wagnerian harmonic virtuosity. Nineteenth-century composers learned that dissonances can be made to resolve not only to consonances, but also, and with interesting results, to weaker dissonances. Here Wagner offers a two-stage resolution from a "Tristan" chord (dissonant) to a dominant-seventh chord (dissonant, but less dissonant) to a six-four chord (still less dissonant). The effect of the extra chord added to the first two sequential cells is twice to transmute the gloomy yearning of the original model into numb desolation. The catatonic way in which Tristan cancels these two extra harmonies before proceeding with the sequence, as shown in example 6 by dotted lines, is another symptom of his breakdown.

This harmonic variation, however, is as nothing compared to the harmonic variation which overcomes this version of the Prelude complex at its destination. The destination is now radically and luminously transformed, as the deceptive cadence by which it is prepared changes, and opens not upon the expected diatonic cello melody, but upon another diatonic melody in another key.[9] The key, A flat, is the key of the love duet, and what Tristan turns to here as he turns to Isolde (he has momentarily recouped from his trauma, though only momentarily) is a nos-

EXAMPLE 7

EXAMPLE 8

talgic recollection of music first heard on that occasion. Dubbed "Felicity" by Lavignac—one of his egregiously Victorian labels—this music coming here and now is replete with irony and pathos. Its meaning deepens as "Felicity" turns to "Death the Liberator" (example 7).

There is a beautiful remote echo of this new destination early in Act III, at the next appearance of the Prelude complex. A "weak" version is heard when Tristan swoons and Kurvenal, fearing for his life, listens anxiously for his heartbeat. As a forecast of Tristan's actual death, this "weak" return obviously serves as a forecast of the "strong" return on that occasion. In technical terms, however, it has more in common with the Act II return—the opening is very quiet; the basic cell receives another new harmonic resolution; recitative (no fewer than ten lines of it, on this occasion) fills the gaps between the cells; and once again the destination is neither the original diatonic cello melody nor the original key. The destination is, in fact, not even diatonic. Oboe and overlapping clarinet play a sweetly attenuated version of Tristan's most recent chromatic motif, first sung at his great epiphany about the love potion ("Ich selbst, ich hab' ihn gebraut!"). This materializes over an excruciatingly prolonged bass F♯ (example 8). But the true, stable destination of the

EXAMPLE 9

Prelude complex comes a phrase or two later, after a new deceptive cadence prepares a long passage in E major. Here Wagner brings a version of the "Felicity" music which was heard at the analogous point in Act II. Tristan is about to begin one of his most moving solos (example 9).

This is admittedly to stretch the term "Prelude complex" and the concept behind it rather far. But all technical and quasi-technical terms have to be stretched hard to keep up with Wagner's mature practice: think of terms such as "leitmotiv," "period," and "tonality."

VII · The "art of transition," Wagner wrote in a much-cited letter of 1859 to Mathilde Wesendonck, was the secret behind his musical form.[10] This essay has attempted to analyze the art of variation that Wagner also developed at that time, in the course of composing the opera so closely bound up with Mathilde.

"Variation" is meant here in the most compendious sense, to cover changes in all possible parameters: melody, harmony, texture, dynamics, rhythm, pace, affect, and others. For flexibility, range, ingenuity, and sheer imaginativeness, it would be hard to cite a richer example of Wagner's art of variation than that applied to the complex train of musical ideas at the beginning of the *Tristan* Prelude. There is nothing quite like it elsewhere in his work, nor, perhaps, in anybody else's. What is special about these variations is that the "theme" consists of so many different elements in a directed series, and that in the variations, while the elements are generally all in place, their affect and that of their series is so richly varied.

On a less technical level, analysis can also point to the way these variations contribute to Wagner's musical dramaturgy. When in the Prelude the "timidest avowal" of love is run through rapidly to its "terrible outpouring," one phase of the opera's action is forecast or epitomized (one thinks, as maybe Wagner did, of the trumpet call in the *Leonore* Overture no. 3). At our first sighting of Tristan soon after the curtain rises, when Brangaene draws the inner curtain on the marquee, a "weak" return of the Prelude complex accompanies Isolde's first oblique reference to her love ("Mir erkoren . . ."). In this compressed, understated return, the third sequential cell is replaced by Isolde's singing of "Todgeweihtes Haupt! todgeweihtes Herz!" Then the cello melody comes with its death-tinged minor-mode inflection (example 2b). The association with death established in this way is reinforced at several other returns, among them another "weak" one in Act I when the women discuss the casket of philtres. Here the recitative "Kennst du die Mutter Künste nicht" and others fill the gaps in the original complex.

As we have seen, the "terrible outpouring" version of the Prelude complex—but without its fateful minor-tinged conclusion—resonates hugely during the drinking of the love potion in Act I, and at Tristan's death in Act III. In the first case, Wagner also labors to project the lovers' confusion and excitement by means of multiple musical gestures tucked in between the elements of the Prelude complex. In the second case, the pathetic reversal of the rhythmic dynamic terminates in the cut-off at Isolde's "Ha!," which depicts the literal death of Tristan but also makes clear that this can be no final conclusion. It is only Tristan who expires in the grip of "the most terrible outpouring of an avowal of hopeless love." Isolde's Transfiguration is required to complete Wagner's scheme.

The Act II return is perhaps the most interesting, registering as it does not an immediate emotional reaction but an emotional state that has had time to sink in. Things have been registering on Tristan for ten minutes, the ten minutes of Marke's monologue. Hence the dryness of the recitative and of the "extra" chords, and hence also the freedom to resolve not in the familiar cello melody but in another, more recent and poignant one. And the reflection of all this in Act III, where Tristan swoons and Kurvenal hovers over him, is at once the quietest and the most subtle of all the returns.

What analysis of this or any other kind cannot do, of course, is direct the way the listener will respond to these returns, to the blunt ones as well as to the subtle. Such responses—of acceptance, submission, enchantment, indifference, rejection—will determine how far we are able to enter into the world-view of *Tristan und Isolde*. Things are safe enough with the first return, the variation within the Prelude itself: if one may judge, as seems fair enough, from the perennial success of the Prelude and Transfiguration in the concert hall, this maintains its canonic status as one of the most unshakably convincing strokes in Wagner. And once the listener-spectator has submitted so far to the famous Wagnerian magic, it is hard to see how she can fail to be thrilled by the return of this music when Tristan is first disclosed, standing silently at the ship's stern, Isolde meanwhile pronouncing her cryptic omens. He may find the magic wearing perilously thin at the kiss at the end of Act I; and the spell may snap completely for a moment at Tristan's death—only to return in full force, it must be hoped, during the Transfiguration.

Most problematic is the crux in Act II: most problematic, and also most critical for our acquiescence to the world-view of *Tristan und Isolde*. Wagner's use of the Prelude complex confirms Tristan's non-response to Marke as a dramatic turning point second to none other in the opera. To be sure, no one drinks, dies, extinguishes torches, or suffers discovery. But Tristan by mentally rejecting the world of Day takes an active, positive step of the first importance. This positivity is crucial, for while it is all very well to say (and, as Wagner does, to show) that Tristan and Isolde have been caught in a permanent and permanently doomed love from before the action started, *Tristan* is a drama and a drama has to hinge on nodes of immediate action. Music which, at the start of the Prelude, had haltingly represented that love returns in an extraordinary variation to clarify the turning point. It is not too much to say that ultimately our response to this variation will determine our belief in Wagner's dramatic vision.

## Notes

1. On the history of the combination and the "Liebestod" title, see *Richard Wagner: Prelude and Transfiguration from "Tristan and Isolde,"* ed. Robert Bailey (Norton Critical Scores; New York, 1985), 36–43.
2. See n. 1. Also included are scores of the Prelude, the Transfiguration (without the vocal part), and Wagner's concert ending to the former.
3. In program notes prepared for concert performances; see ibid., 47–48.
4. Richard Wagner, "On Conducting," in *Three Wagner Essays,* tr. Robert Jacobs (London, 1979), 53–54.
5. See Joseph Kerman, *Opera as Drama,* rev. ed. (Berkeley and Los Angeles, 1988), ch. 8, and *passim*.
6. Ernest Newman, *The Wagner Operas* (New York, 1949), 239.
7. Wagner, "On Conducting," 63.
8. Especially if he also catches the *mitleidig* look that Tristan bestows on the king, as per Wagner's stage direction. This direction presents a difficulty for my reading of this passage.
9. The change in the deceptive cadence is determined by the bass moving down, rather than up, as before: E–Eb rather than E–F.
    Speaking of example 7, Bailey observes that past the upbeat to bar 1 of the Prelude, this is the only time in the opera (including the Prelude) where the initial motif begins with A♮ rather than Ab (*Richard Wagner: Prelude and Transfiguration from "Tristan and Isolde,"* 126). He argues that Wagner wrote A♮ at the beginning of the Prelude to maximize contrast with G♯ in bar 2, this contrast adumbrating the large-scale tonal shift A to A flat which occurs at many important points in the opera. In example 7, the restored A/G♯ contrast highlights G♯ and so supports the new destination of the Prelude complex at this point, A flat (rather than C and A, as before).
    Further support is provided by the "extra" chords. The bass line F–E–D♯ in bars 1–4 of example 7 anticipates the bass E–Eb of the changed deceptive cadence that opens into the new destination.
10. *Richard Wagner to Mathilde Wesendonck,* tr. William Ashton Ellis (New York, 1905), letter 95, 184–90.

ACKNOWLEDGMENTS

I am grateful to the following organizations and publishers for extending permission to reprint:

The American Musicological Society: "A Profile for American Musicology" (*JAMS* 18, 1965).

The British Library: "The *Missa Puer natus est* by Thomas Tallis" (from *Sundry Sorts of Music Books: Essays on The British Library Collections, Presented to O. W. Neighbour on His 70th Birthday*, ed. Chris Banks et al., 1993).

Cambridge University Press: "'Write All These Down': Notes on a Byrd Song" (from *Byrd Studies*, ed. Alan Brown and Richard Turbet, 1992), and "*Tristan und Isolde:* The Prelude and the Play" (to appear in *Richard Wagner: "Tristan und Isolde,"* ed. Carolyn Abbate, forthcoming).

Faber and Faber, Ltd.: "Reading Don Giovanni" (from *The Don Giovanni Book: Myths of Seduction and Betrayal*, ed. Jonathan Miller), © 1990.

*The Hudson Review:* "Auden's *Magic Flute*" (vol. 10, Summer 1957), and "Wagner: Thoughts in Season" (vol. 13, Autumn 1960).

International Musicological Society: "An Italian Musician in Elizabethan England" (paper from the 15th Congress, 1992).

Laaber Verlag: "Taking the Fifth" (from *Das musikalische Kunstwerk, Festschrift Carl Dahlhaus*, ed. H. Danuser et al.), © 1988.

*The New York Review of Books:* "William Byrd and Elizabethan Catholicism," © 1979 Nyrev, Inc.

W. W. Norton & Company, Inc.: "Byrd, Tallis, and the Art of Imitation" (from *Aspects of Medieval and Renaissance Music: A Birthday Offering to Gustave Reese*, ed. Jan LaRue et al.), © 1966, and *"An die ferne Geliebte"* (from *Beethoven Studies*, ed. Alan Tyson), © 1973.

Oxford University Press: "Tovey's Beethoven" (from *Beethoven Studies 2,* ed. Alan Tyson), © 1977, and in conjunction with the Beethovenhaus, Bonn: "Beethoven's Minority" (to appear in *Mozart and Beethoven: Essays in Honour of Alan Tyson,* ed. Sieghard Brandenburg, forthcoming).

Princeton University Press: "Verdi's Use of Recurring Themes" (from *Studies in Music History: Essays for Oliver Strunk,* ed. Harold Powers), © 1968 Princeton University Press.

University of California Press: "*I Lombardi* in San Diego" (*19th-Century Music* 3), © 1980, and "Theories of Late Eighteenth-Century Music" (from *Studies in Eighteenth-Century British Art and Aesthetics,* Ralph Cohen, ed.), © 1985, The Regents of the University of California.

University of Chicago Press: "How We Got into Analysis, and How to Get Out" (*Critical Inquiry* 7), © 1980, and "A Few Canonic Variations" (*Critical Inquiry* 10), © 1983, The University of Chicago. All rights reserved.

Woodrow Wilson International Center for Scholars: "Mozart's Piano Concertos and Their Audience" (symposium paper, 1991).

# INDEX

Beethoven (*continued*)
167, 221–22, 230, 339;
Sonata in E Flat, op. 81a,
232; Sonata in F Minor,
op. 2 no. 1, 221, 223, 235;
Sonata in F Minor, op. 57
(*Appassionata*), 227–28;
Piano Trio in B-Flat Major,
op. 97 (Archduke), 166;
Piano Trio in C Minor,
op. 1 no. 3, 223–24; Quartet in B-Flat Major, op. 130,
187; Quartet in C Major,
op. 59 no. 3, 232; Quartet
in C Minor, op. 18 no. 4,
224; Quartet in C-Sharp
Minor, op. 131, 165–67,
202, 235; Quartet in F
Major, op. 18 no. 1, 236
n.3; Quartet in F Major,
op. 59 no. 1, 63; "Resignation," 173; "Sehnsucht,"
WoO 146, 196–97; Symphony in C Minor (sketch),
Hess 298, 221–22; Symphony No. 3, op. 55
(*Eroica*), 66, 71 n.29, 168,
232; Symphony No. 5,
op. 67, 63–64, 69, 159–61,
168, 207–15, 224, 231, 234,
339–40; Symphony No. 8,
op. 83, 205 n.28; Variations
for Piano in C Minor, WoO
80, 231; Violin Sonata in C
Minor, op. 30 no. 2, 224
Berg, Alban, *Wozzeck*, 269
Bergonzi, Carlo, 303
Berlioz, Hector, 311
Bertati, Giovanni, *Don Giovanni*, 307, 312, 317–18
Blacking, John, 42
Boettcher, Hans, 202, 203 n.3
Bossy, John, 85–86
Bradley, A. C., 158
Brahms, Johannes, 16, 64, 261
Brett, Philip, 126–27, 137–38
n.10
Bruckner, Anton, 264

Budden, Julian, 300, 301
Byrd, William: biography,
80–81, 84–85; and Catholicism, 78–88; compared to
Alfonso Ferrabosco the
Elder, 98–100, 104, 144,
147, 148; compared to
Tallis, 95–97; imitative
style, 95–104; Latin sacred
music, 78–88, 143; musical
style, 81–82, 83–84, 86, 87–
88, 122–23; and Nonsuch,
143, 144; and Sidney, 141;
songs, 106–23. Works: Alleluias, 88; *Aspice, Domine*,
97; *Ave verum corpus*, 122;
*Cantiones quae ab argumento
sacrae vocantur* (1575), 80,
83–84, 95, 98, 101, 127,
142; *Cantiones sacrae* (1589,
1591), 97, 101; *Christus
resurgens*, 137–38 n.10;
*Circumspice Ierusalem*, 82;
"Come to Me, Grief, Forever," 122; "Compel the
Hawk," 123 n.9; *Da mihi
auxilium*, 97; *Deus venerunt
gentes*, 79–80, 82; *Domine,
praestolamur adventum tuum*,
81, 101–4; *Domine, secundum actum meum*, 97, 101,
103; *Emendemus in melius*,
122; *Gradualia*, 86–88, 101,
113; *Haec dicit Dominus*, 82;
"In Angel's Weed," 123 n.9;
"Jerusalem" motets, 82;
*Laententur coeli*, 81–82;
*Laudate, pueri*, 95–96; *Libera
me, Domine, et pone me juxta
te*, 97; Masses, 86, 101, 113;
*Memento, homo*, 93, 96–97,
103; *Miserere* canons, 144;
*Miserere mei Deus*, 142; *Ne
irascaris Domine*, 82, 84;
"Penelope That Longed,"
123 nn.6,9; *Plorans plorabit*,
82; *Psalmes, Sonets, & Songs*
(1588), 106, 107, 117;

*Psalmes, Songs, & Sonnets*
(1611), 107; *Quomodo cantabimus*, 83; "Retire, My
Soul," 107–23; *Songs of Sundrie Natures*, 123 nn.6,9;
"This Sweet and Merry
Month of May," 106; *Unam
petii a Domino*, 87; *Vigilate*,
82; "La virginella," 106;
"Why Do I Use My Paper,
Ink, and Pen," 79, 116–22

Cadenza, 325, 326–27, 331–32
Caldwell, John, 128
Campion, Edmund, 78–80,
82–83
Campion, Thomas, 146
Canon (musical repertory or
standard): compared to repertory, 45, 46–49; created
by performance, 44–45;
impact of oral tradition,
34–36; impact of recording
technology, 43–46; impact
of written music, 34–36,
38, 42
Cantus firmus, in Tallis, 127–
29
Capobianco, Tito, 298–99
Castelli, Ignaz, 173
Castiglione, Giambattista, 140
Catholicism, and Byrd, 77–88
Cavell, Stanley, 21–22
Cecil, William, Lord Burghley, 141
Chapel Royal, 143, 147–48
Charlemagne, 35
Charteris, Richard, 139
Clemens, Jacobus (non Papa),
*Ego flos campi*, 127
Collingwood, R. G., 259
Concerto (classical), 323–30,
333
Concerto rondo, 327–28
Cone, Edward T., 29–30, 39,
55, 286
Cooper, Martin, 179
Coprario, John, 145, 148

19, 21–23, 30–31, 49, 52–53; organicist, 15–19, 42; Schenkerian, 17–18, 42; serial, 20; thematicist, 18, 19, 53–54
Musical expression. *See* Rhetoric
Musical form: in classical concerto, 323–30, 333; and opera translation, 246–47; and Rosen, 53–56, 64–65; sonata form, 53–59, 64–69; in twelve-tone music, 266–68, 270–71; in Wagner, 265–67, 269–71, 347
Musical themes: leitmotiv, 269–70; recurring, 274–87
*Musica transalpina,* 106, 144–46
Music criticism: in the American academy, 19–20, 42–43; definition, 5, 10, 12; and musical analysis, 7–8, 12–16, 19, 21–23, 30–31, 52–53; and music history, 48–49
Musicology, American, 3–5, 7–10, 19–20

Narmour, Eugene, 22–23, 31 n.9, 42
Neighbour, Oliver, 136–37, 148
Newman, Ernest, 341–42
Nietzsche, Friedrich, 262, 263, 264, 265
Noble, Jeremy, 126, 136
Nohl, Ludwig, 177
Nonsuch, 143–144
North, Nigel, 148 n.10
Nottebohm, Gustav, 169, 185, 189–92, 196, 221
Novalis (Friedrich von Hardenberg), 269

Opera: continuous, 312–13; French, 276; Italian, 275–76; translation of libretto, 241–56

Oral tradition, 34–36
Organicism, 15–19, 42, 52–53, 64

Paget, Lord Thomas, 88–89 n.2
Paleotti, Cardinal Gabriele of Bologna, 140
Palisca, Claude, 3–4, 7
Parry, Sir Hubert, 162
Parsons, Robert, 143
Paston, Edward, 126–27
Patrons, 147, 329
Peele, George, *The Old Wives' Tale,* 243
Performance, 44–45, 47–48
Performer, 38–39
Petre, Sir John, 85–86
Philips recordings, 304
Piave, Francesco Maria, 278, 291, 294, 295, 298
Plishka, Paul, 304
Porter, Andrew, 300
Portinaro, Francesco, "Vergine bella," 144
Powers, Harold S., 113
Psalm settings, 90–91

Queen's Musick, 143, 147

Ratner, Leonard G., 60–64, 65
Recalling themes, 274–87
Recording technology, 43–48
Recurring themes, 274–87
Reese, Gustave, 90
Réti, Rudolph, 18, 19, 54
Reynolds, Roger, 45
Rhetoric: in Beethoven, 176–79, 198–200; in Byrd, 84, 88, 97, 101–4, 108, 112, 114–15, 117–22; in Mozart, 315–16; in opera libretto translations, 241–56; and Ratner, 62–63
Rhythm, 336–37, 339–40, 342–44

Riezler, Walter, 164
Ritornello form, 325
Rolland, Romain, 205 n.32
Roncaglia, Gino, 279, 287
Rosen, Charles: and Beethoven, 167, 212–13, 235; criticized by Epstein, 59–60; influenced by Tovey, 52, 60, 155; and Mozart, 330, 331; theory of form, 53–56, 64, 69, 71–72 n.30
Rushton, Julian, 318, 320

Saint-Saëns, Camille, 334 n.11
Salzer, Felix, 20
Sams, Eric, 28–29
San Diego Opera Association, 298–99, 304–5
Sandon, Nick, 137–38 n.10
Savoy, Carlo Emanuele I, duke of, 144
Schenker, Heinrich: aesthetic values, 14, 40; on Beethoven, 71 n.29, 207–8, 212; as musical analyst, 17–18, 22–23, 42, 53–54; on Schumann, 23–26
Schiedermair, Ludwig, 237 n.13
Schindler, Anton, 173
Schmidt-Görg, Joseph, 168–69
Schoenberg, Arnold: musical theory, 16, 18–19, 54, 64; and Wagner, 264–73; *Moses und Aron,* 271–73
Schumann, Clara (*née* Wieck), 28–29
Schumann, Robert: songs, 28–29. Works: "Aus meinen Thränen spriessen," 23–30; "Im wunderschönen Monat Mai," 27–28
Scory, Sylvanus, 141
Scriabin, Alexander, 264
Sechter, Simon, 17
Serialism, 264–71

Designer:  Nola Burger
Compositor:  Dharma Enterprises
Music setter:  George W. Thomson
Text:  10/13 Bembo
Display:  Bembo
Printer:  Malloy Lithographing, Inc.
Binder:  John H. Dekker & Sons